STEPHEN REID is the author of
The Prentice Hall Guide for College Writers
and *Purpose and Process: A Reader for Writers.*
He was for many years the Writing Program
Administrator in the English Department
at Colorado State University, and he
currently helps to mentor new teaching
assistants while teaching a variety of
undergraduate and graduate literature
and composition courses.

PENGUIN ACADEMICS

THE WRITER'S
PURPOSES
A READER FOR COMPOSITION

Stephen Reid

Colorado State University

Prentice Hall

Boston Columbus Indianapolis New York San Francisco Upper Saddle River Amsterdam
Cape Town Dubai London Madrid Milan Munich Paris Montreal Toronto Delhi
Mexico City Sao Paulo Sydney Hong Kong Seoul Singapore Taipei Tokyo

Senior Editor: Brad Potthoff
Editorial Assistant: Nancy C. Lee
Senior Supplements Editor: Donna Campion
Senior Marketing Manager: Sandra McGuire
Senior Media Producer: Stefanie Liebman
Project Manager: Barbara Mack
Project Coordination, Text Design, and Electronic Page Makeup:
  PreMediaGlobal
Operations Specialist: Mary Ann Gloriande
Art Director, Cover: Miguel Ortiz
Cover Designer: Jill Lehan
Cover Photo: "Vibrant Passages" by Fabian Roldan, used by special
  permission of FirstLight International, LLC
Printer and Binder: Edwards Brothers
Cover Printer: Lehigh-Phoenix/Hagerstown

For more information about the Penguin Academics series, please contact us by mail at
Pearson Education, attn: Marketing Department, 51 Madison Avenue, 29th Floor, New York,
NY 10010, or visit us online at www.pearsonhighered.com/english.

For permission to use copyrighted material, grateful acknowledgment is made to the
copyright holders on pages 377–379, which are hereby made part of this copyright page.

Library of Congress Cataloging-in-Publication Data

Reid, Stephen, (date)
    The writer's purposes: a reader for composition/Stephen Reid.
        p. cm. — (Penguin academics)
    Includes bibliographical references and index.
    ISBN-13: 978-0-205-78712-8 (alk. paper)
    ISBN-10: 0-205-78712-6 (alk. paper)
    1. College readers.   2. English language—Rhetoric.   I. Title.
    PE1417.R438 2011
    808'.0427—dc22

                             2010036758

1 2 3 4 5 6 7 8 9 10—EDW—13 12 11 10

Prentice Hall
is an imprint of

www.pearsonhighered.com
ISBN-13: 978-0-205-78712-8
ISBN-10:   0-205-78712-6

contents

Thematic Contents   xv
Preface   xix

CHAPTER 1 Reading: Purposes and Processes   1

Reading Is Not a Spectator Sport   2
Some Myths About Reading   4
Purposes for Reading   5
Processes for Critical Reading   6
Writing Responses   11
Reading and Analyzing Visuals   12
Testing Your Critical Reading Process   15

ELLEN GOODMAN *Honor Society Hypocrisy*   15
Arlene Pfeiffer, a seventeen-year-old honor student, student council president, and unwed mother, is kicked out of her school's honor society after giving birth to her daughter, Jessica. Is the school board guilty of hypocrisy?

MORTIMER ADLER *How to Mark a Book*   20
Active reading should create a conversation between the reader and the writer. "Marking up a book is not an act of mutilation," the author asserts, "but of love."

SHERMAN ALEXIE *The Joy of Reading and Writing*   25
"I learned to read with a *Superman* comic book," Sherman Alexie explains. "I read books I borrowed from the library. I read the backs of cereal boxes. I read auto-repair manuals. ... I loved those books, but I also knew that love had only one purpose. I was trying to save my life."

MALCOLM X *Learning to Read*   29
Malcolm Little explains how he educated himself while in prison by copying entire pages out of a dictionary in order to write letters to Elijah Muhammad and understand the books he read.

TANIA RALLI *Who's a Looter?* 37

Shortly after Hurricane Katrina struck New Orleans, photographers took pictures of people carrying away groceries through the flooded city. In one picture, white residents were described as "*finding* bread and soda" while in another picture a young black man was described as "*looting* a grocery store."

| CHAPTER 2 | Writing: Purposes and Processes   42 |

The Writing Situation   43
Purposes for Writing   44
Audience Analysis   45
Kinds of Writing   46
The Writer's Voice   47
Strategies for Writing   47
Processes for Writing   47
Purpose and Process: One Writer's Essay   50

NICOLLE MIRCOS *My Sister, Kari*   50

The author's essay about her disabled younger sister illustrates how she integrated purpose and process in her prewriting, clustering, rough draft, final draft, and postscript.

PETER ELBOW *Freewriting*   56

A noted teacher, researcher, and writer gives advice about writing: "The most effective way I know to improve your writing is to do freewriting exercises regularly. ... The idea is simply to write for ten minutes. Don't stop for anything. Go quickly without rushing."

ANNE LAMOTT *Shitty First Drafts*   60

Having trouble with those first drafts? Just remember Anne Lamott's advice: "The first draft is the down draft—you just get it down. The second draft is the up draft—you fix it up."

DONALD M. MURRAY *The Maker's Eye: Revising Your Own Manuscripts*   65

"When students complete a first draft, they consider the job of writing done. ... When professional writers complete a first draft, they usually feel that they are at the start of the writing process. When a draft is completed, the job of writing can begin."

AMY TAN *Mother Tongue*   71

"Language is the tool of my trade," writes Amy Tan. "And I use them all—all the Englishes I grew up with." The author of *The Joy Luck Club* prompts us to consider why many Americans look down on people who speak "broken" or "limited" English.

| CHAPTER 3 | Observing | 78 |

Strategies for Reading and Writing Observing Essays   79
Reading an Observing Essay   80
Writing an Observing Essay   81

WILLIAM LEAST HEAT-MOON *West Texas*   88
"I drove on. The low sun turned the mesa rimrock to silhouettes, angular and weird and unearthly; had someone said the far side of Saturn looked just like this, I would have believed him."

ANNIE DILLARD *Lenses*   92
Watching through binoculars as a pair of whistling swans fly over Daleville Pond reminds this Pulitzer Prize-winning writer of her childhood days spent staring at the microscopic life in a drop of pond water.

SAMUEL H. SCUDDER *Take This Fish and Look at It*   96
Samuel Scudder recalls how a famous Swiss naturalist, Louis Agassiz, taught him the skills of observation by having him a fish closely, carefully, and repeatedly.

ROLAND BARTHES AND EMILY PRAGER *Toys and Barbies*   101
According to French philosopher Roland Barthes, children's toys carry with them clues about their cultural and ideological function. Borrowing Barthes's semiotic method, Emily Prager analyzes the cultural myths created and sustained by Barbie.

ROLAND BARTHES *Toys*   102

EMILY PRAGER *Our Barbies, Ourselves*   104

SUEELLEN CAMPBELL *Layers of Place*   106
"All places are astonishingly complex," this author explains. Use her writing exercise to draw on your knowledge, imagination, and memory in order to "build a richly layered portrait of a single space."

ELIZABETH WESTON *Fetal Pig*   113
"Today," her zoology instructor says, "we will dissect the fetal pig." The author feels a wave of fear and nausea overtake her. A headline flashes in her mind: "Girl Sickened by Dead Pig Fails College."

| CHAPTER 4 | Remembering | 116 |

Strategies for Reading and Writing Remembering Essays   117
Reading a Remembering Essay   118
Writing a Remembering Essay   119

DICK GREGORY *Shame*   125

In love with a girl named Helene Tucker and embarrassed by his poverty, the author remembers an incident in a classroom twenty-two years ago that taught him shame.

LAURA WAGNER *Haiti: A Survivor's Story*   129

"I was sitting barefoot on my bed, catching up on ethnographic field notes, when the earthquake hit ... I braced myself in a doorway ... and then a cloud of darkness and cement dust swallowed everything as the house collapsed. I was surprised to die in this way, but not afraid."

HELEN KELLER *The Day Language Came into My Life*   134

The author remembers how, at age seven, her teacher Anne Sullivan arrived and taught her the miracle of language: "Suddenly I felt a misty consciousness as of something forgotten ... and somehow the mystery of language was revealed to me. I knew then that 'w-a-t-e-r' meant the wonderful cool something that was flowing over my hand."

RICHARD RODRIGUEZ *Los Pobres*   137

The Mexican-American author sets out to learn from a summer of hard, physical labor how it feels—and what it means—to be a Mexican alien working in California.

JEANNE WAKATSUKI HOUSTON *Living in Two Cultures*   144

"Because I am culturally neither pure Japanese nor pure American does not mean I am less of a person. It means I have been enriched by the heritage of both." The author recalls her struggles growing up as an Asian female in a *Hakujin* or Caucasian world.

WALTER GOEDEKER *The Wake-Up Call*   150

"There, on the bed, was my best friend hooked to more machines than I had imagined possible. Tubes and wires crisscrossed in an eerie web over his mangled body. He had sustained a massive concussion, a broken leg, a broken arm, and several contusions and lacerations."

| CHAPTER 5 | Investigating   158

Strategies for Reading and Writing Investigating Essays   159
Reading an Investigative Essay   160
Writing an Investigative Essay   161

UNIVERSITY OF UTAH NEWS CENTER *Drivers on Cell Phones Are as Bad as Drunks*   165

"We found that people are as impaired when they drive and talk on a cell phone as they are when they drive intoxicated at the legal blood-alcohol limit," says Professor David Strayer and his University of Utah colleagues Frank Drews and Dennis Crouch.

CLAIRE SUDDATH/REEDLEY *Does Obesity Rehab Work?* 169
"Our national dialogue focuses on obesity prevention, but what do we do for kids who have already gained weight?" The author follows Elizabeth Fedorchalk's efforts to lose weight and change her lifestyle at a weight-loss boarding school.

SARA CORBETT *Rick Steves's Not-So-Lonely Planet* 174
Follow the author as she trails Rick Steves, author of dozens of books and films about travel in Europe, on a blitz of hotels, restaurants, and museums in Lisbon, Portugal.

GLENN C. ALTSCHULER *The E-Learning Curve* 180
Are you thinking about taking a college course online or through distance education? This dean of continuing education at Cornell University advises us to examine the advantages and disadvantages of online courses before we sign on the virtual line.

MARY WHITE *The Beauty Behind Beauty Pageants* 185
The French have a phrase for it: *Il faut souffrir pour être belle.* It is necessary to suffer in order to be beautiful. As the author discovers, nowhere is this more apparent than at a beauty pageant.

CHAPTER 6 | Explaining 192

Strategies for Reading and Writing Explaining Essays 193
Reading an Explaining Essay 194
Writing an Explaining Essay 195

SUZE ORMAN *How to Take Control of Your Credit Cards* 201
The author of many books on finance and host of her own TV show explains how to get control of your credit cards: "I am not saying it will be easy, but there are plenty of strategies that can put you on a path out of credit card hell."

DAVID VON DREHLE *Why Crime Went Away* 207
The author examines the causes of America's dramatic drop in crime and murder rate in the United States. More criminals locked in prisons, increased information on computer networks, and more experience controlling drug cartels, he explains, have reduced crime rates despite high rates of unemployment.

JEAN KILBOURNE *Jesus Is a Brand of Jeans* 214
"Another ad features an attractive young couple in bed. ... However, [the woman's face] is completely covered by a magazine, open to a double-page photo of a car. The man is gazing passionately at the car. The copy reads, 'The ultimate attraction.'"

STEPHEN KING *Why We Crave Horror Movies*   221
"The mythic horror movie, like the sick joke, has a dirty job to do. It deliberately appeals to all that is worst in us. It is morbidity unchained, our most base instincts let free ... and it all happens, fittingly enough, in the dark."

BUD HERRON *Cat Bathing as a Martial Art*   224
Ever wonder how to give a cat a bath? To keep from getting clawed to death, Bud Herron recommends that you dress properly for the job with "canvas overalls tucked into high-top construction boots, a pair of steel-mesh gloves, an army helmet, a hockey face mask, and a long-sleeved flack jacket."

MICHAEL J. JONES *Wine Tasting: How to Fool Some of the People All of the Time*   228
With his tongue firmly in cheek, the author explains the finer points of the "sniff, swirl, and gurgle" technique you can use when tasting a vintage wine on that special occasion.

CHAPTER 7	Evaluating 235

Strategies for Reading and Writing Evaluating Essays   236
Reading an Evaluating Essay   237
Writing an Evaluating Essay   238

CONSUMER REPORTS *Laptops and Desktops*   243
Consumer Reports evaluates the convenience, performance, and price of these slim (13 inches wide), light (3 pounds or less), and inexpensive ($330-$450) laptops.

DAVID SEDARIS *Today's Special*   247
"As a rule," this author explains, "I'm no great fan of eating out in New York restaurants. It's hard to love a place that's outlawed smoking but finds it perfectly acceptable to serve raw fish in a bath of chocolate."

RICHARD ALLEVA *Pocahokum*   251
The visual power of 3-D images is certainly dramatic, but *Avatar* "not only sags but positively rots" when it comes to story and character. The Na'vi are trite escapees from Disney's *Pocahontas*, the author argues, and *Avatar* is remarkable mostly for its "thinness of characterization, predictability of plotting, and poverty of imagination."

ABRAHAM LINCOLN *The Gettysburg Address*   255

GILBERT HIGHET *The Gettysburg Address*   256
Read Lincoln's famous three-minute speech and see if you agree with the author that *The Gettysburg Address* "is one of the greatest speeches in all history."

MARGARET LAZARUS *All's Not Well in Land of The Lion King* 262

The Lion King, the author argues, is not a story about animals. It is "a metaphor for society that originated in the minds of Disney's creators. These bigoted images and attitudes will lodge deeply in children's consciousness."

CRAIG COOLEY *The Two Best Letters on Television* 265

"In the fall of 1994, a new drama hit the airwaves. The title consisted of only two little letters, but it has become one of the most popular shows on television. Its popularity parallels shows such as 'Magnum P.I.,' 'M*A*S*H,' and 'Cheers'. Of course, I'm talking about 'ER.'"

| CHAPTER 8 | Problem Solving | 271 |

Strategies for Reading and Writing Problem-Solving Essays   272
Reading a Problem-Solving Essay   273
Writing a Problem-Solving Essay   274

WENDELL BERRY *Solving for Pattern* 280

What is the difference between a good solution to a problem and a bad solution? Good solutions, the author argues, must promote the harmony, health, and quality of the whole system.

ERIC SCHLOSSER, MARION NESTLE, MICHAEL POLLAN, TROY DUSTER AND ELIZABETH RANSOM, PETER SINGER, AND JIM HIGHTOWER *One Thing to Do About Food* 284

Seven authors explain how to solve America's problems with junk food production and consumption that have lead to skyrocketing rates of obesity and diabetes in children and adults.

MICHAEL BÉRUBÉ *How to End Grade Inflation: A Modest Proposal* 292

Fixing grade inflation could be accomplished, this author argues, simply by converting the range of grades into a 10 point scale and incorporating a "degree of difficulty" factor. This solution would "eliminate faculty capriciousness precisely by factoring it in; and it would involve nothing more than using the numbers we already have at our disposal."

DEBORAH TANNEN *CrossTalk* 295

What happens when women and men attempt to communicate in the workplace? The author, a noted authority on cross-gender communication, offers tips for working women to help keep the lines of communication open.

JULIA ALVAREZ *A White Woman of Color*   301

Writing about her own experience growing up in the Dominican Republic, the author discovers that by accepting many races and color differences "we Latinos can provide a positive multicultural, multiracial model to a divided America."

JENNY SHARPE *The Problem of Dropouts Can Be Solved*   309

"With the combination of a strengthened Head Start program, a strong truancy program, and a wider selection of alternative schools, we can," according to this author, "reduce the problem of high school dropouts."

CHAPTER 9 | Arguing   318

Strategies for Reading and Writing Arguing Essays   319
Reading an Arguing Essay   320
Writing an Arguing Essay   321

DEBORAH TANNEN *The Argument Culture*   330

"We must expand our notion of 'debate' to include more dialogue," this best-selling author suggests. "Instead of asking, 'What's the other side?' we might ask, 'What are the other sides?' Instead of insisting on hearing 'both sides,' let's insist on hearing 'all sides.'"

DAVID KAROLY *Climate Change Science Misinformation*   335

"Let me emphasize that the pattern and magnitude of observed global-scale changes since the mid-20th century cannot be explained by natural climate variability, are consistent with the response to increasing greenhouse gases, and are not consistent with the responses to other factors."

GREGG EASTERBROOK *Some Convenient Truths*   340

Reacting to Al Gore's controversial book, the author argues that reflecting on our history of fighting acid rain and encouraging America's entrepreneurial spirit can help us overcome our gloom and doom attitudes about global climate change.

NEIL L. WATERS *Why You Can't Cite Wikipedia in My Class*   344

"Wikipedia," this author argues, "is not an acceptable citation, even though it may lead one to a citable source."

MARK WILSON *Professors Should Embrace Wikipedia*   349

A professor of geology argues that a wiki site, which can be changed by anyone, can in fact serve to promote the goals of academic knowledge.

MIKE ROYKO *Endorsements Just a Shell Game* 352
Is it ethical for public figures to receive money for selling a product on television when they don't even like the product? The author debates the ethics of television endorsements with his friend, Slats Grobnik.

MARTIN LUTHER KING, JR. *Letter from Birmingham Jail* 356
In his classic 1963 letter to eight Alabama clergymen, America's greatest civil rights leader argues for the timeliness and lawfulness of nonviolent action to gain civil rights for Black Americans.

EMILY SINTEK *Immigration* 373
According to the author, there is a middle ground between those who say immigration policies represent the best of our American heritage and those who say immigration drains our public service programs and takes jobs away from residents.

Credits 377
Index 381

CONTENTS

xiii

thematic contents

RACE AND CULTURAL DIVERSITY

Tania Ralli
Who's a Looter? 37

Nicolle Mircos
My Sister, Kari 50

Amy Tan
Mother Tongue 71

Roland Barthes and Emily Prager
Toys and Barbies 101

Roland Barthes
Toys 102

Emily Prager
Our Barbies, Ourselves 104

Dick Gregory
Shame 125

Laura Wagner
Haiti: A Survivor's Story 129

Richard Rodriguez
Los Pobres 137

Jeanne Wakatsuki Houston
Living in Two Cultures 144

David Sedaris
Today's Special 247

Martin Luther King, Jr.
Letter from Birmingham Jail 356

GENDER ROLES

Ellen Goodman
Honor Society Hypocrisy 15

Roland Barthes and Emily Prager
Toys and Barbies 101

Roland Barthes
Toys 102

Emily Prager
Our Barbies, Ourselves 104

Mary White
The Beauty Behind Beauty Pageants 185

Jean Kilbourne
Jesus Is a Brand of Jeans 214

Margaret Lazarus
All's Not Well in Land of The Lion King 262

Julia Alvarez
A White Woman of Color 301

Deborah Tannen
The Argument Culture 330

TECHNOLOGY AND THE INTERNET

Tania Ralli
Who's a Looter? 37

University of Utah News Center
Drivers on Cell Phones Are as Bad as Drunks 165

Glenn C. Altschuler
The E-Learning Curve 180

Consumer Reports
Laptops and Desktops 243

Neil L. Waters
Why You Can't Cite Wikipedia in My Class 344

Mark Wilson
Professors Should Embrace Wikipedia 349

ENVIRONMENTAL ISSUES

Annie Dillard
Lenses 92

SueEllen Campbell
Layers of Place 106

EDUCATION

Samuel H. Scudder
Take This Fish and Look at It 96

Elizabeth Weston
Fetal Pig 113

Helen Keller
The Day Language Came into My Life 134

Sara Corbett
   Rick Steves's Not-So-Lonely Planet   174

Glenn C. Altschuler
   The E-Learning Curve   180

Suze Orman
   How to Take Control of Your Credit Cards   201

Abraham Lincoln
   The Gettysburg Address   255

Gilbert Highet
   The Gettysburg Address   256

Wendell Berry
   Solving for Pattern   280

LITERACY, WRITING, AND LEARNING

Mortimer Adler
   How to Mark a Book   20

Sherman Alexie
   The Joy of Reading and Writing   25

Malcolm X
   Learning to Read   29

Peter Elbow
   Freewriting   56

Anne Lamott
   Shitty First Drafts   60

Donald M. Murray
   The Maker's Eye: Revising Your Own Manuscripts   65

Amy Tan
   Mother Tongue   71

Helen Keller
   The Day Language Came into My Life   134

Margaret Lazarus
   All's Not Well in Land of The Lion King   262

ADVERTISING AND THE MEDIA

Tania Ralli
   Who's a Looter?   37

Jean Kilbourne
   Jesus Is a Brand of Jeans   214

Richard Alleva
   Pocahokum   251

CONTEMPORARY SOCIAL ISSUES

Tania Ralli
Who's a Looter? 37

University of Utah News Center
Drivers on Cell Phones Are as Bad as Drunks 165

Claire Suddath/Reedley
Does Obesity Rehab Work? 169

Mary White
The Beauty Behind Beauty Pageants 185

Suze Orman
How to Take Control of Your Credit Cards 201

David Von Drehle
Why Crime Went Away 207

Jean Kilbourne
Jesus Is a Brand of Jeans 214

Stephen King
Why We Crave Horror Movies 221

Eric Schlosser, Marion Nestle, Michael Pollan, Troy
Duster, and Elizabeth Ransom, Peter Singer, and Jim
Hightower
One Thing to Do About Food 284

Deborah Tannen
The Argument Culture 330

David Karoly
Climate Change Science Misinformation 335

Greg Easterbrook
Some Convenient Truths 340

Mike Royko
Endorsements Just a Shell Game 352

Emily Sintek
Immigration 373

preface

Reading, especially critical reading, has always been a gateway to effective writing. In our Internet age of digital attractions and distractions, students need, more than ever, to learn to read critically and rhetorically in order to understand how to plan, draft, and revise their own essays. *The Writer's Purposes: A Reader for Composition* is unique in its integrated focus on both reading and writing processes.

The Writer's Purposes begins with a chapter on reading that offers practical advice as well as the experiences of professional writers to help students learn to read critically and rhetorically by considering writers' purpose(s) for writing, their intended audiences, and their strategies. **Chapter 1, Reading**—as well as all the remaining chapters on writers' purposes—offer time-proven strategies to access students' prior experiences and attitudes, to determine a writer's purpose and audience, and to practice questioning a text in the margins, on discussion forums, or in class. Following the initial chapter on reading is **Chapter 2, Writing,** that models for students time-honored writing process advice by professional writers such as Donald Murray, Anne Lamott, and Peter Elbow.

The remaining chapters in *The Writer's Purposes* follow a logical sequence of purposes. **Chapters 3 through 5 (Observing, Remembering, and Investigating)** model for students the descriptive, narrative and investigative skills they need to write their essays. **Chapter 3, Observing,** features classic essays by Annie Dillard, Samuel Scudder, Roland Barthes, as well as more contemporary essays by Emily Prager and SueEllen Campbell. **Chapter 4, Remembering,** models for students how to use personal experience in narrative and even argumentative essays. Classic selections by Helen Keller, Richard Rodriguez, and Dick Gregory are balanced by contemporary essays such as Laura Wagner's *Haiti: A Survivor's Story.* **Chapter 5, Investigating,** shows students how to research and write essays for contemporary audiences in a journalistic format.

Featured topics include cell phones and driving, obesity rehab, online courses, and traveling abroad.

Chapters 6 through 9 (Explaining, Evaluating, Problem Solving, and Arguing) illustrate how professional and student writers write expository and argumentative prose for a variety of audiences and situations. **Chapter 6, Explaining,** shows students how to use the strategies of definition, process analysis, and cause-effect analysis to develop their essays for specific audiences. Essays by contemporary writers such as Suze Orman, David von Drehle, Jean Kilbourne, and Stephen King model these strategies for student writers. **Chapter 7, Evaluating,** shows students how to use criteria supported by evidence and judgments to create evaluations for a variety of audiences. Popular writers such as David Sedaris, Richard Alleva, and Margaret Lazarus contribute evaluative essays on contemporary social and media topics. **Chapter 8, Problem Solving,** models for students how to write proposals that demonstrate an existing problem, propose effective solutions, and offer supporting evidence. This chapter features a wide range of classic and contemporary authors, including Wendell Berry, Eric Schlosser, Michael Pollan, Marion Nestle, Peter Singer, Deborah Tannen, and Julia Alvarez. Finally, **Chapter 9, Arguing,** introduces students to analyzing their audience and context, setting a debatable claim as a thesis, representing and responding to alternative arguments, and supporting their claims with appropriate evidence. This chapter explains traditional pro-con or adversarial argument, Rogerian argument, and constructive argument (which encourages students to look at multiple stakeholders on a controversial issue and seek common ground). Featured writers in this chapter include contemporary authors on the issues of climate change and use of Wikipedia as well as classic argumentative essays by Deborah Tannen, Mike Royko, and Martin Luther King, Jr.

Throughout the chapters in *The Writer's Purposes: A Reader for Composition*, students access their prior knowledge with prereading questions and then follow a critical and rhetorical reading process that includes text annotation and collaborative reading. Students practice their reading processes in every chapter as they read and rhetorically analyze professional essays. Once students have an idea or an assignment for their own writing, the chapters—along with the model professional and student essays—help them develop their own writing processes for their own purpose-driven and audience-based essays. *The Writer's Purposes* provides a compact rhetorical reader for teachers and students who want help with both reading and writing processes. Its blend of classic and contemporary authors and topics and sample student essays for every chapter illustrates how a purpose driven pedagogy for both reading and writing can help students improve their writing for a variety of topics, audiences, and situations.

Acknowledgments

I thank my reviewers, whose many suggestions have greatly improved the text:

Mary Bodelson, Anoka Ramsey Community College; Kevin Carpenter, Kirkwood Community College; Rebecca Hewett, California State University, Bakersfield; Amanda Hiner, Winthrop University; Elizabeth Kleinfeld, Metropolitan State College of Denver; Iraj Omidvar, Southern Polytechnic State University; and Brandon Shaw, Mohawk Valley Community College.

Stephen Reid
Colorado State University

CHAPTER 1

Reading: Purposes and Processes

Y OU *CAN* IMPROVE YOUR WRITING WITHOUT READING a book of essays, but here is what you would be missing:

Imitation is a powerful learning strategy. We learn to cook partly by being in the kitchen and watching our parents or friends put together a meal. We learn how to drive a car partly by observing how others drive. Learning to write essays works the same way. We learn to write, in part, by reading essays written for various purposes and audiences. Notice one key difference, however. We don't learn to cook if we just sit in the kitchen and eat. We have to watch from the cook's point of view; we have to pay attention to what the cook is doing and not be distracted by the wonderful smells coming out of the oven. To learn to drive, we have to imagine ourselves in the driver's seat, doing what the driver does, making decisions and choices. In learning to write, we cannot read passively, hoping just to be entertained or informed. We must learn to read actively, to read with a writer's eye.

Collections of essays offer hundreds of ideas to write about. Faced with an assignment, most of us panic. Why? Basically, because we don't have anything to write about. At first, no ideas come to us. *Nada.* Nothing. Second, when topics do spring to mind (sports, dating, studying, vacations, family, friends), they seem too trivial for a "real" essay. Third, we don't really feel like authorities on anything. (Isn't that, after all, the purpose of college, to let us learn from people who do know?) This collection of essays will help you discover ideas to write about. It will show you that a seemingly trivial subject can become worth writing about. And it will show you how to draw on your powers of observation, memory, and reading to become knowledgeable on your subject.

The processes of reading and writing support each other. If your goal is to become a better writer and thinker, critical reading will help you write more effectively. As you become a more attentive reader of others' essays, you will read and revise your own writing more effectively. Conversely, writing helps you become a more attentive and critical reader. Your first few examinations in college undoubtedly taught you the best way to study for a test. Open the book, read the chapters, and then take the test, right? Wrong. To make sure you know the material, you should be able to *close* the book and still write out the main ideas—and your reactions—in your own words. Learning to read critically, to annotate what you read, and to share your reactions with others will help you synthesize and recall key ideas. Writing is crucial to the reading and learning process; active reading supports the writing process.

Student essays reveal the composing strategies behind the printed page. Seeing how other writers choose a subject, collect information, organize their ideas, and revise their essays will help you compose essays. What situation or context prompted a particular essay? What personal experience motivated the author to write? What was the original purpose? Who was the intended audience? What was the context for this essay or where did it appear? Where did this writer get the examples and information? How did this writer organize the information clearly and logically? How did this writer revise and edit? Seeing the composing processes behind the printed product will help you write more confidently and effectively.

Reading Is Not a Spectator Sport

To read more effectively, you may need to break some old habits.

The Passive Reading Habit

Reading in college demands that you take control of texts before they control you. If you assume that your mind is an empty tablet, ready to be written on, the texts you read will write all over you. To be an active reader, you need to take a *critical stance:* Why should you believe what you read? What makes this writer an authority? What does *authority* mean, anyway? To be an active reader, you need to *connect* what you read to your own experiences. Do this writer's claims connect to your life? Finally, to be an active reader, you need to make *predictions* while you read. How does what a writer says in the first paragraph forecast what will happen in the following paragraph? Read actively. Don't be a spectator—jump right into the action.

The Television Habit

Television, along with the Internet, is arguably the most powerful communication medium in the world. At least the Internet is interactive, allowing you to search, read, and react. But television, because it is so colorful, so fast-paced, and so immediate, can entrance and transfix us. It invites us to become an advertiser's dream: an unthinking, uncritical consumer. The problem is that our passive TV habits carry over into the books and essays we read. You don't need to quit watching television, but you do need to quit watching passively. *You need to break the passive consumer habit, the couch potato trance that television promotes.* Good readers, readers learning to be better writers, readers learning to appreciate and discriminate, read actively. Good readers use the built-in "instant replay" feature of all written texts: They *reread* to engage the text and annotate key features. Good readers also *discuss* what they have read with other readers. Television programs invite us to be passive; reading invites us to be active—and interactive.

The High School Textbook Habit

Because most high schools do not require you to buy and own books, they discourage active reading. You are told not to "mark up" your books. The books are not yours; you must return them at the end of the term. Imagine a coach tossing you a volleyball in gym class and saying, "Now don't hit this too hard. Don't get it dirty. This volleyball is the property of Washington High School." Just as you have to use a volleyball to play the game, you have to use books to learn from them. You need to break the "this-book-is-not-my-property" habit. *Good readers learn how to own books*, to like or hate them, to underline key ideas, to write in the margin, to scribble in the pages, to argue with friends about the ideas. Books need readers armed with pencils and pens to come alive. Books are not really read until they are **re**read and marked up. Good reading must be active and interactive.

The Yellow Highlighter Habit

The first technique most readers learn is to highlight key passages, usually in bright yellow, red, or pink. Although highlighting is better than totally passive reading, too often readers use it as a crutch. They highlight a whole page in neon yellow, hoping that they will remember more. In fact, research shows that you will remember and learn more *if you can connect what you read to what you already know:* "I remember when I felt like that" or "This was the point Professor Brown made in class" or "I really disagree with this." If there is no connection, go ahead and write, "I don't understand any of this!" or "What's the point?" or "Ask about this in class." Written comments in the margin are more effective than highlighting in promoting active, critical reading.

Some Myths About Reading

As you change your habits, you need to re-examine some of your assumptions about reading.

Myth: The best way to read a textbook or an essay is to begin on page one and read straight through until you reach the end.

Reality: The shortest distance between two points is not always a straight line. Your reading will be more effective if you begin by browsing and skimming, getting a feel for the whole essay, chapter, or text. Look at the table of contents, note chapter titles, and skim beginnings of paragraphs. Look for the big picture. Don't let individual trees keep you from seeing the whole forest.

Myth: Textbooks and essays have hidden in them a single, unambiguous message put there by the author.

Reality: Writers do try to communicate some information or idea clearly in their writing, but their actual language may not communicate their intended meaning. Writers cannot transfer ideas directly into their readers' brains. They have to construct meaning as they write, knowing that each reader will respond slightly differently. *The words on the page have meaning only when a reader gives them meaning.

Myth: The reader "decodes" the meaning that the writer puts in the text.

Reality: The text helps readers make meaning, but because readers attach slightly different meanings to individual words or sentences, and because readers connect this language to their own personal and cultural experiences, each reading is unique. To illustrate this point, compare your answer to the following riddle with a classmate's answer: In an automobile accident, a man is killed and his young son is critically injured. The man's son is rushed to a hospital. As the boy is wheeled into the emergency room, the doctor on duty looks at the boy and says, "My God, it's my son!" What was the relationship of the doctor to the injured boy?

Myth: Writers are great, learned people whose authority and wisdom you should bow down to and gratefully accept.

Reality: Writers may be intelligent or wise, but readers should not humble themselves before the "Great One" or uncritically believe the text. Readers must learn to test writers' ideas, question their facts, check up on their information, and challenge their assumptions or conclusions. (That applies to this text, too. For practice, challenge the sentence above with the asterisk.*)

Myth: Reading is a solitary, private activity in which readers try to comprehend written texts.

Reality: Although people do read by themselves, the reading process is not complete until readers *compare* their understanding with other readers. Discussing each essay, sharing annotations of essays, and listening to each other's ideas in class complement the solitary stage of the reading process.

Purposes for Reading

If you are reading this chapter critically, you should have some questions or objections. "Not all reading is alike—I read the comics in a newspaper just for pleasure—what's wrong with that?" "I read the news on the front page just for relaxation and information—that's different from reading a college textbook." "I check my Facebook page every day just to communicate with my friends." You're right. There are, in fact, many purposes for reading. Here are some:

Relaxing and being entertained
Gathering information

Understanding new ideas
Analyzing a problem and possible solutions
Evaluating a product, service, or performance
Agreeing or disagreeing with an argument
Exploring an idea or feeling

When you are reading for relaxation or entertainment, you may just want to be a couch potato, relaxing and enjoying a story or your friends' comments on Facebook. In fact, much writing has entertainment value—humorous anecdotes, original viewpoints, imaginative comparisons, or shocking statistics—designed to get our attention and interest.

Most college courses, however, emphasize critical, interactive reading. Reading information, explanations, evaluations, policy recommendations, or arguments—and then summarizing, responding, and asking questions—is the focus of many courses. *This course focuses on one particular type of critical reading: How to read with a writer's eye.* How to learn more about the craft of writing and thinking by studying the processes and products of other writers. (Critical reading of other writers' essays is only part of the reading/writing process. Another crucial part, learning how to read and revise your own writing *with a reader's eye*, is discussed in the next chapter.)

Processes for Critical Reading

The following are four stages, or dimensions, of a critical reading process. Most good readers agree that they use these strategies, but they also acknowledge that critical reading is a very individual process. Each reader is unique. Each reader has different expectations, different reading habits or learning styles, and different goals for reading. With that important qualification in mind, practice these strategies on the essays that follow in this chapter. See which of these strategies work best for you.

Prereading

The first strategy for critical reading is prereading—what you do before you actually begin reading an essay. Your basic purpose: to get the "big picture" of the subject and author before you read a particular essay.

1. **Write down what you already think or know about the topic.** You will learn and remember more about the essay if you jot down any experiences you've had that are similar or if you record what you think

about a controversial topic *before* you read the essay. Use the Prereading Journal Topic as a prompt for five minutes of freewriting.

2. **If possible, discuss your responses in your Prereading Journal Entry with other members of the class.** Sharing what you know about the subject with others helps activate your prior experiences and knowledge.

3. **Read about the author and the context for this essay.** Who is the author? Why did the writer choose this topic? What prompted the essay? What does the title suggest to you? Who was the original audience for the essay? In what book or magazine was this essay printed? What else has this writer written?

First Reading

During the first reading, read through to the end, noting your reactions and response. Read for enjoyment. Read to satisfy your curiosity. Read for ideas and information that are important to *you*. Imagine you are a reader of the magazine, newspaper, or book in which this essay first appeared.

1. **Get a pencil or pen in your hand.** If you like to play with colors, use a green pen for your first reading. The pen shouldn't slow you down much, but it will enable you to note your important first reactions.

2. **Make quick marks in the margin to record your reactions.** If you like or are surprised by a passage, put a "!" in the margin next to the sentence. If some passage confuses you, put a "?" in the margin. If you don't like something or completely disagree, use a big "X." Put a wavy line under phrases or sentences you find important, striking, or original. Underline any words you want to look up later. Don't let these quick marks interrupt your reading, however.

3. **At the end of your first reading, record your overall reaction to this essay.** Write in your own words the dominant impression, main idea, thesis, or claim that the essay makes.

Annotated Reading

During your second reading, begin to read with a writer's eye: Note in the margins the writer's strategies and techniques.

1. **First, write out your reactions more fully in the margin.** If you put a "!" in the margin, explain in the margin what surprised you. If you

disagreed, explain what you meant by your "X." If you agree with everything the author says, practice *reading against the text:* Note statements in the essay that you *could* reasonably disagree with.

2. **Read from the writer's point of view.** What is the purpose of this essay? What is its main idea or thesis? Who is the audience? What writing strategies did the writer use in this essay? *Bracket at least one sentence or passage illustrating each one of the key features for that particular piece of writing.* For argumentative essays, these features include (a) an introduction that sets the context or background of the argument, (b) a statement or a claim about a controversy, (c) a countering of opposing arguments, (d) some evidence or analysis in support of the writer's claim, and (e) a rational, reasonable tone. Label each of these features in the margins next to the brackets.

3. **Note key features of organization, diction, and style in the margin.** Use roman numerals (I, II, III, IV) to indicate major divisions in the essay. Look up definitions of any underlined words. Comment in the margin on any especially vivid, forceful, memorable, or confusing sentences. Note any figurative language (simile, image, metaphor), historical or literary allusions, or use of irony.

Collaborative Reading

In a small group or in your class as a whole, discuss your annotations and then prepare a collectively annotated version of the essay.

1. **Share your Prereading Journal responses.** What experiences or attitudes toward this subject did your group or class have in common? What differences did you have? How did the essay change your initial attitudes or assumptions?

2. **Compare your annotations.** What did other readers notice that you did not? What did you notice that others may have missed?

3. **Compile a collaboratively annotated version of the essay.** The group or class should agree on the best or most representative marginal comments. One person should then write down the annotations agreed on by the majority of the group or class. (Minority opinions or reactions should also be noted.)

4. **The group or class should then write out several questions it still has about the essay.** Questions may be about any aspect of the essay.

5. **Finally, read the questions in the text following each essay.** Use these questions to supplement your group's critical reading of the

essay: Which of these questions have you already answered? Which questions suggest a new idea to your group or class?

Writing Summaries

Writing out a summary of an essay is an excellent way to practice active, critical reading. Summaries should convey the main ideas, the essential argument, or the key features of a text. Although summaries vary in length and complexity, depending on the writer's purpose and audience, their general purpose is to represent the author's or text's ideas as accurately and faithfully as possible. The following paragraphs illustrate how to write an effective summary, drawing on Mortimer Adler's essay, "How to Mark a Book," which appears later in this chapter.

Paraphrasing

Learning to paraphrase key ideas is essential to writing a good summary. A paraphrase simply restates a passage from a text in different words. The goal of a paraphrase is to accurately recast the author's words in your own language. A good paraphrase retains the meaning of the original text but in a more condensed form.

Original Text: There are two ways in which you can own a book. The first is the property right you establish by paying for it, just as you pay for clothes and furniture. But this act of purchase is only the prelude to possession. Full ownership comes only when you have made it a part of yourself, and the best way to make yourself a part of it is by writing in it.

Paraphrase: Although you can own a book simply by buying it, full ownership is achieved only when you actually write in a book.

Direct Quotation

Often summaries directly quote a few key phrases or sentences from the source. Remember: Any words or phrases within the quotation marks must be accurate, word-for-word transcriptions of the original. In a summary, use direct quotations to convey the key ideas in the essay:

```
Book owners who are afraid to mark in books, Adler
contends, have "a false reverence for paper, bind-
ing, and type." They need to learn to "consume"
books, just as we consume a good steak, "to make
yourself a part of it" by writing in it.
```

Note: Do not quote long sentences. As the preceding example does, condense the original sentence to the most important phrases. Use just a short phrase from a sentence or use an *ellipsis* (three spaced periods . . .) to indicate words that you have omitted.

Original Passage:

"But a great book, rich in ideas and beauty, a book that raises and tries to answer great fundamental questions, demands the most active reading of which you are capable."

Condensed Quotation:

According to Adler, "a great book, rich in ideas and beauty ... demands the most active reading of which you are capable."

Techniques for Summarizing

The purpose of a summary is to give a reader a condensed and objective account of the main ideas and features of a text. Usually, a summary has between one and three paragraphs or between one hundred to three hundred words, depending on the length and complexity of the original essay and the intended audience and purpose. Typically, a summary will do the following:

- **Cite the author and title of the text.** In some cases, the place of publication or the context for the essay may also be included.
- **Indicate the main ideas of the text.** Accurately representing the main ideas (while omitting the less important details) is the major goal of a summary.
- **Use direct quotation of key words, phrases, or sentences.** Quote the text directly for a few key ideas. Paraphrase the other important ideas, using your own words.
- **Include author tags.** Use author tags ("according to Adler," or "as Adler contends") to remind the reader that you are summarizing the author and the text, not giving your own ideas. **Note:** Instead of repeating "Adler says," choose verbs that more accurately represent the purpose or tone of the original passage, such as "Adler argues," "Adler contends," "Adler questions," or "Adler explains."
- **Avoid summarizing specific examples or data.** Unless they help illustrate the thesis or main idea of the text, citing examples is unnecessary.

- **Report the main ideas as objectively as possible.** Represent the author and text as accurately and faithfully as possible. Do NOT include your own thoughts, ideas, evaluations, or responses.

Sample Summary

Read the following summary of "How to Mark a Book" by Mortimer Adler. His essay appears later in this chapter. After you have reread Adler's essay, apply Adler's active reading strategies to this summary. *In the margins of this book, note sentences in the summary that illustrate each of the above six strategies for writing an effective summary:* citing author and title, indicating the main ideas, using occasional direct quotation, including author tags, avoiding summarizing data or examples, and summarizing objectively without adding evaluations, reactions, or responses.

In his essay, "How to Mark a Book," Mortimer Adler argues that the best way to read a book is literally to mark it up, "to write between the lines," to underline key passages, to circle key words, make asterisks, and write in the front papers. Adler admits that we should not write in a library copy of a book or mark up a priceless first edition of *Paradise Lost*. Rather, he recommends that we buy cheap reprint editions so we can "have a conversation" with the author by writing our thoughts and reactions in the margins. Book owners who are afraid to mark in books, Adler contends, have "a false reverence for paper, binding, and type." They need to learn to "consume" books, just as we consume a good steak, "to make yourself a part of it" by writing in it. After giving his own seven strategies for active reading, Adler concludes his essay by reminding his readers that "a great book, rich in ideas and beauty ... demands the most active reading of which you are capable."

Writing Responses

In a summary, your goal is to represent the key ideas of a text without evaluating, commenting, or editorializing. In a response, however, you should give your own reactions and interpretations. The summary should say, "Here's what **the author** is saying." In contrast, the response says, "Here's what **I think** about what the author said." Responding is where you fully activate your critical reading.

Depending on the purpose and intended audience, a response to a text can take several directions. Usually responses will focus on one or more of the following strategies:

- **Agreeing and/or disagreeing with the ideas in the text.** Often, responders react to the ideas or the argument of the essay. In this case, the responders show why they agree and/or disagree with what the author says.
- **Analyzing the effectiveness of the text.** In this case, responders evaluate key features such as the originality of the main idea; the clarity of the organization of the argument; the logical reasoning of an argument; the quality of the supporting evidence; and/or the effectiveness of the author's style, tone, and voice.
- **Interpreting and reflecting on the text.** The responder explains key passages by examining the *underlying assumptions* or the *implications* of the ideas. Often, the responder *reflects* on how his or her own experiences, attitudes, and observations relate to the text.

If you are asked to respond to one of the essays in this textbook, use one or more of these strategies to guide your own essay.

Reading and Analyzing Visuals

Communication in the twenty-first century increasingly depends on our ability to read, understand, and respond to visuals that we encounter on the Internet and on television, in newspapers and magazines, or in advertising. Visual images sometimes occur by themselves, but more typically they occur with some written text and in some social or political context. Like written texts, visual images have a purpose and are directed at a particular audience in a certain context.

Techniques for Reading and Analyzing Visuals

As you read and analyze visuals, always consider the rhetorical situation—the purpose, intended audience, social context, and of course the creator, designer, or user of the visual. Since most visuals appear in the context of accompanying written words or messages, analyzing visuals becomes a key part of critical reading. Use the following techniques to help you read and analyze visuals.

- **Analyzing the composition of the visual by itself.** Describe how the layout, color, contrasts, type face, balance, or use of diagonals draws your attention to some point. Look at the key figures, symbols, and cultural references in the image. What messages are being conveyed? What is the purpose and who is the intended audience?
- **Analyzing the visual in combination with any accompanying text.** Does the accompanying text or caption work to complement the meaning of the visual? How do the words add to or distract from the visual? Do the words and the visual work together to achieve the same purpose for the intended audience?
- **Analyzing the context of the visual.** In what magazine, essay, newspaper, or Web site does the visual appear? What is the historical or cultural context in which the visual appears? What does this context reveal about the purpose and audience of the visual?
- **Analyzing the rhetorical appeals of the visual.** Visuals, like written words, can use appeals to reason, to emotion, and to credibility in order to affect or persuade the reader or viewer. What appeals to logic or reason do the visual and its accompanying text make? What appeals to pathos or emotion does the visual make? Does the visual try to create an ethos of credibility, reliability, or authority? Do these appeals make the visual successful in informing, convincing, or persuading the reader?

The following example illustrates how to use these techniques when reading and analyzing a visual. Before you read the next paragraph, however, study the following visual by photographer Jim Goldberg. Look at the layout of the photograph. Consider lighting, contrasts, and use of diagonals. Who is in the foreground and who in the background? Who is strongly lit by the light from the window and who is in the shadow? What is each figure wearing? What does the caption say? Why is it written in handwriting rather than in a typeface? Write out your own analysis of this visual before you read the following paragraph.

In this image, photographer Jim Goldberg effectively illustrates how a visual and accompanying text can combine to create a more powerful message than either word or image alone. The photograph, taken in San Francisco in 1982, shows the lady of the house, Mrs. Stone, standing in her kitchen with her servant, Vickie Figueroa, standing in the background. The diagonal lines of the white counter and the light from the window send us first to the figure of Mrs. Stone, and then to Ms. Figueroa in the background. This foreground/background contrast sets up a power relationship, confirmed by how Mrs. Stone's hands are

My dream was to became a school teacher.
Mrs Stone is rich.
I have talents but not opportunity.
I am used to standing behind
Mrs Stone.
I have been a servant for 40 years.
Vickie Figueroa.

grasping (and owning) the counter (and thus the kitchen and the house) while Ms. Figueroa's hands are tucked behind her. The contrast also between the pointed and poignant writing and the rather conventional kitchen scene gives the visual a special, combined power. The language in Ms. Figueroa's note supports the power relationship of the image. It is as if Ms. Figueroa is saying, "I am used to standing behind Mrs. Stone, accepting my role, even though I have other dreams." Finally, Goldberg's choice to present the text in what is apparently Ms. Figueroa's own handwriting, complete with crossed out letters, uneven lines, and signature, gives her lost dream of becoming a school teacher remarkable emotional power. If Goldberg had simply put her note in typeface, much of the authenticity and power of the visual would be lost. The image and the text together create an appeal to logic and reason through the document of the actual photograph, which shows these two people standing in a real kitchen. The image and the text also appeal to emotion, however, showing how Ms. Figueroa's dreams contrast so sharply with the reality she seems to accept. Finally, the image and the accompanying text create an ethos of credibility. Goldberg shows his integrity as an artist by creating a highly realistic situation that presents the human emotion without over-dramatizing or editorializing.

Testing Your Critical Reading Process

The sample essay that follows is reprinted twice. Use the unannotated version for your practice. First, write on *one* of the Prereading Journal Topics in your journal or notebook for five minutes. Then follow the instructions for critical reading: Do a first reading and an annotated reading. Annotate in the margins of your book.

When you have finished, compare your annotations to the group annotations that accompany the second reprinting of this essay. You'll quickly see that while you may agree with some of these notes, you will undoubtedly disagree at other points, have different reactions, or make different connections. Your reading should use the same process, but it should *not* have identical annotations.

ELLEN GOODMAN

Honor Society Hypocrisy

Prereading Journal Entry

If you knew a teenager who became pregnant during high school, write about her situation. How old was she? Did she want to have the baby? Did she think about abortion? How did the experience affect her schoolwork? How did her experience affect you?

or

Answer the following question: How should pregnant teenagers in high school be treated by the school administration? (Should they be allowed to compete in athletics? Should they be allowed to be in an honor society? Should schools be required to provide day care?) Explain.

Ellen Goodman is a Pulitzer Prize-winning columnist whose essays and editorials have been syndicated in more than 300 newspapers. Her columns have been published in the Boston Globe, McCall's, *the* Village Voice, *and* Harper's Bazaar. *She has published eight books and collections of essays, including* I know Just What You Mean: The Power of Friendship in Women's Lives *(2000) and* Paper Trail: Common Sense in Uncommon Times *(2004). In "Honor Society Hypocrisy," Goodman recounts one woman's fight in the education arena: Arlene Pfeiffer versus the school board of Marion Center, Pennsylvania. From the title, you can probably guess who wins. But Goodman makes us wonder, "Are all of us really a part of this problem?"*

1   If they ever give a college board test for students of hypocrisy, I am sure that the teenagers of Marion Center, Pa., will score way up in the 700s. Teenagers are always the great hypocrisy spotters in our culture. But in the past few months, they've had a lot of extra practice in this small rural town.

2   The central characters of the case that has put Marion Center on the sociological map include seventeen-year-old Arlene Pfeiffer, her five-month-old daughter, Jessica, the school board, and the National Honor Society.

3   Arlene, a high school senior, was class president for three years, student council president last year and a member of the honor society since tenth grade. But in August, she gave birth to Jessica and decided to keep her. In November, Arlene was kicked out of the honor society by her high school. In January, the school board agreed to her removal. Now Arlene is taking her case to the Human Relations Commission and the Equal Employment Opportunity Commission.

4   What is at issue is not her grades—they have remained high—but two other qualities the honor society demands: "leadership and character." The question is whether an unwed mother had lost her "character," whether she would "lead" others in the wrong direction.

5   It is easy to follow the trail of hypocrisy in this move against Arlene, easy as a multiple choice questionnaire. To begin with, the school didn't strip Arlene of her honor society epaulets because she had sex but because she "got caught." About 37 percent of sixteen-year-old teenagers in this country have had intercourse. Arlene was judged to have less character than those who didn't get pregnant.

6   Then too, if Arlene had not had her baby, she would surely have kept her membership. A little less than half of the teen pregnancies

end in abortion. So she was judged to have less character than a girl who chose abortion.

7   Perhaps it would even have been alright if Arlene had given her baby up for adoption. Or if she had married. No one, for that matter, had ever questioned the character of an unwed teenage father.

8   Indeed, it is difficult to identify exactly what part of Arlene's behavior—sex, pregnancy, motherhood, singleness, none of the above—the school wants to punish. This speaks to the confusion of the adults in this situation.

9   It may well be that these adults—teachers and board members—are suffering from simple hypocrisy. Surely the teenagers in town see it that way. But there may also be a more deeply rooted ambivalence that centers around the word "leadership."

10   A generation ago, unwed pregnancy produced a shotgun marriage, an illegal abortion, or a six-month stay out of town. A decade ago, a pregnant teenager could be barred altogether from school.

11   Now those of us who shepherd kids through the high-risk years know that early parenthood is still the surest, most direct route to a diminished future. But we are told that some of the young mothers who have kept their babies were inspired by fairy tales of Hollywood love-children. Many of us now share an underlying anxiety that if we make unwed motherhood appear acceptable, we may make it more possible, and then more likely. If we pin a medal on Arlene Pfeiffer, does she become a role model?

12   "They said," recalls Arlene Pfeiffer, "that by 'leadership' I might lead others to do it—to get pregnant. But I don't go around saying 'stand in line and get pregnant.'" Nor do girls follow the leader into pregnancy.

13   For all our anxiety, we have no evidence to prove that lifting a sanction produces a bumper crop of babies. On the contrary, we know that teenagers don't get pregnant because they want to. Study after study after study has concluded that they simply take chances.

14   The saga of Arlene Pfeiffer, who mothers by night and gathers honor grades by day, who lives at home with parental support and child care, is an exception. If we are afraid of lauding her success, it is largely because of our own failures. We've done a poor job of discouraging early sexual activity. A poor job at getting teenagers to take more responsibility. A poor job at communicating the real handicaps of early childbearing.

15   As for Arlene, she is pursuing fairness through all the flak of hypocrisy and ambivalence in Marion Center, Pa. I think she's giving the adults a lesson in "character" and "leadership."

Honor Society Hypocrisy

1   If they ever give a college board test for students of hypocrisy, I am sure that the teenagers of Marion Center, Pa., will score way up in the 700s. Teenagers are always the great hypocrisy spotters in our culture. But in the past few months, they've had a lot of extra practice in this small rural town.

Lead-in and introduction

2   The central characters of this case that has put Marion Center on the sociological map include seventeen-year-old Arlene Pfeiffer, her five-month-old daughter, Jessica, the school board and the National Honor Society.

Good lead in. This got my interest. Author also sets up context and situation.

3   Arlene, a high school senior, was class president for three years, student council president last year and a member of the honor society since tenth grade. But in August, she gave birth to Jessica and decided to keep her. In November, Arlene was kicked out of the honor society by her high school. In January, the school board agreed to her removal. Now Arlene is taking her case to the Human Relations Commission and the Equal Employment Opportunity Commission.

!! How can they do that?

4   What is at issue is not her grades—they have remained high—but two other qualities the honor society demands: "leadership and character." The question is whether an unwed mother had lost her "character," whether she would "lead" others in the wrong direction.

The central question of the essay.

5   It is easy to follow the trail of hypocrisy in this move against Arlene, easy as a multiple choice questionnaire. To begin with, the school didn't strip Arlene of her honor society epaulets because she had sex but because she "got caught." About 37 percent of sixteen-year-old teenagers in this country have had intercourse. Arlene was judged to have less character than those who didn't get pregnant.

Good question.

Right!

Source for these statistics?

6   Then too, if Arlene had not had her baby, she would surely have kept her membership. A little less than half of the teen pregnancies end in abortion. So she was judged to have less character than a girl who chose abortion.

7   Perhaps it would even have been alright if Arlene had given her baby up for adoption. Or if she had married.

Yes, double standard here.

No one, for that matter, had ever questioned the character of an unwed teenage father.

8   Indeed, it is difficult to identify exactly what part of Arlene's behavior—sex, pregnancy, motherhood, singleness, none of the above—the school wants to punish. This speaks to the confusion of the adults in this situation.

9   It may well be that these adults—teachers and board members—are suffering from simple hypocrisy. Surely the teenagers in town see it that way. But there may also be a more deeply rooted ambivalence that centers around the word "leadership."

Refuting opposition— the adults' hypocrisy.

10   A generation ago, unwed pregnancy produced a shotgun marriage, an illegal abortion, or a six-month stay out of town. A decade ago, a pregnant teenager could be barred altogether from school.

These were all the wrong solutions.

11   Now those of us who shepherd kids through the high-risk years know that early parenthood is still the surest, most direct route to a diminished future. But we are told that some of the young mothers who have kept their babies were inspired by fairy tales of Hollywood love-children. Many of us now share an underlying anxiety that if we make unwed motherhood appear acceptable, we may make it more possible, and then more likely. If we pin a medal on Arlene Pfeiffer, does she become a role model?

This is true!

But not all of us! Who is "us"?

Good question!

12   "They said," recalls Arlene Pfeiffer, "that by 'leadership' I might lead others to do it—to get pregnant. But I don't go around saying 'stand in line and get pregnant.' " Nor do girls follow the leader into pregnancy.

13   For all our anxiety, we have no evidence to prove that lifting a sanction produces a bumper crop of babies. On the contrary, we know that teenagers don't get pregnant because they want to. Study after study after study has concluded that they simply take chances.

Good reasonable tone here.

What are these studies? Cite a couple.

14   The saga of Arlene Pfeiffer, who mothers by night and gathers honor grades by day, who lives at home with parental support and child care, is an exception. If we are afraid of lauding her success, it is largely because of our own failures. We've done a poor job of discouraging early sexual activity. A poor job at getting teenagers to take more responsibility.

Conclusion

Nice reversal of blame.

Here is Goodman's main idea or thesis.

A poor job at communicating the real handicaps of early childbearing.

15   As for Arlene, she is pursuing fairness through all the flak of hypocrisy and ambivalence in Marion Center, Pa. I think she's giving the adults a lesson in "character" and "leadership."

Audience for this essay: Seems to be more directed at adults and the school board. Purpose of this essay: To persuade the audience that Arlene's problem is as much ours as it is hers.

MORTIMER ADLER

How to Mark a Book

Prereading Journal Entry

Open another textbook you are currently reading. Turn to a chapter or passage you have already read for one of your other classes. Describe, briefly, anything you have written in the text—marginal notes, highlighted passages, or underlined words. Does your method of reading (either with many annotations or with few or none) help you learn and remember? Explain, referring to *specific passages* in your text.

It is ironic that Mortimer Adler, the father of the Great Books Program and promoter of Aristotle and the classics, was a high school dropout. He did attend Columbia University, but he did not receive his BA because he refused to take a required swimming test. Adler did, however, eventually receive a PhD, become an editor for the Encyclopedia Britannica, and has written dozens of books on philosophy and education, including How to Read a Book: The Art of Getting a Liberal Education *(1940),* The Great Ideas: A Synopticon of Great Books of the Western World *(1952), and* Adler's Philosophical Dictionary *(1995). For Mortimer Adler, reading the great books does not mean buying expensive, leather-bound volumes to display behind glass doors. Reading means consuming, as you consume a steak, to "get it into your bloodstream." In "How to Mark a Book," Adler proposes a radical method for reading the classics. "Marking up a book," he claims, "is not an act of mutilation but of love." Read his essay and see if you agree with his method of paying "your respects to the author."*

1   You know you have to read "between the lines" to get the most out of anything. I want to persuade you to do something equally important in the course of your reading. I want to persuade you to "write between the lines." Unless you do, you are not likely to do the most efficient kind of reading.

2   I contend, quite bluntly, that marking up a book is not an act of mutilation but of love.

3   You shouldn't mark up a book which isn't yours. Librarians (or your friends) who lend you books expect you to keep them clean, and you should. If you decide that I am right about the usefulness of marking books, you will have to buy them. Most of the world's great books are available today, in reprint editions, at less than a dollar.

4   There are two ways in which you can own a book. The first is the property right you establish by paying for it, just as you pay for clothes and furniture. But this act of purchase is only the prelude to possession. Full ownership comes only when you have made it a part of yourself, and the best way to make yourself a part of it is by writing in it. An illustration may make the point clear. You buy a beefsteak and transfer it from the butcher's icebox to your own. But you do not own the beefsteak in the most important sense until you consume it and get it into your bloodstream. I am arguing that books, too, must be absorbed in your bloodstream to do you any good.

5   Confusion about what it means to *own* a book leads people to a false reverence for paper, binding, and type—a respect for the physical thing—the craft of the printer rather than the genius of the author. They forget that it is possible for a man to acquire the idea, to possess the beauty, which a great book contains, without staking his claim by pasting his bookplate inside the cover. Having a fine library doesn't prove that its owner has a mind enriched by books; it proves nothing more than that he, his father, or his wife, was rich enough to buy them.

6   There are three kinds of book owners. The first has all the standard sets and best-sellers—unread, untouched. (This deluded individual owns woodpulp and ink, not books.) The second has a great many books—a few of them read through, most of them dipped into, but all of them as clean and shiny as the day they were bought. (This person would probably like to make books his own, but is restrained by a false respect for their physical appearance.) The third has a few books or many—everyone of them dog-eared and dilapidated, shaken and loosened by continual use, marked and scribbled in from front to back. (This man owns books.)

7   Is it false respect, you may ask, to preserve intact and unblemished a beautifully printed book, an elegantly bound edition? Of course not. I'd no more scribble all over a first edition of *Paradise Lost* than I'd give my baby a set of crayons and an original Rembrandt! I wouldn't mark up a painting or a statue. Its soul, so to speak, is inseparable from its body. And the beauty of a rare edition or of a richly manufactured volume is like that of a painting or a statue.

8   But the soul of a book *can* be separated from its body. A book is more like the score of a piece of music than it is like a painting. No great musician confuses a symphony with the printed sheets of music. Arturo Toscanini reveres Brahms, but Toscanini's score of the C-minor Symphony is so thoroughly marked up that no one but the maestro himself can read it. The reason why a great conductor makes notations on his musical scores—marks them up again and again each time he returns to study them—is the reason why you should mark your books. If your respect for magnificent binding or typography gets in the way, buy yourself a cheap edition and pay your respects to the author.

9   Why is marking up a book indispensable to reading? First, it keeps you awake. (And I don't mean merely conscious; I mean wide awake.) In the second place, reading, if it is active, is thinking, and thinking tends to express itself in words, spoken or written. The marked book is usually the thought-through book. Finally, writing helps you remember the thoughts you had, or the thoughts the author expressed. Let me develop these three points.

10   If reading is to accomplish anything more than passing time, it must be active. You can't let your eyes glide across the lines of a book and come up with an understanding of what you have read. Now an ordinary piece of light fiction, like say, *Gone With the Wind*, doesn't require the most active kind of reading. The books you read for pleasure can be read in a state of relaxation, and nothing is lost. But a great book, rich in ideas and beauty, a book that raises and tries to answer great fundamental questions, demands the most active reading of which you are capable. You don't absorb the ideas of John Dewey[1] the way you absorb the crooning of Mr. Vallee.[2] You have to reach for them. That you cannot do while you're asleep.

11   If, when you've finished reading a book, the pages are filled with your notes, you know that you read actively. The most famous *active* reader of great books I know is President Hutchins, of the University of Chicago. He also has the hardest schedule of business activities of any man I know. He invariably reads with a pencil, and sometimes, when he picks up a book and pencil in the evening, he finds himself, instead of making intelligent notes, drawing what he calls "caviar factories" on the margins. When that happens, he puts the book down. He knows he's too tired to read, and he's just wasting time.

12   But, you may ask, why is writing necessary? Well, the physical act of writing, with your own hand, brings words and sentences more sharply

[1]John Dewey (1859–1952) was an educator who believed in learning through experimentation.
[2] Rudy Vallee was a popular singer of the 1920s.

before your mind and preserves them better in your memory. To set down your reaction to important words and sentences you have read, and the questions they have raised in your mind, is to preserve those reactions and sharpen those questions.

13 Even if you wrote on a scratch pad, and threw the paper away when you had finished writing, your grasp of the book would be surer. But you don't have to throw the paper away. The margins (top and bottom, as well as side), the end-papers, the very space between the lines, are all available. They aren't sacred. And, best of all, your marks and notes become an integral part of the book and stay there forever. You can pick up the book the following week or year, and there are all your points of agreement, disagreement, doubt, and inquiry. It's like resuming an interrupted conversation with the advantage of being able to pick up where you left off.

14 And that is exactly what reading a book should be: a conversation between you and the author. Presumably he knows more about the subject than you do; naturally, you'll have the proper humility as you approach him. But don't let anybody tell you that a reader is supposed to be solely on the receiving end. Understanding is a two-way operation; learning doesn't consist in being an empty receptacle. The learner has to question himself and question the teacher. He even has to argue with the teacher, once he understands what the teacher is saying. And marking a book is literally an expression of your differences, or agreements of opinion, with the author.

15 There are all kinds of devices for marking a book intelligently and fruitfully. Here's the way I do it:

16 1. **Underlining:** of major points, of important or forceful statements.

17 2. **Vertical lines at the margin:** to emphasize a statement already underlined.

18 3. **Star, asterisk, or other doo-dad at the margin:** to be used sparingly, to emphasize the ten or twenty most important statements in the book. (You may want to fold the bottom corner of each page on which you use such marks. It won't hurt the sturdy paper on which most modern books are printed, and you will be able to take the book off the shelf at any time and, by opening it at the folded-corner page, refresh your recollection of the book.)

19 4. **Numbers in the margin:** to indicate the sequence of points the author makes in developing a single argument.

20 5. **Numbers of other pages in the margin:** to indicate where else in the book the author made points relevant to the point marked; to

tie up the ideas in a book, which, though they may be separated by many pages, belong together.

21   **6. Circling of key words or phrases.**

22   **7. Writing in the margin, or at the top or bottom of the page, for the sake of:** recording questions (and perhaps answers) which a passage raised in your mind; reducing a complicated discussion to a simple statement; recording the sequence of major points right through the books. I use the end-papers at the back of the book to make a personal index of the author's points in the order of their appearance.

23   The front end-papers are, to me, the most important. Some people reserve them for a fancy bookplate. I reserve them for fancy thinking. After I have finished reading the book and making my personal index on the back end-papers, I turn to the front and try to outline the book, not page by page, or point by point (I've already done that at the back), but as an integrated structure, with a basic unity and an order of parts. This outline is, to me, the measure of my understanding of the work.

24   If you're a die-hard anti-book-marker, you may object that the margins, the space between the lines, and the end-papers don't give you room enough. All right. How about using a scratch pad slightly smaller than the page-size of the book—so that the edges of the sheets won't protrude? Make your index, outlines, and even your notes on the pad, and then insert these sheets permanently inside the front and back covers of the book.

25   Or, you may say that this business of marking books is going to slow up your reading. It probably will. That's one of the reasons for doing it. Most of us have been taken in by the notion that speed of reading is a measure of our intelligence. There is no such thing as the right speed for intelligent reading. Some things should be read quickly and effortlessly, and some should be read slowly and even laboriously. The sign of intelligence in reading is the ability to read different things differently according to their worth. In the case of good books, the point is not to see how many of them you can get through, but rather how many can get through you—how many you can make your own. A few friends are better than a thousand acquaintances. If this be your aim, as it should be, you will not be impatient if it takes more time and effort to read a great book than it does a newspaper.

26   You may have one final objection to marking books. You can't lend them to your friends because nobody else can read them without being distracted by your notes. Furthermore, you won't want to lend

them because a marked copy is a kind of intellectual diary, and lending it is almost like giving your mind away.

27   If your friend wishes to read your *Plutarch's Lives, Shakespeare,* or *The Federalist Papers,* tell him gently but firmly to buy a copy. You will lend him your car or your coat—but your books are as much a part of you as your head or your heart.

QUESTIONS FOR DISCUSSION AND WRITING

1. Adler says that "marking a book is literally an expression of your differences, or agreements of opinion, with the author." Find one statement in the essay you agree with. What in your experience makes you agree with Adler? Find one statement you disagree with and explain why you disagree.

2. Compare Adler's method of reading with the process for reading outlined in this chapter. What points does Adler make that this chapter does not? What methods does this chapter suggest that Adler omits?

3. Find one sentence that best expresses Adler's overall purpose for writing this essay. Is his purpose to entertain you, to give you new information, to explain something, or to persuade you? Does he attempt more than one purpose? Explain.

4. Who is Adler's intended audience? Who would voluntarily buy a book entitled, *How to Read a Book: The Art of Getting a Liberal Education?* Who might be assigned to read it? Who would benefit from reading it?

5. Reread your Prereading Journal Entry. What advice would Adler give you about your reading strategies? What advice would you give him? Then interview a class member about his or her reading strategies. Ask this person to show you a textbook with his or her annotations. What advice would Adler give to this student? What advice does this student have for Adler?

SHERMAN ALEXIE

The Joy of Reading and Writing

Prereading Journal Entry

Write down a list of any books, magazines, or even comics you can remember that you read—or had read to you—in your childhood. Describe your memories of these books, stories, or characters. Which books were your favorites? If any of these books are still available to you, open one of them and read a few pages. (If you remember a title but don't have the book, check your library to see if they have a copy.) What do you think of these books now?

Sherman Alexie, a Spokane/Coeur D'Alene American Indian, grew up on a reservation near Spokane, Washington. After a childhood surgery to relieve hydrocephalitis (water on the brain), Alexie's doctors predicted that Sherman would always be mentally retarded; instead, Alexie learned to read at the age of three and by age five had already read many books, including John Stein- beck's The Grapes of Wrath. *Sherman Alexie has written dozens of articles, poems, and books, including a young adult novel,* The Absolute True History of a Part-Time Indian *(2007); a collection of short stories,* The Lone Ranger and Tonto Fistfight in Heaven *(1993), which was released as the film Smoke Signals; and his latest work, a collection of stories and poems entitled* War Dances *(2009).*

1   I learned to read with a Superman comic book. Simple enough, I suppose. I cannot recall which particular Superman comic book I read, nor can I remember which villain he fought in that issue. I cannot remember the plot, nor the means by which I obtained the comic book. What I can remember is this: I was 3 years old, a Spokane Indian boy living with his family on the Spokane Indian Reservation in eastern Washington state. We were poor by most standards, but one of my parents usually managed to find some minimum-wage job or another, which made us middle-class by reservation standards. I had a brother and three sisters. We lived on a combination of irregular paychecks, hope, fear and government surplus food.

2   My father, who is one of the few Indians who went to Catholic school on purpose, was an avid reader of westerns, spy thrillers, murder mysteries, gangster epics, basketball player biographies and anything else he could find. He bought his books by the pound at Dutch's Pawn Shop, Goodwill, Salvation Army and Value Village. When he had extra money, he bought new novels at supermarkets, convenience stores and hospital gift shops. Our house was filled with books. They were stacked in crazy piles in the bathroom, bedrooms and living room. In a fit of unemployment-inspired creative energy, my father built a set of bookshelves and soon filled them with a random assortment of books about the Kennedy assassination, Watergate, the Vietnam War and the entire 23-book series of the Apache westerns. My father loved books, and since I loved my father with an aching devotion, I decided to love books as well.

3   I can remember picking up my father's books before I could read. The words themselves were mostly foreign, but I still remember the exact moment when I first understood, with a sudden clarity, the purpose of a paragraph. I didn't have the vocabulary to say "paragraph," but I realized that a paragraph was a fence that held words. The words inside a paragraph worked together for a common purpose. They had some specific reason for being inside the same fence. This knowledge delighted me. I began to think of everything in terms of paragraphs. Our reservation was a small paragraph within the United States. My family's house was a paragraph, distinct from the other paragraphs of the LeBrets to the north, the Fords to our south and the Tribal School to the west. Inside our house, each family member existed as a separate paragraph but still had genetics and common experiences to link us. Now, using this logic, I can see my changed family as an essay of seven paragraphs: mother, father, older brother, the deceased sister, my younger twin sisters and our adopted little brother.

4   At the same time I was seeing the world in paragraphs, I also picked up that *Superman* comic book. Each panel, complete with picture, dialogue, and narrative, was a three-dimensional paragraph. In one panel, Superman breaks through a door. His suit is red, blue, and yellow. The brown door shatters into many pieces. I look at the narrative above the picture. I cannot read the words, but I assume it tells me that Superman is breaking down the door. Aloud, I pretend to read the words and say "Superman is breaking down the door." Words, dialogue, also float out of Superman's mouth. Because he is breaking down the door, I assume he says, "I am breaking down the door." Once again, I pretend to read the words and say aloud, "I am breaking down the door." In this way, I learned to read.

5   This might be an interesting story all by itself. A little Indian boy teaches himself to read at an early age and advances quickly. He reads *Grapes of Wrath* in kindergarten when other children are struggling through Dick and Jane. If he'd been anything but an Indian boy living on the reservation, he might have been called a prodigy. But he is an Indian boy living on the reservation, and is simply an oddity. He grows into a man who often speaks of his childhood in the third-person, as if it will somehow dull the pain and make him sound more modest about his talents.

6   A smart Indian is a dangerous person, widely feared and ridiculed by Indians and non-Indians alike. I fought with my classmates on a daily basis. They wanted me to stay quiet when the non-Indian teacher

asked for answers, for volunteers, for help. We were Indian children who were expected to be stupid. Most lived up to those expectations inside the classroom, but subverted them on the outside. They struggled with basic reading in school, but could remember how to sing a few dozen powwow songs. They were monosyllabic in front of their non-Indian teachers, but could tell complicated stories and jokes at the dinner table. They submissively ducked their heads when confronted by a non-Indian adult, but would slug it out with the Indian bully who was ten years older. As Indian children, we were expected to fail in the non-Indian world. Those who failed were ceremonially accepted by other Indians and appropriately pitied by non-Indians.

7 I refused to fail. I was smart. I was arrogant. I was lucky. I read books late into the night, until I could barely keep my eyes open. I read books at recess, then during lunch, and in the few minutes left after I had finished my classroom assignments. I read books in the car when my family traveled to powwows or basketball games. In shopping malls, I ran to the bookstores and read bits and pieces of as many books as I could. I read the books my father brought home from the pawnshops and secondhand stores. I read the books I borrowed from the library. I read the backs of cereal boxes. I read the newspaper. I read the bulletins posted on the walls of the school, the clinic, the tribal offices, the post office. I read junk mail. I read auto-repair manuals. I read magazines. I read anything that had words and paragraphs. I read with equal parts joy and desperation. I loved those books, but I also knew that love had only one purpose. I was trying to save my life.

8 Despite all the books I read, I am still surprised I became a writer. I was going to be a pediatrician. These days, I write novels, short stories, and poems. I visit schools and teach creative writing to Indian kids. In all my years in the reservation school system, I was never taught how to write poetry, short stories, or novels. I was certainly never taught that Indians wrote poetry, short stories, and novels. Writing was something beyond Indians. I cannot recall a single time that a guest teacher visited reservation. There must have been visiting teachers. Who were they? Where are they now? Do they exist? I visit the schools as often as possible. The Indian kids crowd the classroom. Many are writing their own poems, short stories, and novels. They have read my books. They have read many other books. They look at me with bright eyes and arrogant wonder. They are trying to save their lives. Then there are the sullen and already defeated Indian kids who sit in the back rows and ignore me with theatrical precision. The pages of their notebooks are

empty. They carry neither pencil nor pen. They stare out the window. They refuse and resist. "Books," I say to them. "Books," I say. I throw my weight against their locked doors. The door holds. I am smart. I am arrogant. I am lucky. I am trying to save our lives.

QUESTIONS FOR DISCUSSION AND WRITING

1. Alexie says that his first book was probably a comic book of Superman. How did Alexie use the Superman comic books to learn to read? How did learning about paragraphs help him understand the world?
2. In the middle of his essay, Alexie says, "A smart Indian is a dangerous person, widely feared and ridiculed by Indians and non-Indians alike." Near the end of the essay, Alexie says, "I loved those books, but I also knew that love had only one purpose. I was trying to save my life." Explain what Alexie means by these two statements.
3. Explain Alexie's purposes for writing this essay. Is he writing to remember how he learned to read? Is he trying to share the excitement he felt about reading? Is he hoping to persuade other children, Indian or not, to learn to read and write? Does he think he can be successful in achieving these goals?
4. Read the essay in this chapter by Malcolm X, "Learning to Read." In a short essay of your own, explain the similarities and differences between the way Malcolm X learned to read (and why reading was important to him) and how and why Sherman Alexie learned to read. How are the lessons they learned important for all readers?

MALCOLM X

Learning to Read

Prereading Journal Entry

In order to understand how Malcolm X educated himself, try the following: Open a regular collegiate dictionary at random to any page. Instead of copying the whole page, choose just *ten* interesting words on that page. Write out the words and the definitions. Then, in a couple of sentences, describe what you learned from this activity.

Malcolm X was an African-American minister, writer, and activist for human rights. He grew up as a street hustler, was convicted of robbery, and during his seven years in prison became a follower of Elijah Muhammad.

Malcolm X's religious conversion was important in his life, but so also was his nonstop reading, which contributed to his meteoric rise in Muhammad's Black Muslim movement during the 1960s. The Autobiography of Malcolm X *(1965), coauthored with Alex Haley, describes Malcolm's transformation from a young hustler and convict with an eighth-grade education to an articulate spokesman for Black pride and self-esteem. In "Learning to Read," Malcolm X describes how he began his education: He copied, line by line and page by page, the entire dictionary. After learning to read from the dictionary, Malcolm X broadened his scope to include many classics of history and literature. "No university would ask any student to devour literature as I did," Malcolm X says. "I knew right there in prison that reading had changed forever the course of my life. As I see it today, the ability to read awoke inside me some long dormant craving to be mentally alive."*

1   It was because of my letters that I happened to stumble upon starting to acquire some kind of a homemade education.

2   I became increasingly frustrated at not being able to express what I wanted to convey in letters that I wrote, especially those to Mr. Elijah Muhammad. In the street, I had been the most articulate hustler out there—I had commanded attention when I said something. But now, trying to write simple English, I not only wasn't articulate, I wasn't even functional. How would I sound writing in slang, the way I would *say* it, something such as, "Look, daddy, let me pull your coat about a cat, Elijah Muhammad—"

3   Many who today hear me somewhere in person, or on television, or those who read something I've said, will think I went to school far beyond the eighth grade. This impression is due entirely to my prison studies.

4   It had really begun back in the Charlestown Prison, when Bimbi first made me feel envy of his stock of knowledge. Bimbi had always taken charge of any conversations he was in, and I had tried to emulate him. But every book I picked up had few sentences which didn't contain anywhere from one to nearly all of the words that might as well have been in Chinese. When I just skipped those words, of course, I really ended up with little idea of what the book said. So I had come to the Norfolk Prison Colony still going through only book-reading motions. Pretty soon, I would have quit even these motions, unless I had received the motivation that I did.

5   I saw that the best thing I could do was get hold of a dictionary—to study, to learn some words. I was lucky enough to reason also that I

should try to improve my penmanship. It was sad. I couldn't even write in a straight line. It was both ideas together that moved me to request a dictionary along with some tablets and pencils from the Norfolk Prison Colony school.

6   I spent two days just riffling uncertainly through the dictionary's pages. I'd never realized so many words existed! I didn't know *which* words I needed to learn. Finally, just to start some kind of action, I began copying.

7   In my slow, painstaking, ragged handwriting, I copied into my tablet everything printed on that first page, down to the punctuation marks.

8   I believe it took me a day. Then, aloud, I read back, to myself, everything I'd written on the tablet. Over and over, aloud, to myself, I read my own handwriting.

9   I woke up the next morning, thinking about those words—immensely proud to realize that not only had I written so much at one time, but I'd written words that I never knew were in the world. Moreover, with a little effort, I also could remember what many of these words meant. I reviewed the words whose meanings I didn't remember. Funny thing, from the dictionary's first page right now, that "aardvark" springs to my mind. The dictionary had a picture of it, a long-tailed, long-eared, burrowing African mammal, which lives off termites caught by sticking out its tongue as an anteater does for ants.

10   I was so fascinated that I went on—I copied the dictionary's next page. And the same experience came when I studied that. With every succeeding page, I also learned of people and places and events from history. Actually the dictionary is like a miniature encyclopedia. Finally the dictionary's A section had filled a whole tablet—and I went on into the B's. That was the way I started copying what eventually became the entire dictionary. It went a lot faster after so much practice helped me to pick up handwriting speed. Between what I wrote in my tablet, and writing letters, during the rest of my time in prison I would guess I wrote a million words.

11   I suppose it was inevitable that as my word-base broadened, I could for the first time pick up a book and read and now begin to understand what the book was saying. Anyone who has read a great deal can imagine the new world that opened. Let me tell you something: from then until I left that prison, in every free moment I had, if I was not reading in the library, I was reading on my bunk. You couldn't have gotten me out of books with a wedge. Between Mr. Muhammad's teachings, my

correspondence, my visitors . . . and my reading of books, months passed without my even thinking about being imprisoned. In fact, up to then, I never had been so truly free in my life.

12   The Norfolk Prison Colony's library was in the school building. A variety of classes was taught there by instructors who came from such places as Harvard and Boston universities. The weekly debates between inmate teams were also held in the school building. You would be astonished to know how worked up convict debaters and audiences would get over subjects like "Should Babies Be Fed Milk?"

13   Available on the prison library's shelves were books on just about every general subject. Much of the big private collection that Parkhurst had willed to the prison was still in crates and boxes in the back of the library—thousands of old books. Some of them looked ancient: covers faded, old-time parchment-looking binding. Parkhurst . . . seemed to have been principally interested in history and religion. He had the money and the special interest to have a lot of books that you wouldn't have in a general circulation. Any college library would have been lucky to get that collection.

14   As you can imagine, especially in a prison where there was heavy emphasis on rehabilitation, an inmate was smiled upon if he demonstrated an unusually intense interest in books. There was a sizable number of well-read inmates, especially the popular debaters. Some were said by many to be practically walking encyclopedias. They were almost celebrities. No university would ask any student to devour literature as I did when this new world opened to me, of being able to read and *understand*.

15   I read more in my room than in the library itself. An inmate who was known to read a lot could check out more than the permitted maximum number of books. I preferred reading in the total isolation of my own room.

16   When I had progressed to really serious reading, every night at about ten P.M. I would be outraged with the "lights out." It always seemed to catch me right in the middle of something engrossing.

17   Fortunately, right outside my door was a corridor light that cast a glow into my room. The glow was enough to read by, once my eyes adjusted to it. So when "lights out" came, I would sit on the floor where I could continue reading in that glow.

18   At one-hour intervals the night guards paced past every room. Each time I heard the approaching footsteps, I jumped into bed and feigned sleep. And as soon as the guard passed, I got back out of bed onto the

floor area of that light-glow, where I would read for another fifty-eight minutes—until the guard approached again. That went on until three or four every morning. Three or four hours of sleep a night was enough for me. Often in the years in the streets I had slept less than that.

19   The teachings of Mr. Muhammad stressed how history had been "whitened"—when white men had written history books, the black man simply had been left out. Mr. Muhammad couldn't have said anything that would have struck me much harder. I had never forgotten how when my class, me and all of those whites, had studied seventh-grade United States history back in Mason, the history of the Negro had been covered in one paragraph, and the teacher had gotten a big laugh with his joke, "Negroes' feet are so big that when they walk, they leave a hole in the ground."

20   This is one reason why Mr. Muhammad's teachings spread so swiftly all over the United States, among *all* Negroes, whether or not they became followers of Mr. Muhammad. The teachings ring true—to every Negro. You can hardly show me a black adult in America—or a white one, for that matter—who knows from the history books anything like the truth about the black man's role. In my own case, once I heard of the "glorious history of the black man," I took special pains to hunt in the library for books that would inform me on details about black history.

21   I can remember accurately the very first set of books that really impressed me. I have since bought that set of books and I have it at home for my children to read as they grow up. It's called *Wonders of the World*. It's full of pictures of archeological finds, statues that depict, usually, non-European people.

22   I found books like Will Durant's *Story of Civilization*. I read H. G. Wells' *Outline of History*. *Souls of Black Folk* by W. E. B. Du Bois gave me a glimpse into the black people's history before they came to this country. Carter G. Woodson's *Negro History* opened my eyes about black empires before the black slave was brought to the United States, and the early Negro struggles for freedom.

23   J. A. Rogers' three volumes of *Sex and Race* told about race-mixing before Christ's time; and Aesop being a black man who told fables; about Egypt's Pharaohs; about the great Coptic Christian Empires; about Ethiopia, the earth's oldest continuous black civilization, as China is the oldest continuous civilization.

24   Mr. Muhammad's teaching about how the white man had been created led me to *Findings In Genetics* by Gregor Mendel. (The dictionary's

G section was where I had learned what "genetics" meant.) I really studied this book by the Austrian monk. Reading it over and over, especially certain sections, helped me to understand that if you started with a black man, a white man could be produced; but starting with a white man, you never could produce a black man—because the white chromosome is recessive. And since no one disputes that there was but one Original Man, the conclusion is clear.

25   During the last year or so, in the *New York Times*, Arnold Toynbee used the word "bleached" in describing the white man. His words were: "White (i.e., bleached) human beings of North European origin . . . " Toynbee also referred to the European geographic area as only a peninsula of Asia. He said there is no such thing as Europe. And if you look at the globe, you will see for yourself that America is only an extension of Asia. (But at the same time Toynbee is among those who have helped to bleach history. He has written that Africa was the only continent that produced no history. He won't write that again. Every day now, the truth is coming to light.)

26   I never will forget how shocked I was when I began reading about slavery's total horror. It made such an impact upon me that it later became one of my favorite subjects when I became a minister of Mr. Muhammad's. The world's most monstrous crime, the sin and the blood on the white man's hands, are almost impossible to believe. Books like the one by Frederick Olmsted opened my eyes to the horrors suffered when the slave was landed in the United States. The European woman, Fanny Kemble, who had married a Southern white slave owner, described how human beings were degraded. Of course I read *Uncle Tom's Cabin*. In fact, I believe that's the only novel I have ever read since I started serious reading.

27   Parkhurst's collection also contained some bound pamphlets of the Abolitionist Anti-Slavery Society of New England. I read descriptions of atrocities, saw those illustrations of black slave women tied up and flogged with whips; of black mothers watching their babies being dragged off, never to be seen by their mothers again; of dogs after slaves, and of the fugitive slave catchers, evil white men with whips and clubs and chains and guns. I read about the slave preacher Nat Turner, who put the fear of God into the white slave master. Nat Turner wasn't going around preaching pie-in-the-sky and "non-violent" freedom for the black man. There in Virginia one night in 1831, Nat and seven other slaves started out at his master's home and through the night they went from one plantation "big house" to the next, killing, until by the

next morning 57 white people were dead and Nat had about 70 slaves following him. White people, terrified for their lives, fled from their homes, locked themselves up in public buildings, hid in the woods, and some even left the state. A small army of soldiers took two months to catch and hang Nat Turner. Somewhere I have read where Nat Turner's example is said to have inspired John Brown to invade Virginia and attack Harpers Ferry nearly thirty years later, with thirteen white men and five Negroes.

28   I read Herodotus, "the father of History," or, rather, I read about him. And I read the histories of various nations, which opened my eyes gradually, then wider and wider, to how the whole world's white men had indeed acted like devils, pillaging and raping and bleeding and draining the whole world's non-white people. I remember, for instance, books such as Will Durant's *The Story of Oriental Civilization*, and Mahatma Gandhi's accounts of the struggle to drive the British out of India.

29   Book after book showed me how the white man had brought upon the world's black, brown, red, and yellow peoples every variety of the sufferings of exploitation. I saw how since the sixteenth century, the so-called "Christian trader" white man began to ply the seas in his lust for Asian and African empires, and plunder, and power. I read, I saw, how the white man never has gone among the non-white peoples bearing the Cross in the true manner and spirit of Christ's teachings— meek, humble, and Christlike.

30   I perceived, as I read, how the collective white man had been actually nothing but a piratical opportunist who used Faustian machinations to make his own Christianity his initial wedge in criminal conquests. First, always "religiously," he branded "heathen" and "pagan" labels upon ancient non-white cultures and civilizations. The stage thus set, he then turned upon his non-white victims his weapons of war. . . .

31   I have often reflected upon the new vistas that reading opened to me. I knew right there in prison that reading had changed forever the course of my life. As I see it today, the ability to read awoke inside me some long dormant craving to be mentally alive. I certainly wasn't seeking any degree, the way a college confers a status symbol upon its students. My homemade education gave me, with every additional book that I read, a little bit more sensitivity to the deafness, dumbness, and blindness that was afflicting the black race in America. Not long ago, an English writer telephoned me from London, asking questions. One was, "What's your alma mater?" I told him, "Books." You will never catch me with a free fifteen minutes in which I'm not studying something I feel might be able to help the black man.

32   Yesterday I spoke in London, and both ways on the plane across the Atlantic I was studying a document about how the United Nations proposes to insure the human rights of the oppressed minorities of the world. The American black man is the world's most shameful case of minority oppression. What makes the black man think of himself as only an internal United States issue is just a catch-phrase, two words, "civil rights." How is the black man going to get "civil rights" before first he wins his *human* rights? If the American black man will start thinking about his *human* rights, and then start thinking of himself as part of one of the world's great peoples, he will see he has a case for the United Nations.

33   I can't think of a better case! Four hundred years of black blood and sweat invested here in America, and the white man still has the black man begging for what every immigrant fresh off the ship can take for granted the minute he walks down the gangplank.

34   But I'm digressing. I told the Englishman that my alma mater was books, a good library. Every time I catch a plane, I have with me a book that I want to read—and that's a lot of books these days. If I weren't out here every day battling the white man, I could spend the rest of my life reading, just satisfying my curiosity—because you can hardly mention anything I'm not curious about. I don't think anybody ever got more out of going to prison than I did. In fact, prison enabled me to study far more intensively than I would have if my life had gone differently and I had attended some college. I imagine that one of the biggest troubles with colleges is there are too many distractions, too much panty-raiding, fraternities, and boola-boola and all of that. Where else but in a prison could I have attacked my ignorance by being able to study intensely sometimes as much as fifteen hours a day?

QUESTIONS FOR DISCUSSION AND WRITING

1. Try Malcolm X's method of reading on this essay: Look up any unfamiliar names in a dictionary or encyclopedia. (Your dictionary will certainly have Durant, H. G. Wells, and DuBois, but does it have Woodson and Rogers?) What did you learn from these entries that helped you understand this essay?

2. Malcolm X's purposes in this passage are to explain *how* he learned and *what* he learned. Find specific passages that illustrate each purpose. (What other purposes do you find in this essay?)

3. Who is Malcolm X's intended audience for this passage? Educated white people? African-Americans who want to know about the Muslim movement in America? Students? People in prison? Find two specific passages from the essay that seem to identify the intended audience.

4. Explain the differences between Malcolm X's philosophy and Martin Luther King's. (If necessary, read King's *Letter from Birmingham Jail* in Chapter 9.) How, for example, would King's and Malcolm X's opinions about Nat Turner differ?

5. If you have seen Spike Lee's film *Malcolm X*, how does the portrayal of Malcolm in that film differ from the view given in this essay? How might you explain those differences?

6. Malcolm X describes a system of self-education. What are the advantages and disadvantages of that kind of education? Would it work for you? Would it work for you in your major?

TANIA RALLI

Who's a Looter?

Prereading Journal Entry

Write down any memories you have about Hurricane Katrina. Were you affected by the hurricane directly or did you read about it in the newspapers and see media accounts? After writing about your memories, do a Google Images search for "Hurricane Katrina and people." Describe several of the images of people you see there. Explain what conclusions you draw from the pictures you selected.

Tania Ralli has worked as a reporter for the City News Bureau and has contributed articles to the New York Times, the Boston Globe, and the Chicago Tribune. In her article below, which appeared in the New York Times, she describes the reactions of the media and media bloggers to two photographs showing people apparently taking food from grocery stores during the flooding that followed Hurricane Katrina. The controversy was caused not by the photographs themselves but by the captions which suggested that the two white people were "finding" grocery items while a young African American was "looting" a grocery store. As is apparent from this essay, assigning a caption to a photograph is, in fact, a way of "reading" and "interpreting" the picture.

1   Two news photographs ricocheted through the Internet last week and set off a debate about race and the news media in the aftermath of Hurricane Katrina.

Dave Martin/AP Wide World Photos

2   Information from The A.P. photographer described this young man as looting.

3   In a similar visual circumstance, the white couple was described by a different agency's photographer as finding food.

4   The first photo, taken by Dave Martin, an Associated Press photographer in New Orleans, shows a young black man wading through water that has risen to his chest. He is clutching a case of soda and pulling a floating bag. The caption provided by The A.P. says he has just been "looting a grocery store."

5   The second photo, also from New Orleans, was taken by Chris Graythen for Getty Images and distributed by Agence France-Presse. It shows a white couple up to their chests in the same murky water. The woman is holding some bags of food. This caption says they are shown "after finding bread and soda from a local grocery store."

6   Both photos turned up Tuesday on *Yahoo! News*, which posts automatic feeds of articles and photos from wire services. Soon after, a user of the photo-sharing site *Flickr* juxtaposed the images and captions on a single page, which attracted links from many blogs. The left-leaning blog *Daily Kos* linked to the page with the comment, "It's not looting if you're white."

7   The contrast of the two photo captions, which to many indicated a double standard at work, generated widespread anger toward the news media that quickly spread beyond the Web.

Chris Graythen/Getty Images, Inc.

8 On Friday night, the rapper Kanye West ignored the teleprompter during NBC's live broadcast of "A Concert for Hurricane Relief," using the opportunity to lambaste President Bush and criticize the press. "I hate the way they portray us in the media," he said. "You see a black family, it says they're looting. You see a white family, it says they're looking for food."

9   Many bloggers were quick to point out that the photos came from two different agencies, and so could not reflect the prejudice of a single media outlet. A writer on the blog *BoingBoing* wrote: "Perhaps there's more factual substantiation behind each copywriter's choice of words than we know. But to some, the difference in tone suggests racial bias, implicit or otherwise."

10   According to the agencies, each photographer captioned his own photograph. Jack Stokes, a spokesman for The A.P., said that photographers are told to describe what they have seen when they write a caption.

11   Mr. Stokes said The A.P. had guidelines in place before Hurricane Katrina struck to distinguish between "looting" and "carrying." If a photographer sees a person enter a business and emerge with goods, it is described as looting. Otherwise The A.P. calls it carrying.

12   Mr. Stokes said that Mr. Martin had seen the man in his photograph wade into a grocery store and come out with the sodas and bag, so by A.P.'s definition, the man had looted.

13   The photographer for Getty Images, Mr. Graythen, said in an e-mail message that he had also stuck to what he had seen to write his caption, and had actually given the wording a great deal of thought. Mr. Graythen described seeing the couple near a corner store from an elevated expressway. The door to the shop was open, and things had floated out to the street. He was not able to talk to the couple, "so I had to draw my own conclusions," he said.

14   In the extreme conditions of New Orleans, Mr. Graythen said, taking necessities like food and water to survive could not be considered stealing. He said that had he seen people coming out of stores with computers and DVD players, he would have considered that looting.

15   "If you're taking something that runs solely from a wall outlet that requires power from the electric company—when we are not going to have power for weeks, even months—that's inexcusable," he said.

16   Since the photo was published last Tuesday Mr. Graythen has received more than 500 e-mail messages, most of them supportive, he said.

17   Within three hours of the photo's publication online, editors at Agence France-Presse rewrote Mr. Graythen's caption. But the original caption remained online as part of a *Yahoo! News* slide show. Under pressure to keep up with the news, and lacking the time for a discussion about word choice, Olivier Calas, the agency's director of multimedia, asked *Yahoo!* to remove the photo last Thursday.

18   Now, in its place, when readers seek the picture of the couple, a statement from Neil Budde, the general manager of *Yahoo! News*, appears in its place. The statement emphasizes that *Yahoo! News* did not write the photo captions and that it did not edit the captions, so that the photos can be made available as quickly as possible.

19   Mr. Calas said Agence France-Presse was bombarded with e-mail messages complaining about the caption. He said the caption was unclear and should have been reworded earlier. "This was a consequence of a series of negligences, not ill intent," he said.

20   For Mr. Graythen, whose parents and grandparents lost their homes in the disaster, the fate of the survivors was the most important thing. In his e-mail message he wrote: "Now is no time to pass judgment on those trying to stay alive. Now is no time to argue semantics about finding versus looting. Now is no time to argue if this is a white versus black issue."

QUESTIONS FOR DISCUSSION AND WRITING

1. Review Ralli's essay for the key journalistic information that she reports: Who were the photographers? Where and when were these pictures taken? Who do the photographs depict? Who wrote the captions for each picture? Who first noticed how the captions attributed "looting" to African Americans and "finding" to whites?

2. How do the two photographers define the difference between "looting" and "finding"?

3. The final paragraph of Ralli's article quotes a part of Mr. Graythen's explanation of his choice of words. Do you accept his judgment that the context of Katrina is more important than "semantics"? Explain.

4. Google these photographs and the two photographers, Dave Martin and Chris Graythen. What additional information can you find about the circumstances behind the taking of these photographs, their captions, and the reactions of bloggers, journalists, and commentators?

Writing: Purposes and Processes

WILLIAM ZINSSER, AUTHOR OF *ON WRITING WELL* (1994), says that "Writing is a deeply personal process, full of mystery and surprise. No two people go about it in exactly the same way . . . . There is no 'right method.' Any method that will do the job is the right method for you."

Do you agree with that statement? Since critical reading, as we learned in the last chapter, is active, responsive reading, let's cross-examine Zinsser on this point. (Zinsser is not here to defend himself, so you ask the questions and I'll give Zinsser's responses.)

You: I don't know that writing is always "deeply personal." What if I'm just making a grocery list? What's so "deeply personal" about that?

Zinsser (me): OK. You're right. I just meant that the *way* we write is not mechanical or governed by inflexible rules. It depends on who we are. It depends on the situation—who our audience is, what the context is, what we're trying to say, and how we want to say it.

You: I'll agree that writing, especially in a class, is mysterious. I never know what's right and what's wrong. Usually when I do something I like, the teacher dislikes it—and vice versa. To me, that's the "mystery" in writing.

Zinsser (me): I should be clearer. I was talking about the mystery of how we write, not the mystery of how people react to what we've written.

But you're right. Both reading and writing are trial-and-error processes. Each is an art, not a mathematical equation.

You: What bothers me most is that there is no one right method. You say that everybody writes differently, as though that should comfort me. Frankly, it makes me uneasy. How can I learn if there is no "right" way?

Zinsser (me): I think I overemphasized the point. Most writers do agree on some general guidelines: Be guided by your purpose and your intended audience. Think about the kind of writing you are doing and why or where someone would be reading it. Don't believe that you always have to start at the beginning and write to the end. Start anywhere. Just start. Have a plan as you begin writing, an outline or a direction or a strategy, but be willing to change if you get a better idea. Don't worry about spelling and grammar when you're writing a first draft. Focus on getting your ideas down. When you lose the thread of what you're writing, reread what you've written up to that point. Those are guidelines or methods that many writers follow.

You: How about this: If there is no one "right" method of writing, why are there textbooks on writing?

Me: I'll take this one. Good writing textbooks help you discover and practice appropriate options. You should read about several kinds of writing. You should practice writing for a variety of audiences and purposes. You should practice several different invention activities, such as freewriting, clustering, branching, questioning, summarizing, and interviewing. Different strategies will work for different writers and situations, so learn to use what works best for you. Learning to write is learning to diagnose and then solve problems in your writing.

The Writing Situation

To write effectively, you must consider your writing situation. Effective writing depends on your **purpose** and on the main idea or claim you're making. It depends on your **audience** and on your readers' expectations about your writing. It depends on the **kind of writing** you're doing, whether it is a newspaper article, a blog entry, an analysis of a poem, or a research paper for your psychology class. It depends on you as a **writer**. It depends on the **strategies** you're using. The answers to specific questions ("When can I use first person in an essay?" "How detailed should this example be?" "How long should this essay be?" or "Should I use contractions?") depend on you, your purpose, your audience, and what you are trying to write.

Purposes for Writing

First think about purposes for writing that relate specifically to you as a writer. You should benefit, directly or indirectly, from everything you write. You may write a journal just to **express** your feelings and thoughts. You post an entry to a friend's Facebook page, just to **entertain** yourself and your friend. You may take notes in a biology lab or during a field trip to help you see or **observe** something more clearly. You write shopping lists or class notes to help you **remember.** You may also write a story about some event in your life to help you remember. You may read a newspaper or a book, see a film or a television news program, or interview another person to **investigate** something new and **learn.** In each of these cases, writing helps you learn, remember, observe, or discover something new, something that pleases or benefits you. Without those benefits, few writers would want to write anything.

Now think about purposes for writing that relate to your audience. When writers wish to share what they have learned with a specific audience, they have several options. They can write primarily to **inform** their readers about some idea, issue, or event they have read about or investigated. They may wish to **explain** what something is, how it happened, or why it happened. They might want to **persuade** their audience to believe or do something by evaluating a person, product, service, or a piece of literature, film, or art. They might persuade their readers that a serious problem should be solved in a certain way. Finally, they might persuade their readers by arguing for or against a certain issue or claim.

In actual practice, most writers have **multiple purposes** for writing. They may begin by carefully observing a new film, by investigating what film critics have to say about the film, and by remembering other similar films they have seen. They begin, in short, by learning about their topic. Then they may want to inform their audience about the film, to report what the critics are saying. Or they may want to explain the special effects in the film. Or they may want to evaluate the film.

Or they may want to persuade others to see the film—or not to see it. They may, in fact, want to combine several of these purposes.

Remember: Choosing or knowing your purpose(s) will help you decide how to write. How you begin a paper, how you organize it, what kind of evidence you use, what kind of writing style is appropriate—the answers to all of these questions depend on your purpose(s). Teachers and student editors in your class can help you revise your paper only if they know your intended purpose. Purpose (along with the audience and the context) helps guide the whole writing process.

Audience Analysis

The next important element in the writing situation is the intended audience. On some occasions, your essay defines how your readers are likely to respond. If you're writing an autobiographical essay, for example, readers may meet you on your own terms. On other occasions, however, you must accommodate your audience by knowing who they are, what they are likely to believe or know, and what they are expecting. You don't want to bore your readers with information they already have. You don't want to antagonize your readers if you hope that they will accept your proposal. You don't want to use technical language they might not know. (Or you do want to use technical language for experts in the field.) On each writing occasion, analyze your audience by considering the following:

1. **Audience profile.** Who is your intended reader? First decide on the size and interests of your audience. Is it a single person? Is it a small, well-defined group, such as your family? Is it a larger group with well-defined interests, such as the employees in your company? Is it a large, more diverse audience, such as members of your class or readers of *Rolling Stone* magazine? Is it extremely broad and diverse, such as the readers of the *New York Times?* Then describe your readers as accurately as possible. Do they have identifiable roles (businesspeople who read *Forbes* magazine)? Can you identify their age, sex, economic status, ethnic background, or occupational category? All of this information becomes a profile of your intended audience that will help you write.

2. **Audience-subject relationship.** Consider what your audience *knows* about your intended subject. If they are experts, you may

want to review the basics quickly and move right to the important issues. If they are novices, you will have to explain more of the background and avoid technical language. What is your audience's *attitude* toward your position? Are they sympathetic to your ideas or are they more skeptical or even hostile? If they are hostile, you obviously need to establish yourself as a reasonable, caring person who shares some of their ideas and attitudes.

3. **Audience-writer relationship.** Consider your relationship with your audience. Do you know each other? Are you writing for your employer or for your employees? Are you peers—students in the same class or employees in the same company? Who controls the issue you are writing about? If your reader is in power, you will need to be tactful in your criticism and suggestions. If you are in power, you may want to avoid sounding too autocratic.

4. **Writer's role.** Finally, consider your own perspective or role. You may want to tailor this perspective to your audience. If you are trying to persuade your readers to recycle more, an audience of economists might respond better to the idea that recycling can pay for itself; and you could assume a formal role, citing facts, figures, and statistics. But if you are writing to ordinary citizens, you might be more persuasive if you related a more personal story, such as how your experience riding on a trash truck for a day revealed trash that people should be recycling.

Kinds of Writing

How you write also depends on your audience's expectations about the kind of writing you are doing. A grocery list, an office memorandum, an informal essay, a short story or poem, an interview, a news article, a blog or Facebook entry, a legal brief, a letter, an advertisement—these are distinctly different kinds of writing. Each kind of writing creates **expectations** for a certain community of readers about purpose and form. We expect grocery lists to inform us through key words rather than complete sentences. We expect newspaper articles to inform us through relatively short sentences and paragraphs. We expect advertisements to persuade us by means of exaggerated claims and appealing images and language. We expect informal essays to inform or persuade us by means of well-developed paragraphs, some organizing or shaping strategy(s), and appropriate language.

The Writer's Voice

Who you are can also guide your writing. Your "voice," **the personality that you project through your writing,** can attract your reader's interest, gain your reader's patience as you explain a difficult subject, or defuse your reader's hostility as you argue your point. Writers may use colloquial language to project themselves as relaxed, informal, and conversational. Writers may use direct, candid language to project a no-nonsense approach to the subject. They may write in a humorous or ironic tone to show that they, too, recognize absurdities in life. A writer's voice often guides and controls a piece of writing.

Strategies for Writing

Frequently, a strategy for organizing or developing a topic may control a piece of writing. *Typically, strategies are means or methods of carrying out your purpose.* Strategies are ways of thinking and, at the same time, ways of organizing your writing. If you are writing an autobiographical essay, **chronological order** will probably be a strategy you will follow. If you are explaining why you've chosen a certain major to a friend, you may give specific **examples** of the classes you find most interesting. In a history class, if you are explaining how *glasnost* led to the opening of Eastern Europe, you may want to **define** *glasnost*, explain the steps in the **process** that led to the dismantling of the Berlin wall, and explain the **effects** of Gorbachev's policies on East German leaders. If you are evaluating a current film, you may want to **compare and contrast** the film to other recent films of the same type. Chronological order, example, definition, process analysis, comparison and contrast, and cause-and-effect analysis are strategies that can guide your writing.

Processes for Writing

Many writers divide their writing process into stages or dimensions. After assessing their writing situation, they go through four interrelated activities: **collecting** ideas and information, **shaping** or organizing their ideas, **drafting** the piece of writing, and **revising** and editing a final version.

Assessing the Writing Situation

Initially, you should assess the writing situation. Can you decide on a purpose, audience, context, and topic that interest you? Is this an assignment for a teacher or an employer? Who is the audience? Where might this piece of writing appear? What is or should be the purpose for the writing? What role or voice would be appropriate? *Remember:* Even an excellent piece of writing can fail if it is not responsive to the assignment or the intended audience.

Collecting

Collecting involves gathering and recording impressions, images, detailed observations, personal examples, ideas, facts, statistics, and quotations that are relevant to your purpose and audience. Three primary strategies for collecting are **observing** people, places, and events, **remembering** events from your own life, and **investigating** ideas and information in books and through interviews. In this textbook, essays and assignments in Chapters 3, 4, and 5 help you practice these collecting skills.

Shaping

Shaping involves ordering and organizing ideas and information into sentences and paragraphs. Clear organization helps readers understand new ideas, see relationships between ideas and examples, and persuade readers to believe your claim. The essays in this text illustrate how a writer's **thesis or claim** (the main point or idea) works with specific organizational and developmental **strategies** (comparison/contrast, definition, example, process analysis, cause-and-effect analysis, and so forth) to create an essay that flows smoothly and predictably for the reader.

Drafting

Throughout their writing process, most writers are continually writing, taking notes, brainstorming, or drafting a sample paragraph. At some point, however, they sense that they are ready to write out a first version, or assemble various ideas, pieces, and sentences into some whole. The result is a first, or rough, draft. Most writers agree that when this point arrives, they like to plunge ahead, keeping the pencil or word processor moving, sustaining as much momentum as possible. When they become stuck, they reread what they have already written or check their notes, but then they keep moving while the ideas are flowing. The drafting stage is usually not the time to interrupt the train of thought to correct spelling or revise awkwardly worded sentences.

Revising

Revision literally means "re-seeing." When writers revise, they are looking at their writing again, usually from the point of view of their intended audience. Revision includes major changes in content, organization, purpose, audience, or writer's role. Is my organization clear or should I reorganize? Am I just stating or asserting a point without enough examples to show my readers? Have I made transitions between major points or ideas? Are my sentences clear? Revision may require recollecting ideas or information, changing or improving the organization, or writing for a different audience or purpose. Revision also includes editing: fixing spelling, improving awkward sentences, changing word choice, changing punctuation, and correcting mechanics. Writers learn how to revise by rereading their own writing, by reading passages aloud, by listening to the advice of other readers, and by writing alternate versions of a passage and comparing them to the original.

A Reminder About Writing Process(es)

Note the following three points of caution. *First,* no one process exists for all writers. Writers vary these stages or dimensions according to the writing task at hand. *Second,* the stages in the writing process are recursive: Typically, writers collect some information, do some initial shaping, draft a paragraph, go back and collect some more information, revise a portion, change their organization, collect additional information, and so forth. *Finally,* some writers prefer to describe their process in terms of dimensions, since a single idea may affect several stages simultaneously. For example, a shaping strategy (such as comparison/contrast) may provide an organization, suggest some examples for the writer to collect, and indicate how the writer should revise his or her draft.

Purpose and Process: One Writer's Essay

Following are a clustering exercise, a draft, and the final version of an essay by student writer Nicolle Mircos. Notice how Mircos discovers her idea in a journal entry and then uses her clustering exercise to collect ideas and focus her subject. Compare her first draft to the final draft to see how she shaped and revised her essay. Finally, read her postscript to her final essay. How do her comments reveal her purpose for writing, her intended audience, and her writing process? Does she successfully convey her experience and her main idea to you?

NICOLLE MIRCOS

My Sister, Kari

Prereading Journal Entry

Select one moment in your past that changed your life or showed how your life had already changed. What was the event? What were you like before and afterwards?

Student writer Nicolle Mircos writes about her disabled younger sister. "Whenever I try to picture the past," Mircos says, "my sister Kari and the discovery of her musical ability come to mind." Embarrassed by her sister's disability, Mircos one day overhears her sister playing a Neil Diamond song at the piano. Mircos describes the moment that completely changes their relationship.

Rough Draft

"Shut up!" I yelled at my older sister, Kari. "Mom doesn't really like you!" We were having the third argument of that week. With these words; I turned and ran, not wanting to see the tears fall that were making her eyes glisten and her black mascara run down her cheeks. I hated to see her cry because deep down, I still loved her, even though I now knew the truth about her.

I was only eight years old, but going on forty. At that time I believed that there wasn't anything I couldn't understand. So, when my mother explained to me that my sister was mentally retarded because of problems

at birth, I pretended to understand. In actuality, I was confused, shocked and hurt. At first, I thought God was punishing my parents for something they'd done. Then I thought he was punishing me later I decided that he only punish Kari. Why, did not know.

Since the day my mother had explained it to me, I found myself fighting a lot more with her. She was fifteen, but had the mind of a nine year old and I knew how to use that to my advantage now. I was embarrassed to bring friends home with me, afraid that they would notice and say something.

For a long time, I would sneak into her doorway and just watch every move she made. I guess I was trying to see if she really was different than everyone else. The surprising thing was that she was not, she sat and listened to records a lot, like any other fifteen year old.

One day was different. She listened to records like normal, but then suddenly got up and walked straight past me. I followed her downstairs and to the piano. Suddenly, I was shocked to hear the music from her records being played perfectly on the piano. We both played the piano, but I practiced many long hours using music, she had none. I spent many hours with the metronome learning to count and to play rhythms right, she had none. I approached her cautiously not really knowing if I would see a whole new light on her face or maybe the face of Frankenstein's monster staring me in the eyes. Surprisingly enough, she turned to reveal the same face I had made fun of just hours ago. She was smiling, my face expression hadn't changed: I sat down and began to play a game with her. Covering her eyes I played a note and asked her to name it. Several times we tried this in all ranges of the keyboard, she never missed one. On top of all the other talents, she also had perfect pitch. This was something I would never have. It cannot be learned or taught.

It was at that moment that I saw her with new light. I realized that God had given her a gift to help overcome what he had taken away from her. She would never have a boyfriend or go to the prom, but she could listen to the radio and play flawlessly. I sat down with her and she taught me to use my ear and simple left hand chords to play anything without music: I taught her to read notes. Even though she could not tell me the monetary value of a quarter, she could instantly play a B-flat when it appeared on a page.

From that day on, we learned together. I taught her note values and names and she explained how to create accompaniment to right hand melodies. I didn't fight with her anymore. And I am no longer embarrassed to bring friends to meet her. If someone makes fun of her while I am around, I am the first to defend her while standing proudly at her side.

Final Draft

1   "Shut up!" I yelled at my older sister, Kari. "Mom doesn't really like you!" This was the third argument of the week. With these words I turned and ran, not wanting to see the tears fall, making her eyes glisten and her black mascara run down her cheeks. I hated to see her cry. Deep down I still loved her, even though I now knew the truth about her.

2   I was only eight years old, but going on forty. There wasn't anything I couldn't understand. So, when my mother explained to me that my sister was mentally retarded because of problems at birth, I pretended to understand. In actuality, I was confused, shocked, and hurt. At first, I thought God was punishing my parents for some mistake they'd committed. Then, I thought he was punishing me. I lost the older sister to

teach me about makeup, boys, and fashions. Later, I decided that he only punished Kari. Why, I did not know.

3   But the day my mother explained this deficiency to me, I found myself fighting a lot more with Kari. She was fifteen but had the mind of a nine-year-old. I knew how to use that to get her to do chores that I didn't feel like doing. I never invited friends home: The fear of her saying something to embarrass me loomed too great. For a long time, I would sneak into her doorway and just watch every move she made. Often, I would go unnoticed. She was usually oblivious to the outside world. Most of the time she spent her days listening to the radio, almost motionless. I guess I tried to see if she would reveal two heads or maybe three eyes when alone. Surprisingly to me, she did not. On the outside she was normal; inside her circuits were crossed.

4   One day was different. The familiar sounds of music spilled from the radio, but then without warning, she got up and walked straight past me. I followed her as quickly and as quietly as possible downstairs as she led me to the piano. Astoundingly, music spilled from the keys that, until now, only my fingers had touched. I use the term <u>music</u> loosely here because at first, my mind was too garbled to make sense of anything. Each note seemed to have no bearing on any other. A few moments passed before my mind could make sense of notes and actually recognize that she was playing a song from the radio: Neil Diamond's "Hello Again." All at once, it seemed my ear heard each note before its sound wave had even left the piano string. All at once, my preconceived notions of her dropped into a pit deeper than the darkest pit in the ocean. I played the piano, but I practiced many long hours using music. She had no music and practiced none. I spent many hours with the metronome learning to count and to play rhythms right, she spent none. I approached her cautiously, not really knowing if I would see a whole new light on her face or maybe the face of Frankenstein's monster staring me in the eyes. To my surprise, she turned to reveal the same face I had made dampen with tears just hours ago. She turned to reveal a smile. My look of utter amazement remained for several moments before also slipping into a smile.

5   I sat down and began to play a game with her. Covering her eyes, I played a note and asked her to name it. Several times we tried this in all ranges of the keyboard; she never failed. Then, I determined that she also had perfect pitch, something I was not born with and would never have. This gift cannot be learned or taught. This moment I saw her with new light. God had given her a gift to help overcome what he

had taken away from her. She would never have a boyfriend or go to the prom, but she could listen to the radio and play what she'd heard flawlessly. I sat down with her, and she taught me to use my ear and simple left-hand chords to play easy songs without music, and I taught her to read notes. Even though she could not tell me the monetary value of a quarter, she could instantly play a B-flat when it appeared on a page or name one when she heard it played.

6   From that day on, we learned together. I taught her note values and names. She explained how to create accompaniment to right-hand melodies. I didn't start fights with her anymore. I was no longer embarrassed to bring friends to meet her. I still fight with her as all sisters will, but they are no longer fictitiously based on my part. Now, it's difficult to imagine the past when I didn't want to look at her face, afraid that her looks would sting or that her condition would prove contagious. It's difficult because now we are friends, musical partners in a sense. If someone makes fun of her while I am around, I am the first to defend her while standing proudly at her side.

Postscript: Remembering Essay

1. Explain who your audience is and why you think they'll find this paper interesting or useful.

   My audience is anyone who has not necessarily known someone with a problem, but who has had trouble just being around someone who does. It shows how selfish and mean a "normal" person can be to someone less fortunate and hopefully will teach a lesson about treating people nice. Sometimes it takes a special talent, like perfect pitch, for a person to realize underneath God made everyone the same.

2. What dominant impression do you want to leave with your readers?

   First, I want them to see how selfish I was by not wanting people to meet her and starting fights. Then I hope I created a visual enough scene at the piano to show that I have overcome all of that.

3. List one or two sentences from your essay that make a connection between your memory and the present. How do they connect?

It was at that moment—at the piano—that I saw her in a new light. This means that everything I saw in her before had been transplanted into my present feeling of love and admiration for her talent.

4. Collecting and shaping: Which strategies helped you to remember incidents more quickly and clearly? Which strategies helped you most to focus and organize your essay? What problems were you unable to solve?

The journal writings, especially the one about the memory of a song. I also got a lot out of the groupings and clustering exercise. I hope that I put enough sensitivity and warmth into the piano scene.

5. Drafting and revising: What problems did you run into during the actual drafting of your essay? Where did you go back and reshape or redraft portions? Where did your workshop advice help most?

My biggest problem was how to put my true feelings into words that would be sensitive enough for this situation. I changed a lot in the actual body of the essay, especially in the piano scene, to try and make things more vivid.

6. Was your writing process effective for this essay? Why or why not? Assuming that you had the same amount of time to work on this essay, what would you do differently? What would you do the same?

Yes, it helped to bring back the memories of that day a lot more clearly. I would like more time to work in the groups on certain problems. It is always the best help to hear what someone else thinks should be different.

7. What do you like best about your essay? What would you change if you had another day to work on this assignment?

I would try to work a lot more on the part about the girls at the piano. It was so hard for me to get this across. I hope I have done it sufficiently. As for the opening and concluding paragraphs, they came easily to me and I rather like them.

PETER ELBOW

Freewriting

Prereading Journal Entry

Pick one essay you have written recently. Write down what you remember about the course, the assignment, and your topic. Now, try to describe in detail how you got *started* on this essay. What did you do first? What did you do next? What was the first actual writing you did? Did this writing come easily or was it a struggle? Explain.

Peter Elbow was born in New York in 1935, was educated at Williams College and Exeter College, and completed his graduate work at Harvard and at Brandeis University. A former director of writing programs at the State University of New York at Stony Brook, and has written a number of best-selling books about writing including Writing Without Teachers *(1973),* Writing with Power *(1981),* Embracing Contraries: Explorations in Learning and Teaching *(1986), and* What Is English? *(1990). Peter Elbow often acknowledges that he became interested in writing because of his own difficulty in writing. In "Freewriting," which appeared originally in* Writing Without Teachers, *Elbow offers one strategy that helps him overcome his writing block and gets his ideas flowing easily.*

1   The most effective way I know to improve your writing is to do freewriting exercises regularly. At least three times a week. They are sometimes called "automatic writing," "babbling," or "jabbering" exercises. The idea is simply to write for ten minutes (later on, perhaps fifteen or twenty). Don't stop for anything. Go quickly without rushing. Never stop to look back, to cross something out, to wonder how to spell

something, to wonder what word or thought to use, or to think about what you are doing. If you can't think of a word or a spelling, just use a squiggle or else write, "I can't think of it." Just put down something. The easiest thing is just to put down whatever is in your mind. If you get stuck it's fine to write "I can't think what to say, I can't think what to say" as many times as you want; or repeat the last word you wrote over and over again; or anything else. The only requirement is that you *never* stop.

2   What happens to a freewriting exercise is important. It must be a piece of writing which, even if someone reads it, doesn't send any ripples back to you. It is like writing something and putting it in a bottle in the sea. The teacherless class helps your writing by providing maximum feedback. Freewritings help you by providing no feedback at all. When I assign one, I invite the writer to let me read it. But I also tell him to keep it if he prefers. I read it quickly and make no comments at all and I do not speak with him about it. The main thing is that a freewriting must never be evaluated in any way; in fact there must be no discussion or comment at all.

3   Here is an example of a fairly coherent exercise (sometimes they are very incoherent, which is fine):

```
I think I'll write what's on my mind, but the only
thing on my mind right now is what to write for
ten minutes. I've never done this before and I'm
not prepared in any way—the sky is cloudy today,
how's that? now I'm afraid I won't be able to
think of what to write when I get to the end of
the sentence—well, here I am at the end of the
sentence—here I am again, again, again, again, at
least I'm still writing—Now I ask is there some
reason to be happy that I'm still writing—ah yes!
Here comes the question again—What am I getting
out of this? What point is there in it? It's
almost obscene to always ask it but I seem to
question everything that way and I was gonna say
something else pertaining to that but I got so
busy writing down the first part that I forgot
what I was leading into. This is kind of fun oh
don't stop writing—cars and trucks speeding by
somewhere out the window, pens clittering across
peoples' papers. The sky is still cloudy—is it
```

symbolic that I should be mentioning it? Huh? I
dunno. Maybe I should try colors, blue, red, dirty
words—wait a minute—no can't do that, orange, yellow, arm tired, green pink violet magenta lavender
red brown black green—now that I can't think of
any more colors—just about done—relief? maybe.

4   Freewriting may seem crazy but actually it makes simple sense.
Think of the difference between speaking and writing. Writing has the
advantage of permitting more editing. But that's its downfall too. Almost everybody interposes a massive and complicated series of edit-
ings between the time words start to be born into consciousness and
when they finally come off the end of the pencil or typewriter onto the
page. This is partly because schooling makes us obsessed with the
"mistakes" we make in writing. Many people are constantly thinking
about spelling and grammar as they try to write. I am always thinking
about the awkwardness, wordiness, and general mushiness of my natural verbal product as I try to write down words.

5   But it's not just "mistakes" or "bad writing" we edit as we write. We
also edit unacceptable thoughts and feelings, as we do in speaking. In
writing there is more time to do it so the editing is heavier: when
speaking, there's someone right there waiting for a reply and he'll get
bored or think we're crazy if we don't come out with *something*. Most
of the time in speaking, we settle for the catch-as-catch-can way in
which the words tumble out. In writing, however, there's a chance to
try to get them right. But the opportunity to get them right is a terrible
burden: you can work for two hours trying to get a paragraph "right"
and discover it's not right at all. And then give up.

6   Editing, *in itself*, is not the problem. Editing is usually necessary if
we want to end up with something satisfactory. The problem is that editing goes on *at the same time* as producing. The editor is, as it were,
constantly looking over the shoulder of the producer and constantly
fiddling with what he's doing while he's in the middle of trying to do
it. No wonder the producer gets nervous, jumpy, inhibited, and finally
can't be coherent. It's an unnecessary burden to try to think of words
and also worry at the same time whether they're the right words.

7   The main thing about freewriting is that it is *nonediting*. It is an exercise in bringing together the process of producing words and putting
them down on the page. Practiced regularly, it undoes the ingrained
habit of editing at the same time you are trying to produce. It will make
writing less blocked because words will come more easily. You will use
up more paper, but chew up fewer pencils.

8   Next time you write, notice how often you stop yourself from writing down something you were going to write down. Or else cross it out after it's written. "Naturally," you say, "it wasn't any good." But think for a moment about the occasions when you spoke well. Seldom was it because you first got the beginning just right. Usually it was a matter of a halting or even garbled beginning, but you kept going and your speech finally became coherent and even powerful. There is a lesson here for writing: trying to get the beginning just right is a formula for failure— and probably a secret tactic to make yourself give up writing. Make some words, whatever they are, and then grab hold of that line and reel in as hard as you can. Afterwards you can throw away lousy beginnings and make new ones. This is the quickest way to get into good writing.

9   The habit of compulsive, premature editing doesn't just make writing hard. It also makes writing dead. Your voice is damped out by all the interruptions, changes, and hesitations between the consciousness and the page. In your natural way of producing words there is a sound, a texture, a rhythm—a voice—which is the main source of power in your writing. I don't know how it works, but this voice is the force that will make a reader listen to you, the energy that drives the meanings through his thick skull. Maybe you don't *like* your voice; maybe people have made fun of it. But it's the only voice you've got. It's your only source of power. You better get back into it, no matter what you think of it. If you keep writing in it, it may change into something you like better. But if you abandon it, you'll likely never have a voice and never be heard.

10   Freewritings are vacuums. Gradually you will begin to carry over into your regular writing some of the voice, force, and connectedness that creep into those vacuums.

QUESTIONS FOR DISCUSSION AND WRITING

1. Explain Elbow's "rules" for freewriting. How does a writer go about freewriting?

2. Describe Elbow's purpose and intended audience for this essay. What is his main idea? What does he want his reader to believe or do? Who exactly is the "you" he addresses throughout the essay?

3. If voice is created by the sense of the writer speaking to the reader, describe Elbow's voice in this essay. Cite sentences that illustrate how Elbow creates a friendly, informal, but instructive *conversation* with his reader.

4. Review your Prereading Journal Entry. In your writing process, did you do any freewriting as you started this particular essay? Do you think it

might have helped? Explain why you think freewriting would or would not help you as you write.

5. Elbow's writing is smooth and persuasive, but try reading his argument critically. For example, Elbow says in paragraph 7 that freewriting will "make your writing less blocked because words will come more easily." Look again at his own example of freewriting—does it look like his words are coming easily? Earlier, Elbow says that "schooling makes us obsessed with the 'mistakes' we make in writing." Has that been true in your experience, or is Elbow only talking about his experience in school? Choose other statements and examine them critically, in the light of your own experience as a writer.

ANNE LAMOTT

Shitty First Drafts

Prereading Journal Entry

Think about the last paper you wrote for a class. List the steps you took during your writing process. For example, did you begin by reading and taking notes? Did you make an outline or just start writing a draft? After you had a draft, did someone else read it and give you feedback? What steps did you take as you revised the essay?

"Typing fully formed sentences as fast as a court reporter" is the fantasy that most people have about successful writers. The reality, according to Anne Lamott, is that writers struggle to get past that horrid first draft. Lamott's own writing career testifies that success is possible. She is the author of a dozen novels, including Crooked Little Heart *(1997),* Traveling Mercies *(1999), and her latest,* Imperfect Birds *(2010). Her autobiographical and nonfiction works,* Operating Instructions: A Journal of My Son's First Year *(1993),* Bird by Bird: Some Instructions on Writing and Life *(1995), deal engagingly with the connections between writing and raising a child as a single mother. In this selection from* Bird by Bird: Some Instructions on Writing and Life, *Lamott writes humorously of the painful but possible process of getting the first draft down in order to discover something "so beautiful or wild that you now know what you're supposed to be writing about."*

1   Shitty first drafts. All good writers write them. This is how they end up with good second drafts and terrific third drafts. People tend to look

at successful writers, writers who are getting their books published and maybe even doing well financially, and think that they sit down at their desks every morning feeling like a million dollars, feeling great about who they are and how much talent they have and what a great story they have to tell; that they take in a few deep breaths, push back their sleeves, roll their necks a few times to get all the cricks out, and dive in, typing fully formed passages as fast as a court reporter. But this is just the fantasy of the uninitiated. I know some very great writers, writers you love who write beautifully and have made a great deal of money, and not *one* of them sits down routinely feeling wildly enthusiastic and confident. Not one of them writes elegant first drafts. All right, one of them does, but we do not like her very much. We do not think that she has a rich inner life or that God likes her or can even stand her. (Although when I mentioned this to my priest friend Tom, he said you can safely assume you've created God in your own image when it turns out that God hates all the same people you do.)

2   Very few writers really know what they are doing until they've done it. Nor do they go about their business feeling dewy and thrilled. They do not type a few stiff warm-up sentences and then find themselves bounding along like huskies across the snow. One writer I know tells me that he sits down every morning and says to himself nicely, "It's not like you don't have a choice, because you do—you can either type or kill yourself." We all often feel like we are pulling teeth, even those writers whose prose ends up being the most natural and fluid. The right words and sentences just do not come pouring out like ticker tape most of the time. Now, Muriel Spark is said to have felt that she was taking dictation from God every morning—sitting there, one supposes, plugged into a Dictaphone, typing away, humming. But this is a very hostile and aggressive position. One might hope for bad things to rain down on a person like this.

3   For me and most of the other writers I know, writing is not rapturous. In fact, the only way I can get anything written at all is to write really, really shitty first drafts.

4   The first draft is the child's draft, where you let it all pour out and then let it romp all over the place, knowing that no one is going to see it and that you can shape it later. You just let this childlike part of you channel whatever voices and visions come through and onto the page. If one of the characters wants to say, "Well, so what, Mr. Poopy Pants?" you let her. No one is going to see it. If the kid wants to get into really sentimental, weepy, emotional territory, you let him. Just get it all down

on paper, because there may be something great in those six crazy pages that you would never have gotten to by more rational, grown-up means. There may be something in the very last line of the very last paragraph on page six that you just love, that is so beautiful or wild that you now know what you're supposed to be writing about, more or less, or in what direction you might go—but there was no way to get to this without first getting through the first five and a half pages.

5   I used to write food reviews for *California* magazine before it folded. (My writing food reviews had nothing to do with the magazine folding, although every single review did cause a couple of canceled subscriptions. Some readers took umbrage at my comparing mounds of vegetable puree with various ex-presidents' brains.) These reviews always took two days to write. First I'd go to a restaurant several times with a few opinionated, articulate friends in tow. I'd sit there writing down everything anyone said that was at all interesting or funny. Then on the following Monday I'd sit down at my desk with my notes, and try to write the review. Even after I'd been doing this for years, panic would set in. I'd try to write a lead, but instead I'd write a couple of dreadful sentences, xx them out, try again, xx everything out, and then feel despair and worry settle on my chest like an x-ray apron. It's over, I'd think, calmly; I'm not going to be able to get the magic to work this time. I'm ruined. I'm through. I'm toast. Maybe, I'd think, I can get my old job back as a clerk-typist. But probably not. I'd get up and study my teeth in the mirror for a while. Then I'd stop, remember to breathe, make a few phone calls, hit the kitchen and chow down. Eventually I'd go back and sit down at my desk, and sigh for the next ten minutes. Finally I would pick up my one-inch picture frame, stare into it as if for the answer, and every time the answer would come: all I had to do was to write a really shitty first draft of, say, the opening paragraph. And no one was going to see it.

6   So I'd start writing without reining myself in. It was almost just typing, just making my fingers move. And the writing would be *terrible*. I'd write a lead paragraph that was a whole page, even though the entire review could only be three pages long, and then I'd start writing up descriptions of the food, one dish at a time, bird by bird, and the critics would be sitting on my shoulders, commenting like cartoon characters. They'd be pretending to snore, or rolling their eyes at my overwrought descriptions, no matter how hard I tried to tone those descriptions down, no matter how conscious I was of what a friend said to me gently in my early days of restaurant reviewing. "Annie," she said, "it is just a piece of *chicken*. It is just a bit of *cake*."

7   But because by then I had been writing for so long, I would eventually let myself trust the process—sort of, more or less. I'd write a first draft that was maybe twice as long as it should be, with a self-indulgent and boring beginning, stupefying descriptions of the meal, lots of quotes from my black-humored friends that made them sound more like the Manson girls than food lovers, and no ending to speak of. The whole thing would be so long and incoherent and hideous that for the rest of the day I'd obsess about getting creamed by a car before I could write a decent second draft. I'd worry that people would read what I'd written and believe that the accident had really been a suicide, that I had panicked because my talent was waning and my mind was shot.

8   The next day, though, I'd sit down, go through it all with a colored pen, take out everything I possibly could, find a new lead somewhere on the second page, figure out a kicky place to end it, and then write a second draft. It always turned out fine, sometimes even funny and weird and helpful. I'd go over it one more time and mail it in.

9   Then, a month later, when it was time for another review, the whole process would start again, complete with the fears that people would find my first draft before I could rewrite it.

10   Almost all good writing begins with terrible first efforts. You need to start somewhere. Start by getting something—anything—down on paper. A friend of mine says that the first draft is the down draft—you just get it down. The second draft is the up draft—you fix it up. You try to say what you have to say more accurately. And the third draft is the dental draft, where you check every tooth, to see if it's loose or cramped or decayed, or even, God help us, healthy.

11   What I've learned to do when I sit down to work on a shitty first draft is to quiet the voices in my head. First there's the vinegar-lipped Reader Lady, who says primly, "Well, *that's* not very interesting, is it?" And there's the emaciated German male who writes these Orwellian memos detailing your thought crimes. And there are your parents, agonizing over your lack of loyalty and discretion; and there's William Burroughs, dozing off or shooting up because he finds you as bold and articulate as a houseplant; and so on. And there are also the dogs: let's not forget the dogs, the dogs in their pen who will surely hurtle and snarl their way out if you ever *stop* writing, because writing is, for some of us, the latch that keeps the door of the pen closed, keeps those crazy ravenous dogs contained.

12   Quieting these voices is at least half the battle I fight daily. But this is better than it used to be. It used to be 87 percent. Left to its own devices, my mind spends much of its time having conversations with

people who aren't there. I walk along defending myself to people, or exchanging repartee with them, or rationalizing my behavior, or seducing them with gossip, or pretending I'm on their TV talk show or whatever. I speed or run an aging yellow light or don't come to a full stop, and one nanosecond later am explaining to imaginary cops exactly why I had to do what I did, or insisting that I did not in fact do it.

13   I happened to mention this to a hypnotist I saw many years ago, and he looked at me very nicely. At first I thought he was feeling around on the floor for the silent alarm button, but then he gave me the following exercise, which I still use to this day.

14   Close your eyes and get quiet for a minute, until the chatter starts up. Then isolate one of the voices and imagine the person speaking as a mouse. Pick it up by the tail and drop it into a mason jar. Then isolate another voice, pick it up by the tail, drop it in the jar. And so on. Drop in any high-maintenance parental units, drop in any contractors, lawyers, colleagues, children, anyone who is whining in your head. Then put the lid on, and watch all these mouse people clawing at the glass, jabbering away, trying to make you feel like shit because you won't do what they want—won't give them more money, won't be more successful, won't see them more often. Then imagine that there is a volume-control button on the bottle. Turn it all the way up for a minute, and listen to the stream of angry, neglected, guilt-mongering voices. Then turn it all the way down and watch the frantic mice lunge at the glass, trying to get to you. Leave it down, and get back to your shitty first draft.

15   A writer friend of mine suggests opening the jar and shooting them all in the head. But I think he's a little angry, and I'm sure nothing like this would ever occur to you.

QUESTIONS FOR DISCUSSION AND WRITING

1. List the three or four key steps in Lamott's writing process. How are they similar to or different from the steps you described in the Prereading Journal Entry?

2. Lamott has a double purpose in her essay. On the one hand, she wants to explain how she gets beyond her first drafts. On the other, she wants to entertain us with humorous stories about her own trials and tribulations as a writer. Explain how these two purposes relate to each other. How does her humor make her explanation more effective?

3. A writer's voice is her personality as expressed through language. Find three sentences where Lamott's voice is apparent. Make a list of

adjectives that might describe her voice. How does she use her voice to make the essay more effective?

4. Lamott loves to use images and figurative language to enliven her writing. In paragraph 5, for example, she says she sometimes feels "despair and worry settle on my chest like an x-ray apron." Where else does Lamott use similes (comparisons using *like* or *as*)? What other examples of images or figurative language can you find?

5. Choose one of the other authors in this chapter who write about the writing and revising process—Peter Elbow or Donald Murray. How is Lamott's writing process similar to or different from that of one of these other authors? Whose advice seems best suited to *your* writing process? Explain.

6. Interview one of your classmates about his/her writing process. What are the key steps he/she likes to use? Where in the process does he/she usually get hung up? How does he/she work through those problems? Did he/she find Lamott's advice helpful?

DONALD M. MURRAY

The Maker's Eye: Revising Your Own Manuscripts

Prereading Journal Entry

Nancy Sommers, a researcher and writing teacher, says that when students revise their drafts, they mainly change *words* while adult writers change their *ideas* and *organization* as well. Find a rough draft of an essay you have written. Can you refute Sommers' claim that your main concern was only for fixing up spelling and word choice? Can you find places where you changed ideas or revised the organization?

Writing and reading are inextricably connected as we write and revise. "To produce a progression of drafts, each of which says more and says it more clearly," Donald Murray once said, "the writer has to develop a special kind of reading skill." Donald Murray was a Pulitzer Prize-winning journalist, writing teacher, and researcher who also published magazine articles, books of nonfiction, and poetry. He wrote numerous articles on writing processes, and his textbooks on writing include A Writer Teaches Writing *(1984),* Write to Learn *(1987),* Read to Write *(1990),* Shoptalk: Learning to Write with Writers *(1990), and* The Craft of Revision *(2003). "The Maker's Eye," originally published in* The Writer, *shows Murray's lifelong interest in the craft of writing and revising. A key part of writing, Murray says, is rereading and rewriting: "The maker's eye moves back and forth from word to phrase to sentence to paragraph to sentence to phrase to word. The maker's eye sees the need for variety and balance, for a firmer structure, for a more appropriate form. It peers into the interior of the paragraph, looking for coherence, unity, and emphasis, which make meaning clear."*

1   When students complete a first draft, they consider the job of writing done—and their teachers too often agree. When professional writers complete a first draft, they usually feel that they are at the start of the writing process. When a draft is completed, the job of writing can begin.

2   That difference in attitude is the difference between amateur and professional, inexperience and experience, journeyman and craftsman. Peter F. Drucker, the prolific business writer, calls his first draft "the zero draft"—after that he can start counting. Most writers share the feeling that the first draft, and all of those which follow, are opportunities to discover what they have to say and how best they can say it.

3   To produce a progression of drafts, each of which says more and says it more clearly, the writer has to develop a special kind of reading skill. In school we are taught to decode what appears on the page as finished writing. Writers, however, face a different category of possibility and responsibility when they read their own drafts. To them the words on the page are never finished. Each can be changed and rearranged, can set off a chain reaction of confusion or clarified meaning. This is a different kind of reading, which is possibly more difficult and certainly more exciting.

4   Writers must learn to be their own best enemy. They must accept the criticism of others and be suspicious of it; they must accept the praise of others and be even more suspicious of it. Writers cannot depend on others. They must detach themselves from their own pages so that they can apply both their caring and their craft to their own work.

5   Such detachment is not easy. Science fiction writer Ray Bradbury supposedly puts each manuscript away for a year to the day and then rereads it as a stranger. Not many writers have the discipline or the time to do this. We must read when our judgment may be at its worst, when we are close to the euphoric moment of creation.

6   Then the writer, counsels novelist Nancy Hale, "should be critical of everything that seems to him most delightful in his style. He should excise what he most admires, because he wouldn't thus admire it if he

weren't . . . in a sense protecting it from criticism." John Ciardi, the poet, adds, "The last act of the writing must be to become one's own reader. It is, I suppose, a schizophrenic process, to begin passionately and to end critically, to begin hot and to end cold; and, more important, to be passion-hot and critic-cold at the same time."

7   Most people think that the principal problem is that writers are too proud of what they have written. Actually, a greater problem for most professional writers is one shared by the majority of students. They are overly critical, think everything is dreadful, tear up page after page, never complete a draft, see the task as hopeless.

8   The writer must learn to read critically but constructively, to cut what is bad, to reveal what is good. Eleanor Estes, the children's book author, explains: "The writer must survey his work critically, coolly, as though he were a stranger to it. He must be willing to prune, expertly and hard-heartedly. At the end of each revision, a manuscript may look . . . worked over, torn apart, pinned together, added to, deleted from, words changed and words changed back. Yet the book must maintain its original freshness and spontaneity."

9   Most readers underestimate the amount of rewriting it usually takes to produce spontaneous reading. This is a great disadvantage to the student writer, who sees only a finished product and never watches the craftsman who takes the necessary step back, studies the work carefully, returns to the task, steps back, returns, steps back, again and again. Anthony Burgess, one of the most prolific writers in the English-speaking world, admits, "I might revise a page twenty times." Roald Dahl, the popular children's writer, states, "By the time I'm nearing the end of a story, the first part will have been reread and altered and corrected at least 150 times . . . . Good writing is essentially rewriting. I am positive of this."

10   Rewriting isn't virtuous. It isn't something that ought to be done. It is simply something that most writers find they have to do to discover what they have to say and how to say it. It is a condition of the writer's life.

11   There are, however, a few writers who do little formal rewriting, primarily because they have the capacity and experience to create and review a large number of invisible drafts in their minds before they approach the page. And some writers slowly produce finished pages, performing all the tasks of revision simultaneously, page by page, rather than draft by draft. But it is still possible to see the sequence followed by most writers most of the time in rereading their own work.

12   Most writers scan their drafts first, reading as quickly as possible to catch the larger problems of subject and form, then move in closer and closer as they read and write, reread and rewrite.

13   The first thing writers look for in their drafts is *information*. They know that a good piece of writing is built from specific, accurate, and interesting information. The writer must have an abundance of information from which to construct a readable piece of writing.

14   Next writers look for *meaning* in the information. The specifics must build a pattern of significance. Each piece of specific information must carry the reader toward meaning.

15   Writers reading their own drafts are aware of *audience*. They put themselves in the reader's situation and make sure that they deliver information which a reader wants to know or needs to know in a manner which is easily digested. Writers try to be sure that they anticipate and answer the questions a critical reader will ask when reading the piece of writing.

16   Writers make sure that the *form* is appropriate to the subject and the audience. Form, or genre, is the vehicle which carries meaning to the reader, but form cannot be selected until the writer has adequate information to discover its significance and an audience which needs or wants that meaning.

17   Once writers are sure the form is appropriate, they must then look at the *structure*, the order of what they have written. Good writing is built on a solid framework of logic, argument, narrative, or motivation which runs through the entire piece of writing and holds it together. This is the time when many writers find it most effective to outline as a way of visualizing the hidden spine by which the piece of writing is supported.

18   The element on which writers may spend a majority of their time is *development*. Each section of a piece of writing must be adequately developed. It must give readers enough information so that they are satisfied. How much information is enough? That's as difficult as asking how much garlic belongs in a salad. It must be done to taste, but most beginning writers underdevelop, underestimating the reader's hunger for information.

19   As writers solve development problems, they often have to consider questions of *dimension*. There must be a pleasing and effective proportion among all the parts of the piece of writing. There is a continual process of subtracting and adding to keep the piece of writing in balance.

20   Finally, writers have to listen to their own voices. *Voice* is the force which drives a piece of writing forward. It is an expression of the writer's authority and concern. It is what is between the words on the page, what glues the piece of writing together. A good piece of writing is always marked by a consistent, individual voice.

21   As writers read and reread, write and rewrite, they move closer and closer to the page until they are doing line-by-line editing. Writers read their own pages with infinite care. Each sentence, each line, each clause, each phrase, each word, each mark of punctuation, each section of white space between the type has to contribute to the clarification of meaning.

22   Slowly the writer moves from word to word, looking through language to see the subject. As a word is changed, cut, or added, as a construction is rearranged, all the words used before that moment and all those that follow that moment must be considered and reconsidered.

23   Writers often read aloud at this stage of the editing process, muttering or whispering to themselves, calling on the ear's experience with language. Does this sound right—or that? Writers edit, shifting back and forth from eye to page to ear to page. I find I must do this careful editing in short runs, no more than fifteen or twenty minutes at a stretch, or I become too kind with myself. I begin to see what I hope is on the page, not what actually is on the page.

24   This sounds tedious if you haven't done it, but actually it is fun. Making something right is immensely satisfying, for writers begin to learn what they are writing about by writing. Language leads them to meaning, and there is the joy of discovery, of understanding, of making meaning clear as the writer employs the technical skills of language.

25   Words have double meaning, even triple and quadruple meanings. Each word has its own potential for connotation and denotation. And when writers rub one word against the other, they are often rewarded with a sudden insight, an unexpected clarification.

26   The maker's eye moves back and forth from word to phrase to sentence to paragraph to sentence to phrase to word. The maker's eye sees the need for variety and balance, for a firmer structure, for a more appropriate form. It peers into the interior of the paragraph, looking for coherence, unity, and emphasis, which make meaning clear.

27   I learned something about this process when my first bifocals were prescribed. I had ordered a larger section of the reading portion of the glass because of my work, but even so, I could not contain my eyes within this new limit of vision. And I still find myself taking off my glasses and bending my nose towards the page, for my eyes

unconsciously flick back and forth across the page, back to another page, forward to still another, as I try to see each evolving line in relation to every other line.

28   When does this process end? Most writers agree with the great Russian writer Tolstoy, who said, "I scarcely ever reread my published writings, if by chance I come across a page, it always strikes me: all this must be rewritten; this is how I should have written it."

29   The maker's eye is never satisfied, for each word has the potential to ignite new meaning. This article has been twice written all the way through the writing process, and it was published four years ago. Now it is to be republished in a book. The editors make a few small suggestions, and then I read it with my maker's eye. Now it has been re-edited, re-revised, re-read, re-re-edited, for each piece of writing to the writer is full of potential and alternatives.

30   A piece of writing is never finished. It is delivered to a deadline, torn out of the typewriter on demand, sent off with a sense of accomplishment and shame and pride and frustration. If only there were a couple more days, time for just another run at it, perhaps then . . . .

QUESTIONS FOR DISCUSSION AND WRITING

1. Murray's essay has two main parts. The first section gives testimony from professional writers to show how they reread their drafts more critically than student writers. The second part discusses several steps or stages in the revising process, from the initial rereading to publication. Cite paragraph numbers to indicate these two main parts of the essay.

2. Reread the section on "Purposes for Writing" at the beginning of this chapter. Is Murray's purpose in this essay to inform, explain, persuade, explore, or some combination of purposes? Explain, citing specific passages from Murray's essay.

3. Murray's essay originally appeared in an issue of a magazine called The *Writer. Based* on that information and on the essay itself, identify Murray's intended audience. Is he writing to professional writers, to students, to English teachers, to a general audience, or to some combination of the above? Explain your choice(s).

4. One might say that Murray's basic message is "Good readers make good writers." Reread the essay, placing an asterisk (*) next to sentences where Murray connects critical reading with writing or revising. After completing your marginal annotation, explain how reading is important in writing. Use specific sentences from Murray's essay to support your main points.

5. Not everyone's process for writing and revision is or should be the same. Using an essay that you have written recently, describe how your process for writing and revising compares to Murray's process. After describing the similarities and differences, explain how reading Murray's essay gave you some ideas to think about as you work on your next writing project.

Mother Tongue

Prereading Journal Entry

As we grow up, we learn that we can speak one way in one situation, but we have to speak in different ways in other situations. Recall a time when you used the wrong language—too formal or too informal, too slangy or too pompous, too direct or not direct enough. What was the cause of the awkwardness, and how did you feel?

With the publication of her instant classic, The Joy Luck Club *(1989), Amy Tan revealed the world of Chinese-American culture for all her readers. According to Tan, writing the book helped her work through her ambivalence about her Chinese heritage and discover "how very Chinese I was. And how much had stayed with me that I had tried to deny." Since* The Joy Luck Club, *Tan has written dozens of articles and essays and several novels, including* The Kitchen God's Wife *(1991),* The Hundred Secret Senses *(1995), and* The Bonesetter's Daughter *(2001). In "Mother Tongue," which originally appeared in* Threepenny Review *in 1990, Tan writes about "all the Englishes" she grew up with. The title of the essay, "Mother Tongue," refers both to her mother's language and her native language. For Tan, her mother's language was "broken"—something she was initially ashamed of—but was also "perfectly clear, perfectly natural." In this essay, Tan presents a series of examples from her and her mother's life that illustrate how they coped with their "limited Englishes." Tan also helps us see that the perception of these "limitations" may be the result of our own limited and narrow-minded attitudes toward people of different cultural and language backgrounds.*

1   I am not a scholar of English or literature. I cannot give you much more than personal opinions on the English language and its variations in this country or others.

2   I am a writer. And by that definition, I am someone who has always loved language. I am fascinated by language in daily life. I spend a great deal of my time thinking about the power of language—the way it can evoke an emotion, a visual image, a complex idea, or a simple truth. Language is the tool of my trade. And I use them all—all the Englishes I grew up with.

3   Recently, I was made keenly aware of the different Englishes I do use. I was giving a talk to a large group of people, the same talk I had already given to half a dozen other groups. The nature of the talk was about my writing, my life, and my book, *The Joy Luck Club*. The talk was going along well enough, until I remembered one major difference that made the whole talk sound wrong. My mother was in the room. And it was perhaps the first time she had heard me give a lengthy speech, using the kind of English I have never used with her. I was saying things like, "The intersection of memory upon imagination" and "There is an aspect of my fiction that relates to thus-and-thus"—a speech filled with carefully wrought grammatical phrases, burdened, it suddenly seemed to me, with nominalized forms, past perfect tenses, conditional phrases, all the forms of standard English that I had learned in school and through books, the forms of English I did not use at home with my mother.

4   Just last week, I was walking down the street with my mother, and I again found myself conscious of the English I was using, the English I do use with her. We were talking about the price of new and used furniture and I heard myself saying this: "Not waste money that way." My husband was with us as well, and he didn't notice any switch in my English. And then I realized why. It's because over the twenty years we've been together I've often used that same kind of English with him, and sometimes he even uses it with me. It has become our language of intimacy, a different sort of English that relates to family talk, the language I grew up with.

5   So you'll have some idea of what this family talk I heard sounds like, I'll quote what my mother said during a recent conversation which I videotaped and then transcribed. During this conversation, my mother was talking about a political gangster in Shanghai who had the same last name as her family's, Du, and how the gangster in his early years wanted to be adopted by her family, which was rich by comparison. Later, the gangster became more powerful, far richer than my mother's family, and one day showed up at my mother's wedding to pay his respects. Here's what she said in part:

6   "Du Yusong having business like fruit stand. Like off the street kind. He is Du like Du Zong—but not Tsung-ming Island people. The local people call putong, the river east side, he belong to that side local people. That man want to ask Du Zong father take him in like become own family. Du Zong father wasn't look down on him, but didn't take seriously, until that man big like become a mafia. Now important person, very hard to inviting him. Chinese way, came only to show respect, don't stay for dinner. Respect for making big celebration, he shows up. Mean give lots of respect. Chinese custom. Chinese social life that way. If too important won't have to stay too long. He come to my wedding. I didn't see, I heard it. I gone to boy's side, they have YMCA dinner. Chinese age I was nineteen."

7   You should know that my mother's expressive command of English belies how much she actually understands. She reads the *Forbes* report, listens to *Wall Street Week*, converses daily with her stockbroker, reads all of Shirley MacLaine's books with ease—all kinds of things I can't begin to understand. Yet some of my friends tell me they understand 50 percent of what my mother says. Some say they understand 80 to 90 percent. Some say they understand none of it, as if she were speaking pure Chinese. But to me, my mother's English is perfectly clear, perfectly natural. It's my mother tongue. Her language, as I hear it, is vivid, direct, full of observation and imagery. That was the language that helped shape the way I saw things, expressed things, made sense of the world.

8   Lately, I've been giving more thought to the kind of English my mother speaks. Like others, I have described it to people as "broken" or "fractured" English. But I wince when I say that. It has always bothered me that I can think of no way to describe it other than "broken," as if it were damaged and needed to be fixed, as if it lacked a certain wholeness and soundness. I've heard other terms used, "limited English," for example. But they seem just as bad, as if everything is limited, including people's perceptions of the limited English speaker.

9   I know this for a fact, because when I was growing up, my mother's "limited" English limited *my* perception of her. I was ashamed of her English. I believed that her English reflected the quality of what she had to say. That is, because she expressed them imperfectly her thoughts were imperfect. And I had plenty of empirical evidence to support me: the fact that people in department stores, at banks, and at restaurants did not take her seriously, did not give her good service, pretended not to understand her, or even acted as if they did not hear her.

10   My mother has long realized the limitations of her English as well. When I was fifteen, she used to have me call people on the phone to pretend I was she. In this guise, I was forced to ask for information or even to complain and yell at people who had been rude to her. One time it was a call to her stockbroker in New York. She had cashed out her small portfolio and it just happened we were going to go to New York the next week, our very first trip outside California. I had to get on the phone and say in an adolescent voice that was not very convincing, "This is Mrs. Tan."

11   And my mother was standing in the back whispering loudly, "Why he don't send me check, already two weeks late. So mad he lie to me, losing me money."

12   And then I said in perfect English, "Yes, I'm getting rather concerned. You had agreed to send the check two weeks ago, but it hasn't arrived."

13   Then she began to talk more loudly. "What he want, I come to New York tell him front of his boss, you cheating me?" And I was trying to calm her down, make her be quiet, while telling the stockbroker, "I can't tolerate any more excuses. If I don't receive the check immediately, I am going to have to speak to your manager when I'm in New York next week." And sure enough, the following week there we were in front of this astonished stockbroker, and I was sitting there red-faced and quiet, and my mother, the real Mrs. Tan, was shouting at his boss in her impeccable broken English.

14   We used a similar routine just five days ago, for a situation that was far less humorous. My mother had gone to the hospital for an appointment, to find out about a benign brain tumor a CAT scan had revealed a month ago. She said she had spoken very good English, her best English, no mistakes. Still, she said, the hospital did not apologize when they said they had lost the CAT scan and she had come for nothing. She said they did not seem to have any sympathy when she told them she was anxious to know the exact diagnosis, since her husband and son had both died of brain tumors. She said they would not give her any more information until the next time and she would not leave until the doctor called her daughter. She wouldn't budge. And when the doctor finally called her daughter, me, who spoke in perfect English— lo and behold—we had assurances the CAT scan would be found, promises that a conference call on Monday would be held, and apologies for any suffering my mother had gone through for a most regrettable mistake.

15   I think my mother's English almost had an effect on limiting my possibilities in life as well. Sociologists and linguists probably will tell you that a person's developing language skills are more influenced by peers. But I do think that the language spoken in the family, especially in immigrant families which are more insular, plays a large role in shaping the language of the child. And I believe that it affected my results on achievement tests, IQ test, and the SAT. While my English skills were never judged as poor, compared to math, English could not be considered my strong suit. In grade school I did moderately well, getting perhaps B's, sometimes B-pluses, in English and scoring perhaps in the sixtieth or seventieth percentile on achievement tests. But those scores were not good enough to override the opinion that my true abilities lay in math and science, because in those areas I achieved A's and scored in the ninetieth percentile or higher.

16   This was understandable. Math is precise; there is only one correct answer. Whereas, for me at least, the answers on English tests were always a judgment call, a matter of opinion and personal experience. Those tests were constructed around items like fill-in-the-blank sentence completion, such as, "Even though Tom was _____, Mary thought he was _____." And the correct answer always seemed to be the most bland combinations of thoughts, for example "Even though Tom was shy, Mary thought he was charming," with the grammatical structure "even though" limiting the correct answer to some sort of semantic opposites, so you wouldn't get answers like, "Even though Tom was foolish, Mary thought he was ridiculous." Well, according to my mother, there were very few limitations as to what Tom could have been and what Mary might have thought of him. So I never did well on tests like that.

17   The same was true with word analogies, pairs of words in which you were supposed to find some sort of logical, semantic relationship—for example, "*Sunset* is to *nightfall* as _____ is to _____." And here you would be presented with a list of four possible pairs, one of which showed the same kind of relationship: *red* is to *spotlight, bus* is to *arrival, chills* is to *fever, yawn* is to *boring.* Well, I could never think that way. I knew what the tests were asking, but I could not block out of my mind the images already created by the first pair, "*sunset* is to *nightfall*"—and I would see a burst of colors against a darkening sky, the moon rising, the lowering of a curtain of stars. And all the other pairs of words—red, bus, spotlight, boring—just threw up a mass of confusing images, making it impossible for me to sort out something as logical as saying: "A sunset precedes nightfall" is the same as "a chill

precedes a fever." The only way I would have gotten that answer right would have been to imagine an associative situation, for example, my being disobedient and staying out past sunset, catching a chill at night, which turns into feverish pneumonia as punishment, which indeed did happen to me.

18   I have been thinking about all this lately, about my mother's English, about achievement tests. Because lately I've been asked as a writer, why there are not more Asian Americans represented in American literature. Why are there few Asian Americans enrolled in creative writing programs? Why do so many Chinese students go into engineering? Well, these are broad sociological questions I can't begin to answer. But I have noticed in surveys—in fact, just last week—that Asian students, as a whole, always do significantly better on math achievement tests than in English. And this makes me think that there are other Asian-American students whose English spoken in the home might also be described as "broken" or "limited." And perhaps they also have teachers who are steering them away from writing and into math and science, which is what happened to me.

19   Fortunately, I happen to be rebellious in nature and enjoy the challenge of disproving assumptions made about me. I became an English major my first year in college, after being enrolled as premed. I started writing nonfiction as a freelancer the week after I was told by my former boss that writing was my worst skill and I should hone my talents toward account management.

20   But it wasn't until 1985 that I finally began to write fiction. And at first I wrote using what I thought to be wittily crafted sentences, sentences that would finally prove I had mastery over the English language. Here's an example from the first draft of a story that later made its way into *The Joy Luck Club*, but without this line: "That was my mental quandary in its nascent state." A terrible line, which I can barely pronounce.

21   Fortunately, for reasons I won't get into today, I later decided I should envision a reader for the stories I would write. And the reader I decided upon was my mother, because these were stories about mothers. So with this reader in mind—and in fact she did read my early drafts—I began to write stories using all the Englishes I grew up with: the English I spoke to my mother, which for lack of a better term might be described as "simple"; the English she used with me, which for lack of a better term might be described as "broken"; my translation of her Chinese, which could certainly be described as "watered down"; and

what I imagined to be her translation of her Chinese if she could speak in perfect English, her internal language, and for that I sought to preserve the essence, but neither an English nor a Chinese structure. I wanted to capture what language ability tests can never reveal: her intent, her passion, her imagery, the rhythms of her speech and the nature of her thoughts.

22   Apart from what any critic had to say about my writing, I knew I had succeeded where it counted when my mother finished reading my book and gave me her verdict: "So easy to read."

QUESTIONS FOR DISCUSSION AND WRITING

1. In paragraph 2, Tan says that she uses "all the Englishes" she grew up with. List the different Englishes that Tan describes. In what situations do Tan and her mother use each of these Englishes?

2. What main point or points does Tan make in her essay? List several possible main ideas. Upon rereading her essay, which of these ideas seems most important to Tan? Which is most interesting to you? Explain why.

3. Amy Tan uses several specific examples to illustrate how her and her mother's "limited" English affects their lives. Find at least four places where she uses examples from her life. What main idea does each of these examples illustrate?

4. In paragraph 6, Tan gives an extended example of her mother's English. By yourself or in a small group, reread the paragraph. What exactly is she saying? What sentences are still unclear, even after several readings? Is her language confusing or is it "perfectly natural," as Tan claims? Explain.

5. Do you use "different Englishes" in your own life? Do you speak using one style or vocabulary with your parents at home and another with your friends at school? Do you use one style for texting your friends and another on papers you write for classes? Are there other situations in your life where you use a "different" English? Describe one example where you consciously or unconsciously change your language depending on the situation.

6. Reread paragraph 9. Can you think of a situation where you judged a person based on his or her use of nonstandard English? Discuss. Have others judged you, or not taken you seriously, based on your different accent, dialect, or vocabulary? Explain.

Observing

Observing is an initial purpose for many kinds of writing. We observe in order to discover and learn; once we have taught ourselves by close observation, we can explain our subject to others or even persuade them to take a course of action. In every field of study, careful observation triggers the discovery and learning process. In the sciences, researchers design experiments and then carefully observe their data. In business, people record sales figures and observe buying trends. In the humanities, writers carefully observe (read) books, watch dramas, listen to speeches, examine works of art, and chronicle human behavior.

As writers learn about their subjects, they communicate their findings through specific, observed detail that re-creates the subject for their readers. In a sense, observational writing imitates a scientific experiment. The piece of writing creates the data so each reader can conduct the "experiment" for himself or herself. Just as the crucial part of a scientific experiment is the presentation of data, so the essential part of descriptive writing is the re-creation of key sensory detail.

Although specific details or data are essential for descriptive writing, the observed detail must be related to the writer's purpose. Sometimes writers have a purpose before they begin observing their subject: "I want to describe the effects of acid rain on a forest to show my readers the consequences of burning fossil fuels." Sometimes writers discover their purpose only after carefully observing something that catches their interest: "Describing how freshmen live at the University of Moscow let me discover that young people in different cultures are very much alike." Writers should use detail to make a point or create a dominant impression.

Strategies for Reading and Writing Observing Essays

From the *writer's* point of view, observing techniques help the writer see and learn about the subject by observing repeatedly and describing accurately and vividly. From the *reader's* point of view, descriptive writing gives the data, the details, the examples, and the who, what, when, and where of the subject so that the reader reaches a conclusion based on evidence.

As you read the observing essays in this chapter (and write your own), look for the following features of writing about observations:

- **Use of sensory details (sight, sound, smell, touch, taste).** These details include actual *dialogue* as well as the *names* of things. In the desert, for example, a writer may find several kinds of cacti: barrel cactus, hedgehog cactus, or prickly pear cactus.
- **Use of comparisons and images.** Writers often describe what something looks *like:* from a high vantage point, roads in the desert may look like *veins* stretched out across the terrain.
- **Descriptions of what is not there.** Careful observation requires noticing who or what is *not* present or what is *not* happening. Why are there no large plants in the desert? Why is there no water in this river?
- **Descriptions of changes in the subject's form or condition.** Observing a subject over a period of time may reveal crucial changes that are unapparent at first. A mesa may look static and unchanging, but continued observation reveals that the soil is crumbling and decaying. How fast is it eroding? How has it changed in a hundred years?
- **Use of a distinct point of view.** What writers see or sense depends on who they are, what their purpose is in observing, and what experience they bring to the observation. In the desert, a hitchhiker may hear the sound of a faraway truck in the night; a tourist may hear coyotes howling; an Indian may hear a sacred voice calling from the sky.

■ **Focus on a main idea or dominant impression.** All the details in an effective observing essay should add up to a main idea or create a dominant impression.

Reading an Observing Essay

As you practice active, critical reading of observing essays, pay attention to individual bits of description, but also look for the big picture. Keep asking yourself: What main point does the writer want these details to make?

Prereading

Get a feel for the writing situation: Who is the author? What type of essay is it? What is the context and purpose of the essay? The introductory comments in this chapter and the biographical headnote about the author will help orient you. Also explore what you already know about this subject by writing the Prereading Journal Entry at the beginning of each essay.

First Reading

Read the essay quickly, just to get the main idea and to enjoy your reading. If you find an unfamiliar word, underline it to look up later (don't stop to look up these words). If a passage has an especially *vivid description*, place a "!" in the margin. If you are *confused* by a sentence, place a "?" in the margin. If you can't *visualize* what the writer is saying, place an "X" in the margin. Highlight or place a wavy line under passages that suggest the *main idea* or dominant impression of the essay. At the end of your first reading, write one sentence describing your *initial impression* of the essay.

Annotated Reading

During your second reading, write your own questions, reactions, and comments in the margin: "This is especially vivid" or "Why is the writer describing this?" Bracket [ ] and *label* key features of observing essays: sensory details, images, changes, what is not there, point of view, and dominant impression. In the margin, list or outline the major parts of the writer's description. Finally, look up definitions of any words you underlined during your first reading or that catch your attention now.

Collaborative Reading

In a small group or in your class as a whole, share and discuss your annotations. Begin by reading each other's prereading responses. Then share your annotations, noting what other readers noticed that you didn't. Your group or class may focus on one aspect of the essay (the imagery, the style, the point of view, the overall impression) or you may generate questions for further understanding of the whole essay. During (or following) this group discussion, reread key passages to test your understanding of the essay and compare your reactions to what other readers noticed. Check the questions following the essay—do they suggest ideas you haven't considered?

Writing an Observing Essay

Writing an observing essay is basically a matter of opening your eyes—and the rest of your senses. First teach yourself to see; then use what you've seen to teach your reader. Novice writers mistakenly begin with their conclusions and then they rephrase them several times, as if to emphasize their point:

> There doesn't appear to be much out in the desert. Except for some cactus and dirt, the desert looks pretty empty. Basically, it's just a lot of sand, sun, and nothing. But if you really look there are a whole lot of things that will catch your eye. Actually, the desert has some fascinating stuff.

This writer is merely **telling** the reader. Look at the vague, empty language: "*much*," "*some* cactus," "*pretty* empty," "a *lot* of sand," "a *whole lot of things*," and "*fascinating stuff*." Instead, a writer should be **showing** the reader, representing and re-creating the desert for the reader. To do that, writers approach their subjects as artists do, paintbrush or pencil in hand, drawing and recording everything they see. William Least Heat-Moon's essay in this chapter **shows** the reader the desert near the Pecos River in West Texas:

> For a while, I heard only miles of wind against the Ghost; but after the ringing in my ears stopped, I heard myself breathing, then a bird note, an answering call, another kind of bird

song, and another: mockingbird, mourning dove, an
enigma. I heard the high zizz of flies the color of
gray flannel and the deep buzz of a blue bumblebee.
I made a list of nothing in particular:

1. mockingbird
2. mourning dove
3. enigma bird (heard not saw)
4. gray flies
5. blue bumblebee
6. two circling buzzards (not yet, boys)
7. orange ants
8. black ants
9. orange-black ants (what's been going on?)

These details do the writer's work. Least Heat-Moon's description of the birds (some seen, some not seen), the flies, and the ants **show** that there is more to the desert than meets the inexperienced eye.

Details are important, but equally important is the overall point the writer discovers or wishes to make. "Facts are stupid things," naturalist Louis Agassiz reminds us, "until brought into connection with some general law." **Writers construct and arrange observed details so they add up to some dominant impression.** The dominant impression in Moon's essay is the idea that the desert is not "miles of nothing," but contains a special meaning for the traveler who takes the time to look carefully. Writers make meaning by selecting certain details that they want the reader to "see" and then ordering and arranging these details to focus on a dominant impression.

Choosing a Subject for an Observing Essay

Choose some specific person, place, object, or event as the subject for your observing piece. Observe it repeatedly. Your initial purpose is to use your writing to help you observe, discover, and learn about your subject. When you write your essay from your observing notes, focus on some main idea or dominant impression that the observed details will create for your reader.

Possible subjects for an observing essay:

A public place: airport, bar, library, hotel, shop, park, or street
A place on campus: a science lab, art exhibition, greenhouse, veterinary clinic, research library, campus radio station, gymnasium or stadium, or theater

A personal place: your home, your favorite natural spot, your favorite shop or street, or your dormitory or apartment
People: teachers, students, clerks in stores, artists, police officers, disc jockeys, musicians, other writers, or family and friends
Events: sporting events, concerts, theater, films, or classes

As you brainstorm for possible subjects, remember to choose something that you can reobserve during your writing process. No person, place, or event will be exactly the same on the second observation, but you do need to be able to observe it a second or a third time.

Collecting Details for Your Observing Essay

Observing is a collecting strategy, but some tricks of the trade will help you gather details.

Draw your subject. Even if you are not an artist, a *sketch* may help you see more clearly. Pencils make good eyes.

Zoom in for a closer look at your subject. What do you notice when you examine it closely?

Record sounds accurately. If people are talking, record *actual dialogue*. Turn on a tape recorder and notice what it hears that you don't.

Take double-entry notes. Draw a line vertically down the middle of a page. On the left-hand side, write observed details: color, size, shape, behavior, sound, taste, touch, smell. On the right-hand side, write your impressions, reactions, feelings, or questions.

Ask yourself questions about what you are observing. What exactly is this—can you *define* it? How much could this subject change and still be recognizable? How does it *compare* to other related people, places, or events? From what *points of view* is it usually seen? Who usually sees it; who rarely sees it?

Discuss your subject with other people. What do *they* notice when they observe it? How is that different from what you see? Reobserve your subject and compare with your first notes.

Look up your subject in reference material. What are the *names* of the details or parts? What is its *history or biography?* Reobserve your subject to see what else you notice, now that you have background information.

Freewrite or cluster on your subject. What is seen depends on who is doing the seeing. What are your *memories* about this subject? What do you *associate* with this subject?

Shaping Your Observing Essay

To help organize your observing notes, consider your purpose and audience. Your purpose is to help your reader see, notice, observe, and learn from your subject, but what do you want them to focus on? Start by thinking or writing about what you learned from your observations.

Then think about your readers. What order, strategy, or sequence would help them "discover" what you found out? Test several of the following strategies on your subject. See which one(s) work best.

Chronological Order

Two common shapes are the natural time order (A, B, and C) and the flashback order (B, A, and C). What is the natural time order for the event you observed? In what time order did you *notice* certain details about your subject? Would a flashback order be more effective?

In "Lenses," Dillard uses a straightforward chronological order to help shape several paragraphs in her essay. Read paragraph 14, reprinted below. Notice how the italicized words—*when, kept coming, as they neared, then, as they circled on, as they flew, once,* and *when* give a chronological order to the whole paragraph.

```
I lived in that circle of light, in great speed
and utter silence. When the swans passed before
the sun they were distant—two black threads, two
live stitches. But they kept coming smoothly,
and the sky deepened to blue behind them and
they took on light. They gathered dimension as
they neared, and I could see their ardent,
straining eyes. Then I could hear the brittle
blur of their wings, the blur which faded as
they circled on, and the sky brightened to
yellow behind them and the swans flattened and
darkened and diminished as they flew. Once I
lost them behind the mountain ridge; when they
emerged they were flying suddenly very high, and
it was like music changing key.
```

Comparison/Contrast

Reread your collecting notes. If there are striking similarities/differences among parts of your subject, perhaps a comparison/contrast structure will organize your details.

At the end of "Lenses," Annie Dillard compares looking through her binoculars at the whistling swans with looking at the algae in her microscope. Suddenly, the swans flying above the swaying reeds look like the rotifers swimming through the algae.

> I was lost. The reeds in front of me, swaying and
> out of focus in the binoculars' circular field,
> were translucent. The reeds were strands of color
> passing light like cells in water. They were those
> yellow and green and brown strands of pond algae I
> had watched so long in a light-soaked field. My
> eyes burned; I was watching algae wave in a
> shrinking drop; they crossed each other and parted
> wetly. And suddenly into the field swam two
> whistling swans, two tiny whistling swans. They
> swam as fast as rotifers: two whistling swans,
> infinitesimal, beating their tiny wet wings,
> perfectly formed.

Classification

If you are observing people, grouping them according to types may help. At a fast food place, you might classify (and then describe) people by occupation: office workers, students, construction workers, and retired people. You might classify and describe paintings by type: impressionist, cubist, and surrealist.

Figurative Language

Figurative language and images can make your description more vivid. In "West Texas," William Least Heat-Moon relies on figurative language to create both a visual picture and a feeling for the landscape:

> West of the Pecos, a strangely truncated cone rose
> from the valley. In the oblique evening light, its
> silhouette looked *like a Mayan temple,* so perfect
> was its symmetry. I stopped again, started
> climbing, stirring *a panic of lizards* on the way
> up. From the top, the rubbled land below—*veined
> with the highway and arroyos,* topographical relief
> absorbed in the dusk—looked *like a roadmap.*

Titles, Introductions, and Conclusions

Titles, like labels, should indicate the contents of the package. In addition, titles may catch the reader's attention through some imaginative language. Look at the titles of the essays in this chapter. "West Texas" and "Lenses" are merely labels. Look in the table of contents of this reader. Which titles catch your attention?

Introductions help readers anticipate the subject of the essay. Sometimes they set up the context by answering who, what, where, or when questions. At other times, observing essays begin immediately with some description and let the main idea evolve out of the description.

Conclusions for observing essays often focus on the writer's discovery, the main idea, or the dominant impression. In some cases writers give direct statements of the main idea, but just as often the main idea is implied in the details that the writer selects. An idea, word, or phrase that echoes or repeats an idea from the introduction gives an essay a sense of conclusion or closure.

Drafting Your Observing Essay

When you are ready to write a complete draft, begin by *rereading* your collecting notes, focusing on a dominant impression you want the details to create. You may need to reobserve your subject, just to add additional details that support your main idea. If you are not sure about the dominant impression, you may want to start writing, paying attention to what you observe as you write. Once you start writing, try to keep going. Do not stop to look up words—just draw a line and keep going. If you get stuck, go back and reread your collecting notes.

Revising Your Observing Essay

Before you revise, get some feedback from other members of your class. Remember that you should consider their reactions, but do not make changes just because one reader did not like something. Explain your purpose and your audience, and ask your readers to explain *why* they like something, or *why* it should be cut, or *why* you need more details at one place. *You* must make the final decisions. As you revise, keep the following tips in mind.

- **Reconsider your purpose and audience.** Are you doing what you intended? Can you clearly identify your main idea or dominant impression? Have you identified your audience (has it changed since you began writing)?
- **Identify your point of view.** Your dominant impression will probably be related to your point of view: who you are as an observer, what knowledge you bring to your subject, what your attitude toward your subject is.
- **Consider your vantage point.** Do you have a bird's eye view? Are you observing from a low angle? Do you zoom in for a closer look? Would a different vantage point make your observation more vivid or help emphasize your dominant impression?
- **Check your essay for the key features of observing.** Are you using sensory details? Do you include actual dialogue? Do you use the names of things? Have you used comparisons and images to make your description more vivid? Are you describing what is *not* present or *not* happening? Have you described any important changes in your subject's form or condition? Would your essay be improved by using any of these observing techniques?
- **Edit your essay for clear sentences and appropriate word choice, punctuation, usage, or grammar.** When you are relatively satisfied with your observation, reread it primarily for clarity and appropriateness of language. If possible, have another class member read your essay for possible editing changes.

Postscript for Your Observing Essay

When you've finished your essay, write an entry in your journal describing your writing process. Briefly, answer each of the following questions.

1. On what occasions did you observe your subject?
2. Which collecting strategies worked best?
3. Which shaping strategies helped you organize your essay?
4. What was the main idea or dominant impression your essay created?
5. What did this essay teach you about writing?

West Texas

Prereading Journal Entry

Freewrite for five minutes on an experience you have had in a desert or in the country. What were you doing and what did you notice about the land?

or

Describe an incident when you got out of your car to look more closely at a place you had been driving through. Describe the difference between what you saw from your car and what you noticed when you left your car and started walking.

William Least Heat-Moon wrote Blue Highways: A Journey into America *(1982) about his travels around America on the "blue" highways, the secondary roads marked in blue on road maps. His account of the places and people in "down home" America quickly became a best-seller. As one early reviewer of the book commented, "Some men, when they lose their jobs and their wives, take to drink and go to the dogs. When William Least Heat-Moon lost his, he took to the road and . . . wrote a book about his travels in order to find out where he was trying to arrive." Least Heat-Moon traveled in "Ghost Dancing," his van named in memory of the futile ghost dances of the Plains Indians who believed, in the 1890s, that their dances would return the old lands, the bison, and the Indian warriors fallen in battle. Least Heat-Moon has also written* PrairyErth *(1991),* River Horse: The Logbook of a Boat Across America *(1999),* Columbus in the Americas *(2002), and* Roads to Quoz: An American Mosey *(2008).*

"West Texas" is an excerpt from Blue Highways *in which Least Heat-Moon tests the hypothesis that "nothing is out there" in the barren waste of Southwest Texas. He stops one evening, somewhere in western Crockett County, just off Texas highway 29, and records what he sees and feels.*

1   Straight as a Chief's countenance, the road lay ahead, curves so long and gradual as to be imperceptible except on the map. For nearly a hundred miles due west of Eldorado, not a single town. It was the Texas some people see as barren waste when they cross it, the part they later describe at the motel bar as "nothing." They say, "There's nothing out there."

2   Driving through the miles of nothing, I decided to test the hypothesis and stopped somewhere in western Crockett County on the top of a broad

mesa, just off Texas 29. At a distance, the land looked so rocky and dry, a religious man could believe that the First Hand never got around to the creation in here. Still, somebody had decided to string barbed wire around it.

3   No plant grew higher than my head. For a while, I heard only miles of wind against the Ghost; but after the ringing in my ears stopped, I heard myself breathing, then a bird note, an answering call, another kind of bird song, and another: mockingbird, mourning dove, an enigma. I heard the high zizz of flies the color of gray flannel and the deep buzz of a blue bumblebee. I made a list of nothing in particular:

1. mockingbird
2. mourning dove
3. enigma bird (heard not saw)
4. gray flies
5. blue bumblebee
6. two circling buzzards (not yet, boys)
7. orange ants
8. black ants
9. orange-black ants (what's going on?)
10. three species of spiders
11. opossum skull
12. jackrabbit (chewed on cactus)
13. deer (left scat)
14. coyote (left tracks)
15. small rodent (den full of seed hulls under rock)
16. snake (skin hooked on cactus spine)
17. prickly pear cactus (yellow blossoms)
18. hedgehog cactus (orange blossoms)
19. barrel cactus (red blossoms)
20. devil's pincushion (no blossoms)
21. catclaw (no better name)
22. two species of grass (neither green, both alive)
23. yellow flowers (blossoms smaller than peppercorns)
24. sage (indicates alkali-free soil)
25. mesquite (three-foot plants with eighty-foot roots to reach water that fell as rain two thousand years ago)
26. greasewood (oh, yes)
27. joint fir (steeped stems make Brigham Young tea)
28. earth
29. sky
30. wind (always)

4   That was all the nothing I could identify then, but had I waited until dark when the desert really comes to life, I could have done better. To say nothing is out there is incorrect; to say the desert is stingy with everything except space and light, stone and earth is closer to the truth.

5   I drove on. The low sun turned the mesa rimrock to silhouettes, angular and weird and unearthly; had someone said the far side of Saturn looked just like this, I would have believed him. The road dropped to the Pecos River, now dammed to such docility I couldn't imagine it formerly demarking the western edge of a rudimentary white civilization. Even the old wagonmen felt the unease of isolation when they had crossed the Pecos, a small but once serious river that has had many names: Rio de las Vacas (River of Cows—perhaps a reference to bison), Rio Salado (Salty River), Rio Puerco (Dirty River).

6   West of the Pecos, a strangely truncated cone rose from the valley. In the oblique evening light, its silhouette looked like a Mayan temple, so perfect was its symmetry. I stopped again, started climbing, stirring a panic of lizards on the way up. From the top, the rubbled land below—veined with the highway and arroyos, topographical relief absorbed in the dusk—looked like a roadmap.

7   The desert, more than any other terrain, shows its age, shows time because so little vegetation covers the ancient erosions of wind and storm. What appears is tawny grit once stone and stone crumbling to grit. Everywhere rock, earth's oldest thing. Even desert creatures come from a time older than the woodland animals, and they, in answer to the arduousness, have retained prehistoric coverings of chitin and lapped scale and primitive defenses of spine and stinger, fang and poison, shell and claw.

8   The night, taking up the shadows and details, wiped the face of the desert into a simple, uncluttered blackness until there were only three things: land, wind, stars. I was there too, but my presence I felt more than saw. It was as if I had been reduced to mind, to an edge of consciousness. Men, ascetics, in all eras have gone into deserts to lose themselves—Jesus, Saint Anthony, Saint Basil, and numberless medicine men—maybe because such a losing happens almost as a matter of course here if you avail yourself. The Sioux once chanted, "All over the sky a sacred voice is calling."

9   Back to the highway, on with the headlamps, down Six Shooter Draw. In the darkness, deer, just shadows in the lights, began moving toward the desert willows in the wet bottoms. Stephen Vincent Benet:

When Daniel Boone goes by, at night,
The phantom deer arise
And all lost, wild America
Is burning in their eyes.

10   From the top of another high mesa: twelve miles west in the flat valley floor, the lights of Fort Stockton blinked white, blue, red, and yellow in the heat like a mirage. How is it that desert towns look so fine and big at night? It must be that little is hidden. The glistering ahead could have been a golden city of Cibola. But the reality of Fort Stockton was plywood and concrete block and the plastic signs of Holiday Inn and Mobil Oil.

11   The desert had given me an appetite that would have made carrion crow stuffed with salt-bush taste good. I found a Mexican cafe of adobe, with a whitewashed log ceiling, creekstone fireplace, and jukebox pumping out mariachi music. It was like a bunkhouse. I ate burritos, chile rellenos, and pinto beans, all ladled over with a fine, incendiary sauce the color of sludge from an old steel drum. At the next table sat three big, round men: an Indian wearing a silver headband, a Chicano in a droopy Pancho Villa mustache, and a Negro in faded overalls. I thought what a litany of grievances that table could recite. But the more I looked, the more I believed they were someone's vision of the West, maybe someone making ads for Levy's bread, the ads that used to begin, "You don't have to be Jewish."

QUESTIONS FOR DISCUSSION AND WRITING

1. What surprises does the desert hold for Least Heat-Moon? List some of the things he probably didn't expect to find in the desert.

2. In your own words, describe Least Heat-Moon's purpose(s) in this essay. Why is he describing the desert: to entertain us, to inform us about the desert, to persuade us that we should go there, or to explore his almost religious attraction to the desert? Some or all of the above? Which is his principal purpose?

3. Least Heat-Moon mixes naming and literal description with figurative language. Choose one paragraph that you like. What parts are just names and literal descriptions? What parts contain figurative language? Should he use more literal description and less figurative language? Or the reverse? Explain.

4. If you wrote your Prereading Journal Entry about the desert, what did you notice that Least Heat-Moon did not describe? What did he describe that you had not noticed?

5. In the margin of the essay, next to the second paragraph one student wrote: "Passage has a religious theme." Find other passages in this essay that refer or allude to religion. What is Least Heat-Moon saying about the desert, himself, and religion?

ANNIE DILLARD

Lenses

Prereading Journal Entry

If possible, find or borrow a pair of binoculars. Go to a park or just sit outside somewhere. For three minutes, write down what you see without the binoculars. Then look at one area or object through the binoculars. For three minutes, write down what you see.

Annie Dillard was born in Pittsburgh, Pennsylvania, and received her BA and MA from Hollins College. She has published a book of poetry, Tickets for a Prayer Wheel *(1974); columns and essays for* Living Wilderness, Harpers, *and the* Atlantic; *and several books including* Holy the Firm *(1978),* Living by Fiction *(1982),* An American Childhood *(1987),* Modern American Memoirs *(1995), and* The Maytrees *(2007). Dillard established her reputation with the Pulitzer Prize-winning* Pilgrim at Tinker Creek *(1984), which showcases her extensive reading in the natural sciences and her talent for observing nature.* Pilgrim at Tinker Creek *was based on nearly ten years of observations near Roanoke, Virginia, but was written, Dillard explains, not in the great outdoors, but in a library study carrel, working seven days a week for eight months. "Lenses," which appears in* Teaching a Stone to Talk *(1982), recounts two parallel experiences from Dillard's life: as a child, looking through a microscope at animals and plants in a single drop of pond water; and later, as an adult, looking through binoculars at a pair of whistling swans flying over a pond.*

1   You get used to looking through lenses; it is an acquired skill. When you first look through binoculars, for instance, you can't see a thing. You look at the inside of the barrel; you blink and watch your eyelashes; you play with the focus knob till one eye is purblind.

2   The microscope is even worse. You are supposed to keep both eyes open as you look through its single eyepiece. I spent my childhood in Pittsburgh trying to master this trick: seeing through one eye, with both eyes open. The microscope also teaches you to move your hands

wrong, to shove the glass slide to the right if you are following a creature who is swimming off to the left—as if you were operating a tiller, or backing a trailer, or performing any other of those paradoxical maneuvers which require either sure instincts or a grasp of elementary physics, neither of which I possess.

3   A child's microscope set comes with a little five-watt lamp. You place this dim light in front of the microscope's mirror; the mirror bounces the light up through the slide, through the magnifying lenses, and into your eye. The only reason you do not see everything in silhouette is that microscopic things are so small they are translucent. The animals and plants in a drop of pond water pass light like pale stained glass; they seem so soaked in water and light that their opacity has leached away.

4   The translucent strands of algae you see under a microscope—Spirogyra, Oscillatoria, Cladophora—move of their own accord, no one knows how or why. You watch these swaying yellow, green, and brown strands of algae half mesmerized; you sink into the microscope's field forgetful, oblivious, as if it were all a dream of your deepest brain. Occasionally a zippy rotifer comes barreling through, black and white, and in a tremendous hurry.

5   My rotifers and daphniae and amoebae were in an especially tremendous hurry because they were drying up. I burnt out or broke my little five-watt bulb right away. To replace it, I rigged an old table lamp laid on its side; the table lamp carried a seventy-five-watt bulb. I was about twelve, immortal and invulnerable, and did not know what I was doing; neither did anyone else. My parents let me set up my laboratory in the basement, where they wouldn't have to smell the urine I collected in test tubes and kept in the vain hope it would grow something horrible. So in full, solitary ignorance I spent evenings in the basement staring into a seventy-five-watt bulb magnified three hundred times and focused into my eye. It is a wonder I can see at all. My eyeball itself would start drying up; I blinked and blinked.

6   But the pond water creatures fared worse. I dropped them on a slide, floated a cover slip over them, and laid the slide on the microscope's stage, which the seventy-five-watt bulb had heated like a grill. At once the drop of pond water started to evaporate. Its edges shrank. The creatures swam among algae in a diminishing pool. I liked this part. The heat worked for me as a centrifuge, to concentrate the biomass. I had about five minutes to watch the members of a very dense population, excited by the heat, go about their business until—as I

fancied sadly—they all caught on to their situation and started making out wills.

7   I was, then, not only watching the much-vaunted wonders in a drop of pond water; I was also, with mingled sadism and sympathy, setting up a limitless series of apocalypses. I set up and staged hundreds of ends-of-the-world and watched, enthralled, as they played themselves out. Over and over again, the last trump sounded, the final scroll unrolled, and the known world drained, dried, and vanished. When all the creatures lay motionless, boiled and fried in the positions they had when the last of their water dried completely, I washed the slide in the sink and started over with a fresh drop. How I loved that deep, wet world where the colored algae waved in the water and the rotifers swam!

8   But oddly, this is a story about swans. It is not even a story; it is a description of swans. This description of swans includes the sky over a pond, a pair of binoculars, and a mortal adult who had long since moved out of the Pittsburgh basement.

9   In the Roanoke valley of Virginia, rimmed by the Blue Ridge Mountains to the east and the Allegheny Mountains to the west, is a little semiagricultural area called Daleville. In Daleville, set among fallow fields and wooded ridges, is Daleville Pond. It is a big pond, maybe ten acres; it holds a lot of sky. I used to haunt the place because I loved it; I still do. In winter it had that airy scruffiness of deciduous lands; you greet the daylight and the open space, and spend the evening picking burrs out of your pants.

10   One Valentine's Day, in the afternoon, I was crouched among dried reeds at the edge of Daleville Pond. Across the pond from where I crouched was a low forested mountain ridge. In every other direction I saw only sky, sky crossed by the reeds which blew before my face whichever way I turned.

11   I was looking through binoculars at a pair of whistling swans. Whistling swans! It is impossible to say how excited I was to see whistling swans in Daleville, Virginia. The two were a pair, mated for life, migrating north and west from the Atlantic coast to the high arctic. They had paused to feed at Daleville Pond. I had flushed them, and now they were flying and circling the pond. I crouched in the reeds so they would not be afraid to come back to the water.

12   Through binoculars I followed the swans, swinging where they flew. All their feathers were white; their eyes were black. Their wingspan was six feet; they were bigger than I was. They flew in

unison, one behind the other; they made pass after pass at the pond. I watched them change from white swans in front of the mountain to black swans in front of the sky. In clockwise ellipses they flew, necks long and relaxed, alternately beating their wide wings and gliding.

13   As I rotated on my heels to keep the black frame of the lenses around them, I lost all sense of space. If I lowered the binoculars I was always amazed to learn in which direction I faced—dazed, the way you emerge awed from a movie and try to reconstruct, bit by bit, a real world, in order to discover where in it you might have parked the car.

14   I lived in that circle of light, in great speed and utter silence. When the swans passed before the sun they were distant—two black threads, two live stitches. But they kept coming smoothly, and the sky deepened to blue behind them and they took on light. They gathered dimension as they neared, and I could see their ardent, straining eyes. Then I could hear the brittle blur of their wings, the blur which faded as they circled on, and the sky brightened to yellow behind them and the swans flattened and darkened and diminished as they flew. Once I lost them behind the mountain ridge; when they emerged they were flying suddenly very high, and it was like music changing key.

15   I was lost. The reeds in front of me, swaying and out of focus in the binoculars' circular field, were translucent. The reeds were strands of color passing light like cells in water. They were those yellow and green and brown strands of pond algae I had watched so long in a light-soaked field. My eyes burned; I was watching algae wave in a shrinking drop; they crossed each other and parted wetly. And suddenly into the field swam two whistling swans, two tiny whistling swans. They swam as fast as rotifers: two whistling swans, infinitesimal, beating their tiny wet wings, perfectly formed.

QUESTIONS FOR DISCUSSION AND WRITING

1. Dillard's essay is about discovery. What does she learn about the microscopic life in a drop of pond water? What does she learn about the two whistling swans? Why is this essay titled, "Lenses"?

2. What is Dillard's purpose (or purposes) in this essay? Does the essay have a main idea or leave you with a dominant impression? Explain.

3. Comparing and contrasting her two experiences is Dillard's principal shaping strategy in "Lenses." As she explains in the final paragraph, the two swans parallel the "zippy rotifers," and the reeds of the pond recall the strands of algae. List all the other parallels (similarities and differences) you can find between her two experiences.

4. "Lenses" has some technical language, such as the names of algae ("Spirogyra") and the name of microscopic, aquatic animals ("rotifers"). The essay also uses some sophisticated language, such as "purblind" and "apocalypses." How does this language affect Dillard's intended audience? (Did it bother or confuse you as you read the essay?)

5. In an interview, Dillard said that "people want to make you into a cult figure because of what they fancy to be your lifestyle, when the truth is your life is literature! You're writing consciously, off hundreds of index cards. . . . But all this never occurs to people. They think it happens in a dream, that you just sit on a tree stump and take dictation from some little chipmunk." In "Lenses," what parts come from observation and what parts depend on Dillard's knowledge of biology and botany?

6. Compare Dillard's essay, "Lenses," with Least Heat-Moon's essay, "West Texas." Which essay do you like better, and why? Which uses more interesting observed detail? Which essay uses more vivid or imaginative figurative language? Which has a more interesting voice? Explain.

SAMUEL H. SCUDDER

Take This Fish and Look at It

Prereading Journal Entry

If you are currently taking a science class (or have taken one recently), describe any lab experiment where you have had to observe processes and take notes. What was the class, what was the laboratory experiment, and what exactly did you observe and take notes on?

In this essay, Samuel H. Scudder (1837–1911), an American entomologist, narrates his early attempts at scientific observation. Scudder recalls how a famous Swiss naturalist, Louis Agassiz, taught him the skills of observation by having him examine a fish—a haemulon or snapper—closely, carefully, and repeatedly. Agassiz, a professor of natural history at Harvard, taught his students that both factual details and general laws are important. "Facts are stupid things," he said "until brought into connection with some general law." Scudder, writing about his studies under Agassiz, suggests that repeated observation can help us connect facts or specific details with general laws. The essay shows us an important lesson that Scudder learned: To help us see, describe, and connect, "A pencil is one of the best of eyes."

1   It was more than fifteen years ago that I entered the laboratory of Professor Agassiz, and told him I had enrolled my name in the Scientific School as a student of natural history, He asked me a few questions about my object in coming, my antecedents generally, the mode in which I afterwards proposed to use the knowledge I might acquire, and, finally, whether I wished to study any special branch. To the latter I replied that, while I wished to be well grounded in all departments of zoology, I purposed to devote myself specially to insects.

2   "When do you wish to begin?" he asked.

3   "Now," I replied.

4   This seemed to please him, and with an energetic "Very well!" he reached from a shelf a huge jar of specimens in yellow alcohol. "Take this fish," he said, "and look at it; we call it a haemulon; by and by I will ask what you have seen."

5   With that he left me, but in a moment returned with explicit instructions as to the care of the object entrusted to me.

6   "No man is fit to be a naturalist," said he, "who does not know how to take care of specimens."

7   I was to keep the fish before me in a tin tray, and occasionally moisten the surface with alcohol from the jar, always taking care to replace the stopper tightly. Those were not the days of ground-glass stoppers and elegantly shaped exhibition jars; all the old students will recall the huge neckless glass bottles with their leak, wax-besmeared corks, half eaten by insects, and begrimed with cellar dust. Entomology was a cleaner science than ichthyology, but the example of the Professor, who had unhesitatingly plunged to the bottom of the jar to produce the fish, was infectious; and though this alcohol had a "very ancient and fishlike smell," I really dared not show any aversion within these sacred precincts, and treated the alcohol as though it were pure water. Still I was conscious of a passing feeling of disappointment, for gazing at a fish did not commend itself to an ardent entomologist. My friends at home, too, were annoyed when they discovered that no amount of eau-de-Cologne would drown the perfume which haunted me like a shadow.

8   In ten minutes I had seen all that could be seen in that fish, and started in search of the Professor—who had, however, left the Museum; and when I returned, after lingering over some of the odd animals stored in the upper apartment, my specimen was dry all over. I dashed the fluid over the fish as if to resuscitate the beast from a fainting fit, and looked with anxiety for a return of the normal sloppy appearance.

This little excitement over, nothing was to be done but to return to a steadfast gaze at my mute companion. Half an hour passed—an hour—another hour; the fish began to look loathsome. I turned it over and around; looked it in the face—ghastly; from behind, beneath, above, sideways, at three-quarter's view—just as ghastly, I was in despair; at an early hour I concluded that lunch was necessary; so, with infinite relief, the fish was carefully replaced in the jar, and for an hour I was free.

9   On my return, I learned that Professor Agassiz had been at the Museum, but had gone, and would not return for several hours. My fellow-students were too busy to be disturbed by continued conversation. Slowly I drew forth that hideous fish, and with a feeling of desperation again looked at it. I might not use a magnifying-glass; instruments of all kinds were interdicted. My two hands, my two eyes, and the fish; it seemed a most limited field. I pushed my finger down its throat to feel how sharp the teeth were. I began to count the scales in the different rows, until I was convinced that was nonsense, At last a happy thought struck me—I would draw the fish; and now with surprise I began to discover new features in the creature. Just then the Professor returned.

10   "That is right," said he; "a pencil is one of the best of eyes. I am glad to notice, too, that you keep your specimen wet, and your bottle corked."

11   With these encouraging words, he added: "Well, what is it like?"

12   He listened attentively to my brief rehearsal of the structure of parts whose names were still unknown to me; the fringed gill-arches and movable operculum; the pores of the head, fleshy lips and lidless eyes; the lateral line, the spinous fins and forked tail; the compressed and arched body. When I finished, he waited as if expecting more, and then, with an air of disappointment:

13   "You have not looked very carefully; why," he continued more earnestly, "you haven't even seen one of the most conspicuous features of the animal, which is plainly before your eyes as the fish itself; look again, look again!" and he left me to my misery.

14   I was piqued; I was mortified. Still more of that wretched fish! But now I set myself to my task with a will, and discovered one new thing after another, until I saw how just the Professor's criticism had been. The afternoon passed quickly; and when, towards its close, the Professor inquired:

15   "Do you see it yet?"

16   "No," I replied, "I am certain I do not, but I see how little I saw before."

17   "That is next best," said he, earnestly, "but I won't hear you now; put away your fish and go home; perhaps you will be ready with a better answer in the morning. I will examine you before you look at the fish."

18   This was disconcerting. Not only must I think of my fish all night, studying, without the object before me, what this unknown but most visible feature might be; but also, without reviewing my discoveries, I must give an exact account of them the next day. I had a bad memory; so I walked home by Charles River in a distracted state, with my two perplexities.

19   The cordial greeting from the Professor the next morning was reassuring; here was a man who seemed to be quite as anxious as I that I should see for myself what he saw.

20   "Do you perhaps mean," I asked, "that the fish has symmetrical sides with paired organs?"

21   His thoroughly pleased "Of course! Of course!" repaid the wakeful hours of the previous night. After he had discoursed most happily and enthusiastically—as he always did—upon the importance of this point, I ventured to ask what I should do next.

22   "Oh, look at your fish!" he said, and left me again to my own devices. In a little more than an hour he returned, and heard my new catalogue.

23   "That is good, that is good!" he repeated; "but that is not all; go on"; and so for three long days he placed that fish before my eyes, forbidding me to look at anything else, or to use any artificial aid. "Look, look, look," was his repeated injunction.

24   This was the best entomological lesson I ever had—a lesson whose influence has extended to the details of every subsequent study; a legacy the Professor had left to me, as he has left it to so many others, of inestimable value, which we could not buy, with which we cannot part.

25   A year afterward, some of us were amusing ourselves with chalking outlandish beasts on the Museum blackboard. We drew prancing starfishes; frogs in mortal combat; hydra-headed worms, stately crawfishes with gaping mouths and staring eyes. The Professor came in shortly after, and was as amused as any at our experiments. He looked at the fishes.

26   "Haemulons, every one of them," he said; "Mr. _____ drew them."

27   True; and to this day, if I attempt a fish, I can draw nothing but haemulons.

28   The fourth day, a second fish of the same group was placed beside the first, and I was bidden to point out the resemblances and differences

between the two; another and another followed, until the entire family lay before me, and a whole legion of jars covered the table and surrounding shelves; the odor had become a pleasant perfume; and even now, the sight of an old, six-inch worm-eaten cork brings fragrant memories.

29   The whole group of haemulons was thus brought in review; and whether engaged upon the dissection of the internal organs, the preparation and examination of the bony framework, or the description of the various parts, Agassiz's training in the method of observing facts and their orderly arrangement was ever accompanied by the urgent exhortation not to be content with them.

30   "Facts are stupid things," he would say, "until brought into connection with some general law."

31   At the end of eight months, it was almost with reluctance that I left these friends and turned to insects; but what I had gained by this outside experience has been of greater value than years of later investigation in my favorite groups.

QUESTIONS FOR DISCUSSION AND WRITING

1. Apply Scudder's technique of **repeated observation** to Scudder's own essay. Read the essay a second time, carefully, looking for techniques for recording observations. Use a pencil or pen to help you read, by underlining or making brief notes. What do you notice on the **second** reading that you did not see during the first reading?

2. Review your answer to the Prereading Journal Exercise that precedes this essay. After reading Scudder's essay, which of his recommended techniques for observing did you practice during your laboratory session? Which of Scudder's strategies would help you perform and write up future laboratory exercises?

3. What is the purpose of this essay? To inform us about fish? To explain how to learn about fish? To persuade us to follow Professor Agassiz's method? To entertain us with college stories? In your estimation, explain the primary purpose of this essay, citing specific sentences from the essay.

4. Connect Scudder's techniques to those in the other essays in this chapter. Do Annie Dillard, William Least Heat-Moon, or Elisabeth Weston use repeated observation in order to help write their essays? Explain, citing specific examples from at least two of those essays.

Toys and Barbies

Prereading Journal Entry

Select a toy that you played with as a young child—perhaps a doll, a toy car, a set of Legos, or anything else. Describe the toy. What kind of games did you play with this toy? As you reflect on this toy, explain what it meant to you: why you chose it, why you liked it, and why it caught your interest or imagination.

Often called the founder of semiotics, Roland Barthes was born in 1915, in Cherbourg, France, and died in 1980 in a car accident in Paris. He was educated at the Sorbonne and the University of Paris, and he taught in Romania, Egypt, and France. In 1967, he was a visiting professor at Johns Hopkins University. Semiotics focuses on the reading of signs in culture. Everyday objects in popular culture, Barthes argues, carry with them clues about their political or ideological function. For Barthes, objects such as toys "always mean something, and this something is entirely socialized, constituted by the myths . . . of modern adult life." Barthes has written more than twenty books, but one of the most popular, Mythologies, was written in 1967 and translated into English in 1972. In the following selection from Mythologies, Barthes analyzes (i.e., "reads") French toys for clues that reveal how toys help to prepare children to accept the myths or traditions of modern adult life.

Emily Prager was raised in Texas, the Far East, and Greenwich Village. She majored in anthropology at Barnard College and has been a contributing editor for The National Lampoon. She is a short story writer, novelist, and journalist who has written for The Village Voice, Viva, and Penthouse, and has published books of short stories and fiction including A Visit from the Footbinder and Other Stories (1982), Clea and Zeus Divorce (1987), Eve's Tattoo (1991), and Wuhu Diary: On Taking My Adopted Daughter Back to Her Hometown in China (2002). "Our Barbies, Ourselves" appeared in the December 1991 issue of Interview magazine. The occasion for the essay is Prager's discovery that Barbie was designed by a Mr. Jack Ryan, a former husband of Zsa Zsa Gabor and a weapons designer for a missile company. Prager would certainly agree with Barthes that toys "always mean something," and that we can read them both for their private meaning for individuals and for their public, cultural function.

Toys

1   French toys: One could not find a better illustration of the fact that the adult Frenchman sees the child as another self. All the toys one commonly sees are essentially a microcosm of the adult world; they are all reduced copies of human objects, as if in the eyes of the public the child was, all told, nothing but a smaller man, a homunculus to whom must be supplied objects of his own size.

2   Invented forms are very rare: a few sets of blocks, which appeal to the spirit of do-it-yourself, are the only ones which offer dynamic forms. As for the others, French toys *always mean something*, and this something is always entirely socialized, constituted by the myths or the techniques of modern adult life: the army, broadcasting, the post office, medicine (miniature instrument-cases, operating theaters for dolls), school, hair styling (driers for permanent-waving), the air force (parachutists), transport (trains, Citroëns, Vedettes, Vespas, petrol stations), science (Martian toys).

3   The fact that French toys *literally* prefigure the world of adult functions obviously cannot but prepare the child to accept them all, by constituting for him, even before he can think about it, the alibi of a Nature which has at all times created soldiers, postmen, and Vespas. Toys here reveal the list of all the things the adult does not find unusual: war, bureaucracy, ugliness, Martians, etc. It is not so much, in fact, the imitation which is the sign of an abdication, as its literalness: French toys are like a Jivaro head, in which one recognizes, shrunken to the size of an apple, the wrinkles and hair of an adult. There exist, for instance, dolls which urinate; they have an esophagus, one gives them a bottle, they wet their nappies; soon, no doubt, milk will turn to water in their stomachs. This is meant to prepare the little girl for the causality of housekeeping, to "condition" her to her future role as mother. However, faced with this world of faithful and complicated objects, the child can only identify himself as owner, as user, never as creator; he does not invent the world, he uses it: There are, prepared for him, actions without adventure, without wonder, without joy. He is turned into a little stay-at-home householder who does not even have to invent the mainsprings of adult causality; they are supplied to him

ready-made: He has only to help himself, he is never allowed to discover anything from start to finish. The merest set of blocks, provided it is not too refined, implies a very different learning of the world: Then, the child does not in any way create meaningful objects, it matters little to him whether they have an adult name; the actions he performs are not those of a user but those of a demiurge. He creates forms which walk, which roll, he creates life, not property: Objects now act by themselves, they are no longer an inert and complicated material in the palm of his hand. But such toys are rather rare: French toys are usually based on imitation, they are meant to produce children who are users, not creators.

4   The bourgeois status of toys can be recognized not only in their forms, which are all functional, but also in their substances. Current toys are made of a graceless material, the product of chemistry, not of nature. Many are now molded from complicated mixtures; the plastic material of which they are made has an appearance at once gross and hygienic, it destroys all the pleasure, the sweetness, the humanity of touch. A sign which fills one with consternation is the gradual disappearance of wood, in spite of its being an ideal material because of its firmness and its softness, and the natural warmth of its touch. Wood removes, from all the forms which it supports, the wounding quality of angles which are too sharp, the chemical coldness of metal. When the child handles it and knocks it, it neither vibrates nor grates, it has a sound at once muffled and sharp. It is a familiar and poetic substance, which does not sever the child from close contact with the tree, the table, the floor. Wood does not wound or break down; it does not shatter, it wears out, it can last a long time, live with the child, alter little by little the relations between the object and the hand. If it dies, it is in dwindling, not in swelling out like those mechanical toys which disappear behind the hernia of a broken spring. Wood makes essential objects, objects for all time. Yet there hardly remain any of these wooden toys from the Vosges, these fretwork farms with their animals, which were only possible, it is true, in the days of the craftsman. Henceforth, toys are chemical in substance and color; their very material introduces one to a coenaesthesis of use, not pleasure. These toys die in fact very quickly, and once dead, they have no posthumous life for the child.

Our Barbies, Ourselves

1   I read an astounding obituary in the *New York Times* not too long ago. It concerned the death of one Jack Ryan. A former husband of Zsa Zsa Gabor, it said, Mr. Ryan had been an inventor and designer during his lifetime. A man of eclectic creativity, he designed Sparrow and Hawk missiles when he worked for the Raytheon Company, and, the notice said, when he consulted for Mattel he designed Barbie.

2   If Barbie was designed by a man, suddenly a lot of things made sense to me, things I'd wondered about for years. I used to look at Barbie and wonder, What's wrong with this picture? What kind of woman designed this doll? Let's be honest: Barbie looks like someone who got her start at the Playboy Mansion. She could be a regular guest on *The Howard Stern Show*. It is a fact of Barbie's design that her breasts are so out of proportion to the rest of her body that if she were a human woman, she'd fall flat on her face.

3   If it's true that a woman didn't design Barbie, you don't know how much saner that makes me feel. Of course, that doesn't ameliorate the damage. There are millions of women who are subliminally sure that a thirty-nine-inch bust and a twenty-three-inch waist are the epitome of lovability. Could this account for the popularity of breast implant surgery?

4   I don't mean to step on anyone's toes here. I loved my Barbie. Secretly, I still believe that neon pink and turquoise blue are the only colors in which to decorate a duplex condo. And like many others of my generation, I've never married, simply because I cannot find a man who looks as good in clam diggers as Ken.

5   The question that comes to mind is, of course, Did Mr. Ryan design Barbie as a weapon? Because it *is* odd that Barbie appeared about the same time in my consciousness as the feminist movement—a time when women sought equality and small breasts were king. Or is Barbie the dream date of weapons designers? Or perhaps it's simpler than that: Perhaps Barbie is Zsa Zsa if she were eleven inches tall. No matter what, my discovery of Jack Ryan confirms what I have always felt: There is something indescribably masculine about Barbie—dare I say it, phallic. For all her giant breasts and high-heeled feet, she lacks a certain softness. If you asked a little girl what kind of doll she wanted for Christmas, I just don't think she'd reply, "Please, Santa, I want a hard-body."

6   On the other hand, you could say that Barbie, in feminist terms, is definitely her own person. With her condos and fashion plazas and pools and beauty salons, she is definitely a liberated woman, a gal on the move. And she has always been sexual, even totemic. Before Barbie, American dolls were flat-footed and breastless, and ineffably dignified. They were created in the image of little girls or babies. Madame Alexander was the queen of doll makers in the fifties, and her dollies looked like Elizabeth Taylor in *National Velvet*. They represented the kind of girls who looked perfect in jodhpurs, whose hair was never out of place, who grew up to be Jackie Kennedy—before she married Onassis. Her dolls' boyfriends were figments of the imagination, figments with large portfolios and three-piece suits and presidential aspirations, figments who could keep dolly in the style to which little girls of the fifties were programmed to become accustomed, a style that spasm-ed with the sixties and the appearance of Barbie. And perhaps what accounts for Barbie's vast popularity is that she was also a sixties woman: into free love and fun colors, anticlass, and possessed of real, molded boyfriend, Ken, with whom she could chant a mantra.

7   But there were problems with Ken. I always felt weird about him. He had no genitals, and, even at age ten, I found that ominous. I mean, here was Barbie with these humongous breasts, and that was OK with the toy company. And then, there was Ken with that truncated, unidentifiable lump at his groin. I sensed injustice at work. Why, I wondered, was Barbie designed with such obvious sexual equipment and Ken not? Why was his treated as if it were more mysterious than hers? Did the fact that it was treated as such indicate that somehow his equipment, his essential maleness, was considered more powerful than hers, more worthy of the dignity of concealment? And if the issue in the mind of the toy company was obscenity and its possible damage to children, I still object. How do they think I felt, knowing that no matter how many water beds they slept in, or hot tubs they romped in, or swimming pools they lounged by under the stars, Barbie and Ken could never make love? No matter how much sexuality Barbie possessed, she would never turn Ken on. He would be forever withholding, forever detached. There was a loneliness about Barbie's situation that was always disturbing. And twenty-five years later, movies and videos are still filled with topless women and covered men. As if we're all trapped in Barbie's world and can never escape.

8   God, it certainly has cheered me up to think that Barbie was designed by Jack Ryan . . . .

QUESTIONS FOR DISCUSSION AND WRITING

1. In one sentence, state the main idea or thesis of Barthes' essay. In a second sentence, state the main idea or thesis of Prager's essay. How are these statements similar? How are they different?

2. Explain what Barthes means in the first two sentences of paragraph 3. What, specifically, does he mean by each of the following phrases: "toys *literally* prefigure the world of adult function"; "the alibi of a Nature which has at all times created soldiers, postmen, and Vespas"; and "things the adult does not find unusual: war, bureaucracy, ugliness, Martians"? How do these phrases relate to Barthes' theme that "French toys *always mean something*"? What, according to Barthes, is the function of toys?

3. What does Prager like most about her Barbie? What problems or questions does she have about Barbie?

4. Identify places in her essay where Prager seems to criticize Barbies and their function in our culture. Find other places, however, where Prager is trying to avoid stepping "on anyone's toes." Why is she both critical and yet sympathetic? How might this strategy be related to her purpose?

5. Barthes' essay was published in a book called *Mythologies* while Prager's essay appeared in the magazine *Interview*. What might be differences between these two audiences? Explain how the differences (or similarities) in the subject matter, the sentence style, the vocabulary, and the specific examples and details help address a similar or different audience for each essay.

6. At the end of her essay, Prager says, "It's as if we're all trapped in Barbie's world and can never escape." What does Prager mean by this statement? How would Barthes react to this statement? Would he agree or disagree? What is your response to Prager and Barthes? Write an essay in which you represent Prager, Barthes, and yourself engaged in a conversation about the key issues raised in these two essays.

SUEELLEN CAMPBELL

Layers of Place

Prereading Journal Entry

Think about a place that you know well, perhaps a place that you have lived for an extended period of time or a place that you know very well.

Interdisciplinary Studies in Literature and Environment 13.2 (Summer 2006). Copyright © 2006 by the Association for the Study of Literature and Environment.

Instead of describing it, research it online. Whether it is a city place, a rural or mountain scene, or even a place on the water or the ocean, every place has a history. Search online for information about the objects at this place, the biology or zoology, the people who have been there, and the changes it has undergone in the last ten years or the last century. When you've collected this information, explain how this information changes the way you see or understand this place.

SueEllen Campbell teaches courses at Colorado State University in nature and environmental literature, twentieth-century fiction and non-fiction, and literary theory. Her publications include Bringing the Mountains Home *(2001) and* Even Mountains Vanish: Searching for Solace in an Age of Extinction *(2003). She is the author of articles about American environmental literature and ecocriticism and is now working on a guide to landscapes in nature and culture. She is co-editor of the University of Virginia Press ecocritical book series "Under the Sign of Nature" and is co-director of Changing Climates @ Colorado State University.*

1   There's something compellingly immediate about places. Dirt, trees, houses, mosquitoes, a barking dog, the weight of the air: these things are so physical, so *present*. Our personal reactions and associations draw us into their powerful orbits, too: I camped here on my honeymoon; I caught tadpoles in this pond when I was a child; in this forest, I always feel smothered. Because such sensory and emotional elements create our ordinary experiences of place, they can make us feel that our understanding is complete.

2   Yet all places are astonishingly complex. They are finely and intricately laminated, not only with the immediate and personal, but also with what we don't see that is present, with what is past and future, even with what is somewhere else. With a little work, we can learn to recognize many more of those layers. When we do, our comprehension of what makes a place becomes immeasurably richer—not necessarily more comforting, but certainly more thorough.

3   What follows here is an exercise I've been developing over the last several years, one that draws on knowledge, imagination, memory, and curiosity to build towards a richly layered portrait of a single place. I've used various versions in a senior-level nature writing workshop, in a lunch-hour seminar for faculty and graduate students in my university's College of Natural Resources, at a session on "Imagining Invisible Landscapes" at the 2005 ASLE conference, and as a continuing

series of prompts for my own thinking. Following the exercise itself, I'll add a few brief comments.

The Exercise

4   Today I'm going to ask you to think about how layered and compli cated places are—and how many different ways we have to perceive, think about, and understand them.

5   This exercise is divided into stages, and I'd like you to try to think about just one thing at a time.

6   Choose one place that you know well, maybe a place you love. Put yourself there in your imagination and memory. Choose your season, time of day, and weather. Now settle in: sit down in a particular spot; close your eyes, take a deep breath, quiet your mind.

7   In your imagination, open your eyes. Look around you. Choose just one part of what you see to focus on, something close enough to you to fit into this room, maybe close enough to touch. This will be the "place" you'll be thinking about for the next forty-five minutes or so.

1. What do you actually see, with your eyes, right now? Forget what you know and think only about what you see. Be concrete, detailed, and straight-forward—the visual facts, but precise. Avoid metaphors. If you don't know or can't remember something, think instead about questions you could investigate. Think about lines, shapes, sizes, balance, design. Think about textures. Think about colors—their shades, intensity, variations, how they reverberate against or meld into each other. Think about what painters call "values"—if you were to shift into black and white vision, what would be lightest, what darkest, what in the middle. Stay concrete and detailed. Think about light and shadow, how they change colors, how sometimes how they move.

   Imagine that you have a few other lenses at hand: zoom in close, use binoculars, a magnifying glass, a microscope. Or zoom back, use a wide-angle lens or a telescope. Look up. Look down. Hang your head upside down. Take your glasses off. Put on rose-colored sunglasses. Squint.

8   Think about how all these visual parts go together.

2. Pay attention to the rest of your body, how your whole body is in this place. Listen carefully: what do you hear? Breathe through your mouth, then through your nose: what do you smell? Put your nose right up against something you've been looking at: what do you

smell now? Pay attention to your skin—your face, your hands, the parts of you that are touching something solid: what is touching your skin, what is it sensing? Are you aware of your bones, your muscles? How does the air feel going into your lungs? Can you feel your heart beating? Touch something you've been looking at—with your finger tips, with your face. How does it feel against your body? Taste something. How does it taste? Again, stay as concrete as you can. If you need a metaphor, which at this point you may well, make it plain and direct. Be detailed. And again, if you don't know, ask a question.

3. I asked you to choose a place that you know well. How, why, do you know this place? How do you feel about it? Think about the story of your relationship with this place: When did you first meet? How did your relationship develop? Was it love at first sight? A gradual friendship? Any quarrels, rough spots, temporary separations? What memories does this place hold for you? Lots of tiny ones full of ordinary daily details? A few big dramatic ones? What other emotions does this place evoke for you? Be as concrete as possible—avoid big words like "peaceful" or "hopeful." Are your memories and emotions about this place deeply personal and idiosyncratic, or are they things you'd expect other people to share? Do you think that your own identity, or your sense of yourself, the shape of your life, how you matter to yourself, is somehow tied up with the identity of this place? How so? How did this happen?

4. Has anyone painted this place, or made some other kind of visual art in response to it, or written a poem or a story or an essay or a book about it? To what effect? What human events have happened here—during your lifetime, in the last two or three centuries, since humans first arrived in the vicinity? Who has lived here, or spent time here, and how? How has this place been tied to events happening elsewhere, through commerce or politics? Who owns it, who controls what happens to it? How have different parts of our culture thought about this place, or other places much like it? Is it a kind of place we have typically valued, or not? What have humans done to hurt it, or to help it? What do you mean by "hurt" and "help"? What threatens it, or its inhabitants, now? Pollution, poverty, warfare, invasive species, habitat loss, climate change, strip mining, deforestation, desertification, suburban sprawl, volcanic explosions, hurricanes, golf course or ski area development, disease? What forces are working to fight these threats? What lines

of connection, influence, or effect could you trace going out from here to other places, or coming in from them?

5. What is sharing this place with you, right now? Make a quick list of things you can see: people, plants, other animals, birds, insects. What kinds of lives do all these creatures live? How do they manage to live here? How much water is around you, in what forms, doing what? What's the temperature? How bright is the light? What's the air like? Dry? Humid? Still? Windy? What's the ground like beneath you? What kind of rock, or soil, or plant cover? What is here that you can't see—because it's underground or inside something else, because it's so small, because our human senses can't respond to it? What if you had Superman-like X-ray eyes? How do all these elements of this scene interact with each other?

6. What happens here when you're not around? What would likely be here at another time of the day or another part of the year? How long has this place been the way it is now—with its current form and current inhabitants? What was it like here a hundred years ago? Twenty thousand years ago, when average global temperatures were roughly ten degrees Fahrenheit lower than they are now? Five million years ago? A hundred million? If you could drill a core straight down beneath you all the way through the crust, what stories would that core tell?

9   What might it be like here fifty or a hundred years from now? What might happen as the planet continues warming, say another four or six degrees Fahrenheit, as some fairly conservative models predict, making it warmer than it's been since humans evolved? More rain? Drought? What other changes might follow shifts in temperature and moisture?

7. Does this place *matter*? Why? How? Think big now: cosmically, philosophically, spiritually. What would be lost to the world or just to you if it were destroyed tomorrow? Might this place have anything to teach us, any kind of wisdom we might want? What does it know that we don't, about life on this planet, about time, maybe about endurance or fortitude or change? What happens to the place itself when we start asking giant questions like these? Does it disappear? Become richer and more brilliant?

8. Finally, think a little bit about what happens when you do this exercise. Which parts were the easiest for you, which the hardest, and why? Where do you have the most questions, the fewest

observations or facts or ideas? What happens in your head when you do these as a series? How do these ways of thinking affect each other? Do they illuminate each other? Converse with each other? Did any parts help you remember or imagine something that you could have included in one of the earlier parts? What's the effect of the accumulation of all of them? What would change if you focused on a different place? Why did you choose the one you did?

Versions, Strategies, and Results

10   Other versions of this exercise are easy to imagine. Indoors or outside, involving writing or not, lasting an hour, a day, a whole term, for beginners or professionals, scientists or artists or humanists, focused on the place where the exercise is occurring or on somewhere else—there are many possible variables. The order above is the one I used for an audience of ASLE members accustomed to thinking about cultural issues; for the College of Natural Resources faculty, I asked the science-based questions before the cultural ones; for beginning students, it might be best to open with questions about feelings, then work towards more concrete observations and harder speculations. The wording of the initial charge (choose a place that [. . .].) is also variable and critical: choose a place that you fear, think of the place you spent most time as a child, think about where you live now, such different openers would produce quite different responses. And of course there are many other questions to ask, with many different possible ways to focus.

11   What follows the exercise will also vary by circumstances. One might have students type up their notes and turn them in, choose high points and craft a short essay, or use their unanswered questions to direct their research for a larger project. A good conversation can also ensue. As one ASLE listener said, debriefing might be important; he had chosen to think about a seriously threatened place he couldn't find a way to help protect and so had found the exercise very painful. A graduate student in ecology told me she, too, had found it painful: she'd realized that not only could she not answer most of the questions about the place she'd chosen, but worse, she couldn't answer them about any place. A senior wildlife biologist, on the other hand, remarked that although he'd thought about all those things separately, he had never put them together. The final paragraph

of the exercise above might serve as a template for a follow-up conversation.

12   One final note. I've also found such sets of questions helpful in teaching environmental literature, since they can help clarify what individual books do and don't address; indeed, they often illuminate books I teach in my other literature classes as well, since place usually matters in one way or another. And I use them as reminders for my own creative, critical, and scholarly activities: they partly developed from the work I did for my last book (*Even Mountains Vanish: Searching for Solace in an Age of Extinction*), and they are helping drive the research for the guide to landscapes in nature and culture I'm writing now in collaboration with Richard Kerridge. For those of us who are working to help preserve what's important about our environment, I believe, it is both ethically and practically important to try to see the complexities of particular places as comprehensively and clearly as we can, and these questions are tools to help us do so.

QUESTIONS FOR DISCUSSION AND WRITING

1. Campbell begins her exercise by asking readers to imagine what they "see" and then what you "hear," "smell," "feel" or "touch" in this place. If you tried this exercise, were you able to reproduce these sensory details about a place that you held only in your memory? Would you have preferred to begin with part three, your memory or your story about this place? Why or why not?

2. How did you respond to the question that your identity might be related to the identity of the place? How can a place have an "identity" that relates to your own identity?

3. Question 4 in the exercise asks you to explore the history of this place. While you can think about the history of a place just by using your memory, also use some research tools to find out about the history of the place. What can you find in an online search or a search through library databases?

4. Campbell discusses a variety of people who might practice with this exercise: students of the environment, ecology students, biologists, and writers. What other courses are you currently taking or have taken recently where specific and detailed observations of a place are important? Choose one of those courses and write about a place that would be important for that field of study.

Fetal Pig

Prereading Journal Entry

Write for five minutes about a class that was initially difficult or traumatic but later became one of your favorite subjects. Explain the causes of your fear. What events changed your attitude?

Elizabeth Weston, a student at Colorado State University, majored in zoology. She was co-editor of the college yearbook and wished to become a "science writer for a news organization, translating scientific discoveries into terms the general public can understand." In "Fetal Pig," Weston selects a subject she describes as "one of the worst but most enlightening experiences" she had in college. Required by her zoology course to dissect a fetal pig preserved in formaldehyde, Weston musters her courage and enters the fascinating world of biology.

One Writer's Observing Process

Rough Draft

I remember being a sociology major as a timid freshman. Now there was logic behind this choice, I hated science passionately. I don't know exactly when I began to detest the subject. All I know is by college I wanted nothing to do with it.

Colorado State had other plans for me. The science requirement was staring me straight in the face. Like many science haters, I decided to get the worst over early. Zoology 110 was my fate. I vividly recall crying before laboratory after hearing we had to dissect a fetal pig. Still I went. There it was in front of me, a tiny bluish grey baby pig in the fetal position. Barely developed ears held tightly to its large head, just above never opened eyes. That was it, the tears flooded my vision. I tried to cover it up, but the instructor spotted me from across the huge, cold lab. I felt so ridiculous and childish as he approached, but this scientist assured me that compassion was a rare but exceptional trait of a scientist. Suddenly the formaldehyde didn't make me nauseated, and the dissection gave me a chance to see firsthand one of the most incredible things this world offers, life. From that day forward, my curiosity about life and the workings of our world has exploded. All thanks to a scientist with that rare quality of compassion.

Final Draft

Fetal Pig

1   I hate science. Every slimy, theoretical, mathematical experiment makes my skin crawl. I'm not certain what events led to this conclusion, all I know is that I want nothing to do with it. Colorado State had other plans for me. The science requirement was staring me straight in the face, and unfortunately, no amount of whining or pleading seemed to change the minds of advisors. I reluctantly chose Zoology 110 as my fate.

2   So here I sit slumped over the hard black table top marked for posterity by students long since gone. My emotions pass through every extreme but somehow always avoid that content feeling when you know everything will work out. A slow glance around the room reveals cold stainless steel instruments that belong in a B grade horror movie. A human skeletal replica looms in the far corner as if to remind us of our frailty and to keep a watchful eye to prevent any grotesque acts that might be attempted in the name of black humor. I pull my gaze to the front of the laboratory where a stocky man, wearing a starched lab coat oddly matched with green Converse sneakers, is preparing to speak.

3   "Today we will dissect the fetal pig."

4   A headline flashes in my mind, "Girl Sickened By Dead Pig Fails College." My heartbeat quickens; I am actually frightened.

5   Mustering all the courage I can, I timidly reach into the bucket holding the tiny corpses. I hold my breath and turn my head so I won't be asphyxiated by the nauseating formaldehyde fumes. Looking at my motionless rival, I feel sympathy for the never born baby now held in a plastic bag womb. Utilizing my forceps I remove the piglet from the baggie. Its barely formed ears are pinned snugly against its head as if this world was far too loud. Never opened eyes sleep serenely over the snout, the smooth tongue protruding. Uncalcified bones twist painfully, creating distorted limbs too weak to ever support the infant's weight, and the tail is only an accumulation of tissue lacking all resemblance to the characteristically spiraled pig's tail. Curled in fetal position, like a human baby, I'd believe it was only napping if only the skin weren't so icy and blue.

6   The innocence of my victim paralyzes me except for the warm tear I feel trickle down my cheek. Another breaks free from the boundary of my eye. Embarrassed, I hurriedly attempt to wipe them away. Too late, the instructor has spotted me. He strides across the room and ends up at my side.

7   "You know, Elizabeth, compassion is a rare quality in a scientist, but definitely an exceptional one."

8   His words hang precariously in my mind. Could this be true? I let the thought sink into my head. Now for some reason the formaldehyde isn't quite so malodorous and the skin not as clammy and lifeless.

9   "If you'd prefer you can just watch the dissection," the TA suggests kindly.

10   "That's okay, I think I'd like to do this."

11   Methodically I cut the thick skin revealing the wonders that reside within. My curiosity peaks with each new discovery. Uninflated lungs ready to fill with air, a perfect miniature heart, tiny kidneys and liver waiting to fulfill their intended functions: the tiny body is miraculous. As the end of the two hour period draws near, I gently place the baby back into the bag and tenderly lay him in the bucket. Aware that I have uncovered something that fascinates me, I smile and turn to see the instructor who nods at me with a grin.

QUESTIONS FOR DISCUSSION AND WRITING

1. Is Weston's purpose to describe in detail the fetal pig or to tell you about herself and her feelings? Explain, referring to specific sentences in the essay.

2. What specific details or images convey Weston's sense of fear and hatred? What specific details communicate her sense of wonder?

3. Explain how Weston might respond to animal rights activists who suggest that fetal pig dissections are cruel and should be done with computer simulations.

4. Following Weston's model, recall a discovery you made about science, either by yourself or in a science class. Re-create the conditions as closely as possible and observe more closely what is happening. Describe this event, using both your memories and observations.

5. One reader of Weston's essay felt the essay ended too abruptly, that Weston's change in attitude happened too fast for the reader. Working by yourself or in groups, revise the conclusion in order to *show* the author's change more gradually and more completely. You may need to add an extra paragraph or two.

CHAPTER

Remembering

REMEMBERING, LIKE OBSERVING, IS AN INITIAL PURPOSE for writing and learning as well as a strategy that serves other purposes. Sometimes our initial purpose—remembering—remains our final purpose: We write about our past experiences to share a part of our life with another person. At other times, remembering leads to some larger purpose for our writing: We use specific examples from our personal experience to explain what something is, to propose a solution to a problem, or to explore a difficult question.

Personal experience makes writing effective in two ways. First, it enables the reader to *connect* with the writer and his or her experiences. When it triggers a similar experience, the reader thinks, "Yes, I can identify with that." If the reader hasn't had a similar experience, showing the experience helps the reader visualize and understand: "That hasn't happened to me, but I can see how important it was." Second, specific examples from personal experience act as *evidence* to illustrate a point. In a scientific experiment, researchers prove a point by demonstrating that in 95 out of 100 cases, a vaccine prevented a certain disease. In an essay, writers use personal experience not to prove that something happens in all or most cases, but to *show that it did happen in this one case*. Readers may be convinced if the example fairly represents other similar cases. A writer explaining how drinking causes automobile accidents, for example, needs to give just one vivid illustration to persuade a reader that tragedy can result.

In this chapter, however, the focus is on the autobiographical narrative itself. Each essay tells a brief story, but it focuses on some *main idea* that shows how an experience changed the writer. In the best essays, writers do not *tell* their readers about the events—they *show* the events. They re-create the places, scenes, people, and dialogue so that the story itself reveals that main idea.

Strategies for Reading and Writing Remembering Essays

As you read the remembering essays in this chapter and recall events from your own life to write about, keep the following key strategies in mind.

- **Use of detailed observation of people, places, and events.** Effective remembering essays build on observing strategies. Writers recall *sights, sounds, smells, tactile feelings, tastes*. Writers use actual or re-created *dialogue*. They give actual *names* of people and places—even if they have changed the names in their account.

- **Creation of specific scenes set at an actual time and place.** Instead of describing the outcome of an important event or describing a habitual action ("We used to sit in class a lot and cause trouble"), writers re-create an event by setting it in a specific *time* and *space*. In his essay reprinted in this chapter, "Shame," Dick Gregory sets the scene vividly for his readers: "It was on a Thursday. I was sitting in the back of the room, in a seat with a chalk circle drawn around it."

- **Use of important changes, contrasts, or conflicts.** The main idea or dominant impression in autobiographical accounts often grows out of *changes* in people or places, *conflicts* between people, or *contrasts* between the past and the present.

- **Focus on connections between past events, people, or places and the present.** Often in autobiographical accounts, the main point crystallizes when the writer makes *connections* between the past and the present. Writing about his experiences in school, Gregory says, "I guess I would have gotten over Helene by summertime, but something happened in that classroom that made her face hang in front of me for the next twenty-two years."

- **Creation of a main idea or dominant impression.** The details, specific scenes, accounts of changes or conflicts, and connections between past and present should point to a *single main idea* or *dominant impression* for the passage as a whole.

Reading a Remembering Essay

Reading other people's accounts of important people, places, and events in their lives may be the most enjoyable kind of reading we do. Everyone likes to see how other people live and discover how their lives are different from ours—and yet the same, too. Curiosity propels us into the story, and the power of the narrative keeps us interested.

After a first or second reading, however, we may want to tell our own story, to make it as entertaining, suspenseful, vivid, or dramatic as the account we just read. At this point, we reread the account *with a writer's eye*, looking for those strategies and tricks that make that particular narrative effective. The following strategies will help you understand the craft of storytelling.

Prereading

Think about your own life. Do the Prereading Journal Entry. Writing about your own life *before* you read will help you enjoy the passage more and see the author's strategies for writing an autobiographical essay. In addition, read about the author, his or her life, and the time and place the author describes.

First Reading

The first reading should be for your enjoyment. If you come across an unknown word, underline it. If you are puzzled by a passage, put a "?" in the margin. If you read a vivid or interesting passage, put a "!" in the margin, but keep reading. Highlight or place a wavy line under or next to key passages, but don't allow these marks to detract from your enjoyment of the story. *At the end of the first reading, write a sentence describing your initial impression.*

Annotated Reading

As you reread the essay, read to understand what happened. Don't just highlight or underline passages—write your *reactions* and *questions* in the margin: "This scene is especially memorable" or "Why does the writer describe this incident?" Also read with a writer's eye. Bracket [ ] and label the key features of writing about memories. Finally, note in the margin any sentences that seem to give the writer's *main idea* or dominant impression for the passage as a whole. When necessary, look up definitions of any unfamiliar words.

Collaborative Reading

In a small group or in your class as a whole, share your reading experiences and annotations. Trade journal entries and discuss each other's experiences. Then exchange your books and read each other's annotations. Your group or class should discuss the various annotations and then agree on the ones that illustrate *consensus* reactions to the essay. One person in the group or class should record in the margin the best annotations from the group or class. At the bottom of the essay, write out the *main idea or dominant impression* created by the essay. After compiling a collective annotation of the essay, list ideas, questions, and interpretations for further reading or writing about the essay. A group or class recorder should write down at least two such ideas or questions.

Writing a Remembering Essay

Writing a remembering essay requires much more than just remembering. In your mind, memories are vivid sets of pictures. To show these pictures to your reader, however, you must re-create each image and scene, painstakingly, frame by frame. Imagine that you are a Disney cartoonist: You must draw dozens of separate sketches which will then be flipped through in a matter of a second or two, creating the illusion for your readers of a Technicolor trip through your past.

As you write about your memories, think about which scenes or sketches should be fully drawn, set in an actual time and place, and which should be presented as habitual actions, blurred and impressionistic. Specific scenes are those that occur only once. They happen on a specific day. They re-create key events by using detailed description and actual dialogue. They may even present the thoughts of the central character.

Use your observing skills to set the scene for specific events. Often, just a detail or two, a specific sight, sound, or smell will give your scene an authentic ring. In "Shame," Gregory describes the chair he sat in with a chalk circle drawn around it. He describes how he was shaking, scared to death. He describes the teacher, opening her book and calling out names alphabetically. Without such details in your sketches, readers will not see a vivid picture.

Finally, keep arranging and rearranging these pictures until they tell a story, focused by some dominant impression, main idea, or central discovery. They may present some conflict—and then resolve it. They may present a question—and then show your answer or discovery. They may show a scene from the past and contrast that past with the present.

Choosing a Subject for a Remembering Essay

Write an essay about an important person, place, event, scene, or object in your life. Your purpose is to *re-create* key scenes containing some conflict/resolution and, in the process, show *why* these memories are important. Begin by assuming that you are writing these memories for a family member or good friend.

As you begin writing and planning, look for an angle or a way to **focus** your experience. Your essay will be about yourself, but it may take place in only one day, or perhaps only an hour. It may focus on a certain person, a place that is important, or an object. Or, instead of focusing on one thing, look for several experiences linked by a **single thread:** three days at school, two different but really similar friends, or three weird but prophetic dreams. Finally, look for an **uncommon subject** or a **unique point of view** that has the power to surprise your reader.

Collecting Memories and Ideas

Try some of the following collecting strategies. If you already have a topic, these strategies may help you remember more. If you don't have a topic, they may suggest one.

Go to the library or Google a popular magazine issue published when you were five, ten, or fifteen years old.

What memories do the articles and even the advertisements evoke?

Draw a sketch of the place, person, or object you're writing about. Or get out a map of a place you've visited and want to remember.

Dig out old pictures of yourself, family, or friends. Write a journal entry about a picture that catches your attention.

If possible, visit a business, a school, a house where you used to live or work. What personal memories does it evoke? Then observe it objectively: What does it probably look like to a stranger?

Interview friends or family members in person, on Facebook, or on email about your topic. What do they remember about these events?

Try brainstorming: Just begin writing about your subject and write nonstop, whatever comes into your mind. Don't worry about whether it really makes sense; just keep writing.

Do a looping exercise: Brainstorm for five minutes. Then stop and reread what you have written. Underline the sentence or idea that is most interesting. Then write for five more minutes, using that sentence as your starting point. Stop and reread your second brainstorm. Underline the most interesting sentence. Use that sentence as the starting point for your last five-minute brainstorm.

For clustering, start with a clean piece of paper. Write your person, place, or scene in the center of the page and circle it. Draw several inch-long spokes or lines out from that center circle. Draw a circle or oval at the end of each spoke. Then write in these circles whatever ideas, scenes, people, events, or objects pop into your mind. Again, draw spokes out from several of these circles and write key words or phrases. Keep this clustering exercise going until you've identified several important scenes, people, places, or ideas. (See Nicolle Mircos's clustering exercise in Chapter 2, page 50.)

Shaping Your Remembering Essay

Several of the following shaping strategies may help you organize your memories. For each strategy, read the examples from the essays in this chapter and then write a few notes showing how each strategy might apply to your topic. After you have made some notes for each of these strategies, decide which one(s) work best for your topic.

Chronological Order

Usually writers follow a natural time order (A, B, and C), but you may wish to try a flashback or inverted order (B, A, and C).

In "Living in Two Cultures," Jeanne Wakatsuki Houston signals her natural time order with occasional phrases at the beginning of paragraphs.

In remembering myself as a small child. . . .
After the war . . . my world drastically changed.
As I passed puberty and grew more interested in boys. . . .
When I met my blond samurai. . . .
When we were first married. . . .
When my mother visited us, as she often did. . . .
How my present attitudes will affect my children . . . remains to
    be seen.

Conflict/Resolution

Your remembering essay may have one central conflict or it may have several related conflicts, each showing your main idea. These conflicts may be resolved immediately, or resolved only with the passage of time, or only partially resolved. *As you work with your own topic, identify the conflict(s) and resolution(s) contained in your memories.*

In Dick Gregory's essay, "Shame," the conflict between Richard's love for Helene and his embarrassing poverty is stated at the beginning of the essay: "I never learned hate at home, or shame. I had to go to school for that." The conflict focuses the story until the resolution when the boy walks out of school and doesn't go back for a long time.

Comparison/Contrast

At the heart of a remembering essay is a comparison or contrast between the person you were then and the person you are now. Look for similarities or common threads between people, places, things, images, or memories. Look also for key changes in another person, place, thing, or attitude.

In "Living in Two Cultures," Houston contrasts her Japanese family traditions with the expectations of her Caucasian husband: "When we first married I wondered if I should lay out his socks and underwear every morning like my mother used to do for my father. But my brothers' warning would float up from the past: don't be subservient to Caucasian men or they will take advantage."

Image

Look for key images that may connect or illuminate scenes. Once you've found an image that evokes your feelings or experiences, you may be able to use it several times to organize and shape your essay.

In "Shame," Dick Gregory says he is "pregnant with poverty." In "*Los Pobres,*" Richard Rodriguez uses the image of *los pobres* several times to create a vivid image of the Mexican workers. Used repeatedly, key images can focus and shape an entire essay.

Tone and Voice

Tone is the writer's attitude toward his or her subject. In a remembering essay, a writer may write with a nostalgic tone, or a bitter tone, or a philosophical, accepting tone. *Voice* is the writer's personality as revealed in the essay. In a remembering essay, writers sometimes use an adult voice, reflecting on their experiences, or sometimes a child's voice. A writer's voice may be emotional, conversational, and colloquial, or it may be impersonal and detached. Tone and voice overlap, but together they help a reader re-create the attitude and personality of the writer.

In "Shame," we occasionally hear the voice of a child in Dick Gregory's account: "The teacher thought I was stupid. Couldn't spell, couldn't read, couldn't do arithmetic. Just stupid." In contrast, Richard Rodriguez's voice in *"Los Pobres"* is more sophisticated yet vulnerable:

> "The dark sweating faces turned toward me as I spoke. They stopped their work to hear me. Each nodded in response. I stood there. I wanted to say something more. But what could I say in Spanish, even if I could have pronounced the words right?"

Dialogue

Wherever possible, *use actual dialogue* to re-create key scenes from your memories. Even if you cannot accurately reproduce conversation from years ago, your remembered dialogue will re-create what was important to you. (When you write dialogue, use quotation marks and indent each time a different character speaks.)

Gregory's dialogue in "Shame" re-creates the climax of his story:

I stood up and raised my hand.
  "What is it now?"
  "You forgot me."
  She turned toward the blackboard. "I don't have time to be playing with you, Richard."
  "My Daddy said he'd. . . ."
  "Sit down, Richard, you're disturbing the class."
  "My Daddy said he'd give . . . fifteen dollars."
  She turned and looked mad. "We are collecting this money for you and your kind, Richard Gregory. If your Daddy can give fifteen dollars you have no business being on relief."

Drafting Your Remembering Essay

After you've collected some possible characters, scenes, or places for your essay and tried several of the shaping strategies, you are ready to write a draft. Begin by rereading your notes and ideas. If the first five minutes of writing does not seem to be going in the right direction, save what you've written and start again. Once you begin writing, try to keep writing—without stopping to look up spelling or check punctuation. If you get stuck, go back and reread what you have written and pick up the thread.

Revising Your Remembering Essay

Use feedback from your readers to help you revise, but if you are in doubt, trust your own judgment. This essay must be your story, not theirs. However, if they don't get your point or cannot vividly see key scenes, then work more on re-creating those memories on the page. As you revise, keep the following tips in mind.

- **Re-examine your purpose and audience.** Are you doing what you intended? Should you write for a different audience?
- **Reread your essay for dominant impression or main idea.** Did your readers understand why this memory was important for you? You probably don't want a flat statement explaining the "moral" of the story, but the importance of the narrative must be clear.
- **Look for specific scenes, set in time and place.** Avoid just telling about key events. Show them. Check the essay for specific scenes, located in time and space, which use actual dialogue and detailed observation.
- **Where is the central conflict and resolution?** Can it be made clearer for the reader? Is it *shown* (not just told) in the specific scenes?
- **Have a reader describe the essay's voice and tone.** Does your reader's description match what you intended to convey? Should you change any sentences to make your intended voice or tone clearer?
- **Edit and proofread the essay.** Reread the essay for clarity of sentences, spelling, punctuation, grammar, or problems in mechanics.

Postscript for Your Remembering Essay

When you've finished your essay, write a journal entry that answers the following questions about your writing process. Hand in this entry with all the drafts of your essay.

1. What idea or collecting strategy helped you decide on your topic?
2. Which of the shaping strategies worked best for your essay? Which strategies didn't work? Why not?
3. What problems did you have during your drafting? What worked out well?
4. What worked best about your writing process? What was just busy-work and got in your way?
5. If you had another day to work on this essay, what would you change?

DICK GREGORY

Shame

Prereading Journal Entry

Freewrite for five minutes about an experience in school that caused you embarrassment, disappointment, or disgrace.

Dick Gregory—track star, civil rights activist, candidate for the mayor of Chicago, and vegetarian activist for the obese—is best known as the first black comedian to perform for white audiences. "Where else in the world but America," he said of his 1960s Playboy Club performances, "could I have lived in the worst neighborhoods, attended the worst schools, rode in the back of the bus, and got paid $5,000 a week just for talking about it?" His various causes are reflected in his books: From the Back of the Bus *(1962),* No More Lies: The Myth and Reality of American History *(1971),* Dick Gregory's Political Primer *(1972),* Murder in Memphis: The FBI and the Assassination of Martin Luther King *(1993), and* Callus on My Soul: A Memoir *(2000). "Shame," a selection from Gregory's best-selling* Nigger: An Autobiography *(1964), describes an episode from his childhood in St. Louis. "We ain't poor; we're just broke," Gregory's mother used to say, but "Shame" reveals the truth: "Poor is a state of mind you never grow out of."*

1   I never learned hate at home, or shame. I had to go to school for that. I was about seven years old when I got my first big lesson. I was in love with a little girl named Helene Tucker, a light-complexioned little girl with pigtails and nice manners. She was always clean and she was smart in school. I think I went to school then mostly to look at her.

I brushed my hair and even got me a little old handkerchief. It was a lady's handkerchief, but I didn't want Helene to see me wipe my nose on my hand. The pipes were frozen again, there was no water in the house, but I washed my socks and shirt every night. I'd get a pot, and go over to Mister Ben's grocery store, and stick my pot down into his soda machine. Scoop out some chopped ice. By evening the ice melted to water for washing. I got sick a lot that winter because the fire would go out at night before the clothes were dry. In the morning I'd put them on, wet or dry, because they were the only clothes I had.

2   Everybody's got a Helene Tucker, a symbol of everything you want. I loved her for her goodness, her cleanness, her popularity. She'd walk down my street and my brothers and sisters would yell, "Here comes Helene," and I'd rub my tennis sneakers on the back of my pants and wish my hair wasn't so nappy and the white folks' shirt fit me better. I'd run out on the street. If I knew my place and didn't come too close, she'd wink at me and say hello. That was a good feeling. Sometimes I'd follow her all the way home, and shovel the snow off her walk and try to make friends with her Momma and her aunts. I'd drop money on her stoop late at night on my way back from shining shoes in the taverns. And she had a Daddy, and he had a good job. He was a paper hanger.

3   I guess I would have gotten over Helene by summertime, but something happened in that classroom that made her face hang in front of me for the next twenty-two years. When I played the drums in high school it was for Helene and when I broke track records in college it was for Helene and when I started standing behind microphones and heard applause I wished Helene could hear it, too. It wasn't until I was twenty-nine years old and married and making money that I finally got her out of my system. Helene was sitting in that classroom when I learned to be ashamed of myself.

4   It was on a Thursday. I was sitting in the back of the room, in a seat with a chalk circle drawn around it. The idiot's seat, the trouble-maker's seat.

5   The teacher thought I was stupid. Couldn't spell, couldn't read, couldn't do arithmetic. Just stupid. Teachers were never interested in finding out that you couldn't concentrate because you were so hungry, because you hadn't had any breakfast. All you could think about was noontime, would it ever come? Maybe you could sneak into the cloakroom and steal a bite of some kid's lunch out of a coat pocket. A bite of something. Paste. You can't really make a meal of paste, or

put it on bread for a sandwich, but sometimes I'd scoop a few spoonfuls out of the paste jar in the back of the room. Pregnant people get strange tastes. I was pregnant with poverty. Pregnant with dirt and pregnant with smells that made people turn away, pregnant with cold and pregnant with shoes that were never bought for me, pregnant with five other people in my bed and no Daddy in the next room, and pregnant with hunger. Paste doesn't taste too bad when you're hungry.

6   The teacher thought I was a troublemaker. All she saw from the front of the room was a little black boy who squirmed in his idiot's seat and made noises and poked the kids around him. I guess she couldn't see a kid who made noises because he wanted someone to know he was there.

7   It was on a Thursday, the day before the Negro payday. The eagle always flew on Friday. The teacher was asking each student how much his father would give to the Community chest. On Friday night, each kid would get the money from his father, and on Monday he would bring it to the school. I decided I was going to buy me a Daddy right then. I had money in my pocket from shining shoes and selling papers, and whatever Helene Tucker pledged for her Daddy I was going to top it. And I'd hand the money right in. I wasn't going to wait until Monday to buy me a Daddy.

8   I was shaking, scared to death. The teacher opened her book and started calling out names alphabetically.

9   "Helene Tucker?"

10   "My Daddy said he'd give two dollars and fifty cents."

11   "That's very nice, Helene. Very, very nice indeed."

12   That made me feel pretty good. It wouldn't take too much to top that. I had almost three dollars in dimes and quarters in my pocket. I stuck my hand in my pocket and held onto the money, waiting for her to call my name. But the teacher closed her book after she called everybody else in the class.

13   I stood up and raised my hand.

14   "What is it now?"

15   "You forgot me."

16   She turned toward the blackboard. "I don't have time to be playing with you, Richard."

17   "My Daddy said he'd. . ."

18   "Sit down, Richard, you're disturbing the class."

19   "My Daddy said he'd give . . . fifteen dollars."

20 She turned around and looked mad. "We are collecting this money for you and your kind, Richard Gregory. If your Daddy can give fifteen dollars you have no business being on relief."

21 "I got it right now, I got it right now, my Daddy gave it to me to turn in today, my Daddy said . . ."

22 "And furthermore," she said, looking right at me, her nostrils getting big and her lips getting thin and her eyes opening wide, "we know you don't have a Daddy."

23 Helene Tucker turned around, her eyes full of tears. She felt sorry for me. Then I couldn't see her too well because I was crying, too.

24 "Sit down, Richard."

25 And I always thought the teacher kind of liked me. She always picked me to wash the blackboard on Friday, after school. That was a big thrill, it made me feel important. If I didn't wash it, come Monday the school might not function right.

26 "Where are you going, Richard?"

27 I walked out of school that day, and for a long time I didn't go back very often. There was shame there.

QUESTIONS FOR DISCUSSION AND WRITING

1. Is the source of Richard's shame his poverty, his lack of a father, his "troublemaking" behavior, his teacher, his love for Helene, or some combination? Explain.

2. What are Gregory's purposes in this selection? To describe a traumatic moment from his childhood? To criticize his teacher and the school system? To explain the effects of poverty and racial prejudice? Explain.

3. Which paragraphs show Gregory re-creating key events from his past life? Which paragraphs show Gregory describing typical or habitual actions in the past? Which paragraphs show Gregory reflecting on those events?

4. Are the reflective or "adult" parts of this story told in a different style (sentences, vocabulary, voice) than the parts that re-create actual events from Gregory's life? Explain, referring to specific passages.

5. Create a time line for this story. First, list in chronological order all the events referred to or described in the story—including events that occur before the story begins. Where on this time line does Gregory's story open?

6. Reread your Prereading Journal Entry. Does that incident have a potential political point? Could you use your account to make a larger point about the use of power in families, schools, or society? Revise your journal entry into a longer account about that incident in your life.

Haiti: A Survivor's Story

Prereading Journal Entry

Journals are a great place to write down what is happening to you on a daily basis. If you keep a journal, write in a blog, or post regularly on Facebook, reread your entries until you find an event that you find interesting. Write a longer entry on that day, event, or person.

Laura Wagner graduated from Yale University in 2004 with a degree in History of Science and History of Medicine. She is currently is a graduate student studying medical anthropology, human rights, gender and sexual violence, and Haiti diaspora at the University of North Carolina, Chapel Hill. Wagner was living and conducting research in Port-au-Prince when on January 12, 2010, an earthquake of 7.0 on the Richter scale destroyed thousands of buildings and killed over a hundred thousand people. In her essay, which appeared in Salon.com, Wagner recalls in detail what life was like in Haiti, before, during, and after the earthquake. In her essay, Wagner describes how, in the "aftermath of the earthquake, there was great personal kindness and sacrifice, grace and humanity in the midst of natural and institutional chaos and rupture."

1   I was sitting barefoot on my bed, catching up on ethnographic field notes, when the earthquake hit. As a child of the San Francisco area, I was underwhelmed at first. "An earthquake. This is unexpected," I thought. But then the shaking grew stronger. I had never felt such a loss of control, not only of my body but also of my surroundings, as though the world that contained me were being crumpled.

2   I braced myself in a doorway between the hallway and the kitchen, trying to hold on to the frame, and then a cloud of darkness and cement dust swallowed everything as the house collapsed. I was surprised to die in this way, but not afraid. And then I was surprised not to be dead after all. I was trapped, neither lying down nor sitting, with my left arm crushed between the planks of the shattered doorway and my legs pinned under the collapsed roof. Somewhere, outside, I heard people screaming, praying and singing. It was reassuring. It meant the world hadn't ended.

3   I want you to know that, before the earthquake, things in Haiti were normal. Outside Haiti, people only hear the worst — tales that are

cherry-picked, tales that are exaggerated, tales that are lies. I want you to understand that there was poverty and oppression and injustice in Port-au-Prince, but there was also banality. There were teenage girls who sang along hilariously with the love ballads of Marco Antonio Solís, despite not speaking Spanish. There were men who searched in vain for odd jobs by day and told never-ending *Bouki* and *Ti Malis* stories and riddles as the sun went down and rain began to fall on the banana leaves. There were young women who painted their toenails rose for church every Sunday, and stern middle-aged women who wouldn't let me leave the house without admonishing me to iron my skirt and comb my hair. There were young students who washed their uniforms and white socks every evening by hand, rhythmically working the detergent into a noisy foam. There were great water trucks that passed through the streets several times a day, inexplicably playing a squealing, mechanical version of the theme from "Titanic," which we all learned to ignore the same way we tuned out the overzealous and confused roosters that crowed at 3 a.m. There were families who finished each day no further ahead than they had begun it and then, at night, sat on the floor and intently followed the Mexican telenovelas dubbed into French. Their eyes trained on fantastic visions of alternate worlds in which roles become reversed and the righteous are rewarded, dreaming ahead into a future that might, against all odds, hold promise.

4   I need to tell you these things, not just so that you know, but also so I don't forget.

5   I think I was under the rubble for about two hours. Buried somewhere in what had been the kitchen, a mobile phone had been left to charge, and now it kept ringing. The ringtone was sentimental, the chorus of a pop love song. There was something sticky and warm on my shirt. I thought it was sòs pwa, a Haitian bean soup eaten over rice, which we'd had for lunch. I thought it was funny, that sòs pwa was leaking out of the overturned refrigerator and all over me. I thought, "When I get out, I will have to tell Melise about this." Melise was the woman who lived and worked in the house. I spent a large part of every day with her and her family — gossiping and joking, polishing the furniture with vegetable oil, cooking over charcoal and eating pounded breadfruit with our hands. She said my hands were soft. Her palms were so hard and calloused from a lifetime of household work that she could lift a hot pot with her bare hands. She called me her third daughter. I thought Melise would laugh to see me drenched in her sòs pwa from the bottom hem of my shirt up through my bra. It took me some

time to figure out that what I thought was sòs pwa was actually my blood. I wrung it out of my shirt with my free right hand. I couldn't tell where it was coming from.

6 Melise did not make it out of the house. She died, we assume, at the moment of collapse. According to others, who told me later, she cried out, "*Letènel, oh letènel!*" and that was all. (The word is Creole for the French "l'Eternal," a cry out to God.) She had been folding laundry on the second floor — the floor that crumbled onto the first floor, where I was pinned, thinking wildly of sòs pwa. Melise worked and lived in that house for 15 years. She dreamed of one day having her own home and being free. She talked about it all the time. She died in the wreckage of a place she did not consider her home.

7 I want to write everything down – those mundane remembrances of how life was before — because as time passes I am afraid that people will become fossilized, that their lives and identities will begin to be knowable only through the facts of their deaths. My field notes are buried in that collapsed house. Those notes are an artifact, a record of a lost time, stories about people when they were just people — living, ordinary people who told dirty jokes, talked one-on-one to God, blamed a fart on the cat, and made their way through a life that was grinding but not without joy or humor, or normality. I don't want my friends to be canonized.

8 I had been in Port-au-Prince for a total of six months, conducting research on household workers and human rights. As a young American woman not affiliated with any of the large organizations that dominate the Haitian landscape, I was overwhelmed every day by the fierce generosity of Haitians. People who had little were eager to share their food, their homes, their time, their lives. Now I'm cobbling together this narrative — these nonconsecutive remembrances — in surreal and far-removed settings: first a hospital bed in South Miami, then a Cinnabon-scented airport terminal, now a large public university during basketball season. I can't do anything for those same people who gave of themselves so naturally and unflinchingly. My friends, who for months insisted on sharing whatever food they had made, even if I had already eaten, promising me "just a little rice" but invariably giving more. My friends, who walked me to the taptap stop nearly every day.

9 Now that the first journalistic burst has ended, now that the celebrity telethons have wrapped, the stories you hear are of "looters" and "criminals" set loose on a post-apocalyptic wasteland. This is the same story that has always been told about Haiti, for more than 200

years, since the slaves had the temerity to not want to be slaves any-more. This is the same trope of savagery that has been used to strip Haiti and Haitians of legitimacy since the Revolution. But at the mo-ment of the quake, even as the city and, for all we knew, the govern-ment collapsed, Haitian society did not fall into Hobbesian anarchy. This stands in contradiction both to what is being shown on the news right now, and everything we assume about societies in moments of breakdown.

10   In the aftermath of the earthquake, there was great personal kind-ness and sacrifice, grace and humanity in the midst of natural and in-stitutional chaos and rupture. My friend Frenel, who worked cleaning and maintaining the house, appeared within minutes to look for sur-vivors. He created a passage through the still-falling debris using only a flashlight and a small hammer — the kind you would use to nail a picture to a wall. Completely trapped, the nerves in my left arm dam-aged, I could not help him save me. He told me, calmly, "Pray, Lolo, you must pray," as he broke up the cement and pulled it out, piece by piece, to free me. Once I was out, he gave me the sandals off his own feet. As I write this, I am still wearing them. At the United Nations compound, where Frenel ultimately guided and left me, everyone sat together on the cracked asphalt, bleeding and dazed, holding hands and praying as the aftershocks came. A little boy who had arrived alone trembled on my lap. Another family huddled under the same metallic emergency blanket with us. Their child looked at me, warily — a foreigner, covered in blood and dusted white with cement powder. His grandmother told him, *"Ou mèt chita. Li malad, menm jan avek nou."* You can sit. She's sick, too, just like us.

11   Social scientists who study catastrophes say there are no natural disasters. In every calamity, it is inevitably the poor who suffer more, die more, and will continue to suffer and die after the cameras turn their gaze elsewhere. Do not be deceived by claims that everyone was affected equally — fault lines are social as well as geological. After all, I am here, with my white skin and my U.S. citizenship, listening to birds outside the window in the gray-brown of a North Carolina win-ter, while the people who welcomed me into their lives are still in Port-au-Prince, within the wreckage, several of them still not ac-counted for.

12   As I sat waiting to be flown out, trying to convince myself that I was just another injured person using up scant food and resources, a non-Haitian man whom I presumed worked for the U.N. approached me.

13 "Can you do me a favor?" he asked. "Could you write something down?"

14 I nodded, and he handed me a pen and paper.

15 "Tear the paper in half, and on the first half write 'unidentified local female' in block letters. Then on the second piece of paper write the same thing."

16 I looked up. There were bodies loaded into the back of a pickup truck. The woman's floral print dress was showing and her feet were hanging out. There were not enough sheets and blankets for the living patients, never mind enough to adequately wrap the dead. The U.N. guy looked at me and sort of smiled as I numbly tore the paper and wrote.

17 "After all, you need something to do. All the bars are closed," he said.

18 I stared at the bodies on the truck, and I hated him. I did not know which, if any, of my friends had survived. I imagined the people I love — Marlène, one of my best friends, or Damilove, the mother of my goddaughter – wrapped up in some scrap of cloth with their feet hanging out and some asshole tagging them with a half-piece of scrap paper that says they are anonymous, without history, unknown.

19 I am telling you two things that seem contradictory: that people in Haiti are suffering horribly, and that Haitians are not sufferers in some preordained way. What I mean is that suffering is not some intrinsic aspect of Haitian existence, it is not something to get used to. The dead were once human beings with complex lives, and those in agony were not always victims.

20 In Haiti I was treated with incredible warmth and generosity by people who have been criminalized, condemned, dehumanized and abstractly pitied. They helped me in small, significant ways for the six months I was there, and in extraordinary ways in the hours after the quake. Now I cannot help them. I cannot do anything useful for them from here, except to employ the only strategy that was available to us all when we were buried in collapsed houses, listening to the frantic stirrings of life aboveground: to shout and shout until someone responds.

QUESTIONS FOR DISCUSSION AND WRITING

1. In the middle of her essay, Wagner explains that she wanted to write everything down because she is afraid that people in Haiti "will become fossilized." Explain what she means by this statement.

2. Later in her essay, Wagner says that we should not be "deceived by claims that everyone was affected equally—fault lines are social as well as geological." What exactly does she mean here?

3. Remembering essays recall specific people, places and events, but they often offer reflections on the meaning of those events. Find one paragraph where Wagner relates her memories of a specific event. Then find a paragraph where she is reflecting on the meaning of her experience. Explain how both kinds of paragraphs work to achieve her purpose.

4. Review the strategies for reading and writing a remembering essay at the beginning of this chapter. Which of those five strategies does Wagner do especially well? Which might she use or develop more to improve her essay? Explain your choices.

5. Review your response to the prewriting journal entry at the beginning of this chapter. Which of the five remembering strategies did you try in your entry? Which could you work on if you were to do a revised draft? Explain your responses.

HELEN KELLER

The Day Language Came into My Life

Prereading Journal Entry

Write for five minutes, recalling your earliest memories of reading or writing. Focus on a specific book that you read or something that you wrote. Where were you? What were you reading or writing? Why do you think you remember that particular time?

At the age of eighteen months, Helen Keller (1880-1968) lost her sight and hearing as a result of an illness. During the next five years of her childhood, Keller became increasingly wild and unruly as she struggled against her dark and silent world. In "The Day Language Came into My Life," Keller re-members how, at age seven, her teacher, Anne Sullivan, arrived and taught her the miracle of language. After learning sign language and Braille, Keller began her formal schooling and—with continued help from Sullivan—eventu-ally graduated with honors from Radcliffe College. In her adult years, Keller became America's best-loved ambassador for the blind and disabled. She met nearly every American president, traveled to dozens of countries to speak on behalf of blind and deaf people, and wrote several books, including

The Story of My Life *(1903),* The World I Live In *(1908), and* Midstream: My Later Life *(1930). The story of Anne Sullivan's teaching is told in William Gibson's Pulitzer Prize-winning play,* The Miracle Worker.

1   The most important day I remember in all my life is the one on which my teacher, Anne Mansfield Sullivan, came to me. I am filled with wonder when I consider the immeasurable contrast between the two lives which it connects. It was the third of March 1887, three months before I was seven years old.

2   On the afternoon of that eventful day, I stood on the porch, dumb, expectant. I guessed vaguely from my mother's signs and from the hurrying to and fro in the house that something unusual was about to happen, so I went to the door and waited on the steps. The afternoon sun penetrated the mass of honeysuckle that covered the porch and fell on my upturned face. My fingers lingered almost unconsciously on the familiar leaves and blossoms which had just come forth to greet the sweet southern spring. I did not know what the future held of marvel or surprise for me. Anger and bitterness had preyed upon me continually for weeks and a deep languor had succeeded this passionate struggle.

3   Have you ever been at sea in a dense fog, when it seemed as if a tangible white darkness shut you in, and the great ship, tense and anxious, groped her way toward the shore with plummet and sounding-line, and you waited with beating heart for something to happen? I was like that ship before my education began, only I was without compass or sounding-line and had no way of knowing how near the harbor was. "Light! Give me light!" was the wordless cry of my soul, and the light of love shone on me in that very hour.

4   I felt approaching footsteps. I stretched out my hand as I supposed to for my mother. Someone took it, and I was caught up and held close in the arms of her who had come to reveal all things to me, and, more than all things else, to love me.

5   The morning after my teacher came she led me into her room and gave me a doll. The little blind children at the Perkins Institution had sent it and Laura Bridgman had dressed it; but I did not know this until afterward. When I had played with it a little while, Miss Sullivan slowly spelled into my hand the word "d-o-l-l." I was at once interested in this finger play and tried to imitate it. When I finally succeeded in making the letters correctly I was flushed with childish pleasure and pride. Running downstairs to my mother I held up my hand and made the letters for doll. I did not know that I was spelling a word or even that words existed; I was simply making my fingers go in monkeylike

imitation. In the days that followed I learned to spell in this uncomprehending way a great many words, among them pin, hat, cup and a few verbs like sit, stand and walk. But my teacher had been with me several weeks before I understood that everything has a name.

6　　One day, while I was playing with my new doll, Miss Sullivan put my big rag doll into my lap also, spelled "d-o-l-l" and tried to make me understand that "d-o-l-l" applied to both. Earlier in the day we had had a tussle over the words "m-u-g" and "w-a-t-e-r." Miss Sullivan had tried to impress it upon me that "m-u-g" is mug and that "w-a-t-e-r" is water, but I persisted in confounding the two. In despair she had dropped the subject for the time, only to renew it at the first opportunity. I became impatient at her repeated attempts and, seizing the new doll, I dashed it upon the floor. I was keenly delighted when I felt the fragments of the broken doll at my feet. Neither sorrow nor regret followed my passionate outburst. I had not loved the doll. In the still, dark world in which I lived there was no strong sentiment or tenderness. I felt my teacher sweep the fragments to one side of the hearth, and I had a sense of satisfaction that the cause of my discomfort was removed. She brought me my hat, and I knew I was going out into the warm sunshine. This thought, if a wordless sensation may be called a thought, made me hop and skip with pleasure.

7　　We walked down the path to the well-house, attracted by the fragrance of the honeysuckle with which it was covered. Someone was drawing water and my teacher placed my hand under the spout. As the cool stream gushed over one hand she spelled into the other the word water, first slowly, then rapidly. I stood still, my whole attention fixed upon the motions of her fingers. Suddenly I felt a misty consciousness as of something forgotten – a thrill of returning thought; and somehow the mystery of language was revealed to me. I knew then that "w-a-t-e-r" meant the wonderful cool something that was flowing over my hand. The living word awakened my soul, gave it light, hope, joy, set it free! There were barriers still, it is true, but barriers that could in time be swept away.

8　　I left the well-house eager to learn. Everything had a name, and each name gave birth to a new thought. As we returned to the house every object which I touched seemed to quiver with life. That was because I saw everything with the strange, new sight that had come to me. On entering the door I remembered the doll I had broken. I felt my way to the hearth and picked up the pieces. I tried vainly to put them together. Then my eyes filled with tears; for I realized what I had done, and for the first time I felt repentance and sorrow. I learned a great many new words that day. I do not remember what they all were; but I do know that *mother, father, sister, teacher* were among them – words that were to make the world blossom for me, "like Aaron's rod, with flowers." It would have been difficult to find a happier child than I was as I lay in my crib at the close of that eventful day and lived over the joys it had brought me, and for the first time longed for a new day to come.

QUESTIONS FOR DISCUSSION AND WRITING

1. Helen Keller's books have been translated into more than fifty languages. Explain why you believe her story, as illustrated in this essay, has such universal appeal.
2. In paragraph 3, Keller uses an analogy to explain her feelings and her state of mind before language opened her life. Identify the extended comparison. What "difficult concept" does Keller explain through her analogy?
3. A century ago, when Helen Keller was learning to read and speak, people who were blind and deaf were actually classified by the law as "idiots." Describe one experience you have with a person with disabilities. Based on your experience, how have Americans' attitudes toward people with some disability improved? What laws have changed or been enacted to support these changes?
4. On the Internet or in your library's databases, gather information or articles on the education of deaf and/or blind children. What educational methods are used? What new technologies help children with these disabilities?

RICHARD RODRIGUEZ

Los Pobres

Prereading Journal Entry

Describe an experience in which your expectations about a job did not match the reality of the experience. Set the context, describe your expectations, and then narrate events from one or two specific days that showed how the reality did not meet your expectations.

In Hunger of Memory: The Education of Richard Rodriguez *(1982), Richard Rodriguez describes how his education changed forever his under-privileged minority status. The son of Spanish-speaking Mexican-American*

RODRIGUEZ / LOS POBRES

immigrants, Rodriguez learned English in the Sacramento school system, received an MA degree from Stanford, and eventually earned a PhD in English literature at Berkeley. Instead of accepting one of many teaching offers from prestigious schools, however, Rodriguez chose to leave academic life, on the grounds that he was benefiting as a minority when the "genuinely disadvantaged," the "people who cannot read or write," were ignored by the system. Rodriguez has published a number of essays in magazines such as Harper's *and* The American Scholar, *and several books including* Days of Obligation: An Argument with My Mexican Father *(1992) and* Brown: The last Discovery of America *(2002). In "Los Pobres," an excerpt from* Hunger of Memory, *Rodriguez describes a summer job he took in order to understand the hard, manual labor that is routine for many other Mexican-Americans. Rodriguez discovers, however, that chopping out tree stumps and shoveling all day cannot help him understand the lives of the other Mexican workers— the poor, the powerless, the silent ones. Through the events of that summer, Rodriguez realizes that he can never really be one of "los pobres."*

1   I went to college at Stanford, attracted partly by its academic reputation, partly because it was the school rich people went to. I found myself on a campus with golden children of western America's upper middle class. Many were students both ambitious for academic success *and* accustomed to leisured life in the sun. In the afternoon, they lay spread out, sunbathing in front of the library, reading Swift or Engels or Beckett. Others went by in convertibles, off to play tennis or ride horses or sail. Beach boys dressed in tank tops and shorts were my classmates in undergraduate seminars. Tall tan girls wearing white strapless dresses sat directly in front of me in lecture rooms. I'd study them, their physical confidence. I was still recognizably kin to the boy I had been. Less tortured perhaps. But still kin. At Stanford, it's true, I began to have something like a conventional sexual life. I don't think, however, that I really believed that the women I knew found me physically appealing. I continued to stay out of the sun. I didn't linger in mirrors. And I was the student at Stanford who remembered to notice the Mexican-American janitors and gardeners working on campus.

2   It was at Stanford, one day near the end of my senior year, that a friend told me about a summer construction job he knew was available. I was quickly alert. Desire uncoiled within me. My friend said that he knew I had been looking for summer employment. He knew I needed some money. Almost apologetically he explained: It was something I probably wouldn't be interested in, but a friend of his, a contractor,

needed someone for the summer to do menial jobs. There would be lots of shoveling and raking and sweeping. Nothing too hard. But nothing more interesting either. Still, the pay would be good. Did I want it? Or did I know someone who did?

3   I did. Yes, I said, surprised to hear myself say it.

4   In the weeks following, friends cautioned that I had no idea how hard physical labor really is. ("You only *think* you know what it is like to shovel for eight hours straight.") Their objections seemed to me challenges. They resolved the issue. I became happy with my plan. I decided, however, not to tell my parents. I wouldn't tell my mother because I could guess her worried reaction. I would tell my father only after the summer was over, when I could announce that, after all, I did know what "real work" is like.

5   The day I met the contractor (a Princeton graduate, it turned out), he asked me whether I had done any physical labor before. "In high school, during the summer," I lied. And although he seemed to regard me with skepticism, he decided to give me a try. Several days later, expectant, I arrived at my first construction site. I would take off my shirt to the sun. And at last grasp desired sensation. No longer afraid. At last become like a *bracero*. "We need those tree stumps out of here by tomorrow," the contractor said. I started to work.

6   I labored with excitement that first morning—and all the days after. The work was harder than I could have expected. But it was never as tedious as my friends had warned me it would be. There was too much physical pleasure in the labor. Especially early in the day, I would be most alert to the sensations of movement and straining. Beginning around seven each morning (when the air was still damp but the scent of weeds and dry earth anticipated the heat of the sun), I would feel my body resist the first thrusts of the shovel. My arms, tightened by sleep, would gradually loosen; after only several minutes, sweat would gather in beads on my forehead and then—a short while later—I would feel my chest silky with sweat in the breeze. I would return to my work. A nervous spark of pain would fly up my arm and settle to burn like an ember in the thick of my shoulder. An hour, two passed. Three. My whole body would assume regular movements; my shoveling would be described by identical, even movements. Even later in the day, my enthusiasm for primitive sensation would survive the heat and the dust and the insects pricking my back. I would strain wildly for sensation as the day came to a close. At three-thirty, quitting time, I would stand upright and slowly let my head fall back, luxuriating in the feeling of tightness relieved.

7   Some of the men working nearby would watch me and laugh. Two or three of the older men took the trouble to teach me the right way to use a pick, the correct way to shovel. "You're doing it wrong, too fucking hard," one man scolded. Then proceeded to show me—what persons who work with their bodies all their lives quickly learn—the most economical way to use one's body in labor.

8   "Don't make your back do so much work," he instructed. I stood impatiently listening, half listening, vaguely watching, then noticed his work-thickened fingers clutching the shovel. I was annoyed. I wanted to tell him that I enjoyed shoveling the wrong way. And I didn't want to learn the right way. I wasn't afraid of back pain. I liked the way my body felt sore at the end of the day.

9   I was about to, but, as it turned out, I didn't say a thing. Rather it was as that moment I realized that I was fooling myself if I expected a few weeks of labor to gain me admission to the world of the laborer. I would not learn in three months what my father had meant by "real work." I was not bound to this job; I could imagine its rapid conclusion. For me the sensations of exertion and fatigue could be savored. For my father or uncle, working at comparable jobs when they were my age, such sensations were to be feared. Fatigue took a different toll on their bodies—and minds.

10   It was, I know, a simple insight. But it was with this realization that I took my first step that summer toward realizing something even more important about the "worker." In the company of carpenters, electricians, plumbers, and painters at lunch, I would often sit quietly, observant. I was not shy in such company. I felt easy, pleased by the knowledge that I was casually accepted, my presence taken for granted by men (exotics) who worked with their hands. Some days the younger men would talk and talk about sex, and they would howl at women who drove by in cars. Other days the talk at lunchtime was subdued; men gathered in separate groups. It depended on who was around. There were rough, good-natured workers. Others were quiet. The more I remember that summer, the more I realize that there was no single *type* of worker. I am embarrassed to say I had not expected such diversity. I certainly had not expected to meet, for example, a plumber who was an abstract painter in his off hours and admired the work of Mark Rothko. Nor did I expect to meet so many workers with college diplomas. (They were the ones who were not surprised that I intended to enter graduate school in the fall.) I suppose what I really want to say here is painfully obvious, but I must say it nevertheless: The men of that summer were middle-class Americans. They certainly didn't constitute an oppressed

society. Carefully completing their work sheets; talking about the fortunes of local football teams; planning Las Vegas vacations; comparing the gas mileage of various makes of campers—they were not *los pobres* my mother had spoken about.

11   On two occasions, the contractor hired a group of Mexican aliens. They were employed to cut down some trees and haul off debris. In all, there were six men of varying age. The youngest in his twenties, the oldest (his father?) perhaps sixty years old. They came and they left in a single old truck. Anonymous men. They were never introduced to the other men at the site. Immediately upon their arrival, they would follow the contractor's directions, start working—rarely resting—seemingly driven by a fatalistic sense that work which had to be done was best done as quickly as possible.

12   I watched them sometimes. Perhaps they watched me. The only time I saw them pay me much notice was one day at lunch-time when I was laughing with the other men. The Mexicans sat apart when they ate, just as they worked by themselves. Quiet. I rarely heard them say much to each other. All I could hear were their voices calling out sharply to one another, giving directions. Otherwise, when they stood briefly resting, they talked among themselves in voices too hard to overhear.

13   The contractor knew enough Spanish, and the Mexicans—or at least the oldest of them, their spokesman—seemed to know enough English to communicate. But because I was around, the contractor decided one day to make me his translator. (He assumed I could speak Spanish.) I did what I was told. Shyly I went over to tell the Mexicans that the *patron* wanted them to do something else before they left for the day. As I started to speak, I was afraid with my old fear that I would be unable to pronounce Spanish words. But it was a simple instruction I had to convey. I could say it in phrases.

14   The dark sweating faces turned toward me as I spoke. They stopped their work to hear me. Each nodded in response. I stood there. I wanted to say something more. But what could I say in Spanish, even if I could have pronounced the words right? Perhaps I just wanted to engage them in small talk, to be assured of their confidence, our familiarity. I thought for a moment to ask them where in Mexico they were from. Something like that. And maybe I wanted to tell them (a lie, if need be) that my parents were from the same part of Mexico.

15   I stood there.

16   Their faces watched me. The eyes of the man directly in front of me moved slowly over my shoulder, and I turned to follow his glance

toward *el patrón* some distance away. For a moment I felt swept up by that glance into the Mexicans' company. But then I heard one of them returning to work. And then the others went back to work. I left them without saying anything more.

17   When they had finished, the contractor went over to pay them in cash. (He later told me that he paid them collectively—"for the job"— though he wouldn't tell me their wages. He said something quickly about the good rate of exchange "in their own country.") I can still hear the loudly confident voice he used with the Mexicans. It was the sound of the *gringo* I had heard as a very young boy. And I can still hear the quiet, indistinct sounds of the Mexican, the oldest, who replied. At hearing that voice I was sad for the Mexicans. Depressed by their vulnerability. Angry at myself. The adventure of the summer seemed suddenly ludicrous. I would not shorten the distance I felt from *los pobres* with a few weeks of physical labor. I would not become like them. They were different from me.

18   After that summer, a great deal—and not very much really— changed in my life. The curse of physical shame was broken by the sun; I was no longer ashamed of my body. No longer would I deny myself the pleasing sensations of my maleness. During those years when middle-class Black Americans began to assert with pride, "Black is beautiful," I was able to regard my complexion without shame. I am today darker than I ever was as a boy. . . . My skin, in itself, means nothing. I stress the point because I know there are people who would label me "disadvantaged" because of my color. They make the same mistake I made as a boy, when I thought a disadvantaged life was circumscribed by particular occupations. That summer I worked in the sun may have made me physically indistinguishable from the Mexicans working nearby. (My skin was actually darker because, unlike them, I worked without wearing a shirt. By late August my hands were probably as tough as theirs.) But I was not one of *los pobres*. What made me different from them was an attitude of *mind*, my imagination of myself.

19   I do not blame my mother for warning me away from the sun when I was young. In a world where her brother had become an old man in his twenties because he was dark, my complexion was something to worry about. "Don't run in the sun," she warns me today. I run. In the end, my father was right—though perhaps he did not know how right or why—to say that I would never know what real work is. I will never know what he felt at his last factory job. If tomorrow I worked at

some kind of factory, it would go differently for me. My long education would favor me. I could act as a public person—able to defend my interests, to unionize, to petition, to speak up—to challenge and demand. (I will never know what real work is.) I will never know what the Mexicans knew, gathering their shovels and ladders and saws.

20   Their silence stays with me now. The wages those Mexicans received for their labor were only a measure of their disadvantaged condition. Their silence is more telling. They lack a public identity. They remain profoundly alien. Persons apart. People lacking a union obviously, people without grounds. They depend upon the relative good will or fairness of their employers each day. For such people, lacking a better alternative, it is not such an unreasonable risk.

21   Their silence stays with me. I have taken these many words to describe its impact. Only: the quiet. Something uncanny about it. Its compliance. Vulnerability. Pathos. As I heard their truck rumbling away, I shuddered, my face mirrored with sweat. I had finally come face to face with *los pobres*.

QUESTIONS FOR DISCUSSION AND WRITING

1. At the end of paragraph 17, Rodriguez senses the distance he felt from *los pobres:* "I would not become like them. They were different from me." Why can't he become like them? How, exactly, are they different?

2. Remembering essays are often shaped by an *expectations-versus-reality* pattern. Where in *"Los Pobres"* does Rodriguez focus clearly on the differences between what he thought would happen and what actually happened?

3. Writers of remembering essays often focus on a few specific scenes clearly set in time and place. List the specific days (key scenes) from the summer of work that Rodriguez describes. Which scenes most effectively convey how he felt?

4. Who is Rodriguez's audience? Do you think the experiences Rodriguez describes are more interesting to white readers than to members of an ethnic minority? Why or why not?

5. In order to bring key scenes to life, writers of remembering essays use dialogue and sensory detail. Which scenes contain the best detail and dialogue? How do these strategies engage the reader in the writer's memories?

6. *"Los Pobres"* is about Rodriguez's summer of physical labor, but it is also about power, authority, and education. In which paragraphs or

scenes is this theme most clearly stated? According to Rodriguez, how does his "attitude of mind," his education, confer power and authority?

7. Write about a time in your life when you felt like *los pobres,* like an outsider. What was the situation? What made you feel different? What made you feel powerless? How did you cope with this situation and what did you learn?

JEANNE WAKATSUKI HOUSTON

Living in Two Cultures

Prereading Journal Entry

We all play multiple roles, behaving one way with our parents, another way with friends, and a third way with members of the opposite sex. Describe two or three different roles that you play, indicating how the roles are different and for whom you play each role.

Following the bombing of Pearl Harbor on December 7, 1941, many Japanese-American citizens were sent to prison camps. Although the U.S. government said that the Japanese were just being "detained" for their own protection, the widespread fear was that they might become spies or even fight against the United States. Jeanne Wakatsuki, "interned" with her family during World War II at Manzanar near Death Valley, described her experiences in Farewell to Manzanar: A True Story of Japanese American Experience During and After the World War II Internment *(1973). Houston has also written* Beyond Manzanar: Views of Asian-American Womanhood *(1985) and* The Legend of Fire Horse Woman *(2003). "Living in Two Cultures" describes Houston's experiences growing up in California after the war. The essay shows how the conflict between the traditional Japanese customs and the "Hakujin" or "All-American" culture in California created a "double standard" for Houston's self-image as a Japanese-American female.*

1   The memories surrounding my awareness of being female fall into two categories: those of the period before World War II, when the family made up my life, and those after the war, when I entered puberty and my world expanded to include the ways and values of my Caucasian peers. I did not think about my Asian-ness and how it influenced my self-image as a female until I married.

2   In remembering myself as a small child, I find it hard to separate myself from the entity of the family. I was too young to be given "duties" according to my sex, and I was unaware that this was the organizational basis for operating the family. I took it for granted that everyone just did what had to be done to keep things running smoothly. My five older sisters helped my mother with domestic duties. My four older brothers helped my father in the fishing business. What I vaguely recall about the sensibility surrounding our sex differences was that my sisters and I all liked to please our brothers. More so, we tried to attract positive attention from Papa. A smile or affectionate pat from him was like a gift from heaven. Somehow, we never felt this way about Mama. We took her love for granted. But there was something special about Papa.

3   I never identified this specialness as being one of the blessings of maleness. After all, I played with my brother Kiyo, two years older than myself, and I never felt there was anything special about him. I could even make him cry. My older brothers were fun-loving, boisterous and very kind to me, especially when I made them laugh with my imitations of Carmen Miranda dancing or of Bonnie Baker singing "Oh, Johnny." But Papa was different. His specialness came not from being male, but from being the authority.

4   After the war and the closing of the camps, my world drastically changed. The family had disintegrated; my father was no longer godlike, despite my mother's attempt to sustain that pre-war image of him. I was spending most of my time with my new Caucasian friends and learning new values that clashed with those of my parents. It was also time that I assumed the duties girls were supposed to do, like cooking, cleaning the house, washing and ironing clothes. I remember washing and ironing my brothers' shirts, being careful to press the collars correctly, trying not to displease them. I cannot ever remember my brothers performing domestic chores while I lived at home. Yet, even though they may not have been working "out there," as the men were supposed to do, I did not resent it. It would have embarrassed me to see my brothers doing the dishes. Their reciprocation came in a different way. They were very protective of me and made me feel good and important for being a female. If my brother Ray had extra money, he would sometimes buy me a sexy sweater like my Caucasian friends wore, which Mama wouldn't buy for me. My brothers taught me to ride a bicycle and to drive a car, took me to my first dance, and proudly introduced me to their friends.

5   Although the family had changed, my identity as a female within it did not differ much from my older sisters who grew up before the war. The males and females supported each other but for different reasons. No longer was the survival of the family as a group our primary objective; we cooperated to help each other survive "out there" in the complicated world that had weakened Papa.

6   We were living in Long Beach then. My brothers encouraged me to run for school office, to try out for majorette and song leader, and to run for queen of various festivities. They were proud that I was breaking social barriers still closed to them. It was acceptable for an Oriental male to excel academically and in sports. But to gain recognition socially in a society that had been fed the stereotyped model of the Asian male as cook, houseboy or crazed kamikaze pilot was almost impossible. The more alluring myth of mystery and exotica that surrounds the Oriental female made it easier, though no less inwardly painful, for me.

7   Whenever I succeeded in the *Hakujin* world, my brothers were supportive, whereas Papa would be disdainful, undetermined by my obvious capitulation to the ways of the West. I wanted to be like my Caucasian friends. Not only did I want to look like them, I wanted to act like them. I tried hard to be outgoing and socially aggressive and to act confidently, like my girlfriends. At home I was careful not to show these personality traits to my father. For him it was bad enough that I did not even look very Japanese: I was too big, and I walked too assertively. My breasts were large, and besides that I showed them off with those sweaters the *Hakujin* girls wore! My behavior at home was never calm and serene, but around my father I still tried to be as Japanese as I could.

8   As I passed puberty and grew more interested in boys, I soon became aware that an Oriental female evoked a certain kind of interest from males. I was still too young to understand how or why an Oriental female fascinated Caucasian men, and of course, far too young to see then that it was a form of "not seeing." My brothers would warn me, "Don't trust the *Hakujin* boys. They only want one thing. They'll treat you like a servant and expect you to wait on them hand and foot. They don't know how to be nice to you." My brothers never dated Caucasian girls. In fact, I never really dated Caucasian boys until I went to college. In high school, I used to sneak out to dances and parties where I would meet them. I wouldn't even dare to think what Papa would do if he knew.

9   What my brothers were saying was that I should not act toward Caucasian males as I did toward them. I must not "wait on them" or allow them to think I would, because they wouldn't understand. In other words, be a Japanese female around Japanese men and act *Hakujin*

around Caucasian men. This double identity within a "double standard" resulted not only in a confusion for me of my role or roles as female, but also in who or what I was racially. With the admonitions of my brothers lurking deep in my consciousness, I would try to be aggressive, assertive and "come on strong" toward Caucasian men. I mustn't let them think I was submissive, passive and all giving like Madame Butterfly. With Asian males I would tone down my natural enthusiasm and settle into patterns instilled in me through the models of my mother and my sisters. I was not comfortable in either role.

10   Although I was attracted to males who looked like someone in a Coca-Cola ad, I yearned for the expressions of their potency to be like that of Japanese men, like that of my father: unpredictable, dominant, and brilliant—yet sensitive and poetic. I wanted a blond samurai.

11   When I met my blond samurai, during those college years in San Jose, I was surprised to see how readily my mother accepted the idea of our getting married. My father had passed away, but I was still concerned about her reaction. All of my married brothers and sisters had married Japanese-American mates. I would be the first to marry a Caucasian. "He's a strong man and will protect you. I'm all for it," she said. Her main concern for me was survival. Knowing that my world was the world of the *Hakujin*, she wanted me to be protected, even if it meant marriage to one of them. It was 1957, and interracial couples were a rare sight to see. She felt that my husband-to-be was strong because he was acting against the norms of his culture, perhaps even against his parent's wishes. From her vantage point, where family and group opinion outweighed the individual's, this willingness to oppose them was truly a show of strength.

12   When we first married I wondered if I should lay out his socks and underwear every morning like my mother used to do for my father. But my brothers' warning would float up from the past: don't be subservient to Caucasian men or they will take advantage. So I compromised and laid them out sporadically, whenever I thought to do it . . . . which grew less and less often as the years passed. (Now my husband is lucky if he can even find a clean pair of socks in the house!) His first reaction to this wifely gesture was to be uncomfortably pleased. Then he was puzzled by its sporadic occurrence, which did not seem to coincide as an act of apology or because I wanted something. On the days when I felt I should be a good Japanese wife, I did it. On other days, when I felt American and assertive, I did not.

13   When my mother visited us, as she often did when she was alive, I had to be on good behavior, much to my husband's pleasure and

surprise. I would jump up from the table to fill his empty water glass (if she hadn't beat me to it) or butter his roll. If I didn't notice that his plate needed refilling, she would kick me under the table and reprimand me with a disapproving look. Needless to say, we never had mother-in-law problems. He would often ask, with hope in his voice, "When is your mother coming to visit?"

14   My mother had dutifully served my father throughout their marriage, but I never felt she resented it. I served my brothers and father and did not resent it. I was made to feel not only important for performing duties of my role, but absolutely integral for the functioning of the family. I realized a very basic difference in attitude between Japanese and American cultures toward serving another. In my family, to serve another could be uplifting, a gracious gesture that elevated oneself. For many white Americans, it seems that serving another is degrading, an indication of dependency or weakness in character, or a low place in the social ladder. To be ardently considerate is to be "self-effacing" or apologetic.

15   My father used to say, "Serving humanity is the greatest virtue. Giving service of yourself is more worthy than selling the service or goods of another." He would prefer that we be maids in someone's home, serving someone well, than be salesgirls where our function would be to exchange someone else's goods, handling money. Perhaps it was his way of rationalizing and giving pride to the occupations open to us as Orientals. Nevertheless, his words have stayed with me, giving me spiritual sustenance at times when I perceived that my willingness to give was misconstrued as a need to be liked or an act of manipulation to get something.

16   My husband and I often joke that the reason we have stayed married for so long is that we continually mystify each other with responses and attitudes that are plainly due to our different backgrounds. For years I frustrated him with unpredictable silences and accusing looks. I felt a great reluctance to tell him what I wanted or what needed to be done in the home. I was inwardly furious that I was being put into the position of having to *tell* him what to do. I felt my femaleness, in the Japanese sense, was being degraded. I did not want to be the authority. That would be humiliating for him and for me. He, on the other hand, considering the home to be under my dominion, in the American sense, did not dare to impose on me what he thought I wanted. He wanted me to tell him or make a list, like his parents did in his home.

17   Entertaining socially was also confusing. Up to recent times, I still hesitated to sit at one head of our rectangular dining table when my husband sat at the other end. It seemed right to be seated next to him, helping him serve the food. Sometimes I did it anyway, but only with our close friends who didn't misread my physical placement as psychological subservience.

18   At dinner parties I always served the men first, until I noticed the women glaring at me. I became self-conscious about it and would try to remember to serve the women first. Sometimes I would forget and automatically turn to a man. I would catch myself abruptly, dropping a bowl of soup all over him. Then I would have to serve him first anyway, as a gesture of apology. My unconscious Japanese instinct still managed to get what it wanted.

19   Now I just entertain according to how I feel that day. If my Japanese sensibility is stronger, I act accordingly and feel comfortable. If I feel like going all-American, I can do that, too, and feel comfortable. I have come to accept the cultural hybridness of my personality, to recognize it as a strength and not weakness. Because I am culturally neither pure Japanese nor pure American does not mean I am less of a person. It means I have been enriched with the heritage of both.

20   How my present attitudes will affect my children in later years remains to be seen. My world is radically different from my mother's world, and all indications point to an even wider difference between our world and our children's. Whereas my family's and part of my struggle was racially based, I do not foresee a similar struggle for our children. Their biracialism is, indeed, a factor in their identity and self-image, but I feel their struggle will be more to sustain human dignity in a world rapidly dehumanizing itself with mechanization and technology. My hope is they have inherited a strong will to survive, that essential trait ethnic minorities in this country have so sharply honed.

QUESTIONS FOR DISCUSSION AND WRITING

1. Explain which of the following phrases best expresses the central focus of Houston's essay: "learning new values that clashed with those of my parents," "my self-image as a female," or "the entity of the family." Defend your choice with references to the rest of the essay.

2. Is Houston's purpose to explain how living in two cultures shaped her life? Does she have a larger political purpose or point to make, as Rodriguez does? Explain.

3. If you liked this essay, explain why you are a good audience for this essay. If you disliked this essay, explain why you are an inappropriate reader. If you disliked this essay, what could Houston have done to get your interest—apart from changing the *subject* of the essay?

4. Create a time line for Houston's essay. List, in chronological order, all the events described or referred to in the essay. Where does Houston begin her story? Does she use flashback, or do all events occur in chronological order?

5. Compare Houston's ability to adjust to her two cultures with Rodriguez's experiences with the Mexican aliens. Which writer fits in most comfortably with both worlds? Cite specific passages to support your conclusion.

6. Write an autobiographical essay about you and your family, describing how female and male *expectations and roles* differed. Or describe how your *values* contrasted with those of your parents. Focus on several specific incidents illustrating differing roles or values and showing how you adjusted to those differences.

WALTER GOEDEKER

The Wake-Up Call

Prereading Journal Entry

Describe an accident involving drunk driving that happened to you, a friend or family member, or someone in your community. What were the circumstances? What was the outcome? How might this accident have been prevented?

Walter Goedeker was studying civil engineering at Mohawk Valley Community College when he wrote this essay for his instructor, Marie Czarnecki. He decided to write about something that happened to him and his best friend, Dave. As Goedeker explains, "I cannot recall when we met; it seems as if we were always friends." When he started this remembering assignment, Goedeker relates, he stared at his computer for nearly an hour before he put a word down. "I knew what I wanted to say, but didn't have a clue where to start. Then I began to freewrite. I simply wanted to get my thoughts down as they came to me, realizing that I would organize and weed out the 'junk' later." Goedeker explains that his goal was to engage the reader with the "closeness of our relationship" in order to drive home his point about alcohol abuse. Reprinted here are Goedeker's rough draft, with his revision notes and changes, followed by the final version of his essay.

I would like to share a little story with you about an event that I had experienced that changed my life forever. Although I wouldn't mind just getting to the point, first I would like to fill you in on some of the details.

One typical day of my senior year of high school, my buddy and I once again found ourselves caught up in a serious dilemma. "What do you want to do tonight, Bud?" asked my best friend, Dave. "I don't care, what do you want to do?" I replied, as I had countless other times to the same question. Then we both looked at each other and without a word, a grin stretched across our faces and we both blurted out simultaneously, "party!" So party we did, for the last three years of high school. Our parents were not all that happy about our little outings, but what did they know about being a teenager in the eighties? The way we figured it, as long as we brought home decent grades, they shouldn't have anything to bitch about. We would work at local farms after school to give us enough cash to fund our habits. Our needs were quite simple, beer and gas (in that order). We would cruise around listening to tunes, looking for something interesting to do almost every night. Some nights you would get lucky and run into some of the boys and girls sucking down on some frostys on some seldom traveled back road. Next we would start a small fire, and bingo, instant party. Dave was always the life of the party. His sense of humor was like a cross between Robin Williams and George Carlin. He never failed to have you in stitches at some point in the night. He was quite a smooth talker when it came to the ladies too. Hell, he could talk the Pope into a subscription to Playboy. The fact that he was a Tom Cruise look-alike didn't hurt him any. The jocks used to call him "pretty boy," the girls used to just call him. They didn't call him that when I was around, they knew better. If you messed with him, you were messing with me, and they knew it.

Getting home was a different story. It was scary sometimes, but we always made it. The next day I would pick him up and discuss the events of the evening on our way to school. We didn't hang out with a lot of people in school, but the friends we had were a wild bunch to say the least. You name it, we did it, listen to tunes, camping, fishing, riding dirt bikes, working on vehicles, partying, and driving around drunk without a care in the world. After we graduated, he took off to the Navy and I went to the Air Force. We kept in touch religiously, writing and calling. When the opportunity arose, I would fly down to see him, and he did likewise. We soon developed a new ritual, sending each other compilations of the latest music we were listening to at the time. It was always a wonderful sight to see that little brown package in my mailbox. A couple of years later, he ended up stationed in Bethesda, Maryland while I was working in N.Y.C. I will never forget the day that I returned to the construction office and the foreman told me that I had a call. The number was one that I had never seen. I dialed the phone and the voice on the other end said, "Bethesda Naval Hospital. How may I help you?" I gave my name and the next thing she asked was, "Thank God, do you have any family or friends situated in or around Bethesda, Maryland?" My heart rate shot up and my stomach tightened like a tourniquet, I couldn't speak as I stood there with my mouth hanging open, my brain racing with thought. "Are you there?" she said, "Yes," I managed to stammer out. She asked me a few questions about a man that the police found tangled up in a demolished Chevette, a few miles from the hospital with no identification. The only lead they had was a phone number written on a cassette sleeve. My number. I was in a state that I had never experienced in my whole life. My whole body was rigid, as the adrenalin surged through my veins. The next thing that I remember was this woman asking me for any identifying marks, "A tattoo," I replied. I then described his tattoo to her. "That's him," she said. I was stunned but I managed to give her all the information that she needed, also I got the address for the hospital. Next, I had to make the hardest phone call of my life, to call his parents and tell them that their only son was in critical condition in the hospital. After the call, I immediately left work, got changed, and headed for Maryland.

The five hour drive didn't even seem to have happened as I tried to prepare myself for what was yet to come. Upon arrival I met his parents in the hall. They had flown in just two hours before. As we embraced, we were all speechless. There are no words for what we were feeling, just tears. I turned to the door and the nurse held her hand out and said, "Family only." Before I could say a word, Dave's mom said, "He's his brother," and I went into the room. There on the bed, was my best friend hooked to more machines than I had imagined possible. Tubes and wires crisscrossed in an eerie web over his mangled body. He had sustained a massive concussion, a broken leg, a broken arm, several contusions and lacerations. He needed 180 stitches, 60 of which were on his face. He had some nerve damage to his face, so his facial muscles were all bunched up in spots, and drooping lifelessly in others.

He looked up at me and tried to say something but couldn't. All he could do was kind of a half smile as a few tears trickled down his cheek. I held his hand and forced a smile onto my face and said, "Ah man, I came all the way down here for this? I thought you would be in bad shape." He gave me his best smile and hugged me. I stayed there for two weeks and he made great improvement. A month later he was back home. He hardly remembers any of it but that accident had changed both of us for life. He had fallen asleep at the wheel after a night of drinking. That night wasn't supposed to be different from any other partying night but it was. He told me that after drinking and driving for so many years that he started to feel that he was invincible. I knew how he felt. God must have decided to give him a second chance. After 14 months Dave has fully recovered. The scars are hardly noticeable, his bones healed perfectly. The doctors said it was nothing short of a miracle.

Today he is presently working at a hospital in Myrtle Beach, while enrolled in nursing school. He has since gotten married, had a son and has been an active member of A.A. for four and one-half years. Both of our lives have changed so much over the years, but we are still best friends. When we get together, we sip on a few colas and chat about the old times. We just happen to both have our birthdays on November 6, so I will be sending out his compilation soon. I am always overjoyed to see that little brown package coming to my mailbox, for more reasons than one.

Final Draft

The Wake-Up Call

1   One typical day of my senior year of high school, my buddy and I once again found ourselves caught up in a serious dilemma. "What do you want to do tonight bud?" asked my best friend, Dave. "I don't care, what do you want to do?" I replied, as I had countless other times to the same question. Then we both looked at each other and without a word, grins stretched across our faces and we both blurted out simultaneously, "Party!" So party we did, throughout the entire last year of high school.

2   Our parents were not all that happy about our little outings, but what did they know about being a teenager in the eighties? Back then we figured as long as we brought home decent grades, they shouldn't have anything to complain about.

3   After school, we would work at local farms or perform odd jobs for elderly folks in the community to earn enough cash to fund our habits. Most of our interests didn't require much money, probably because we

didn't have a whole lot of money to start with. We spent our spare time either in the woods or hanging out on the shore of a secluded lake on his father's farm. Our material needs were quite simple: cassettes, beer and gas (in that order). We both had a keen interest in music. Almost every night, we would cruise around listening to our latest musical discoveries and drink a few beers.

4 Some nights we would get lucky and run into some of our friends pursuing similar interests on some desolate back road. Oftentimes we would start a small fire, gather around it, and "shoot the shit" as we called it. Different people would be in and out all night, often until the wee hours of the morning. Dave always counted on me to get him home . . . and one way or another, I always did.

5 Dave was always the life of the party. His sense of humor was like a cross between Robin Williams's ability for improv, and George Carlin's searing wit. He was quite a smooth talker as well. When it came to the ladies, it was truly magical to watch him work. Hell, he could talk the Pope into buying a subscription to <u>Playboy</u>. He was around 5'6" with short jet black hair and baby blue eyes that sparkled with life. His bright smile seemed to be a permanent fixture on his face. In school, the jocks used to call him "Pretty Boy." The girls used to just call him.

6 The two of us had known each other our whole lives. He lived right over the hill from me, so we saw each other nearly every day. It was uncanny the way we could hold entire conversations with only a few key words and a whole lot of body language. You name it, we did it—listened to tunes, went camping, fishing, and riding dirt bikes, worked on vehicles, partied, and, I now regret, drove around drunk without a care in the world.

7 After we graduated, he enlisted in the Navy, and I went to the Air Force. We kept in touch religiously, writing or calling several times a month. Whenever the opportunity arose, I would fly down to see him, and he did likewise.

8 Soon thereafter, we developed a new ritual, sending each other compilations of our latest musical discoveries. We kept this up for quite some time. It was always a welcome sight to see that little brown package in my mailbox. It soon became like a game, or a race, to see who could find some fresh tunes that we could introduce to each other.

9 A couple of years later, he ended up stationed in Bethesda, Maryland, while I was working in N.Y.C. I will never forget the day that I returned to the construction office and the foreman told me that

I had received a long distance call. The number was one that I had never seen. I dialed the phone and the voice on the other end said, "Bethesda Naval Hospital, how may I help you?" I gave her my name and the next thing she said was, "Thank God, do you have any family or friends situated in, or around Bethesda, Maryland?"

10   My heart rate shot up as my stomach tightened like a tourniquet. I found myself speechless as I stood there with my mouth hanging open, my brain racing with thought.

11   "Are you there?" she asked.

12   "Yes," was all that I managed to stammer out. A few moments later I did my best to regain my composure. I then asked, "What is wrong?"

13   She then proceeded to tell me about a young man that the police had found tangled up in a demolished automobile a few miles from the hospital. He had no identification and was completely incoherent. The only lead they had to go on was a phone number written on a cassette sleeve. My number. My whole body was rigid as the adrenalin surged through my veins. Then came the most horrifying question of all.

14   "Could you please tell me about some kind of identifying mark? A scar, or a birthmark maybe?" My mind raced, and then somehow beyond my conscious control, almost instantly I replied, "A tattoo." I then described his tattoo to her. I could describe it quite well. I had been there when he received it and I witnessed the Hell he had to pay when his parents saw it. "That's him," she replied. I was stunned, but I managed to give her all the information that she needed. I asked for the address to the hospital before I hung up.

15   Next, I had to make the hardest phone call of my life. I had to call his parents and tell them that their only son was in critical condition in a hospital 600 miles from home. After the call, I immediately left work, got changed, and headed for Maryland.

16   The five hour drive sped past, as I tried to prepare myself for what was to come. Upon arrival, I met his parents in the hallway. They had flown in just two hours before. The three of us embraced each other in the busy corridor, oblivious to the hustle and bustle around us. There were no words to describe what we were feeling, just tears. I turned to the door and the nurse held her hand out and said, "Family only." Before I could say a word, Dave's mom said, "This is his brother," and I went into the room.

17   There, on the bed, was my best friend hooked to more machines than I had imagined possible. Tubes and wires crisscrossed in an eerie web over his mangled body. He had sustained a massive concussion, a

broken leg, a broken arm, and several contusions and lacerations. He had received 180 stitches, 60 of which were on his face. He had suffered some nerve damage to his face so his facial muscles were all bunched up in spots and were drooping lifeless in others.

18   He looked up at me and tried to say something but couldn't. He gave me his best attempt at a smile as a few tears trickled down his cheeks. I held his hand and forced a smile onto my face and said, "Ah, man, I came all the way down here for this? I thought you would be in bad shape. You'll be out of here in no time." In the back of my mind, I knew that those words couldn't be much further from the truth. He just gave me his best smile and hugged me. I don't remember how long it was before I let go.

19   I stayed there for two weeks. He made a great deal of progress in that short period. When I left, he was already becoming semi-independent. A month later, he was back home. The doctor told us that his recovery was nothing short of a miracle. I must agree. A higher power must have decided to give him a second chance. After fourteen months, Dave had fully recovered. The scars were hardly noticeable, and his bones have healed perfectly. Maybe my higher power was giving me a wake-up call as well.

20   Today, he hardly remembers any of his ordeal. Nonetheless, that accident changed both of us for life. He had fallen asleep at the wheel after a night of drinking. That night wasn't supposed to be different from any other night of partying, but it was. He later told me that after drinking and driving for so many years, he started to feel that he was invincible. It was always the other guy that gets hurt or nailed by the cops. If he read about someone in the paper that got a D.W.I., he figured that it was just some schmuck that couldn't handle his booze. I knew how he felt.

21   These days I see those people in a whole new perspective. I see them as people—someone's child or parent or perhaps someone else's best friend.

22   I am happy to say that today Dave is working at a hospital in Myrtle Beach, while enrolled in nursing school. He has chosen this profession to help give other people their second chances. He has since gotten married, had a son and has been an active member of Alcoholics Anonymous for four and one-half years. An active DRY member.

23   Both of our lives have changed so much over the years, but we are still best friends. These days when we get together, we sip on a few colas instead of beers and chat about the old times. It is a shame that it

took this kind of tragedy for us to realize that we could enjoy our adult lives without watching them go by through bloodshot eyes.

24 We just happen to both have our birthdays on November 6. This means that soon I will be sending out the traditional compilation. These days, I am overjoyed to see that little brown package arrive in my mailbox, for more reasons than one.

QUESTIONS FOR DISCUSSION AND WRITING

1. Explain the significance of the title of the essay. Who actually receives the wake-up call? Who learns the most from this wake-up call—Dave or the writer? Do they learn equally from the events portrayed in the essay? Explain.

2. Explain Goedeker's purpose for this essay. Is he just remembering an important episode in his life? Is he trying to explain the effects of alcoholism? Is he trying to persuade his readers that excessive drinking or driving drunk should be avoided? Explain your choice(s) by referring to specific passages in the essay.

3. Reread Goedeker's essay looking for important *changes* in the key characters, *contrasts* between past and present, and *conflicts* between characters. What changes, contrasts, or conflicts could be further developed to make the essay more effective?

4. Compare the opening paragraphs of Goedeker's rough draft and his final version. Which beginning more effectively gets the reader's attention? Does the revised beginning also focus the reader's attention on the main purpose of the essay? Explain.

5. What part of this narrative did you find most memorable and effective? Which part(s) needed additional showing detail? What specific descriptions would you suggest that the writer add?

6. Assume that Goedeker is revising the final version of his essay to make his essay more effective. What specific suggestions would you give him? What scenes should have more showing detail? Where should he cut passages? What might be missing from the story that you as a reader would like explained further?

Investigating

INVESTIGATING—ALONG WITH OBSERVING AND REMEMBERING—is a third initial purpose for writing. Writers investigate in order to learn—through summaries of written accounts, interviews, surveys, and direct observation. Then, they usually **report** what they have learned to their readers. As a result of an investigation, however, a writer's purpose may shift from reporting information to arguing for or against an issue, or to proposing a solution to a problem. For example, writers interested in alternative energies may summarize articles on solar generation of electricity and interview experts to better inform themselves—and then their readers—about a complex issue. They could even decide later to argue for tougher controls on coal-fired generating plants or to propose a plan to increase solar electric generation in their city or state. Although the investigative essays in this chapter illustrate how to gather evidence as you write for a variety of purposes, this chapter focuses just on **investigating** a topic and **reporting** what the writer learns to a specific audience.

Investigative writing should *inform* readers, not take a stand, argue for or against, or editorialize. Its hallmark is objectivity. True objectivity is not possible (or desirable, some would say), but good reporters try to present information accurately to their readers. Objective reporting is a matter of intent, personal integrity, and method. Writers of investigative reports should *intend* to focus not on their own opinions but on other people's ideas, opinions, and arguments. In doing so, however, they may need to acknowledge their own biases or emotions. They should also maintain their *personal integrity* around topics that trigger their own prejudices. Preconceived opinions should not disable writers' intent to "tell it like it is." Finally, writers of investigative reports should use the *methods* of accurate investigating and reporting: checking facts, finding multiple witnesses, quoting accurately, and summarizing surveys and other reports thoroughly and fairly.

Investigative reporting takes a variety of forms. Investigative writers sometimes merely summarize longer written reports or scientific studies, and in that case their purpose is to condense and highlight the study, usually for a general audience. In a longer investigation, writers may summarize many written sources, conduct their own interviews, gather information from surveys, observe people and events firsthand, and report on their investigations. In that case, they become the principal investigators rather than just summarizers of other studies. In either case, their final purpose is to report their findings to a specific audience.

Strategies for Reading and Writing Investigating Essays

As you read the essays in this chapter, look for the following techniques for gathering information and reporting it to an audience.

- **A title and "lead" that get the reader's attention and interest.** Investigative reporters recognize that readers may flip the page if their report does not have an interesting or succinct title and a lead-in that invites the reader to read the article. Titles such as "Drivers on Cell Phones are as Bad as Drunks" trigger the reader's curiosity.
- **Presentation of basic who, what, when, where, why, and how information.** Readers expect to find basic information early in the report, and they expect the information to be reliable and accurate.
- **Summarizing, quoting, or reporting information from oral or written sources.** Investigative reporters use interviews, surveys, summaries, paraphrases, and accurate quotations from their sources.
- **Focus on some key question or questions.** Effective investigative writing collects information that relates to a key question: what something means or is, when or how it happened, how or

why something happened, or who did it. Are drivers who use cell phones as impaired as drunk drivers? What goes on behind the scenes at a beauty pageant? The key question becomes the main idea or focus of the report.

- **Language that is readable, interesting, and accurate.** Investigative reports should be easily read and understood by the intended audience. Where appropriate, use graphics, diagrams, or visuals to illustrate important points.

Reading an Investigative Essay

Prereading

Begin by writing what you already know about the topic of the article. Whether the article is about cell phones or bloggers, write down anything you know about the subject. You'll find it interesting to compare what you wrote before you read the article with what you learned after you read the article. Then find out about the author, the occasion for this article, and the audience for which the article was written.

First Reading

Your first reading should be for enjoyment, to satisfy your curiosity about the subject. If some passage confuses you, put a "?" in the margin. If you like a passage or are surprised by the information, put a "!" in the margin. Highlight or put a wavy line under any key passages. Underline any words you want to look up later, but don't let these brief marks interrupt your reading. *At the end of this reading, write out the question that this investigative report answers.*

Annotated Reading

For your annotated reading, write your own reactions in the margin: "I didn't know that"; "How did the writer get that information?"; or "This part is boring." Be sure to read with a writer's eye. Bracket and label key features of investigative reports: title, lead-in, who-what-when-where information, examples of clear or interesting style, and focus of the investigation. In the margin, list or outline the main parts of the report or the key stages in the writer's investigation. When necessary, look up definitions of words.

Collaborative Reading

In your class or small group, share your Prereading Journal Entries. What, collectively, did the class or your group already know about the subject? Appoint a recorder to make a collaborative annotation for this essay by compiling the best annotations. At the end of the essay, write the central question that the report addresses. When you have finished the collaborative annotation, write down two questions you or your group still has about the article.

Writing an Investigative Essay

As you prepare to write an investigative essay, keep three important points in mind.

First, you will be practicing particular **investigative skills,** such as reading and summarizing, interviewing and taking notes, listening and writing down dialogue, doing online searches, or conducting surveys and organizing responses. You will use your skills of observing other people and places and remembering your experiences, but now the focus is on what you learn from *written sources* and from *other people.* Although you may include your own experiences during the investigation, you are the investigator, not the subject of the investigation.

Second, your **primary purpose** is **to report** what you discover to your intended audience. Although you will probably form an opinion about your topic or subject during your investigation, you should *not* editorialize, argue for one side or the other, offer your solutions to problems you discover, or evaluate your subject. Your primary purpose should be to **inform** your readers about the subject. You should attempt to report objectively, even if that means reporting your own biases or limited perspectives. You may report other people's judgments or opinions, but as the investigator, you should not argue for any particular position or belief.

Third, an investigation requires asking—and then answering—questions that your readers might have about your subject. You will provide answers to basic who, what, when, where, why, and how questions, but your report should **focus on** the answer(s) to a single basic question about a specific subject: How does cell phone use impair drivers? Should students take online courses in college? What is the best program for treating obesity?

Choosing a Subject for an Investigative Essay

Your first thought may be that you have to investigate something weird and unknown, like the feeding habits of the aardvark. However, your investigation may be more successful (and much easier) if you investigate some everyday object or phenomenon, or an ordinary person. Look for something interesting, unusual, or surprising in your everyday life.

Investigate some aspect of your favorite hobby: cars, fashion, cooking, scuba diving, photography, listening to music, gaming, or watching television. In your library or online, browse through magazines or Web sites related to your hobby to get a sense of a possible audience. Interview a friend to find out what he or she would like to know about your hobby. Find some written sources and informed people you could interview about your basic question.

Investigate something related to your business or place of work. How is this business organized? Who is a key person you could interview or profile? Survey your customers on their reactions to your service or product. How does your company advertise itself online?

In a class you are currently taking, what idea, concept, person, performance, or product could you investigate? Initially, discuss the idea with a classmate. Then informally interview or email your teacher: What angle or focus does he or she suggest? What other books or sources does this teacher suggest? Try to frame your investigative question.

Review the essays you have read so far in this text. Then make a "curiosity list." What topics discussed in your favorite essays might you investigate?

Collecting Information

Begin by stating your investigative question: For your hobby, it might be, "Can netbooks replace laptops for watching video or gaming?" or "How can I make a digital scrapbook?" For a class, your question might be, "What marketing strategies has the McDonald's franchise used to retain their market share?" or "Who is Jon Krakauer and how did he write *Into the Wild?*" You will probably modify your central question as you collect information, but you need a focus for your initial investigation.

Once you have a tentative question, try the following collecting strategies.

- Ask the reporter's "wh" questions about your topic: Who? What? When? Where? Why? How? (*Note:* You may ask each "wh" question several times: Who conducted the recent research on the effects of cell phone use on drivers? Who were the subjects who were tested in this research? How was driver behavior measured? How was this behavior compared to driving under the influence?)
- Interview people who are knowledgeable on your topic. You may use early interviews to help you focus your investigative question, or you may interview experts after you know more about your topic. For your interview, be sure to make an *appointment*. Prepare for your interview by writing down the *questions* you want to ask. At key points in your interview, try *restating* the point your interviewee has just made: "Are you saying that . . . ?" or "OK. So you believe that . . . ?" During your interview, bring a *tape recorder* and/or take *careful notes*. You may also conduct an interview by email if the person is busy and cannot see you in person.
- Use your library databases and sources. While you may want to begin your research by doing a Google search and checking on Wikipedia, you will find more authoritative and reliable information by checking your library's online databases. Take an orientation tour of your library. Ask your teacher or reference librarian for databases or sources that might be appropriate for your investigation. *When you find a source, be sure to email yourself the article or the link.* In class, you can practice summarizing information from articles without plagiarizing.
- Write a questionnaire if you need to know the attitudes, preferences, or opinions of a group of people. (Be sure to test your questionnaire on friends or members of your class before you distribute it.)

Shaping Your Investigative Essay

Test the following shaping strategies to see which one(s) will help you organize your information and present it clearly to your readers.

Chronological Order of Your Investigation

Writers often follow the natural chronological order of their investigation. They describe their investigation and what they found, step-by-step.

Process Analysis

When investigative writers ask *how* something happens, they often turn to process analysis. A step-by-step description of some process can easily organize material in an investigative essay.

Other shaping strategies may help organize your information. Sometimes writers of investigative articles answer the question "Why?" by describing the **causes or effects** that relate to their topic. Other writers use **comparison or contrast** to organize their ideas.

Drafting Your Investigative Essay

Before you begin drafting, write your central *investigative question* at the top of the page. Use this question to keep you focused as you write. If you have extensive information, you may need to make a brief *outline* before you begin writing: What are you going to discuss first, second, next, or last?

Revising Your Investigative Essay

After you have finished a first draft and let it sit for a day or so, you are ready to begin revising. As you revise, keep the following tips in mind.

- **Compare your essay to your central investigative question.** Does your essay answer the question you intended to answer? (You may need to change the question or some parts of the essay to make them fit.)
- **Check the essay for your purpose.** Remember that you should be reporting information to your readers, *not* arguing for or against any particular idea.
- **Reconsider your audience.** If you have a specific magazine or Website in mind for your audience, skim through an article similar to yours. Reread your essay. Are you being too technical in places? Do you need to be more specific in other places? Where do your readers need more information?
- **Revise your title or your lead-in.** Titles and opening sentences should describe your topic and get your reader's attention. Jot down two additional titles. Do you still like your first choice? Ask your peer readers about your lead-in. Do you have some attention-getting *example, statistic, play on words, quotation* from some expert, or *question* that plays on your reader's curiosity?
- **Reread your opening paragraphs for answers to "wh" questions.** Do you give basic who, what, when, and where information for your readers early in your essay?
- **Do you have transitions in the opening sentences of body paragraphs?** Look for key words or transitions that signal your organization to your

reader. Are there key chronological words? Do key phrases indicate that you are investigating cause or effect? Make sure your shaping strategy is apparent to your readers.

■ **Check the accuracy of your summaries, paraphrases, and direct quotations against your notes or your photocopies.** Direct quotations must be accurate, word-for-word transcriptions. Be sure to identify your sources and give proper credit.

■ **Revise and edit sentences to improve clarity and avoid errors.** Use your peer readers' reactions and check your handbook to simplify sentences and correct any errors in spelling, punctuation, or usage.

Postscript for Your Investigative Essay

When you have finished your essay, answer the following questions about your composing process.

1. What sources of information (your own observations, interviews, surveys, printed articles, and books) were most helpful?
2. How did your central investigative question change from your first idea to its final form?
3. Which shaping strategies were most helpful in organizing your essay?
4. What did you learn about investigating techniques as you wrote this essay?
5. What do you like best about your final version? What would you change if you had more time?

UNIVERSITY OF UTAH NEWS CENTER

Drivers on Cell Phones Are as Bad as Drunks

Prereading Journal Entry

Nearly everyone has a story about using cell phones while driving, whether you had—or nearly had—an accident caused by someone else using a cell phone while driving, or because you were using one yourself. Provide information in your journal entry that gives answers to the key who, what, when, where, and why questions.

The following report, prepared by the University of Utah News Center, describes a research study on the effects of driving while using cell phones. The article presents the results of a study conducted by psychology Professor David Strayer and his colleagues Frank Drews and Dennis Crouch. Notice how this report cites the authors of this study, gives the research methodology, and summarizes the detailed findings of the study.

1   Three years after the preliminary results first were presented at a scientific meeting and drew wide attention, University of Utah psychologists have published a study showing that motorists who talk on handheld or hands-free cellular phones are as impaired as drunken drivers.

2   "We found that people are as impaired when they drive and talk on a cell phone as they are when they drive intoxicated at the legal blood-alcohol limit" of 0.08 percent, which is the minimum level that defines illegal drunken driving in most U.S. states, says study co-author Frank Drews, an assistant professor of psychology. "If legislators really want to address driver distraction, then they should consider outlawing cell phone use while driving."

3   Psychology Professor David Strayer, the study's lead author, adds: "Just like you put yourself and other people at risk when you drive drunk, you put yourself and others at risk when you use a cell phone and drive. The level of impairment is very similar."

4   "Clearly the safest course of action is to not use a cell phone while driving," concludes the study by Strayer, Drews and Dennis Crouch, a research associate professor of pharmacology and toxicology. The study was set for publication June 29 in the summer 2006 issue of *Human Factors: The Journal of the Human Factors and Ergonomics Society.*

5   The study reinforced earlier research by Strayer and Drews showing that hands-free cell phones are just as distracting as handheld cell phones because the conversation itself – not just manipulation of a handheld phone – distracts drivers from road conditions.

6   *Human Factors* Editor Nancy J. Cooke praised the study: "Although we all have our suspicions about the dangers of cell phone use while driving, human factors research on driver safety helps us move beyond mere suspicions to scientific observations of driver behavior."

7   The study first gained public notice after Strayer presented preliminary results in July 2003 in Park City, Utah, during the Second International Driving Symposium on Human Factors in Driver Assessment, Training and Vehicle Design. It took until now for the study to be completed, undergo review by other researchers and finally be published.

Key Findings: Different Driving Styles, Similar Impairment

8 Each of the study's 40 participants "drove" a PatrolSim driving simulator four times: once each while undistracted, using a handheld cell phone, using a hands-free cell phone and while intoxicated to the 0.08 percent blood-alcohol level after drinking vodka and orange juice. Participants followed a simulated pace car that braked intermittently.

9 Both handheld and hands-free cell phones impaired driving, with no significant difference in the degree of impairment. That "calls into question driving regulations that prohibited handheld cell phones and permit hands-free cell phones," the researchers write.

10 The study found that compared with undistracted drivers:

- Motorists who talked on either handheld or hands-free cell phones drove slightly slower, were 9 percent slower to hit the brakes, displayed 24 percent more variation in following distance as their attention switched between driving and conversing, were 19 percent slower to resume normal speed after braking and were more likely to crash. Three study participants rear-ended the pace car. All were talking on cell phones. None were drunk.

- Drivers drunk at the 0.08 percent blood-alcohol level drove a bit more slowly than both undistracted drivers and drivers using cell phones, yet more aggressively. They followed the pace car more closely, were twice as likely to brake only four seconds before a collision would have occurred, and hit their brakes with 23 percent more force. "Neither accident rates, nor reaction times to vehicles braking in front of the participant, nor recovery of lost speed following braking differed significantly" from undistracted drivers, the researchers write.

11 "Impairments associated with using a cell phone while driving can be as profound as those associated with driving while drunk," they conclude.

Are Drunken Drivers Really Less Accident-Prone Than Cell Phone Users?

12 Drews says the lack of accidents among the study's drunken drivers was surprising. He and Strayer speculate that because simulated drives were conducted during mornings, participants who got drunk were well-rested and in the "up" phase of intoxication. In reality, 80 percent of all fatal alcohol-related accidents occur between 6 p.m. and 6 a.m. when drunken drivers tend to be fatigued. Average blood-alcohol levels in those accidents are twice 0.08 percent. Forty percent of the roughly 42,000 annual U.S. traffic fatalities involve alcohol.

13   While none of the study's intoxicated drivers crashed, their hard, late braking is "predictive of increased accident rates over the long run," the researchers wrote.

14   One statistical analysis of the new and previous Utah studies showed cell phone users were 5.36 times more likely to get in an accident than undistracted drivers. Other studies have shown the risk is about the same as for drivers with a 0.08 blood-alcohol level.

15   Strayer says he expects criticism "suggesting that we are trivializing drunken-driving impairment, but it is anything but the case. We don't think people should drive while drunk, nor should they talk on their cell phone while driving."

16   Drews says he and Strayer compared the impairment of motorists using cell phones to drivers with a 0.08 percent blood-alcohol level because they wanted to determine if the risk of driving while phoning was comparable to the drunken driving risk considered unacceptable.

17   "This study does not mean people should start driving drunk," says Drews. "It means that driving while talking on a cell phone is as bad as or maybe worse than driving drunk, which is completely unacceptable and cannot be tolerated by society."

ABSTRACT

Objective: The objective of this research was to determine the relative impairment associated with conversing on a cellular telephone while driving. Background: Epidemiological evidence suggests that the relative risk of being in a traffic accident while using a cell phone is similar to the hazard associated with driving with a blood alcohol level at the legal limit. The purpose of this research was to provide a direct comparison of the driving performance of a cell phone driver and a drunk driver in a controlled laboratory setting. Method: We used a high-fidelity driving simulator to compare the performance of cell phone drivers with drivers who were intoxicated from ethanol (i.e., blood alcohol concentration at 0.08% weight/volume). Results: When drivers were conversing on either a handheld or hands-free cell phone, their braking reactions were delayed and they were involved in more traffic accidents than when they were not conversing on a cell phone. By contrast, when drivers were intoxicated from ethanol they exhibited a more aggressive driving style, following closer to the vehicle immediately in front of them and applying more force while braking. Conclusion: When driving conditions and time on task were controlled for, the impairments associated with using a cell phone while driving can be as profound as those associated with driving while drunk. Application: This research may help to provide guidance for regulation addressing driver distraction caused by cell phone conversations.

QUESTIONS FOR DISCUSSION AND WRITING

1. Reread the first few paragraphs of this article. What key investigative question are the University of Utah psychologists trying to answer? Write out this statement in the form of a question.
2. Reports of research should also provide the results of the research. What conclusions do the University of Utah researchers offer? Cite specific sentences from key paragraphs of this report that describe the conclusions of the study.
3. Reports on research should also indicate the methodology used in the study: How was the experiment set up? If there were human subjects, what were they asked to do? How were the variables measured? Were there "controls" to ensure objectivity of measurement? In what paragraphs does the writer report on the methodology of the study? Describe the methodology.
4. What appears below is the the abstract of the original research article by David Strayer, Frank Drews, and Dennis Crouch as it appeared in the academic journal, *Human Factors*. Cite specific examples from this abstract to show how the language and vocabulary is appropriate for readers of an academic journal. How does this language differ from the above University of Utah report (reprinted above) which was intended for a more general audience? Cite specific examples of sentences and vocabulary to support your answer.

CLAIRE SUDDATH/REEDLEY

Does Obesity Rehab Work?

Prereading Journal Entry

In your journal, write down everything you can remember that you have had to eat over the last seven days. Are you on a particular diet? If so, describe how what you have eaten this week relates to your diet. Do your entries for this week represent your dietary goals, or are there changes you want to make?

Claire Suddath/Reedley is a journalist who currently writes articles for Time *magazine. Of the dozens of articles she has written, some recent titles include "Mourning the Death of Handwriting," "A Brief History of Mickey*

Mouse," "Cute Things Falling Asleep," and "Facebook: 25 Things I Didn't Want to Know About You." In "Does Obesity Rehab Work?" Suddath/Reedley turns from writing humorous articles about Facebook to investigating a serious social problem: childhood obesity. Her investigative question focuses not on obesity prevention but on finding out what programs currently exist for children who already face problems with obesity.

1   Elizabeth Fedorchalk was tired of being fat. She had been trying to lose weight since elementary school, but diets never made a difference. She wasn't husky. She wasn't big-boned. By age 16, the 5-ft. 5-in., 291-lb. high school junior from Holts Summit, Mo., was undeniably obese. And each year, it was only getting worse.

2   Fedorchalk's diet was abysmal. She skipped breakfast, ate lunch at school — usually chicken strips and fries — and frequently had dinner at McDonald's: a burger and more fries. She drank nondiet soda and snacked on potato chips and Little Debbie cakes. She never exercised because, between school and extracurricular activities, she claimed she didn't have time. "It got to where I didn't like sports anymore," Fedorchalk says. "I'd get out of breath and get upset because mentally I wanted to do so much, but physically I couldn't." She gained 45 lb. in 2009 alone.

3   She had high cholesterol, and her weight put her at risk for hypertension, heart disease, sleep apnea and Type 2 diabetes. By any measure, Fedorchalk was in poor health. But look around. She is hardly alone.

4   In the past 30 years, obesity rates among U.S. children have more than tripled. A flurry of antiobesity legislation has taken aim at environmental factors that have contributed to the epidemic, and Michelle Obama's sweeping new Let's Move campaign to end childhood obesity will most likely inspire further changes in the coming years. But while healthier school lunches and public-service announcements may help future generations stay fit, they won't make someone like Fedorchalk thin. Our national dialogue focuses on obesity prevention, but what do we do for kids who have already gained the weight?

5   As Fedorchalk's weight climbed, her parents feared for her wellbeing. "We couldn't communicate with her or get her to change her habits," says her mother Michele. Family members decided there was nothing they could do for her at home; she needed professional help. In September, they sent her to Wellspring Academy, a residential weight-loss facility in Reedley, Calif. For families like the Fedorchalks, Wellspring offers a commodity often in short supply: hope. But turning that hope into a long-term remedy for teen obesity isn't easy.

Weight-Loss Boarding School

6   When marathon runner and educator Ryan Craig opened Well-spring Academy in 2004, it was the only residential obesity-treatment center of its kind. (Others existed mostly in clinical settings.) A former board member of the Aspen Education Group — one organization behind those wilderness programs for troubled teens — Craig learned about the staggering U.S. obesity rates and saw an enormous untapped market for a weight-loss school.

7   Wellspring Academy houses about 75 students in grades 8 through 12, all at various stages of weight loss. Students can enroll at any time and must stay at least four months. They live together in dorms, just like at traditional boarding schools.

8   Aside from regular academic classes and sessions with staff therapists, kids participate in simple exercise routines like walking 10,000 steps (5 miles) each day. The school's weight-loss program was designed by Northwestern University Medical Center professor Daniel Kirschenbaum, who used to run a number of clinical obesity programs in Chicago-area hospitals. Students are served three perfectly proportioned meals a day and are asked to note everything they eat in a journal. Calorie and fat counts are displayed on a whiteboard in Wellspring's cafeteria, making it easy for kids to copy them down. The diet, which allows for unlimited access to fruits and vegetables, works out to about 1,300 calories per day and results in 1 to 5 lb. of weight loss a week, depending on the student. Wellspring claims its students lose an average of 25% of their starting weight and 70% maintain or continue their weight loss a year after leaving the academy.

9   Every meal at Wellspring is basically a fat-free re-creation of something unhealthy. In their nutrition and cooking classes, kids learn to make mozzarella sticks with fat-free cheese and PB&J sandwiches with imitation peanut butter. They're nowhere near as tasty as the original versions, but the kids seem to like them, and at least they don't feel deprived. "A lot of parents ask me why we don't serve organic health foods," says Craig, "to which I say, is your kid really going to eat that?"

No Easy Answers

10   A program as progressive as Wellspring's is bound to have some kinks. Like most other weight-loss programs, Wellspring is not covered by any health insurance plan. Many families find themselves taking out loans to pay the $6,250-per-month tuition. "A lot of parents use their kids' college money," says Craig. Its prohibitively high cost makes the

place inaccessible to many Americans who could benefit, especially since the highest obesity rates are found in low-income areas. But Wellspring kids are far from wealthy. Fedorchalk's mother and father, who work at a nursing home and Walmart, respectively, struggle to pay the bill. Freddy Fahl, 16, attends the school courtesy of a several-thousand-dollar student loan taken out by his mother Debi DeShon.

11   Fahl arrived at Wellspring in September. He was up to 351 lb., having gained 40 lb. a year for three years straight. "His weight was completely out of control," says DeShon. Last year, Fahl was even denied health insurance because of his weight. "He was 16, and I thought, O.K., I have two more years with him. Am I willing to send my child into the world at 400 lb.?"

12   When he stayed on the diet, Fahl lost an average of 4 lb. per week. But he found himself cheating whenever he could. While visiting his brother off campus one weekend, he went to Taco Bell and ate "almost everything" on the menu. At another outing to a restaurant, he ordered pie. Over Christmas break, he managed to lose weight, but only because his mother kept him on the program. When he returned to campus in January, he mysteriously started gaining. His therapist wonders whether he didn't smuggle in some candy.

13   Fahl's weaknesses mirror one of Wellspring's: its success hinges on the parents. Craig hosts family workshops and urges parents to rid their homes of unhealthy foods. Yet despite the thousands of dollars they spend on tuition, only some Wellspring parents are willing to change their behavior. In medical studies, family-based behavioral treatments have proved almost twice as effective as those that involve only the child. "You can't have a successful program if the parent is telling the kid not to eat chips while he's sitting there eating ice cream," says Leonard Epstein, a clinical psychologist and professor at the University at Buffalo.

14   After they leave Wellspring, students remain in contact with their therapists for six months to help them readjust to the real world. They have been spoon-fed diet-friendly meals for so long that they are often unsure how to act at birthday parties and pizza nights.

15   Which points to another problem: the fat-free diet. It's difficult to maintain and, over the long term, nutritionally unsound; humans need fat to survive. "People don't lose any more weight on a low-fat diet than they do on a high-fat one," says David Ludwig, director of the obesity program at Children's Hospital Boston.

16   "This is the only area of our program that is controversial," Craig acknowledges. But he adds that kids need something they can understand, and they understand fat.

17   The school's self-reported 70% success rate is based on voluntary
follow-up assessments with former students, most of whom agree to
participate. A rate that high is almost unheard-of in the diet world.
Only 7% of dieters finish Jenny Craig's one-year program, while
Weight Watchers counts people who stay even a few pounds under
their starting weight as a triumph. But these programs lack the comprehensive approach of Wellspring. Research indicates that therapy-
based obesity treatment can be three times as effective as traditional
diet-and-exercise models. But how many people can run off to rehab
for six months? "The outcome is probably better [at Wellspring] than if
the program were applied to the general public. The people who can go
to that school are a small sliver of the population," says Kerri Boutelle,
associate professor of pediatric psychiatry at University of California at
San Diego.

After Wellspring

18   Fedorchalk and Fahl have been at Wellspring for nearly six months
and have lost 72 and 82 lb., respectively. Fedorchalk dropped eight dress
sizes — from a size 22 to a 14 — and although she's still considered obese
at 219 lb., for the first time in her life she can shop at what she calls
"skinny people" stores. She counts fat grams obsessively and adheres to
her diet whenever she's at a restaurant. On a recent visit to an Olive
Garden, it took her 20 minutes to find something on the menu she could
eat. She is also exercising regularly. "Whenever I'd try to do a sport at
home, there'd always be really skinny people who were always really good
at it, and I'd feel kind of awkward," she says. "Here I can give 100% without looking stupid." In November, she and Fahl walked a half marathon.

Fahl was scheduled to leave Wellspring on Jan. 15, but he was still
struggling with the program, and DeShon didn't think he was ready to
come home. Two days before his departure, she told him he had to
stay. "I did my part," Fahl complained. "Why can't I lose the rest of the
weight at home?"

19   That's a lot easier said than done, of course. "It's way harder than
they ever tell you it will be," says Ganzy McCorvey, 19, who lost 104 lb.
at Wellspring in 2007, only to gain half of it back. "I felt really guilty
making my mom eat the same things as me. And then there were my
friends, who always wanted to go to Wendy's." Other former Wellspring students experienced similar roller-coaster cycles of losses
and gains.

20   Wellspring is no miracle cure. Even the most advanced kids at the
academy are far from thin. But they are healthier, and they have been

empowered with the uncommon gift of hope. Nobody is destined to be fat forever, says Fedorchalk. "Even if you do mess up, even if you do fall, what matters is you get back up again. You can always start anew at the next meal."

QUESTIONS FOR DISCUSSION AND WRITING

1. Although Suddath/Reedley focuses primarily on Wellspring Academy and its methods for treating obesity, she does give some background information and statistics about the obesity epidemic. Which paragraphs contain this background information? Should she give more facts and statistics about obesity in America? Why or why not?

2. Investigative essays should answer key questions about the who, what, where, when, how and why of the subject. Where does Suddath/Reedley answer each of these questions? (Cite specific examples and paragraphs.) Does she give sufficient information about Wellspring Academy and its success with its students? What other questions do you have?

3. Writers of investigative reports rely on research, interviews, surveys, and direct observation. Which of these kinds of information gathering did Suddath/Reedley probably use to write her article? Whom did she interview? Cite specific examples from her article to support each of your choices.

4. Write your own investigative report on diets or weight-loss programs that you, your friends, or family members have tried. Use a variety of information gathering strategies: surveys, interviews, online and library research, and direct observation. Find a newspaper, magazine, or online site that would be appropriate for your article and write for that particular audience.

SARA CORBETT

Rick Steves's Not-So-Lonely Planet

Prereading Journal Entry

If you have taken a trip outside of the United States—or even a trip to some far off state—describe your trip. If you consulted a guide book, travel site, or online Web site, explain what book or site you consulted. What did you learn about your destination before you left? Did you actually go to some of the attractions you read about? What was your opinion of the usefulness of the travel advice you received?

Rick Steves is a best-selling travel writer and host of the popular Rick Steves' Europe *television series. He has authored over forty travel books about Europe, and his* Rick Steves' Italy *has been for several years the best-selling international guidebook sold in the U.S. His interests in travel have expanded into a weekly radio show, walking tour podcasts, foreign language phrasebooks, and snapshot guides. His* Europe Through the Backdoor *has been updated for the past twenty years, and a new book,* Travel as a Political Act *(2009) describes how travel can become a force for international understanding. The following excerpt is taken from a longer profile of Rick Steves by Sara Corbett that appeared in the* New York Times Magazine. *Sara Corbett is a contributing writer to the* New York Times *and has written articles on a variety of subjects, including "A Cutting Tradition," "Patients without Borders," "A Prom Divided," and "Can the Cellphone Help End Global Poverty?"*

1   The guy is just another tourist. Or that's how it appears, anyway, to Cristina, the prim Portuguese woman holding down the front desk at the Residencia Roma, a spartan three-star hotel on a quiet side street in Lisbon. No two tourists are the same, of course, but there is something familiar, even iconic, in this man's eager-beaver smile, his unstylish windbreaker and leather walking shoes, his broken-spined guidebook to Spain and Portugal. Like most Americans, he doesn't pretend to speak anything but English. He inquires about rates — 60 euros for a double — then asks to see a room. Cristina shrugs, hands the man a key and waves him toward a set of stairs leading up into the hotel's interior, unaware that she has just set a dervish loose in her establishment.

2   Safely beyond her gaze, Rick Steves accelerates up the stairs and rockets down a dim hallway, quickly shedding all pretense of leisure. This is what he calls a "blitz," a 10-minute undercover rampage during which he will poke mattresses and inspect toilet seats, prowling the hotel like an unleashed hound. Earlier in the day, as we ate breakfast together, Steves had spelled out his plan for seeing Lisbon. "We'll just blitz the Bairro Alto and the castle, then the restaurants," he said, spooning yogurt into his mouth at double the pace most of us think of as normal. "And after that, we'll blitz the museums." With this, he peered under the breakfast table at my feet, adding, "I hope those shoes are comfortable."

3   Dashing through the Residencia Roma qualifies as an unscheduled side blitz, but its small sign caught Steves's eye as he passed by on the street, and he couldn't resist taking a look. This is often how it goes with Steves, who has written 27 eponymous guidebooks to Europe, stars in a public-television travelogue series called "Rick Steves' Europe" and also runs Europe Through the Back Door, a $20-million-a-year tour business he started in his hometown of Edmonds, Wash. At the age of 49, he is a methodical, even obsessive, planner, but he remains a sucker for a worthy diversion. In many respects, this is the root of Steves's character: a fastidious mind coupled with an explorer's sense of whimsy. After 30 years of professional travel, he has built a fortune from veering off course, discovering and expertly promoting what he calls the "backdoors" to Europe — the alleyway pension, the forgotten Alpine village, the poorly lighted restaurant with the souvlaki to die for.

4   On camera and off, Steves comes across as a perambulating, mildly mischievous Mister Rogers, relentlessly chipper and almost painfully square, delivering feel-good messages about travel with an earnestness that could be mistaken for naïveté. "This is fun!" he bubbles when he is having fun. "Wouldya look at that?" he exclaims, happening upon a pretty view or a pigeon-covered plaza.

5   This enthusiasm has found a fertile audience, even in an era when many Americans have grown more afraid of traveling abroad. Last year, . . . Rick Steves still managed to sell more than 600,000 guidebooks and sign up some 5,000 people for his company's bus tours. For the last three years, Steves's guide to Italy has outsold those from Frommer's, Fodor's and Lonely Planet; several of his foreign phrase books — which include translations like "If you don't slow this taxi down, I will throw up" — have become more popular than Berlitz.

6   Like any good guru, Steves has figured out how to churn out a message that is both infectious and profitable. His travel philosophy, published on a single page in each of his guidebooks, calls for his readers to skip most luxuries in order to have a more authentic experience, but above all he demands they be "fanatically positive and militantly optimistic." Politically speaking, Steves is a bit of a fox in the henhouse; he has earned the trust of older and less cosmopolitan Americans with his methodical research and good cheer and, in large part, by keeping his liberal leanings just under the radar. A sought-after speaker, he has given the keynote address at both the AARP convention and that of NORML, the National Organization for the Reform of Marijuana Laws.

(To the former, he dispensed tips on getting senior discounts at youth hostels. To the latter, he lauded pot smoking as a way of traveling vicariously: "You can read National Geographic about an ascent of Mount Everest, and that's kind of exciting, but if you have a little help, you're almost there.")

7   Back at home in Washington State, Steves has a wife, Anne, and two teenage children, who sometimes accompany him on his travels. His earliest trips to Europe came during his own adolescence, when he accompanied his parents, who owned a piano import business in Edmonds, on visits to German factories. While finishing a business degree at the University of Washington in 1978, Steves discovered the art of backpacking in Europe, taking extended summer trips on a shoestring.

8   To finance these trips, he began teaching a "Europe 101" course through the University of Washington's Experimental College, where he was surprised to see older travelers show up looking for advice. His course handbook gradually thickened into something he could sell as an all-purpose guide to Europe, and before long he was running itinerary-less minibus tours through the continent, putting up paying customers of all ages in hostels, empty bomb shelters and a 50-cents-a-night communal tent in the Munich Botanical Gardens. Steves remembers it all fondly as "a cross between Woodstock and a slumber party."

9   Since then, his enterprise has grown more corporate — he employs 60 people in Edmonds and another 25 international tour guides — but only somewhat less frugal. "Back then, I had a personal crusade to put 'soft' Americans into miserable hotel rooms," Steves wrote in a 1999 memoir, "if only to understand how comfortable they had it back home." In the interest of building a broader following and a measurable income, Steves eventually made a few concessions (his books now include reviews of three- and four-star hotels), but he has remained staunchly moralistic about the advantages of cheap travel. "Spending money only builds a thicker wall between you and what you came to see," he says.

10   He is also clear about what he expects his middle-American congregants to see while in Europe, which is an alternative universe to the one in which they live. In his books and TV shows, Steves tirelessly champions Europe for its lack of gun violence and devotion to the bicycle. He recommends a certain hash bar in Amsterdam and explains that the city's prostitutes are licensed and unionized — protected by

"the law, not pimps." And he once brought a tour group to meet his cousin in Oslo "so they could chat about what it's like to have enforced paternity leave."

11   It is hard to say to what extent the Rickniks are internalizing Steves's politics, but each time he strays too far from the feel-good part of travel into more controversial territory, there are those ready to remind him of his place. "I'm looking for a good hotel and a memorable bite to eat . . . not some sort of out-of-place editorial," one reader wrote in an Amazon.com review. A number of fans sent angry e-mail messages after reading an essay Steves wrote and published on his Web site last fall, criticizing what he perceived as American ethnocentrism and lack of vision in world politics. "It seems you are a person," sniffed one, "who has been corrupted by many trips to Europe."

12   When it comes to practical advice, however, Steves's word continues to pass for gospel. A positive review in one of his books can easily double the business at a small hotel or restaurant. And when he goes off the beaten path, he now has thousands of eager tourists following behind him. Some travelers complain that when they show up to eat the grilled sardines at a hole-in-the-wall joint Steves recommends in Barcelona or when, heeding his advice, they rush through Rome in order to better savor the sleepy Cinque Terre region of Italy's northwest coast, they are confronted with about the last thing they want to see: hordes of other Americans doing exactly the same.

13   One of Steves's great discoveries is Gimmelwald, a Swiss village of 140 dairy farmers tucked between peaks of the Alps and accessible by only gondola or on foot. When Steves first backpacked through in the late 70's, it was little more than a rest stop for a seasonal trickle of European hikers. But after years of appearing in his guidebooks, the village is now visited by nearly 20,000 out-of-towners annually, and more than a few dairy farmers have reinvented themselves as innkeepers. Inside the world's great cities, Steves's opinion is no less transformative. When he described his favorite street in Paris, a narrow lane in the Seventh Arrondissement called Rue Cler, as so French "I feel like I must have been a poodle in a previous life," its cafes were quickly choked with American tourists. Among some Parisians, the street is now half-jokingly referred to as Rue Rick Steves.

14   Steves acknowledges the paradox in opening Europe's "backdoors" to the masses, but maintains that the people who buy his books or travel with his tour company — "our people," he likes to call them — are a cut above the average marauding tourist. At the very least, he

claims to be pushing a quieter, curiosity-driven form of tourism, one where the aim is getting to know, and maybe even learn from, some real Europeans, not just those paid to serve beer and take tickets. "People go to the cultural zoo," he says. "They get hung up on it. 'Show me a thatched roof! Show me a guy in lederhosen!' It's like visiting a game preserve. But I say, Stow your camera and be there. Pick grapes. Go to church. Buy something at the market."

15   Somewhere along the way, Steves lost the young backpacker audience to the hipper, more freewheeling guides like Lonely Planet and the Rough Guide series, but what remained — a market of aging baby boomers who find both safety and adventure in Steves's nerdy gallivanting — has proved to be touristic gold. Steves criticizes his competitors in the guidebook market (namely the informative but bland Fodor's and Frommer's guides) as "so dry they make your lips chap," adding, "It's like their writers are not allowed to have a personality."

16   Steves's personality, by contrast, dominates every page of his own literature. His smiling photo is splashed across his books, newsletters and brochures. He publishes a free newsletter offering travel advice and a raft of advertisements for various products sold on his Web site, from travel pillows and luggage locks to DVD's and special Rick Steves maps. But what he is selling more than anything is a quirky but thoroughly vetted travel experience, road-tested by Steves himself. It is debatable whether his legions of grown-up backpackers will be the kind of influence-wielding ambassadors he hopes them to be in Europe — not to mention whether they'll return home having soaked up his political viewpoints — but Steves takes obvious delight in the fact that in this day and age they're out there traveling at all.

17   On my last day with Steves, we climb on board a ferryboat to visit the small fishing village of Porto Brand-o, which sits across the Tagus River. The boat is empty except for a few weathered Portuguese women returning home from the market. There is not a tourist in sight. As the boat pitches and rolls over the strong current, Steves excuses himself, gets up from his seat and disappears toward the bow of the ferry. A few minutes later, he returns, wearing an enormous grin. He pulls out his guidebook and scribbles a note in the margins. When I ask what he has written, what gem he has turned up for the multitude of his readers who will make this voyage as soon as the next edition is out, he lifts his book. "Tall men can use the urinal with their head out the porthole," he intones. Looking more than a little satisfied, he adds, "I'll get letters on that one, saying: 'I did that! That's cool!' "

QUESTIONS FOR DISCUSSION AND WRITING

1. Typically, a profile of a person focuses on describing that person's accomplishments but also strives to convey a sense of the person's character and personality. Find three examples from three different paragraphs in Corbett's profile that describe Rick Steves's personality. In your own words, how would you describe his personality?

2. Writers of profiles gather their material through background research, reading the person's books, reading biographies, conducting interviews, and sometimes following that person through a typical day's activity. Which of these strategies does Corbett use in writing her profile of Steves? Cite specific passages from her article to support your choices.

3. Corbett writes her profile of Steves for the *New York Times Magazine*. Find a copy of the magazine online or in your library and skim some sample articles from a current issue. What are typical topics and for what audience are these articles written. Do you consider yourself a member of this audience? Explain why or why not.

4. Review the five strategies for reading and writing an investigative essay discussed earlier in this chapter. Taking each strategy separately, explain whether Corbett does a good job with that particular strategy. For example, the first strategy is to write a title and a lead paragraph that gets the reader's interest and attention. Do you think Corbett does a good job with her title and lead? Comment on Corbett's effectiveness with each of the five strategies.

5. Choose a person that you might like to write a profile about. Do some research online and in the library about this person's background, achievements, and personality. Then write out a plan you might follow for writing a profile of this person. What magazine or online site would you select to publish your profile? Who would be your audience? How might you go about conducting an interview with this person? Write out a plan you might follow for writing a profile on this person.

GLENN C. ALTSCHULER

The E-Learning Curve

Prereading Journal Entry

If you have taken a course online or through a distance education program, describe your experiences with that course. What were the strengths and weaknesses of the course? Would you take such a course online again? Why or why not?

As dean of the School of Continuing Education and Summer Sessions at Cornell University, Glenn Altschuler is the author of Changing Channels: America in TV Guide *(1992) as well as a regular column appearing in the New York Times on negotiating college. Topics he has recently explored include internships in college, faculty advising, admissions, and cheating. In the following essay, taken from his New York Times column, Altschuler reports on the strengths and weaknesses of online education. "Distance education is definitely not for every student," Altschuler says, "but it can provide a successful learning experience if the class is small, the virtual materials are well designed, and the student has regular contact with the professor."*

1   In the information age, knowledge is power, and higher education helps secure both. With college credentials come jobs, promotions and salary increases. Little wonder that many full- and part-time workers are going back to school and that distance learning—with the prospect of taking courses in the company lounge or, better yet, at home in PJ's in front of a PC—has expanded significantly in the last few years.

2   With 90,000 nontraditional students enrolled, the University of Phoenix is now the largest private university in the United States. Christopher Byron, a columnist for Bloomberg News, calls Phoenix Online "the single greatest improvement in higher education since the condom." Traditional institutions have followed suit, creating separate for-profit corporations to deliver their courses online. According to a report by the International Data Corporation, e-learning will increase 33 percent a year from 1999 to 2004, making online instruction a $12 billion business.

3   But while many remain bullish on the long-term prospects of e-learning, the momentum has slowed. In the spring, responding to what it called the realities of the private market, Unext, a high-profile distance learning company, laid off 12 percent of its workers. Other companies have shed employees or closed shop altogether.

4   "We are now seeing a bit of a reality check, kind of like the dot-com shake-up," said J. Richard Gividen, president of the consulting company Distance Learning Integrators.

5   As they discover the high costs of producing and providing staff for online courses, colleges and universities are reassessing as well—Temple University in Philadelphia closed its e-learning venture several months ago. Even when the cost of developing a distance learning course is kept to a relatively modest $5,000 to $15,000, it is

difficult, at the moment, to turn a profit, according to new studies at six universities commissioned by the Alfred P. Sloan Foundation. With venture capital less available than in the heady late 90s, administrators and trustees have become reluctant to pour more endowment money into for-profit enterprises whose profitability is in doubt.

6   Prospective students remain skeptical, too, specifically about the quality of education they will receive online. Only 9 of 15,000 U.A.W. Ford employees in Ohio took advantage of a $4,200 grant provided by the company for distance education, according to Thomas Shostak, dean of lifelong learning at Ohio University.

7   Adapting a variant of Yogi Berra's explanation of the difficulty reserving a table at his favorite restaurant—"nobody goes there anymore; it's too crowded"—many potential customers believe they get more personal attention when they take classes in residence than when they take them over the Internet. In a recent marketing strategy report for eCornell, Cornell's new distance learning company, only 30 percent of the respondents expected to receive the same or better interaction with instructors in the technology-enabled courses.

8   Although online learning is in its infancy and the pedagogy is constantly evolving, students can sort out available options now, increasing the likelihood of getting quality instruction.

9   As dean of continuing education at Cornell, which is independent of eCornell, I advise those who ask about distance learning to first identify their goal. If it is the acquisition of a specific skill (say, reading a spreadsheet) or preparing for a career change (say, to get certified in software applications), it may not be necessary to take courses that carry academic credit. If it is to rack up a few credits to transfer to a residential degree program, students must make sure that the bricks-and-mortar institution from which they plan to graduate actually accepts credits completed online.

10   And if the aim is a degree, it is especially important to know all the requirements. Some institutions, for example, require several residency weekends in addition to distance learning courses. Not every student can (or wants to) leave family and work, but those who do tend to complete degrees at a higher rate than those who don't. Degree candidates should also find out as much as they can about the online course provider.

11   Begin by "following the dots," Sara Dulaney Gilbert recommends in "How to Be a Successful Online Student" (McGraw-Hill, 2001), adding, "If the name of the organization is followed by .edu or .org, it is rarely a purely commercial venture or potential rip-off." Lists of

accredited institutions are available from the Council for Higher Education Accreditation (chea@chea.org). Accrediting bodies say they hold technology-mediated courses to the same standards as traditional courses.

12   Modes of instruction, quality and workload vary, and prestigious institutions (some of which, alas, are as obsessed with profits as the for-profits) do not necessarily offer the best distance learning programs. Richard L. Hoeg, manager of technical education and engineering information services for Honeywell Labs, is emphatic about how students should proceed: "Never enroll in an e-learning program unless you can sample a segment of an actual course—not a demo," he said. Many institutions now permit prospective students to sit in on a class, or might supply e-mail addresses of current students who can supply a candid evaluation.

13   Since support services are as important as course content, students should compare provisions for it. "Generally speaking," Mr. Shostak said, "the more chances the student has to interact with the instructor, the more successful he or she will be." Will the professor be available to answer questions and evaluate exams, or have these tasks been assigned to a teaching assistant? At Empire State College, the State University of New York's arm for nontraditional students, instructors are expected to respond to all requests from students within 48 hours, according to Meg Benke, director of its Center for Distance Learning. The University of Wisconsin at Madison provides advising, admissions, registration, bookstore and technical assistance to online students via the Web, e-mail, fax and telephone. Help desks are usually open dawn to midnight Monday to Saturday.

14   Students must also decide between courses in which students and faculty members meet together in real time (synchronously) or in which e-learning can take place any time (asynchronously). Although courses with no set meeting time may be more convenient, they can also make distance learning distant learning. "Not having to be at class, I tended to wait until the last minute to do the work," one online student at Ohio University admitted. Others complain about not being able to interrupt a presentation with a question, or to get to know classmates.

15   The dropout rate for students in asynchronous courses is substantial, says Mr. Gividen of Distance Learning Integrators. To address the sense of isolation, these courses now provide discussion boards, virtual student lounges, assignments to be completed by teams and teachers'

e-mail addresses. Empire State students are encouraged to log on every day and required to do so twice a week.

16   Most important, many institutions now limit class size. To maximize interaction, no more than 25 students should be enrolled, and even this group should be broken up into smaller teams for some assignments, according to online course planners.

17   Because competition for customers is fierce, Ms. Gilbert says, online courses are "going to force institutions of all kinds to focus on the student more than they are accustomed to having to do."

18   In my experience, e-learning may actually encourage some personality types to get more involved. In the distance learning course I teach, "Popular Culture in Modern America, 1950-Present," e-mail seems to embolden students to make more (and more critical) comments than in face-to-face instruction.

19   Courses enhanced by technology support multiple learning styles and give students fluency with electronic information as basic tools of life. I can supplement my lectures with Web links to Elvis singing, John Wayne killing Indians, Mexicans and bad guys, and John Updike reading from one of his novels. Distance learning courses can also eliminate some of the barriers of the real world. The naked eye cannot see the convective heat loss from a leaf, but visual displays of the phenomenon have been created for the Internet.

20   Then again, I have had adventuresome students discover, rather late in the game, that they could not find sufficient material in the libraries of Singapore to write a research paper about American popular culture.

21   I'm not prepared to say that virtual is better than face-to-face education, or even as good. But it's here to stay, and informed and highly motivated consumers can make good use of it.

QUESTIONS FOR DISCUSSION AND WRITING

1. Describe Altschuler's multiple purposes in writing this essay. Is he reporting on the current state of distance education? Is he giving advice to prospective students? Is he advocating distance education? Is he reminding educators that distance education has its problems? Cite specific sentences to support your response.

2. Reread the article and list the sources Altschuler uses in gathering his information. What information comes from his personal experience? What other sources does he cite? Does he always identify the background or credentials of each of his sources?

3. Altschuler is addressing a wide audience consisting of students, teachers, educational administrators, and readers interested in education generally. Find specific sentences in Altschuler's essay in which he addresses each of these members of his audience. Does Altschuler focus on one of these groups more than the others? Explain.

4. Many "traditional" college courses today use some of the electronic features of online education, such as Web sites for courses, e-mail, chat rooms, and discussion forums. If you have taken one of those courses, explain how these virtual features added to or distracted from the format of that class.

5. Write an investigative essay on the state of online education at your own college. Research your college catalogue. Interview administrators at your school who coordinate online education. Talk to professors who teach such courses and to students who have taken them. Report your findings in the form of an article to appear in your campus newspaper.

MARY WHITE

The Beauty Behind Beauty Pageants

Prereading Journal Entry

Think of a job, sport, or hobby you have. What goes on before the performance, during practice, at rehearsals, or at business meetings that the general public may not know about? For other members of your class, explain what happens "behind the scenes."

When Mary White was a student in a composition class at Oklahoma State University, she wrote about appearance versus reality at a beauty pageant. After reading several articles and interviewing Lisa Scott, a seventeen-year-old participant, White reports on what goes on behind the scenes—how much money contestants spend on their clothes, how they suffer embarrassment and pain, and how they sacrifice dignity for the chance at a modeling career.

Mary White's Notes

Purpose: To inform the public of the trauma, pain, and money involved in the pageant. As beautiful and glamorous as pageants appear, not all of the preparation is smiles and roses.

Audience: The general public who sees only the final performance, either live or on television.

Brief Outline:

I.   Introduction
II.   Learning to be beautiful
III. The clothes
IV.   The look
V.   The pain
VI.   That night
VII. Conclusion

Article: "Let Tom Edison Be the Judge." U.S. News and World Report 5, June 1989: 13.

Article: Let Tom Edison Be the Judge

1   Victorians tried to cover them up, feminists tried to dress them down and Stalinists tried to throw them out, but no one can stop those indomitable beauty contests. Last week, even the Soviets succumbed, picking their first Miss U.S.S.R. before thousands of screaming fans.

2   Forerunners of this *glasnost* glamour girl were chosen 700 years ago from a neighboring empire. Marco Polo reported that Genghis Khan's grandson, Kublai Khan, augmented his love nest by ordering a jury of officers to identify the land's most beautiful girls. Those getting the highest rating—20—were summoned to his court. Meanwhile, European villagers chose the fairest May queen each spring.

3   The modern beauty pageant would have originated with P. T. Barnum in 1854 had Victorian America not shuddered at the thought of women displaying themselves. Ever the showman, Barnum turned his plan for a parade of beauties into a contest for best portrait. Rehoboth Beach, Del., dared the first Miss United States competition in 1880 (with Thomas Edison judging), and Atlantic City, N.J., caught the wave in 1921, crowning the first Miss America. In the next few decades, the voices of puritanism faded, only to be replaced in the '70s by feminists arguing that, as men's equals, women shouldn't be judged like heifers. But millions of young contestants with Cinderella dreams weren't dissuaded and, with even the prudish Evil Empire now worshiping the female form, they may never be.

Rough Draft

Beauty pageants aren't always what they seem. It seems that being a contestant in a pageant today is as difficult as being a neurosurgeon, and almost as stressful. These women are put through an incredible amount of pain, embarrassment, and schooling, just to make them beautiful. The amount of money spent on dresses alone is enormous, not to mention make-up, hair, and shoes. Recently, I attended a pageant and was astonished to learn that not all of what you see on stage is real.

It is not uncommon for a beauty pageant contestant to attend school to learn proper etiquette for a pageant. "I have been in a pageant class all semester. This is just like a final," said Lisa Scott, contestant of the Carl Albert Junior College Scholarship pageant. "In class they taught us how to walk, how to smile, and how to answer the judges," said Lisa. The class is a "dry run" of the actual pageant. They are given the rules in class as well as a support group of other contestants. "Talent is the most important part. It counts 40% of the points. In class they teach you how to act talented, even if you aren't. . . . Well, in reality, I guess they teach you to act beautiful even if you are not," Lisa smiled.

Everyone knows that clothes are an important part of pageants, but few people realize how difficult it is to find an appropriate pageant dress. "It is hard to find a dress that is beautiful, but not too showy. Or find one that is beautiful, not too showy, and doesn't cost a small fortune. It is even harder to find all of those things in a dress that fits. I got super lucky. All of my dresses were marked down, but they all had to be altered from sizes 11 to 13 to size 1 or 3," Lisa recited. Lisa was correct. She only spent $700 on two dresses, but it is not uncommon for contestants to spend $1500 to $6000 on one dress. Finding the right dress, the right size, and the right price are all obstacles that the viewer never sees.

Another startling fact that the public isn't aware of is the pain associated with being pageant beautiful. When asked about the "pageant pain," Lisa said this: "I am really enjoying the pageant atmosphere, but I haven't been able to feel my left big toe for 3 days now. And I have no skin left under my arms from taping my chest up." Numb toes are common among contestants. Contestants are encouraged to buy tight shoes, or shoes that are too small so they won't slip or the contestant won't take large steps. The raw skin under the arms is even more common. All but one of the contestants in the Carl Albert Junior College pageant had to tape their chests for cleavage. The taping was done with duct tape and medical tape. Pads were placed underneath their breasts to produce a fuller look. Every contestant wore a bustier instead of a regular bra. "It really does make us look better. It is uncomfortable though," Lisa said. Some contestants taped their stomachs and rear ends also. "It (the taping) is all done to give a firmer, more smooth look. Once everyone is taped and dressed, they look completely different."

Firm grip is used on the contestants rear ends to keep their swimsuits down. "Firm grip doesn't really hurt, but it is sticky and hard to get off."

Pageant night is the grande finale. Pageant mothers run around backstage doing make-up, fixing hair, looking for another set of pads, doing motherly type things. The audience sits in the auditorium watching the stage, waiting for the games to begin. Backstage, contestants help tape each other, and utter encouraging words. They sit in front of mirrors, trying to cover up bags under their eyes. A pageant mother runs around with Vaseline so that the contestants lips won't stick to their teeth from smiling too much. The hair is taken out of rollers and the hair dressers go to work on it.

Final Draft

The Beauty Behind Beauty Pageants

1   Sitting in front of the television or sitting in the audience, all of the pageant contestants look absolutely breathtaking. Every girl has just the right figure, smile, poise, and grace it takes to be the next Miss Whatever. The sad truth is that although the contestants say they are living a dream, the dream turns out to be more like a nightmare. It seems that being a contestant in a pageant today is as difficult as being a successful lawyer in Washington, D.C., or even as difficult as being a professional athlete, where the competition is so fierce to be number one. These women are put through an incredible amount of schooling, embarrassment, and pain just to make them beautiful. The money they spend on one dress alone is enormous, not to mention the cost of make-up, hair, nails, and shoes. Recently, I attended a pageant and talked with one of the contestants. I was astonished to learn that not all of what I saw on stage was real.

2   It is not at all uncommon for a contestant to go to school to learn proper pageant etiquette. "I have been in pageant class all semester. This is just like the final exam," said Lisa Scott, contestant in the Carl Albert Junior College Scholarship Pageant. The pageant is associated with the Miss America Scholarship Pageant. The winner of the CAJC Pageant has the opportunity to participate in the Miss Oklahoma Scholarship Pageant. If the girl should win the title of Miss Oklahoma, she is then off to the Miss America Scholarship Pageant. "In class they taught us how to walk, smile, and answer the questions we are asked by the judges," said Lisa. The class is a dry run of the actual pageant. The contestants are given the rules of the pageant in class as well as the support of their fellow contestants. "Talent is the most important part of the contest; it counts forty percent of the points. In class they teach

you how to act talented even if you are not . . . well . . . I guess, truthfully, they teach you to act beautiful even if you aren't," Lisa says as she flashes her pageant smile.

3   Everyone knows that clothes are an important part of pageant competition. Few people, however, realize how difficult it is to find an appropriate pageant dress. "It is hard to find a dress that is beautiful but not showy. It is even harder to find a dress that is beautiful, not showy and doesn't cost a small fortune. It is just about a miracle to find a dress that is all of those things and fits. I got super lucky. All of my dresses were marked down, but they all had to be altered." Lisa was correct in using the word "lucky." She spent about seven hundred dollars total on her two pageant dresses. It is not uncommon for a contestant to spend anywhere from one thousand to six thousand dollars on just one dress. Finding the right dress, at the right price, and in the right size are all obstacles that the pageant viewer never sees.

4   Another startling fact about pageants that the general public is not aware of is the pain involved in being beautiful. When asked about pageant pain Lisa said this: "I am really enjoying the pageant atmosphere, but I haven't been able to feel my big toe for three days. I have no skin left under my arms from taping my chest up." Numb toes are fairly common among pageant contestants. Contestants are encouraged to buy shoes that are too small so they will not slip. Having small shoes also cuts down on the size of steps the girl takes. The raw skin is even more common. All but one of the contestants in the Carl Albert Junior College Scholarship Pageant had to tape their chests up for cleavage. The taping was done with duct tape and medical tape. Pads were placed underneath their breasts to produce a fuller look. Every contestant wore bras that gave extra support for their new cleavage. "It really does make us look better; it is uncomfortable though," Lisa said. Some contestants taped their stomachs and their behinds. "It is all done to give a firmer, more smooth look to the contestant. Once everyone is dressed they look completely different." Firm grip is used on the contestants' behinds to keep their swimsuits in place. "Firm grip doesn't hurt but it is sticky and hard to get off." It is apparent that the beauty that is seen on stage is not all real. The beauty seen on stage is an enhancement of what society thinks should be there.

5   The modern beauty pageant would have originated with P. T. Barnum in 1854 ("Let Tom Edison Be the Judge"). Victorian women, however, shuddered at the thought of displaying themselves publicly ("Let Tom Edison"). Mr. Barnum would not be put off by this and turned his

beauty pageant into a "best portrait" contest ("Let Tom Edison"). The best portrait contest is still a part of pageantry today. The contestants are judged on their poise, talent, diction, individual beauty, and on the way they photograph. The First Miss United States Pageant was held in 1880 with Thomas Edison judging ("Let Tom Edison"). The first Miss America Pageant was held in Atlantic City, New Jersey, in 1921.

6   Since those first pageant nights, the glamour as well as competition has increased. Pageant mothers run around backstage doing hair, fixing make-up, looking for mislaid items, and offering words of encouragement. The audience sits in the auditorium waiting for the games to begin. Backstage the contestants offer suggestions and support to each other. Contestants sit in front of mirrors trying to cover the bags under their eyes, hoping that this night will be the beginning of a great modeling career.

7   Finally, all preparations are done, and the dresses are on. Everyone is picture perfect. The contestants move through the parade like they have been doing this for years. The spotlight falls on the winner and a sigh is let out among the contestants. Everyone congratulates the winner and wipes away the tears of joy and disappointment. When asked if she would participate in another pageant Lisa, who placed second runner-up in the CAJC pageant, said this: "Well . . . a lot of people have told me tonight that I have a lot of potential. They have said I need to mature some. I am only seventeen. With more improvement, I could really do well in another pageant."

8   Pageants have been the gateway for many career openings and they have been a source of entertainment for people for years. Not everyone, however, believes that pageants serve a worthy purpose. According to model Kaylan Pickford, "A beauty contest is not a guarantee of launching you as a model, even if you win. The whole experience could be very degrading" (93). She believes that dignity is the most important thing when it comes to being beautiful. It would seem very difficult to be dignified with a taped chest and Vaseline-coated teeth.

9   Not everyone's attitudes about pageants are the same. The fact is the public encourages women to be beautiful no matter what it costs, whether it be money, pain, or time. Pageants have been enjoyed by millions over the years. Contestants compete in them year after year, trying to look just a little better in hopes of winning the coveted title of Miss . . . .

WORKS CITED

"Let Tom Edison Be the Judge." *U.S. News and World Report* 5, June 1989: 13.
Pickford, Kaylan. "Beauty Pageants Are Only Skin Deep." *50 Plus*, Oct. 1986: 92–93.
Scott, Lisa D. Interview. 28 October 1989.

QUESTIONS FOR DISCUSSION AND WRITING

1. List the basic who, what, when, where, and how information that White gives in her essay.
2. Reread White's statement of purpose in her notes. Which parts of her thesis (trauma, pain, money) does her essay most effectively and least effectively show? Cite specific sentences to support your answer.
3. Who is White's audience? Write a different lead-in for White's essay that would also appeal to her audience.
4. Which shaping strategies (chronological order, process analysis, causal analysis, comparison) does White use to organize her essay? Would another shaping strategy also work?
5. If White asked for your help revising this paper, what changes in content would you suggest to make this paper more effective? More of White's own observations backstage? Interviews with other contestants or mothers? More references to feminists' arguments about beauty contests?
6. Reread your Prereading Journal Entry. If you wanted to write an investigating paper on this topic, how might you proceed? What would you read? Whom might you interview? What might you observe?

Explaining

EXPOSITORY WRITING, OR WRITING THAT EXPLAINS, USES a variety of strategies: analysis (dividing a subject into its parts to explain the whole), classification (grouping ideas, people, or things into similar categories), comparison and contrast (noting similarities and differences), definition (placing limits on the meaning of a word or idea), process analysis (explaining how to do something, or how it happens), and causal analysis (explaining the causes or effects of ideas or events). Each of these strategies represents a way of thinking, a way of showing the relationships between ideas, events, or people. Expository writing typically uses several of these strategies to help explain the subject to a reader.

In a sense, expository writing is like doing math problems. Writers must show their work and their thinking, not just give the "answers." Writers explaining how to tune an engine must *show* all the steps in the process. Writers explaining the effects of excessive credit card debt should *show* examples of actual people who have run into financial difficulty because of their debt. An effective explanation makes a generalization and then supports that main idea with examples, illustrations, facts, or other data. *Showing the specific examples* and then *explaining the relationship between the specific case and the general idea* is the principal task of the expository writer.

Strategies for Reading and Writing
Explaining Essays

As you read the expository essays in this chapter, look for the following key features of expository writing.

- **Beginning with an attention-getting title and lead-in.** Since readers are busy and easily distracted, expository writing should appeal to their curiosity or self-interest. The lead and/or the title should pique their interest in the subject.
- **Statement of the thesis or main idea early in the essay.** Expository writing should present no mysteries for the reader. The reader should not wonder, "Why is this writer telling me this?" Writers present the thesis early and demonstrate that idea in the essay.
- **Definition of key terms or ideas or description of what something is.** If one purpose of an essay is to explain what something is, writers use definition and description to explain the subject to their reader. What is a computer "modem" and how did it get its name? What characterizes a Japanese conversation and how is it different from an American conversation?
- **Analysis of the steps in the process.** If one purpose of the essay is to explain some process or show how to do something, writers use process analysis. A writer might explain to school children what happens during photosynthesis (a descriptive process) or explain to novice cooks the best way to cook fried chicken (a prescriptive or how-to process).
- **Analysis of causes or effects.** If one purpose of an essay is to show the relationship between causes and effects, writers use causal analysis to explain their subject. Typically, writers show how an event or a condition has several causes (What are the causes of alcoholism among college students?) or how an event or a condition has multiple effects (How does prejudice in the workplace affect women's salaries?)
- **Demonstration of main ideas with examples or specific data.** The heart of expository writing is the demonstration. Without specific illustrations, firsthand observation, remembered examples, facts, statistical data, or quotations from written sources or interviews, expository writing will not explain anything to its readers.

■ **Use of transitions to show connections between main points.** Clarity is a primary goal of exposition, so writers use transitions (*first, second, then, although, moreover, on the one hand, while, after, next, in addition, finally*) to show key relationships to their readers.

Reading an Explaining Essay

Prereading

Determine what you already know about the subject *before* you begin reading an essay. If you had to define the idea of a "good friend," what would it be? If you had to explain why you think advertising is deceptive, what would you say? Writing what you already know about the subject of a particular essay will help you connect with the subject. In addition, finding out about the author and the occasion for the essay will help you understand the intended relationship between writer and reader. Is the writer an expert, explaining SDS to medical students? Is the writer a journalist, informing readers how SDS is or is not transmitted? Your Prereading Journal Entry and the information about the author and the article will help answer those questions.

First Reading

During your first reading, concentrate on understanding the writer's explanation. If some passage is confusing, place a "?" in the margin. If you like an idea or an example, put a "!" in the margin. If the writer is wrong about some point, put a "X" in the margin. Highlight or put a wavy line under any key passages. Underline words you need to look up later. At the end of your first reading, state in a single sentence the writer's main idea: "This essay explains how television detracts from the quality of family life."

Annotated Reading

For your annotated reading, begin by writing your reactions to the essay. Which passages were the clearest? If a passage was not clear, did you miss something on the first reading or did the writer fail to give a good example or fail to use simple, clear language? Write your reactions in the margin: "I liked this example" or "This idea still isn't clear to me." In addition to writing your reactions, read with a writer's eye. Which explaining techniques were the most effective? Least effective? Bracket [ ] and label key features of expository essays: beginning with a clear title, lead-in, and thesis; use of definition, process analysis, or causal analysis; sufficient use of specific examples and data; and effective use of transitions. When necessary, look up definitions of words that you underlined or that catch your attention now.

Collaborative Reading

In your class or small group, share your Prereading Journal Entries. Based on the journal entries, does your class or group represent the intended audience for this essay? Was the writer addressing people more informed on the subject? Less informed? Appoint a recorder to compile typical annotations from the class or group. Annotate one copy of the essay with your collected notes. At the end of the essay, write out a statement of the writer's *thesis*. When you have finished the collective annotations, write at least two questions you or your group has about this essay.

Writing an Explaining Essay

In an explaining essay, your *purpose* is to explain the what, how, and why that surround a subject: what something is, how to do something, how something usually happens, and/or why something happens. You are writing to an *audience* that may be interested in the subject or may not be very informed on the subject. If the audience is already interested or knowledgeable, you need to show them that you have a certain angle or a special understanding that they may not have considered. If they don't know about the topic, you should arouse their curiosity and show them why they need to understand the subject.

To succeed with your readers, you must meet their expectations. In expository writing, readers have three key expectations: They expect you to state the **main idea** or thesis, to use **specific support,** and to **organize** your explanation coherently. First, readers are busy and impatient. They want to know the main idea. Their first question is, "Why is the writer telling me this?" By the time they've read for two or three minutes, they expect to know what your point is. Second, your readers want general statements to be supported with specific examples, statistics, quotations, detailed descriptions, images, or brief narratives from your experience. Third, readers appreciate a sense of order, of progression, of organization. They like to see that you first define a term and then explain it, that you discuss x and then compare it to y; that you explain that x has three key causes or effects. They want you to show the steps (1, 2, 3, and 4) in the process, and explain events in a chronological order.

Finally, don't forget that you are a person explaining something to another person. In an informal essay, your personality or **voice** can make your explanation worth reading. You may use *I* in your essay; you may want to describe why *you* are curious about the subject; you may want to show your readers what (and how) *you learned* about your subject. You will most likely want to share some of your own experience. If your audience can relate to you, they will more easily understand your ideas and explanations.

Choosing a Subject for an Explaining Essay

The questions following the essays in this chapter suggest some ideas for an explaining essay, but here are other possibilities.

Start an **authority list.** In your journal, write down topics that you know about, that you are an authority on. Perhaps a hobby, a subject you have studied, a place you have been, or a person you know could become the subject for your explaining essay.

Reread your **class notes** from your other courses for subjects you could explain. Since you are still studying this subject, you might not feel comfortable writing a technical explanation for your professor, but perhaps a friend who is not taking the class might be your audience. Pick an idea, term, process, phenomenon, or event and explain it to your friend.

Find a **specialized magazine**—in the library or online—that focuses on one of your favorite subjects or hobbies. There are magazines devoted to cars, fashion, cooking, skiing, sports, interior decorating, gardening, religion, fishing, sewing, vegetarian diets, aerobics—the list is almost endless. Browse through magazine shelves in your bookstore or grocery store. Ask your librarian for magazines that focus on your interests. Look through several issues to find possible topics.

Collecting Ideas and Examples

Use the observing, remembering, and investigating skills you've practiced in the previous chapters. Start by **observing** a place that is relevant to your explaining paper. If you're writing about cars, visit a showroom to get the flavor of a new car place. If you're describing vegetarian diets, go to a restaurant that serves vegetarian food. If you're explaining an idea from your biology class, describe your classroom, or the professor, or the laboratory. Next, write two pages in your journal **remembering** all your experiences with this subject. In your explaining essay, you can then take the best memories and experiences and use them as *specific examples* to support your main idea. Finally, begin **investigating** your subject: Read an article on your topic, interview an expert, or conduct a survey. These collecting skills will help you focus your subject and generate the specific support that your readers expect.

As you work on your subject, ask key questions. The answers to the following questions will suggest additional support you can use, but they will also help you to shape and organize your essay.

To explain **what** something is or means, answer the following questions:

How can you describe it?
What examples of it can you find?
What is it similar to? What is it unlike?
What are its parts? What is its function?
How can it be classified? Is it a type of something?
Which of these questions is most useful to your audience?

To explain **how** to do something or **how** something happens, answer the following questions:

What are necessary conditions or equipment for the process?
What are the key steps in the process?
Do or should the steps occur in a specific sequence?
If any steps or events were omitted, would the outcome change?
Which steps are most important?
Which steps or events does your audience most need to know?

To explain **why** something happens, answer the following questions:

Do several causes (1, 2, 3) lead to one effect?
Does one cause lead to several effects (1, 2, 3)?
What is the order of the causes or effects?
Is there an action or situation that would prevent an effect?
What causes or effects need clarification for your audience?

Shaping Your Explaining Essay

As you collect ideas and examples and think about shaping and organizing, *narrow* and *focus* your subject into a topic suitable for your purpose, audience, and occasion. If you're writing a short essay about automobile repair for a friend, do not try to explain how to overhaul the whole engine. Instead, *narrow* your explanation to a limited operation, such as setting the engine's timing. If you are writing about an effective diet, *focus* on some angle appropriate for your audience: a weight loss diet that is not only low in fat but is also good for your heart.

Test the following shaping strategies against your particular topic. Some of these strategies may suggest an idea or example to include in your essay, while others may suggest how to organize your whole essay.

Example

Most explaining essays can be developed by examples. Remember: An example is one specific incident, located in time and space, which illustrates your point. Don't begin your example by saying, "That happened to me often" or "I used to do that a lot." Instead, describe an incident that happened at a specific time. Show the scene, just as you would in a remembering essay.

Definition

Definition can organize a whole essay, but more likely it will help you develop a small part of your essay. Defining key terms and ideas helps explain your ideas to a specific reader. Definitions thus form the basis for the writer's explanation

Classification

Classification is a process of sorting individual items into the groups, categories, or classes to which they belong. We can classify university students by their major (Music, Engineering, Business, History, English) or by race or culture (Asian, Black, Hispanic, Anglo). We can classify automobiles by price (luxury, moderately priced, inexpensive) or by body type (sports car, sedan, truck, or van).

Process Analysis

Process analysis explains how to do something (how to make great fried chicken, or how to study for a class) or how something typically happens (how the electoral college works or how photosynthesis works).

Causal Analysis

Analysis and discussion of causes and effects can organize a whole essay. A writer might explain why an airplane crashed by devoting a paragraph to each of the possible causes: bad weather, engine problems, and pilot error. Or the writer might explain how a single cause, such as an air traffic controller's failure to understand a pilot's request, causes the plane to circle the airport, run out of fuel, and eventually crash several miles short of the runway.

Voice

A writer's voice, used with other shaping strategies, can organize an entire essay.

Introductions

Introductions to explaining essays often have three key features:

Lead-in: An example, statement, definition, statistic, quotation, short narrative, or a description that gets the reader's *interest.*

Thesis: A statement of the writer's main idea; a *promise* to the reader that the essay fulfills.

Essay map: A sentence or phrase that *previews* or *lists* the main subtopics that the writer plans to discuss.

Conclusions

Conclusions connect your main examples and evidence to your thesis. In addition to re-emphasizing the thesis, conclusions often wrap up the essay by *echoing* some word, phrase, or idea from the introductory paragraph.

Drafting Your Explaining Essay

First, reread your prewriting notes. What is your purpose and who is your audience? What examples do you intend to use? Which shaping strategy will work best for your essay? Especially for a long essay, write a brief outline or list of the order of your main points. Some writers prefer to have their lead-in, thesis, and map written before drafting the body of their essay; other writers prefer to compose the introduction last, after they have written the body of the essay.

Revising Your Explaining Essay

When you have finished writing your draft—and have let it sit for a day or so—have another reader review your essay. Be sure to explain your purpose, audience, and the primary shaping strategy you are using. As you revise your essay, take your reader's advice as you review the following checklist.

- **Compare your thesis sentence with your conclusion.** If your conclusion states your main idea more clearly than your thesis, revise your thesis to make it fit your conclusion. Most writers discover what they want to say as they write, so your conclusion usually more accurately reflects the purpose and focus of your essay.
- **Check your introductory paragraphs.** Do you have an interesting *lead-in* to catch your reader's attention? Does your *essay map* preview the main points in the essay?
- **Have you defined key words for your audience?** Definitions may include a *description* of an object, a *comparison* to something similar or different, a description of the object's *purpose or function*, or an *example* of its use.
- **In a process analysis, explain each step clearly for your reader.** Have you described the equipment or ingredients for your process? Make clear to your reader which steps or parts of the sequence are *most* or *least* important.
- **In a causal analysis, explain how or why each cause contributes to the effect.** Are there other possible causes for your effect that your readers will know about? Are there other possible effects of your cause?
- **Review your essay for overall coherence.** Body paragraphs often begin with a *transition* from the previous idea as well as a statement of that paragraph's topic. Check the opening sentences in each body paragraph: Is the main idea of that paragraph clear? Is there a smooth transition from the previous paragraph?
- **Edit your essay.** Revise for clarity of sentences and appropriate word choice, punctuation, usage, and grammar. Correct any spelling errors.

Postscript for Your Explaining Essay

When you finish your essay, answer the following questions. Be sure to hand in this postscript with your completed essay.

1. In your essay, what is/are your main purpose or purposes? Who is your intended audience?

2. Does your essay explain **what** (definition), **how** (process analysis), **why** (causal analysis), or some combination? Refer to specific paragraphs in your essay to support your answer.

3. What parts or stages in your writing process (getting an idea, collecting, shaping, drafting, and revising) caused you the most trouble as you wrote this essay? Which parts were the easiest?

4. What do you like best about your finished product? What do you like least? Cite one paragraph that you like best and one paragraph that you like least.

SUZE ORMAN

How to Take Control of Your Credit Cards

Prereading Journal Entry

Describe your experiences with credit cards. Do you have a credit card? What was your age when you first opened one? Did your family or friends advise you about using a credit card? Are you able to pay off your credit card bill each month? Do you use a debit card instead? Do you have family members who got into debt using their credit cards? Explain.

The author of several best-selling books, including The Money Book for the Young, Fabulous & Broke *(2005),* Women and Money: Owning the Power to Control Your Destiny *(2007), and* Suze Orman's Action Plan *(2010), Suze Orman was born in 1951 in Chicago, earned a degree in social work from the University of Illinois, and started her career not as a financial expert but as a waitress in Berkeley, California. After working at a restaurant for seven years, she talked her way into a job as a financial advisor with Merrill Lynch. She then started her own business and published her first book,* You've

Earned It, Don't Lose It (1999). *Six of her most recent books have been* New York Times *bestsellers. Now that she is young(ish), fabulous, and very wealthy, Suze Orman has her own TV show, and she appears on* Oprah, *the* Today Show, The View, *and* Larry King. *She is also the winner of two Emmy Awards for her PBS specials and has been the recipient of the most GRACIE Awards in the history of the AWRT (American Women in Radio and Television).* "How to Take Control of Your Credit Cards" *appeared originally as one of her regular columns for* Money Matters *on Yahoo! Finance.*

1   I'm all for taking credit where credit is due, but when it comes to credit cards, way too many of you are overdoing it. For Americans who don't pay their entire credit card bill each month, the average balance is close to $4,000. And when we zoom in on higher-income folks—those with annual incomes between $75,000 and $100,000—the average balance clocks in at nearly $8,000. If you're paying, say, 18 percent interest on an $8,000 balance, and you make only the 2 percent minimum payment due each month, you are going to end up paying more than $22,000 in interest over the course of the 54 years it will take to get the balance down to zero.

2   That's absolute insanity.

3   And absolutely unnecessary.

4   If you have the desire to take control of your credit card mess, you can. It's just a matter of choice. I am not saying it will be easy, but there are plenty of strategies that can put you on a path out of credit card hell. And as I explain in the accompanying sidebar, even those of you who can't seem to turn the corner and become credit responsible on your own, can get plenty of help from qualified credit counseling services.

How to Be a Credit Card Shark

5   If you overspend just because you like to buy buy buy on credit, then you are what I call Broke by Choice. You are willfully making your own mess. I am not going to lecture you about how damaging this is; I'm hoping the fact that you're reading this article means you are ready to make a change.

6   But I also realize that some of you are Broke by Circumstance. I actually tell young adults in the dues-paying stage of their careers to lean on their credit cards if they don't yet make enough to always keep up with their bills. But the key is that if you rely on your credit cards to make ends meet, you must limit the plastic spending to true necessities, not indulgences. Buying groceries is a necessity. Buying dinner for you and your pals at a swank restaurant is an indulgence you can't afford if it will become part of your unpaid credit card balance.

7   But whether you are broke by choice or by circumstance, the strategy for getting out of credit card debt is the same: to outmaneuver the card companies with a strategy that assures you pay the lowest possible interest rate, for the shortest possible time, while avoiding all of the many snares and traps the card companies lay out for you.

8   Here's how to be a Credit Card Shark.

Take an Interest in Your Rate

9   The average interest rate charged on credit cards is 15 percent, with plenty of folks paying 18 percent, 20 percent, or even more. If you carry a balance on any credit cards, your primary focus should be to get that rate down as low as possible.

10   Now then. If you have a FICO score of at least 720, and you make at least the minimum payment due each month, on time, you should be able to negotiate with your current credit card issuer to lower your rate. Call 'em up and let them know you plan to transfer your entire balance to another card with a lower rate—more on this in a sec—if they don't get your rate down.

11   If your card issuer doesn't step up to the plate and give you a better deal, then do indeed start shopping around for a new card with a sweet intro offer. For those of you with strong FICO scores, a zero-rate deal ought to be possible. You can search for top card deals at the Yahoo! Finance Credit Card Center.

12   Don't forget, though, that the key with balance transfer offers is to find out what your rate will be when the intro period expires in six months to a year. If your zero rate will skyrocket to 20 percent, that's a crappy deal, unless you are absolutely 100 percent sure you will get the balance paid off before the rate changes. (And if you got yourself into card hell in the first place, I wouldn't be betting on you having the ability to wipe out your problem in just six months . . .)

13   Once you are approved for the new low- or zero-rate card, move as much of your high-rate balances onto this new card. But don't—I repeat, do NOT—use the new card for new purchases. Hidden in the fine print on these deals are provisions stating, first, that any new purchases you make on the card will come with a high interest rate, and second, that you'll be paying that high interest on the entirety of your new purchase charges until you pay off every last cent of the balance transfer amount. This, to put it mildly, could really screw up your zero-rate deal. So please, use the new card only to park your old high-rate debt, and not to shop with.

14 Another careless mistake you can make is to cancel your old cards. Don't do that either. Those cards hold some valuable "history" that's used to compute your FICO credit score. If you cancel the cards, you cancel your history, and your FICO score can take a hit. If you are worried about the temptation of using the cards, just get out your scissors and give them a good trim. That way you can't use 'em, but your history stays on your record.

Coddle Your New Card

15 When you do a balance transfer, you need to protect your low rate as if it were an endangered species—because if the credit card issuer has anything to say about it, it will be. Look, you don't really think the card company is excited about charging you no interest, do you? How the heck do they make money off of that? They only offer up the great deal to lure you over to their card. Then they start working overtime trying to get you to screw up so they have an excuse to change your zero interest rate, often to as much as 20 percent or more.

16 And the big screw-up they are hoping you don't know about is buried down in the fine print of your card agreement: make one late payment and you can kiss your zero deal good-bye. Even worse is that card companies are now scouring all your credit cards—remember, they can check your credit reports—to see if you have been late on any card, not just their card. So even if you always pay the zero-rate card on time, if you are late on any other card, your zero deal can be in jeopardy.

17 That's why I want you to make to make sure every credit card bill is paid ahead of schedule. Don't mail it in on the day it is due; that's late. Mail it in at least five days early. Better yet, convert your card to online bill pay so you can zap your payments over in time every month. And remember, it's only the minimum monthly payment that needs to be paid. That's not asking a lot.

Dealing with High-Rate Debt

18 Okay, I realize not everyone is going to qualify for these low-rate balance transfer deals, so let's run through how to take control of your cards if you are stuck with higher rates.

19 I want you to line up all your cards in descending order of their interest rates. Notice I said the card with the highest interest rate comes first. Not the one with the biggest balance.

20 Your strategy is to make the minimum monthly payment on every card, on time, every month. But your card with the highest interest

rate gets some special treatment. I want you to pay more than the minimum amount due on this card. The more you can pay, the better; but everyone should put in, at the minimum, an extra $20 each month. Push yourself hard to make that extra payment as large as possible. It can save you thousands of dollars in interest charges over time.

21 Keep this up every month until your card with the highest rate is paid off. Then turn your attention to the card with the next highest rate. In addition to the usual monthly minimum payment due on that second card, I want you to add in the entire amount you were previously paying on the first card (the one that's now paid off). So let's say you were paying a total of $200 a month on your original highest-rate card, and making a $75 monthly minimum on the second card. Well, now you are going to fork over $275 a month to the second card. And, of course, you'll continue to make the minimum monthly payment due on any other cards. Once your second card is paid off, move on to the third. If your monthly payment on that second card was $275, then that's what you should add to the minimum payment due on your third card. Get the idea? Rinse and repeat as often as needed, until you have all your debt paid off. For some of you this may take a year, for others it may take many years. That's okay. Just get yourself moving in the right direction and you'll be amazed how gratifying it is to find yourself taking control of your money rather than letting it control you.

22 And be sure to keep an eye on your FICO credit score. As you pay down your card balances—and build a record of paying on time—your score is indeed going to rise. Eventually your score may be high enough to finally qualify for a low-rate balance transfer offer.

Is Credit Counseling Right for You?

23 There is plenty of help available if you can't seem to get a solid grip on dealing with your credit card debt. But not all the help is good. Given that so many Americans are drowning in card debt, it's really no surprise that some enterprising—and underhanded—folks have figured out a way to make money off of this epidemic by charging high fees for counseling and advice.

24 So you need to make sure you choose an honest and fair credit counseling service. Start by getting references from the National Foundation for Credit Counseling.

25 Next, make an appointment to talk with a counselor face-to-face. A good counselor will question you thoroughly and in detail

about your financial situation before proposing anything. . If you are simply told right off the bat that you need a Debt Management Plan (see below), you should run out the door PDQ. That firm is not interested in truly helping you. They just want to hit you up with a bunch of fees.

26   A good counselor is also going to require that you attend education classes. This is not punishment! On the contrary, it's the best help you can get. Quite often, you can make the changes necessary to take control of your credit card spending just by learning a few good habits.

QUESTIONS FOR DISCUSSION AND WRITING

1. Writers of effective explaining essays focus their thesis for a specific audience. Describe the audience Orman addresses in her essay. Which sentences help you identify this audience? Which sentences in Orman's essay most clearly express her thesis for this audience?

2. Explaining essays typically use definition of terms, explanation of processes, and analyses of causes and effects. Find at least one example of each of the following strategies in Orman's essay: definition, process analysis, and causal analysis. In each case, decide if the information Orman gives is clear to you. Where do you need additional information or clarification?

3. To connect with her readers, Orman uses the second person, "you," and she uses informal language such as "you and your pals," "call 'em up," "more on this in a sec," and "sweet intro offer." Find other examples of informal language in her essay. Does this language work for her audience? Does it make the subject of finances more lively and readable? Explain.

4. Find one of the offers for credit cards that you, a friend, or a family member has recently received. Study the fine print. Then, in your own words, explain what the key points in the fine print mean in language that another member of your class can understand. Is Orman right about the "many snares and traps" that the card companies set for their customers?

5. Do some research online or in your library databases about recent reforms of credit card abuses. How do these regulations help reduce some of the more blatant abuses of credit card companies? Which of their unregulated practices can still lead to abusive lending practices? In what ways should credit card companies be further regulated?

DAVID VON DREHLE

Why Crime Went Away

Prereading Journal Entry

In your experience, have crime rates in your city or neighborhood risen or dropped in the past decade? If you are aware of possible increases or decreases in crime, is your opinion based on personal experiences, what your friends say, what you see on television, what you read in the media, or some combination of these?

David Von Drehle is a journalist with a prominent writing career. He was born in Denver in 1961, educated at the University of Denver and Oxford University, and has been a longtime writer for the Washington Post. He has earned Distinguished Writing Awards from the American Bar Association and the American Society of Newspaper Editors. Among his books are The Lowest of the Dead: Inside Death Row *(1995),* Dead Wrong: A Death Row Lawyer Speaks Out against Capital Punishment *(1998), and* Triangle: The Fire that Changed America *(2003). In the following article, which appeared in* Time *magazine in 2010, Von Drehle tries to explain why crime rates in the U.S. have decreased despite a recession and high unemployment. Possible causes include better police work, changing demographics, and high incarceration figures; however, as Von Drehle explains, precise cause and effect relationships in issues as complex as crime rates are difficult to determine.*

1   Health care, climate change, terrorism — is it even possible to solve big problems? The mood in Washington is not very hopeful these days. But take a look at what has happened to one of the biggest, toughest problems facing the country 20 years ago: violent crime. For years, Americans ranked crime at or near the top of their list of urgent issues. Every politician, from alderman to President, was expected to have a crime-fighting agenda, yet many experts despaired of solutions. By 1991, the murder rate in the U.S. reached a near record 9.8 per 100,000 people. Meanwhile, criminologists began to theorize that a looming generation of so-called superpredators would soon make things even worse.

2   Then, a breakthrough. Crime rates started falling. Apart from a few bumps and plateaus, they continued to drop through boom times and recessions, through peace and war, under Democrats and Republicans. Last year's murder rate may be the lowest since the mid-1960s,

according to preliminary statistics released by the Department of Justice. The human dimension of this turnaround is extraordinary: had the rate remained unchanged, an additional 170,000 Americans would have been murdered in the years since 1992. That's more U.S. lives than were lost in combat in World War I, Korea, Vietnam and Iraq — combined. In a single year, 2008, lower crime rates meant 40,000 fewer rapes, 380,000 fewer robberies, half a million fewer aggravated assaults and 1.6 million fewer burglaries than we would have seen if rates had remained at peak levels.

3   There's a catch, though. No one can convincingly explain exactly how the crime problem was solved. Police chiefs around the country credit improved police work. Demographers cite changing demographics of an aging population. Some theorists point to the evolution of the drug trade at both the wholesale and retail levels, while for veterans of the Clinton Administration, the preferred explanation is their initiative to hire more cops. Renegade economist Steven Levitt has speculated that legalized abortion caused the drop in crime. (Fewer unwanted babies in the 1970s and '80s grew up to be thugs in the 1990s and beyond.)

4   The truth probably lies in a mix of these factors, plus one more: the steep rise in the number of Americans in prison. As local, state and federal governments face an era of diminished resources, they will need a better understanding of how and why crime rates tumbled. A sour economy need not mean a return to lawless streets, but continued success in fighting crime will require more brains, especially in those neighborhoods where violence is still rampant and public safety is a tattered dream.

The Lockup Factor

5   In his book *Why Crime Rates Fell*, Tufts University sociologist John Conklin concluded that up to half of the improvement was due to a single factor: more people in prison. The U.S. prison population grew by more than half a million during the 1990s and continued to grow, although more slowly, in the next decade. Go back half a century: as sentencing became more lenient in the 1960s and '70s, the crime rate started to rise. When lawmakers responded to the crime wave by building prisons and mandating tough sentences, the number of prisoners increased and the number of crimes fell.

6   Common sense, you might think. But this is not a popular conclusion among criminologists, according to Conklin. "There is a tendency, perhaps for ideological reasons, not to want to see the connection," he says.

Incarceration is to crime what amputation is to gangrene — it can work, but a humane physician would rather find a way to prevent wounds and cure infections before the saw is necessary. Prison is expensive, demoralizing and deadening. "Increased sentencing in some communities has removed entire generations of young men" from some minority communities, says San Francisco police chief George Gascón. "Has that been a factor in lowering crime? I think it probably has. I think it also probably has had a detrimental effect on those communities."

7   Prisoners leave saddened parents, abandoned mates, fatherless children. Of course, in many cases, those families are better off with their violent relatives behind bars. But a court system that clobbers first-time offenders with mandatory sentences — sometimes for nonviolent crimes — will inevitably lock up thousands of not-so-bad guys alongside the hardened criminals. Not everyone agrees on the definition of a nonviolent criminal, but studies have estimated that as many as one-third of all U.S. prison inmates are in that category, most of them locked up on drug charges.

8   R. Dwayne Betts may be one of those not-so-bad guys, sentenced to nine years in an adult prison on a first offense at age 16. It's hard to know if a less severe punishment would have worked. Betts hijacked a stranger's car at gunpoint, which is a dangerous and depraved thing to do. But he also showed signs of promise, having earned his high school diploma a year ahead of schedule. Betts gradually learned to navigate the violence and boredom of prison and emerged in 2006 ready to launch a respectable life, enrolling in college, getting married and writing a book called A Question of Freedom. He looks on those prison years as a costly void, "a waste of society's time and money in the sense that I didn't get any rehabilitation or any educational opportunities." Most inmates, Betts continues, can't do what he has done; they don't have the tools. "I was fortunate in that I knew how to read, I liked books, was pretty intelligent, and I knew I had no intention of being locked up for the rest of my life."

9   With government budgets hammered red by the Great Recession, the high cost and human toll of the lock-'em-up strategy has made it hard to sustain. California lawmakers decided last month to cut the number of state prisoners by 6,500 in the coming year. Other states are already at work, on a smaller scale. In 2008, the most recent year for which data are available, 20 states reduced their prisoner counts by a total of nearly 10,000 inmates. As a result, according to the Justice Department, the number of state and federal prisoners grew by less

than 1% nationwide — the smallest increase in nearly a decade. (The number of blacks behind bars is, in fact, falling as the rate of incarceration among African Americans has dropped nearly 10% from its peak.)

The Data-Processing Factor

10   In interviews with police chiefs across the country, *Time* heard the same story again and again. It is the saga of a revolution in law enforcement, a new way of battling the bad guys, and it begins, at least in some tellings, with a colorful New York City transit cop named Jack Maple. He worked the subways back when the city was averaging four, five, almost six murders a day, and even though the experts informed him that crime was inseparable from such "root causes" as poverty and despair, Maple developed a theory that the key cause was criminals. If police collected and analyzed enough data, they could figure out where the criminals liked to operate and when they tended to be there. Voilà: go there and arrest them, and crime would go down.

11   Maple sold his boss, William Bratton, on the idea of data-driven policing, and when Bratton was promoted to police commissioner under New York City Mayor Rudolph Giuliani in 1994, his ideas went citywide. They evolved into CompStat, a real-time database of crime statistics and other intelligence useful for pinpointing trouble spots and targeting resources. CompStat put precinct captains and district commanders in the hot seat, and results followed. Crime plummeted. The city of fear became one of the safest major cities in America, and Commissioner Bratton landed on the cover of *Time*.

12   A new survey of retired New York City police supervisors, however, confirms what many skeptics have suspected for years. Pressure from the twice-weekly CompStat reviews inspired a certain amount of fudging (exactly how much is unknown). Police hunted for bargains on eBay so that they could adjust theft reports to reflect lower values of stolen goods, magically transforming major crimes into minor ones. A fight involving a weapon — aggravated assault — might become a mere fistfight by the time the police report was filed. Nevertheless, behind the gamesmanship was a genuine drop in crime. (Murder is down an astonishing 80% from its peak in New York City, and it's very hard to fudge a murder.) Similar declines have been recorded in many other cities.

13   Versions of CompStat now shape police work in metropolitan areas from coast to coast. In the Maryland suburbs of Washington, for example, Prince George's County chief Roberto Hylton sings the praises of "a technology that we call Active Crime Reporting, which provides information every 15 minutes, so I can see, even from a laptop away

from work, the whole crime picture of the county. I can shift resources. It actually provides me with the trends, patterns that have occurred the previous week, previous day, maybe even the previous year." Paired with a program to improve trust and communication between police and crime-plagued communities, the data-driven approach is working, Hylton says.

The New Economy of Crime

14   Criminologists will tell you, however, that the tale of CompStat is not the whole story. New York City's crime rate actually began to drop a couple of years before Giuliani became mayor. And rates began falling in cities without CompStat at about the same time — though not as rapidly as in New York. For while police were changing tactics, the criminals were shifting gears too.

15   The high-crime hell of the 1980s and early '90s was a period of chaos in the illegal drug trade. Powder cocaine was generally measured and sold in multiple-dose amounts behind locked doors, but crack was relatively cheap and highly portable. Upstart young dealers saw an opening and shouldered their way into a business long dominated by established kingpins. Trading valuable drugs for ready cash in plain sight was a recipe for robbery and intimidation. Dealers armed themselves for protection, and soon every teenage squabble in crack territory carried a risk that bullets would fly.

16   From that low point, the drug business has settled down in most cities. Distribution is better organized. Crack use has fallen by perhaps 20%, according to UCLA criminal-justice expert Mark Kleiman, as younger users have turned against a drug that had devastated their neighborhoods. Opiates and marijuana are illegal, just like cocaine, but they don't turn users into paranoid, agitated, would-be supermen. "A heroin corner is a happy corner" where junkies quietly nod off, says David Simon, creator of the TV series *The Wire*, who used to cover cops for the Baltimore *Sun*.

17   Criminologist Conklin believes that two statistics in particular — median age and the unemployment rate — help explain the ebb and flow of crime. Violence is typically a young man's vice; it has been said that the most effective crime-fighting tool is a 30th birthday. The arrival of teenage baby boomers in the 1960s coincided with a rise in crime, and rates have declined as America has grown older. The median age in 1990, near the peak of the crime wave, was 32, according to Conklin. A decade later, it was over 35. Today, it is 36-plus. (It is also true that today's young men are less prone to crime. The juvenile crime rate in 2007, the most recent available, was the lowest in at least a generation.)

18   "The effect of unemployment," Conklin adds, "is problematic." Indeed it is. Heather MacDonald of the Manhattan Institute dissected this issue in a recent *Wall Street Journal* op-ed. "As the economy started shedding jobs in 2008," she wrote, "criminologists and pundits predicted that crime would shoot up, since poverty, as the 'root causes' theory holds, begets criminals. Instead, the opposite happened. Over 7 million lost jobs later, crime has plummeted to its lowest level since the early 1960s." To MacDonald, this is proof that data-driven police work and tougher sentencing are the answer to crime — not social-welfare programs. Conklin thinks it may be too soon to tell. "The unemployment rate began to spike less than a year ago. We may yet see the pressure show up in crime rates," he says. It's fair to say, though, that the belief in a simple cause-and-effect relationship between income and crime has worn pretty thin.

19   The danger of chronic joblessness is that jobs are a part of the social fabric. Ideally, they connect people to constructive projects and well-ordered institutions. They foster self-discipline and reward responsibility. Some optimists theorize that crime rates might continue to drop in coming years as police pit their strength against a dwindling army of criminals. In his recent book, *When Brute Force Fails*, UCLA's Kleiman argues that new strategies for targeting repeat offenders — including reforms to make probation an effective sanction rather than a feckless joke — could cut crime and reduce prison populations simultaneously. Safer communities, in turn, might produce more hopeful and well-disciplined kids. It's a sweet image to contemplate in this sour era, but a lack of jobs is a cloud over the picture.

20   A more realistic view might be the one dramatized in Simon's HBO series, *The Wire*. In 60 episodes spread across five seasons from 2002 to 2008, the program humanized this tangled question of crime fighting with penetrating sophistication. CompStat-obsessed politicians fostered numbers-fudging in the ranks. Cool-headed drug lords struggled to tame their war-torn industry. Gangs battled for turf under the nodding gaze of needy junkies. Prisons warehoused the violent and nonviolent with little regard for who could be rehabilitated. It made for award-winning drama, but it also was a reminder that in every American city, neighborhoods remain where violence still reigns and it simply isn't safe to walk around. And national crime statistics mean nothing to the millions of people who live there.

21   In those places, the crime problem isn't solved; the fight is scarcely begun. To the many factors that have combined to cool the

nation's violent fever, more must be added — more creativity, more pragmatism, more honest concern for the victims of inner-city crime. It's a daunting prospect. The will to keep working on the most persistent pockets of lawlessness will be severely tested in this era of unbalanced budgets. You might be tempted to say it's hopeless. But that's what people were saying 20 years ago, just before progress broke through.

QUESTIONS FOR DISCUSSION AND WRITING

1. Reread Von Drehle's article and list the major causes he discusses that have contributed to a reduced crime rate. For each of these causes, however, Von Drehle analyzes both the significance of the cause as well as possible problems with assuming that this cause is a main or major factor in reducing crime. Based on your analysis, rate these causes (first, second, third, etc.) according to their probable effect on reducing crime. Explain your choices.

2. Von Drehle, as a journalist, does extensive research and fact gathering in order to write this article. Reread his article to determine whom he interviewed in order to gather his information and what his major sources were. List the people and resources he references in his article. As a reader, are you convinced by his analysis and research?

3. In his next-to-last paragraph, Von Drehle discusses the popular crime show, *The Wire*. Do you think that information and episodes from a television series constitute reliable evidence to help analyze increases or decreases in crime rates? Explain why you think this paragraph does or does not belong in an article attempting to explain causes of decreasing crime to readers of *Time* magazine.

4. Can you imagine other possible causes for reduction in crime rates? Do rising rates of education help contribute to lower crime rates? Might increased gun ownership contribute to less rather than more crime? Could improved technologies in communication (computers, televisions, Web cameras on streets and in businesses, cell phones, social networking, Google searches, Twitter, or other technologies) play a significant role?

5. Write your own essay on trends in crime rates in your own city, town, or campus. Focus on a particular type of crime to help narrow your investigation. Consider rates of rape on your campus or in your town, rates of petty theft or burglaries, rates of identity theft or white collar crimes, or domestic abuse rates. Research online and in your library databases, but also find local experts to interview. Explain what are the most important causes that have led to these changes in crime rates.

JEAN KILBOURNE

Jesus Is a Brand of Jeans

Prereading Journal Entry

Make a list of the purchases you have made in the last few days. Try to make the list as inclusive as you can—groceries, clothes, coffee, fast food, purchases at shops, malls, and even online purchases. Where you can remember, indicate the brand of each product. With a list of the brand name products you purchased, try to recall any advertisements you have seen about this product. Do you think you would have purchased these brands if you had not seen any advertisements for these products?

A graduate of Wellesley College with an education doctorate from Boston University, Jean Kilbourne is the award-winning author of Can't Buy My Love: How Advertising Changes the Way We Think and Feel *(1999) and* So Sexy, So Soon *(2008). She is internationally recognized for her work on alcohol and tobacco advertising and for her analysis of images of women in advertising. She is also known for her award-winning documentary,* Killing Us Softly. *Kilbourne has appeared on hundreds of radio and TV programs, including* All Things Considered, *the* Today Show, *and* Oprah. *The* New York Times Magazine *recently named her as one of the three most popular speakers on college campuses. The following essay appeared in the September 2006 issue of* New Internationalist *and was accompanied by eleven sample advertisements, two of which are reproduced with this article.*

1   A recent ad for Thule car-rack systems features a child in the back-seat of a car, seatbelt on. Next to the child, assorted sporting gear is carefully strapped into a child's carseat. The headline says: "We Know What Matters to You." In case one misses the point, further copy adds: "Your gear is a priority."

2   Another ad features an attractive young couple in bed. The man is on top of the woman, presumably making love to her. However, her face is completely covered by a magazine, open to a double-page photo of a car. The man is gazing passionately at the car. The copy reads, "The ultimate attraction."

3   These ads are meant to be funny. Taken individually, I suppose they might seem amusing or, at worst, tasteless. As someone who has studied ads for a long time, however, I see them as part of a pattern: just

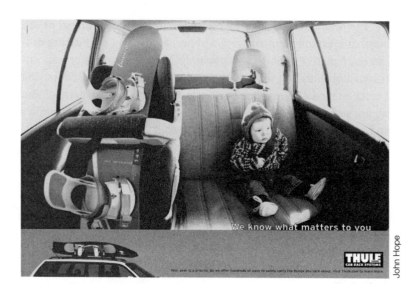

We know what matters to you

THULE
CAR RACK SYSTEMS

Your gear is a priority. So we offer hundreds of ways to safely carry the things you care about. Visit Thule.com to learn more.

two of many ads that state or imply that products are more important than people. Ads have long promised us a better relationship via a product: *buy this and you will be loved.* But more recently they have gone beyond that proposition to promise us a relationship with the product itself: *buy this and it will love you.* The product is not so much the means to an end, as the end itself.

4   After all, it is easier to love a product than a person. Relationships with human beings are messy, unpredictable, sometimes dangerous. "When was the last time you felt this comfortable in a relationship?" asks an ad for shoes. Our shoes never ask us to wash the dishes or tell us we're getting fat. Even more important, products don't betray us. "You can love it without getting your heart broken," proclaims a car ad. One certainly can't say that about loving a human being, as love without vulnerability is impossible.

5   We are surrounded by hundreds, thousands of messages every day that link our deepest emotions to products, that objectify people and trivialize our most heartfelt moments and relationships. Every emotion is used to sell us something. Our wish to protect our children is leveraged to make us buy an expensive car. A long marriage simply provides the occasion for a diamond necklace. A painful reunion between a father and his estranged daughter is dramatized to sell us a phone system. Everything in the world – nature, animals, people – is just so much stuff to be consumed or to be used to sell us something.

6   The problem with advertising isn't that it creates artificial needs, but that it exploits our very real and human desires. Advertising promotes a bankrupt concept of *relationship*. Most of us yearn for committed relationships that will last. We are not stupid: we know that buying a certain brand of cereal won't bring us one inch closer to that goal. But we are surrounded by advertising that yokes our needs with products and promises us that *things* will deliver what in fact they never can. In the world of advertising, lovers are things and things are lovers.

7   It may be that there is no other way to depict relationships when the ultimate goal is to sell products. But this apparently bottomless consumerism not only depletes the world's resources, it also depletes our inner resources. It leads inevitably to narcissism and solipsism. It becomes difficult to imagine a way of relating that isn't objectifying and exploitative.

Tuned In

8   Most people feel that advertising is not something to take seriously. Other aspects of the media are serious – the violent films, the trashy talk shows, the bowdlerization of the news. But not advertising! Although much more attention has been paid to the cultural impact of advertising in recent years than ever before, just about everyone still feels personally exempt from its influence. What I hear more than anything else at my lectures is: "I don't pay attention to ads... I just tune them out... they have no effect on me." I hear this most from people wearing clothes emblazoned with logos. In truth, we are all influenced. There is no way to tune out this much information, especially when it is designed to break through the 'tuning out' process. As advertising critic Sut Jhally put it: "To not be influenced by advertising would be to live outside of culture. No human being lives outside of culture."

9   Much of advertising's power comes from this belief that it does not affect us. As Joseph Goebbels said: "This is the secret of propaganda: those who are to be persuaded by it should be completely immersed in the ideas of the propaganda, without ever noticing that they are being immersed in it." Because we think advertising is trivial, we are less on guard, less critical, than we might otherwise be. While we're laughing, sometimes sneering, the commercial does its work.

10   Taken individually, ads are silly, sometimes funny, certainly nothing to worry about. But cumulatively they create a climate of cynicism that

is poisonous to relationships. Ad after ad portrays our real lives as dull and ordinary, commitment to human beings as something to be avoided. Because of the pervasiveness of this kind of message, we learn from childhood that it is far safer to make a commitment to a product than to a person, far easier to be loyal to a brand. Many end up feeling romantic about material objects yet deeply cynical about other human beings.

Unnatural Passions

11   We know by now that advertising often turns people into objects. Women's bodies – and men's bodies too these days – are dismembered, packaged and used to sell everything from chainsaws to chewing gum, champagne to shampoo. Self-image is deeply affected. The self-esteem of girls plummets as they reach adolescence partly because they cannot possibly escape the message that their bodies are objects, and imperfect objects at that. Boys learn that masculinity requires a kind of ruthlessness, even brutality.

12   Advertising encourages us not only to objectify each other but to feel passion for products rather than our partners. This is especially dangerous when the products are potentially addictive, because addicts do feel they are in a relationship with their substances. I once heard an alcoholic joke that Jack Daniels was her most constant lover. When I was a smoker, I felt that my cigarettes were my friends. Advertising reinforces these beliefs, so we are twice seduced – by the ads and by the substances themselves.

13   The addict is the ideal consumer. Ten percent of drinkers consume over sixty percent of all the alcohol sold. Most of them are alcoholics or people in desperate trouble – but they are also the alcohol industry's very best customers. Advertisers spend enormous amounts of money on psychological research and understand addiction well. They use this knowledge to target children (because if you hook them early they are yours for life), to encourage all people to consume more, in spite of often dangerous consequences for all of us, and to create a climate of denial in which all kinds of addictions flourish. This they do with full intent, as we see so clearly in the 'secret documents' of the tobacco industry that have been made public in recent years.

14   The consumer culture encourages us not only to buy more but to seek our identity and fulfillment through what we buy, to express our individuality through our 'choices' of products. Advertising corrupts

relationships and then offers us products, both as solace and as substitutes for the intimate human connection we all long for and need.

15   In the world of advertising, lovers grow cold, spouses grow old, children grow up and away – but possessions stay with us and never change. Seeking the outcomes of a healthy relationship through products cannot work. Sometimes it leads us into addiction. But at best the possessions can never deliver the promised goods. They can't make us happy or loved or less alone or safe. If we believe they can, we are doomed to disappointment. No matter how much we love them, they will never love us back.

16   Some argue that advertising simply reflects societal values rather than affecting them. Far from being a passive mirror of society, however, advertising is a pervasive medium of influence and persuasion. Its influence is cumulative, often subtle and primarily unconscious. A former editor-in-chief of *Advertising Age*, the leading advertising publication in North America, once claimed: "Only eight percent of an ad's message is received by the conscious mind. The rest is worked and reworked deep within, in the recesses of the brain."

17   Advertising performs much the same function in industrial society as myth did in ancient societies. It is both a creator and perpetuator of the dominant values of the culture, the social norms by which most people govern their behavior. At the very least, advertising helps to create a climate in which certain values flourish and others are not reflected at all.

18   Advertising is not only our physical environment, it is increasingly our spiritual environment as well. By definition, however, it is only interested in materialistic values. When spiritual values show up in ads, it is only in order to sell us something. Eternity is a perfume by Calvin Klein. Infiniti is an automobile, and Hydra Zen a moisturizer. Jesus is a brand of jeans.

19   Sometimes the allusion is more subtle, as in the countless alcohol ads featuring the bottle surrounded by a halo of light. Indeed products such as jewelry shining in a store window are often displayed as if they were sacred objects. Advertising co-opts our sacred symbols in order to evoke an immediate emotional response. Media critic Neil Postman referred to this as "cultural rape."

20   It is commonplace to observe that consumerism has become the religion of our time (with advertising its holy text), but the criticism usually stops short of what is at the heart of the comparison. Both advertising and religion share a belief in transformation, but most religions believe that this requires sacrifice. In the world of advertising,

enlightenment is achieved instantly by purchasing material goods. An ad for a watch says, "It's not your handbag. It's not your neighborhood. It's not your boyfriend. It's your watch that tells most about who you are." Of course, this cheapens authentic spirituality and transcendence. This junk food for the soul leaves us hungry, empty, malnourished.

Substitute Stories

21   Human beings used to be influenced primarily by the stories of our particular tribe or community, not by stories that are mass-produced and market-driven. As George Gerbner, one of the world's most respected researchers on the influence of the media, said: "For the first time in human history, most of the stories about people, life and values are told not by parents, schools, churches, or others in the community who have something to tell, but by a group of distant conglomerates that have something to sell."

22   Although it is virtually impossible to measure the influence of advertising on a culture, we can learn something by looking at cultures only recently exposed to it. In 1980 the Gwich'in tribe of Alaska got television, and therefore massive advertising, for the first time. Satellite dishes, video games and VCRs were not far behind. Before this, the Gwich'in lived much the way their ancestors had for generations. Within 10 years, the young members of the tribe were so drawn by television they no longer had time to learn ancient hunting methods, their parents' language or their oral history. Legends told around campfires could not compete with Beverly Hills 90210. Beaded moccasins gave way to Nike sneakers, and 'tundra tea' to Folger's instant coffee.

23   As multinational chains replace local character, we end up in a world in which everyone is Gapped and Starbucked. Shopping malls kill vibrant downtown centers locally and create a universe of uniformity internationally. We end up in a world ruled by, in John Maynard Keynes's phrase, the values of the casino. On this deeper level, rampant commercialism undermines our physical and psychological health, our environment and our civic life, and creates a toxic society.

24   Advertising creates a world view that is based upon cynicism, dissatisfaction and craving. Advertisers aren't evil. They are just doing their job, which is to sell a product; but the consequences, usually unintended, are often destructive. In the history of the world there has never been a

propaganda effort to match that of advertising in the past 50 years. More thought, more effort, more money goes into advertising than has gone into any other campaign to change social consciousness. The story that advertising tells is that the way to be happy, to find satisfaction – and the path to political freedom, as well – is through the consumption of material objects. And the major motivating force for social change throughout the world today is this belief that happiness comes from the market.

QUESTIONS FOR DISCUSSION AND WRITING

1. Reread your Prereading Journal Entry on the products you have purchased recently. How would you judge the effects of advertising on your purchases? Would you agree that you are like many of the people Kilbourne hears from who say that they don't pay attention to ads—they just tune them out, or would you agree with advertising critic Sut Jhally who says, "To not be influenced by advertising would be to live outside of culture. No human being lives outside of culture."?

2. At one point in her essay, Kilbourne says that "advertising promotes a bankrupt concept of *relationship*." What does Kilbourne mean by this statement? Is this statement actually the thesis of her article? Explain why or why not.

3. In her articles and books, Kilbourne often wants to persuade girls and women that because advertisements objectify women, they contribute to unhealthy self-images for women. Where in this essay do you see Kilbourne making this argument? Where does her argument focus on issues other than self-image? What is her overall argument?

4. Kilbourne is writing an essay that attempts to persuade her readers that advertising *causes* certain *effects*. List the *effects* of advertising that she describes. What examples, images, statistics, or testimony by experts does she give as support for each of these possible effects? Which effects is she able to support with specifics and which need more support in order for the reader to be convinced? Explain.

5. Advertising, Kilbourne claims, "creates a toxic society." Look up *The Story of Stuff* on Google, and watch the video made by Annie Leonard. In what ways are Kilbourne's and Leonard's messages similar? In what ways are they different?

Why We Crave Horror Movies

Prereading Journal Entry

If you have read a novel by Stephen King, explain why you did (or did not) like the book. If you liked the novel, explain exactly why you found the book interesting. Exactly what is it that attracts you to (or repels you from) a Stephen King novel?

It may be hard for Stephen King fans to believe that his first major novel, Carrie, *was published in 1975, over thirty-five years ago. Although Stephen King established his reputation with early classics such as* The Shining *(1977) and* The Stand *(1978), he continues his amazingly prolific career with award-winning novels such as* Bag of Bones *(1998) and* Black House *(2001). His more recent publications also include his best-selling* On Writing: A Memoir of the Craft *(2000),* From a Buick 8 *(2002),* Lisey's Story *(2006), and* Just after Sunset *(2008). "With Stephen King," says critic Chelsea Yarbro, "you never have to ask 'Who's afraid of the big bad wolf?'— You are. And he knows it." But why are we attracted to the things we fear? As one reader put it, "Why, somebody please tell me, was I holding on to his book so hard that my knuckles had begun to turn white?" In the following essay, King explains that we indulge in horror in order "have fun," but it is "a very peculiar sort of fun, indeed."*

1   I think we're all mentally ill; those of us outside the asylums only hide it a little better—and maybe not all that much better, after all. We've all known people who talk to themselves, people who sometimes squinch their faces into horrible grimaces when they believe no one is watching, people who have some hysterical fear—of snakes, the dark, the tight place, the long drop . . . and, of course, those final worms and grubs that are waiting so patiently underground.

2   When we pay our four or five bucks and seat ourselves at tenth-row center in a theater showing a horror movie, we are daring the nightmare. Why? Some of the reasons are simple and obvious. To show that we can, that we are not afraid, that we can ride this roller coaster. Which is not to say that a really good horror movie may not surprise a scream out of us at some point, the way we may scream when the roller coaster twists through a complete 360 or plows through a lake at the

bottom of the drop. And horror movies, like roller coasters, have always been the special province of the young; by the time one turns 40 or 50, one's appetite for double twists or 360-degree loops may be considerably depleted.

3   We also go to re-establish our feelings of essential normality; the horror movie is innately conservative, even reactionary. Freda Jackson as the horrible melting woman in *Die, Monster, Die!* confirms for us that no matter how far we may be removed from the beauty of a Robert Redford or a Diana Ross, we are still light-years from true ugliness.

4   And we go to have fun.

5   Ah, but this is where the ground starts to slope away, isn't it? Because this is a very peculiar sort of fun, indeed. The fun comes from seeing others menaced—sometimes killed. One critic has suggested that if pro football has become the voyeur's version of combat, then the horror film has become the modern version of the public lynching.

6   It is true that the mythic, "fairy-tale" horror film intends to take away the shades of gray. . . . It urges us to put away our more civilized and adult penchant for analysis and to become children again, seeing things in pure blacks and whites. It may be that horror movies provide psychic relief on this level because this invitation to lapse into simplicity, irrationality and even outright madness is extended so rarely. We are told we may allow our emotions a free rein . . . or no rein at all.

7   If we are all insane, then sanity becomes a matter of degree. If your insanity leads you to carve up women like Jack the Ripper or the Cleveland Torso Murderer, we clap you away in the funny farm (but neither of those two amateur-night surgeons was ever caught, heh-heh-heh); if, on the other hand, your insanity leads you only to talk to yourself when you're under stress or to pick your nose on your morning bus, then you are left alone to go about your business . . . though it is doubtful that you will ever be invited to the best parties.

8   The potential lyncher is in almost all of us (excluding saints, past and present; but then, most saints have been crazy in their own ways), and every now and then, he has to be let loose to scream and roll around in the grass. Our emotions and our fears form their own body, and we recognize that it demands its own exercise to attain proper muscle tone. Certain of these emotional muscles are accepted—even

exalted—in civilized society; they are, of course, the emotions that tend to maintain the status quo of civilization itself. Love, friendship, loyalty, kindness—these are all the emotions that we applaud, emotions that have been immortalized in the couplets of Hallmark cards and in the verses (I don't dare call it poetry) of Leonard Nimoy.

9   When we exhibit these emotions, society showers us with positive reinforcement; we learn this even before we get out of diapers. When, as children, we hug our rotten little puke of a sister and give her a kiss, all the aunts and uncles smile and twit and cry, "Isn't he the sweetest little thing?" Such coveted treats as chocolate-covered graham crackers often follow. But if we deliberately slam the rotten little puke of a sister's fingers in the door, sanctions follow—angry remonstrance from parents, aunts and uncles; instead of a chocolate-covered graham cracker, a spanking.

10   But anticivilization emotions don't go away, and they demand periodic exercise. We have such "sick" jokes as, "What's the difference between a truckload of bowling balls and a truckload of dead babies?" (You can't unload a truckload of bowling balls with a pitchfork . . . a joke, by the way, that I heard originally from a ten-year-old). Such a joke may surprise a laugh or a grin out of us even as we recoil, a possibility that confirms the thesis: If we share a brotherhood of man, then we also share an insanity of man. None of which is intended as a defense of either the sick joke or insanity but merely as an explanation of why the best horror films, like the best fairy tales, manage to be reactionary, anarchistic, and revolutionary all at the same time.

11   The mythic horror movie, like the sick joke, has a dirty job to do. It deliberately appeals to all that is worst in us. It is morbidity unchained, our most base instincts let free, our nastiest fantasies realized . . . and it all happens, fittingly enough, in the dark. For those reasons, good liberals often shy away from horror films. For myself, I like to see the most aggressive of them— *Dawn of the Dead*, for instance—as lifting a trap door in the civilized forebrain and throwing a basket of raw meat to the hungry alligators swimming around in that subterranean river beneath.

12   Why bother? Because it keeps them from getting out, man. It keeps them down there and me up here. It was Lennon and McCartney who said that all you need is love, and I would agree with that.

13   As long as you keep the gators fed.

QUESTIONS FOR DISCUSSION AND WRITING

1. Stephen King gives several reasons why we crave horror films. List at least four of the reasons he gives in the first half of the essay. Which of these reasons most closely describes why you watch horror films—if in fact you do?

2. One of Stephen King's purposes in this essay is to make a philosophical statement about the nature of human beings. According to King, what is the essential nature of human beings? How does King's notion of humanity contrast with the more popular civilized notions about human beings?

3. One of King's strategies is to suggest, as he does in paragraph 2, that the reasons why we watch horror films are "simple and obvious." Are the reasons he gives simple and obvious? Do you watch horror films for the anticivilized motives that King suggests? Does King's strategy make you more likely to agree with his stated reasons and explanations? Why or why not?

4. Although King's audience is anyone who watches or is fascinated by horror, he focuses particularly on younger readers or viewers. Where in his essay does King address his younger audience?

5. King chooses to write his essay in the first person plural, using "we" throughout the essay. Find several passages where King uses the first person plural address. How does this strategy make his overall argument more effective than using the more common first person singular "I" or even using the third person? Explain.

6. Many activities, hobbies, or sports—rock climbing, contact sports, gymnastics, taking difficult courses, learning to fly, snowboarding, giving a speech—have an element that is challenging but perhaps irrational or difficult to explain. If you have an activity that is mentally or physically dangerous, scary, or risky, write an essay explaining why you do what you do.

BUD HERRON

Cat Bathing as a Martial Art

Prereading Journal Entry

If you have ever trained an animal—cat, dog, horse, pig, or any other animal—to do some specific task, describe the steps in that process to someone interested in learning the finer points of training. What are the preparatory stages, what are the key steps, and what are the pitfalls to avoid?

Howard "Bud" Herron was for many years the publisher of The Republic, a newspaper in Columbus, Indiana. He originally wrote "Cat Bathing" for the Saturday Evening Post, but it was posted on the Internet and circulated in e-mails and posted on dozens of Web pages until it became a classic. In the humorous tradition of a James Thurber, Mark Twain, or Dave Barry, Herron explains, with serious purpose but exaggerated details, the specific steps to bring a cat, soap, and water together for a brief but exciting, almost Olympic battle. One of the most interesting tourist attractions in Key West, Florida, is—or used to be—a troupe of trained cats. They were trained to sit on their perches, jump through hoops, and even jump over fire and water obstacles. At sunset, hundreds of tourists would gather and watch the spectacle, not believing that cats could be trained without external force to do anything on command. Herron's essay also appeals to our incredulity that cats could somehow be dragged to water and given a bath—without inflicting permanent bodily harm on either the cat or the owner. Perhaps there are other successful approaches—such as a strong sedative for the cat—but Herron shows that, with the proper preparation and frame of mind, a cat can be successfully bathed, rinsed, and dried.

1   Some people say cats never have to be bathed. They say cats lick themselves clean. They say cats have a special enzyme of some sort in their saliva that works like new, improved Wisk—dislodging the dirt where it hides and whisking it away.

2   I've spent most of my life believing this folklore. Like most blind believers, I've been able to discount all the facts to the contrary: the kitty odors that lurk in the corners of the garage and dirt smudges that cling to the throw rug by the fireplace. The time comes, however, when a man must face reality, when he must look squarely in the face of massive public sentiment to the contrary and announce: "This cat smells like a port-a-potty on a hot day in Juarez." When that day arrives at your house, as it has at mine, I have some advice you might consider as you place your feline friend under your arm and head for the bathtub:

3   ▪ Know that although the cat has the advantage of quickness and lack of concern for human life, you have the advantage of strength. Capitalize on that advantage by selecting the battlefield. Don't try to bathe him in an open area where he can force you to chase him. Pick a very small bathroom. If your bathroom is more than four feet

square, I recommend that you get in the tub with the cat and close the sliding-glass doors as if you were about to take a shower. (A simple shower curtain will not do. A berserk cat can shred a three-ply rubber curtain quicker than a politician can shift positions.)

4 ▪ Know that a cat has claws and will not hesitate to remove all the skin from your body. Your advantage here is that you are smart and know how to dress to protect yourself. I recommend canvas overalls tucked into high-top construction boots, a pair of steel-mesh gloves, an army helmet, a hockey face mask, and a long-sleeved flak jacket.

5 ▪ Prepare everything in advance. There is no time to go out for a towel when you have a cat digging a hole in your flak jacket. Draw the water. Make sure the bottle of kitty shampoo is inside the glass enclosure. Make sure the towel can be reached, even if you are lying on your back in the water.

6 ▪ Use the element of surprise. Pick up your cat nonchalantly, as if to simply carry him to his supper dish. (Cats will not usually notice your strange attire. They have little or no interest in fashion as a rule. If he does notice your garb, calmly explain that you are taking part in a product testing experiment for J. C. Penney.)

7 ▪ Once you are inside the bathroom, speed is essential to survival. In a single liquid motion, shut the bathroom door, step into the tub enclosure, slide the glass door shut, dip the cat in the water, and squirt him with shampoo. You have begun one of the wildest 45 seconds of your life.

8 ▪ Cats have no handles. Add the fact that he now has soapy fur, and the problem is radically compounded. Do not expect to hold on to him for more than two or three seconds at a time. When you have him, however, you must remember to give him another squirt of shampoo and rub like crazy. He'll then spring free and fall back into the water, thereby rinsing himself off. (The national record for cats is three latherings, so don't expect too much.)

9 ▪ Next, the cat must be dried. Novice cat bathers always assume this part will be the most difficult, for humans generally are worn out at this point and the cat is just getting really determined. In fact, the drying is simple compared to what you have just been through. That's because by now the cat is semi-permanently affixed to your right leg. You simply pop the drain plug with your foot, reach for your towel and wait. (Occasionally, however, the cat will end up clinging to the top of your army helmet. If this happens, the best

thing you can do is to shake him loose and to encourage him toward your leg.) After all the water is drained from the tub, it is a simple matter to just reach down and dry the cat.

10   In a few days the cat will relax enough to be removed from your leg. He will usually have nothing to say for about three weeks and will spend a lot of time sitting with his back to you. He might even become psychoceramic and develop the fixed stare of a plaster figurine. You will be tempted to assume he is angry. This isn't usually the case. As a rule he is simply plotting ways to get through your defenses and injure you for life the next time you decide to give him a bath. But at least now he is clean.

QUESTIONS FOR DISCUSSION AND WRITING

1. Herron doesn't actually list the basic steps in giving a cat a bath, but we can reconstruct the main steps in his recommended process. Reread his essay and then list and describe the key steps in the process.

2. In order to appeal to its audience, humor on the Internet needs to be short and succinct. Readers are not going to scroll through pages of a long-winded essay. They want something that gets their attention quickly and provides an amusing break in the day. How well does Herron succeed in writing a humorous piece suitable for the Internet? Cite specific passages from the essay to support your explanation.

3. As writers such as Dave Barry know, humor often depends on exaggeration. Herron's essay is jam-packed with exaggerated descriptions and details. List phrases from the essay where Herron makes us laugh by exaggerating parts of his instructions. Which parts did you find the funniest?

4. Humorists love to use vivid language, comparisons, and images to create impressive word images for their readers. In paragraph 1, for example, Herron uses a simile—a comparison using *like* or *as*—when he says that his "cat smells like a port-a-potty on a hot day in Juarez." List all the other similes or uses of figurative language you can find in the essay. Which of these did you find especially humorous? Explain.

5. Write your own "how-to" essay on some subject you know well. Think of activities you are familiar with and then imagine you are writing to readers who know something about your subject, but don't know the particular steps in the process of doing something or making something. You may be either humorous or serious, but be sure the steps in your process are clear, specific, and complete. Answer all the relevant *who, what, when, where, how,* and *why* questions.

Wine Tasting: How to Fool Some of the People All of the Time

Prereading Journal Entry

Describe some esoteric activity such as preparing gourmet foods, selecting and serving vintage wines, or appreciating fine art, classical music, or jazz. What should novices know about this activity? What should they learn to do—or not do?

Michael Jones, an international business major at Colorado State University, decided to write his essay on wine tasting. Rather than describe the process in sophisticated language for the wine aficionado, Jones adds some humor to his essay by creating a fictitious history about the origins of the ritual. As his teacher Emily Golson explains, when she read his paper aloud in class, everyone was smiling. When she asked how many people believed what Jones had written, almost every student raised his or her hand. Although Jones quickly admitted that he invented most of his history of wine tasting, his essay shows how to appreciate wine—without becoming too snobbish about the whole process.

Postscript on the Writing Process

1. How did you decide on this topic?

    My topic was somewhat suggested to me by a friend. He suggested that I write about wine making. I refined that to wine tasting.

2. How did you actually write the paper?

    I found myself writing this paper under self-imposed deadlines, such as having to have two pages done before dinner, or before classes started. I found this paper very entertaining to write. Although I did need to consult a few friends on the actual techniques of wine tasting, I wrote the paper with a hint of satire. The best place this can be seen is in the history paragraph. The entire history that I have recorded is fictitious and is not intended to parallel any person or event.

3. What did you like best about your paper?

> The strength is the introduction to the wine-tasting ritual with an edge of humor applied. This lighthearted approach makes the ritual more accessible to the average reader, instead of just the wine aficionado. I try to use a tone of humor to let people realize that the techniques of wine tasting, though taken very seriously by some, should be a source of entertainment and exploration by the novice.

First Two Paragraphs of Rough Draft

1   It never fails, you've finally got a date with the person you've been watching all semester. They're coming over for dinner tonight; the lasagna is in the oven, the salad is in the refrigerator, and you're at the liquor store wondering what the difference is between the four different brands of Bardolino wine. They're all red, and have the same amount of wine in each bottle, but the difference in price is as much as eleven dollars. You could be frugal and buy the cheapest bottle, saving enough money for a cheap six-pack and a pizza later in the week, or you could go for broke and buy the most expensive, but with your luck, they won't like it, and you've wasted that extra money, or they won't be able to tell the difference, and again, you can kiss that pizza and beer good-bye. You've wasted ten minutes already, staring at labels printed in Italian (after all, you are having lasagna) and have five minutes to decide before you have to get back to clean the bathroom. You finally give up and choose one of the medium priced bottles, get home, and get everything ready. They show up, you uncork the bottle, and pour the first glass to taste it. You swirl and swish it as if rinsing with a fluoride wash, hopefully impressing this person beyond belief. Do you know what you're doing? Most likely not, but it's all a show, isn't it?

2   Before we get started, let's take a look at where wine tasting got its start. In 1637, in the wine cellar of an influential nobleman's estate outside of Paris, the host and his two guests were inadvertently locked in by a faithful manservant. Jean-Pierre, the nobleman, resigned the three of them to the fact that they were there for the night. Francois and Michelle suggested that they become comfortable and partake of some of the fine wine available. While on their third bottle, and no longer worried about their present situation, or whether or not the world would revolve another inch, they noticed, in their giddy state, the color

cast from the wine by the candles, and started comparing the colors with various shades of flowers, or as it became later in the night, the fleshtones of certain women known to them. They also began swishing and swirling the wine about their mouths, at first to remove the particles of beef and cabbage from between their teeth, but later to see who could make the most obnoxious or outrageous noises. One term, the "nose of the wine," was originally derived when Francois, when caught in a fit of laughter with a mouthful of wine, was able to expel wine through his nostril, and give in great detail the experience he got from it. Since then, the actual technique has changed in judging the wine's nose. Weeks later, while reuniting at an elite restaurant in Paris, Francois, Jean-Pierre, and Michelle joyfully engaged in a reenactment of their wining experiments from the estate's cellar. During their meal, they cooed over the color of the wine, again using descriptions from their collective imaginations. And while they swirled, sniffed, and gurgled, the nobles of Paris looked on in amazement at a ritual in which they had not yet been introduced. The aristocrats, being of the elitist mindset, soon adopted the sniff, swirl, and gurgle techniques, and elevated it to a level high above its farcical beginnings.

230

Final Draft

Wine Tasting: How to Fool Some of the People All of the Time

1   It never fails, you've finally got a date with that certain person you've been watching all semester. They're coming over for dinner tonight. The lasagna is in the oven, the salad is in the refrigerator, and you're at the liquor store wondering what the difference is between the four different brands of Bardolino wine. They're all red and have the same amount of wine in each, but the difference in price is as much as eleven dollars. You could be frugal and buy the cheapest bottle, saving enough money for a cheap six-pack and a pizza later in the week, or you could go for broke and buy the most expensive. But with your luck, they won't know the difference, and your pizza and beer fund is drained. You've wasted ten minutes already, staring at labels printed in Italian (after all, you are having lasagna) and have five minutes to decide before you have to get back to clean the bathroom. You finally give up and choose one of the medium-priced bottles, get home, and get everything ready. They show up, you open the bottle, and pour the first glass to taste it. You swirl and swish it as if rinsing with a fluoride wash, hopefully impressing this person beyond belief. Do you know what you

are doing? Most likely not, but it's all a show, isn't it? Well, let's take a look at wine tasting and where it got its start to find out.

2   In 1637, in the wine cellar of an influential nobleman's estate outside of Paris, the host and his two guests were inadvertently locked in by a faithful manservant. Jean-Pierre, the nobleman, resigned his guests to the fact that they were there for the night. Francois and Michelle suggested that they become comfortable and partake in some of the fine wine available. While on their third bottle, and no longer worried about their present situation, they noticed, in their giddy state, the color cast from the wine by the candles. At this point, they started comparing the colors with various shades of flowers, or as it became later in the night, the fleshtones of certain women known to them. They also began swishing and swirling the wine about their mouths, at first to remove the particles of beef and cabbage from between their teeth, but later to see who could make the most obnoxious or outrageous noises. One term, the "nose of the wine," was originally derived when Francois, caught in a fit of laughter with a mouthful of wine, was able to expel through his nostrils a noseful of wine, and give in great detail the experience he got from it. Weeks later, while reuniting at an elite restaurant in Paris, Francois, Jean-Pierre, and Michelle joyfully engaged in a reenactment of their winning experiments from the estate's cellar. During their meal, they cooed over the color of the wine, again using descriptions from their collective imaginations. And while they swirled, sniffed, and gurgled, the nobility of Paris looked on in amazement at a ritual to which they had not yet been introduced. The aristocrats, being of the elitist mindset, soon adopted the sniff, swirl, and gurgle technique and elevated it to a level high above its farcical beginnings.

3   The aristocrats' education—and yours—begins with the uncorking of the wine. This involves, simply, removing the cork, but removing it in one piece. Don't try to screw the corkscrew in any spot of the cork and yank that sucker out of there. Instead, position the corkscrew in the middle of the cork, and gently pull the cork straight out of the bottle. If the cork is pulled at an angle, it could possibly break, making you look like an inexperienced clod.

4   Now that the bottle is open, your first urge may be to sniff the cork. Try to suppress this urge, because I can tell you exactly what it smells like, cork. That's right, a cork smells like a cork, and a wet dog smells like a wet dog. If you must do something with the cork, "inspect" it to

see if it is extremely dry, or if it is encrusted with a dried substance. In the case of the former, it is a sign of not having been stored on its side, very typical for lower-end wines. And with the latter, it tells you that the cork was not tight, and some of the wine leaked out and dried, which is possible with any wine, and will not hurt it at all.

5   Before you start "tossing down" a few glasses of wine, give some consideration to the wine itself. It has been cooped-up in the bottle for years, and finally has a chance for some fresh air. What you need to do next is let the wine "breathe," as this will soften, or take away the bitterness of the wine. The traditionalists say to let it stand in the bottle for some time, usually no longer than twenty minutes. Think about it, however. Letting a whole bottle of wine try to aerate itself through a three-quarters of an inch hole is like breathing through your nose when it's stuffed up from a cold; it's not very efficient. Instead, pour the wine into glasses, half of a glass is usually enough, and let the wine breathe there. It is much more effective, and you can begin drinking it sooner, because there is less wine to breathe and more surface area in contact with the air.

6   The sniff, swirl, and gurgle technique is by far the funnest part of the predrinking ritual, and it is at this point that you can recover from any minor *faux pas* that you may have made. The actual order is to swirl, then sniff, and lastly to gurgle the wine in your mouth. The swirling of the wine in the glass is to, again, aerate the wine, and also to observe the color of the wine. At this point you can become very creative in describing the wine's color, and use images of the sun setting over the rolling waves of the ocean. Possibly the color would remind you of the flushed cheeks of a young man or woman. However you describe it, use more than just "Yep, it's red all right." The sniffing of the wine is used to determine its "nose" or bouquet. The actual technique has changed since its conception back in 1637. Nowadays, all you need to do is inhale the vapors of the wine through your nose. With this you get the first impression of the wine, whether it will be hearty and strong, or light and sweet. During this, the rolling of the eyes is appropriate; however, too much eye play is theatrical and should be avoided. Again, be creative in describing its bouquet.

7   The final step in the triad is the gurgling, or swishing of the wine in the mouth. The purpose of this step is to introduce the wine to your tastebuds, which are located on your tongue. So by swishing the wine around your mouth, you are actually moving the wine around your

tongue. Remember this, because all too often people get carried away and act as if they are rinsing while at the dentist's office. Also, do not swallow too soon, for it is in the mouth that the wine will be tasted, and in the stomach where it will be felt, and it will reach the stomach soon enough. Enjoy the taste, and the aftertaste of the wine, because that is the reason you chose wine in the first place.

8   Now that the tasting ritual is completed, you and your guests are ready to enjoy dinner with the marvelous wine that you have chosen. And the purpose of all this that you have gone through? To impress someone, of course. Because by the time you finish the bottle, you won't care what the wine's bouquet was like, or whether or not the color was tantalizing to the eyes. But you are now armed with the knowledge and technique that can charm the shorts off any ritual-fearing person. Even the Maitre d' will look down his nose at you with an air of approval.

QUESTIONS FOR DISCUSSION AND WRITING

1. In your own words, state the thesis of this essay. What sentence(s) in the essay best express this thesis?

2. Jones's purpose is to explain wine tasting and at the same time entertain the reader. Which paragraphs in the essay most successfully accomplish one or both of these purposes?

3. What primary shaping strategy does Jones use to organize his essay? What different processes does Jones explain? What terms related to wine tasting does Jones define?

4. Jones uses words such as "sucker," "funnest," "clod," and "Yep." In the context of this paper and each particular sentence, is this colloquial or conversational language appropriate or effective? Explain your decision.

5. In his postscript, Jones says that his "lighthearted approach makes the ritual more accessible to the average reader, instead of just the wine aficionado." Where is Jones most or least successful at addressing his audience?

6. Assume that you are helping Jones edit wordiness out of his sentences. The following sentences could be phrased more concisely (fewer words) without changing the meaning. Revise each sentence, and then decide whether you would recommend that Jones use your revisions.

```
"The aristocrats, being of the elitist mindset,
soon adopted the sniff, swirl, and gurgle
```

technique and elevated it to a level high above
its farcical beginnings."

"In the case of the former, it is a sign of not
having been stored on its side, very typical for
lower-end wines."

"Before you start 'tossing down' a few glasses
of wine, give some consideration to the wine
itself."

CHAPTER 7

Evaluating

We ARE ALL CRITICS. WHETHER WE ARE PRAISING A movie we saw last week or discussing recent political events, dispensing criticism is a national pastime. When we exercise our right to free speech, most of the time we are evaluating a person, product, performance, or work of art.

When we write a formal evaluation, however, the stakes are a bit higher. If we're writing an evaluation of some historical event for a class, our grade may depend on the outcome. If we're evaluating the competition for our employer, our job may depend on careful research. If we're evaluating a political candidate, the future may hinge on our careful judgment. We should learn, therefore, what separates a statement of opinion that may make *us* feel good from an evaluation that will actually persuade *others*.

Formal written evaluations are not mere statements of opinion. First, evaluations contain a careful *description* of the person, product, performance, or event being evaluated. Readers need to know exactly what thing or event is being evaluated. Second, evaluations usually *consider both good and bad points*. They do not advertise or hype the subject. An evaluation sells the writer's critical judgment by acknowledging virtues and faults—and weighing them in the balance. Third, evaluations persuade a specific audience by using *criteria* (standards of judgment) that experts on the subject agree are important. If filmgoers agree that a good escape film should have an entertaining plot, stereotyped good and bad characters, and an exotic setting, then the writer has three criteria (ideal standards) by which to judge a specific film.

Finally, evaluations give *specific evidence* to support the writer's judgments: citations of specific characters, dialogue, or scenes from a Toni Morrison novel for example; or references to specific people and events related to a historical event.

As the essays in this chapter illustrate, evaluations vary widely in length, style, and format. Book critiques, television and film reviews, and evaluations of products have slightly different styles and formats that are designed to appeal to their different audiences. A consumer article may be written in simple, direct language, with separate headings for each criterion. A film review, on the other hand, may have a literary style with implied criteria. We determine style and format by knowing our audience and the magazine, newspaper, or book that might publish our evaluation. All evaluations establish criteria, balance strengths and weaknesses, and use supporting evidence, but each uses a particular style to appeal to the intended audience.

Strategies for Reading and Writing Evaluating Essays

Because evaluative writing must both inform and persuade an audience, it uses techniques of observing and explaining. It demonstrates what the person, product, object, or performance is and then explains its virtues and faults. As you read the essays in this chapter, pay attention to the following techniques for writing evaluations.

- **Description of the person, product, performance, or work of art.** Since most reviews and evaluations are intended for readers who are not familiar with a particular subject, writers usually provide background information: who, what, when, and where. A critique of a film, for example, gives the director and the principal actors, the context of the story and some of the plot, the filming location (perhaps), and may explain when and where the film is currently showing.

- **Statement of an overall claim about the subject.** The claim about the overall value is the thesis of the critique or review. It considers the virtues and faults and renders an overall judgment. The overall claim may be that the film is worth seeing for the special effects, even though the plot is not believable.

- **Use of criteria for the evaluation.** A criterion is a standard of judgment. It is the ideal case, against which the writer measures his or her particular subject. Thus, for a film, "plot" is not a criterion, but "fast-moving and entertaining plot" is a possible criterion for an adventure film.

■ **Separate judgment for each criterion.** If a writer's criteria for judging a family restaurant are pleasant decor, quick service, nutritious food, and moderate prices, then the writer will make a separate judgment in each of these areas. (Remember: Criteria is plural, referring to several standards; criterion is singular, referring to one standard of judgment.)

■ **Each judgment supported with evidence.** Writers typically use their own careful observation and description of the subject for evidence, but they may also use the results of interviews and surveys, quotations from authorities, or data from experiments.

■ **Criteria, style, and format adjusted to the particular audience.** Writers anticipate which criteria are most acceptable for the subject and the audience, and they present their claims in an appropriate format and style.

Reading an Evaluating Essay

As you read the essays in this chapter, use the following strategies for active, critical reading.

Prereading

Begin by writing down what you already know about the subject. The Prereading Journal Entry may suggest a topic. However, if you aren't familiar with that particular product, service, or performance, choose a similar subject and write some notes for an evaluation of it. It's important to record what *you* think before you are influenced by a particular critique or review. Then read the headnotes about the author and the topic for background and context: Understanding the writer's situation, his or her purpose and audience, and some biographical details will make your reading more effective.

First Reading

Read for information and enjoyment, as you would an article you picked up in a magazine. If some passage is confusing, place a "?" in the margin. If you disagree with a criterion or a judgment, place an "X" in the margin. If you especially enjoy some sentence or insight (or are surprised by the information or judgment), put a "!" in the margin. Highlight or put a wavy line under any key passages. Underline any words you want to look up later. *When you finish reading, write the overall claim that the writer makes.*

Annotated Reading

For your critical reading, write your own observations and reactions in the margin: "This is a full description. I can visualize it," "I disagree here," "This evidence is persuasive," or "Why doesn't this writer discuss. . . ?" Also read with a writer's eye, noting key features of writing evaluations. Place brackets around one passage containing *background description*, around the sentence stating the *overall claim*, and around *one criterion*, the writer's *judgment*, and the accompanying *evidence*. Identify each of these key features in the margin. List the writer's criteria or outline the critique. When necessary, look up definitions of the words you've underlined.

Collaborative Reading

In your class or small group, share your Prereading Journal Entries. What did other class members think about this subject *before* they read this evaluation? After reading the essay, were group members convinced of the writer's overall claim based on the evidence presented? Appoint a recorder to write down your ideas. Then read each other's marginal annotations and compile a jointly annotated version of the essay. Finally, when your group or class has completed a collaborative annotation, write one or two questions that you still have about this review or critique—questions that you'd like to investigate in further reading of this essay or that you'd like to discuss in class.

Writing an Evaluating Essay

As you write your own evaluation of a product, service, performance, or person, remember the following important tips:

1. Choose a subject you are already relatively knowledgeable about. You don't have to be Jeff Gordon or Jimmie Johnson to write about cars or Steven Spielberg to write about films, but you should have experience with the subject you are evaluating.

2. To become more expert, have your subject close at hand so you can *reobserve* it as you write. For films or television programs, use a video cassette to review key scenes. For books, essays, art objects, places, and commercial products, reread key passages, reobserve the object, or retest the product. *Do not write an evaluation wholly from memory.*

3. Review the key features of evaluative writing: You must *describe* the product, service, or performance so your audience knows what you are evaluating. You must state an *overall claim*: What is this subject's overall value? To support your overall claim, you establish *criteria* (standards of value), you make a *judgment* about each separate criterion (meets or doesn't meet the standard), and you give supporting *evidence* for your judgment. Finally, make your criteria and supporting evidence appropriate for your *audience*. Readers of *Film Quarterly*, for example, expect more sophisticated judgments and evidence than do the readers of a local newspaper.

4. Consider your audience as you write. First, be sure to check your criteria with your potential readers. Will they agree with your criteria for a restaurant, a book or essay, a commercial product, or a performance? Your readers may forgive you if your judgment differs from theirs, but not if you have inappropriate or uninformed criteria for your judgments. Second, remember that you have a "double audience": Some readers will know your product, film, restaurant, book, or event, so they will be reading to compare their reactions with yours. Other readers will know about the subject, but they will *not* have seen this particular product or performance. Keep both of these readers in mind as you write.

Choosing a Subject for an Evaluating Essay

If your instructor has left the topic open, you might begin with some fairly obvious possibilities: a review of a restaurant, film, book, piece of art, product, dramatic performance, television program, and so forth.

Before you rush out to the local video store, however, consider your own interests. What hobbies or outside interests do you have? What are you already an "expert" on? What jobs have you held, and what could you evaluate about your job?

Finally, check through the class notes for your current classes: What are you studying in other classes you could evaluate? You might choose a work of literature, a piece of art, a piece of equipment in your lab, a particularly good teacher, or even the course itself.

Collecting Examples and Criteria

For evaluative essays, use the observing, remembering, and investigating skills already practiced in Chapters 3, 4, and 5. Collect information by *observing* your subject several times, taking careful notes. List, brainstorm, or freewrite on your *memories* associated with this subject. Check in *written sources* (books, articles, and newspapers) for evaluations, reviews, and consumer articles. *Interview* any friends, teachers, and businesspeople who might have relevant information or opinions. If appropriate, conduct an informal *survey* to determine the opinions of other people about your subject.

As you collect information, note possible *criteria* for evaluating your subject. You must have information to support your judgments about each criterion. If you are writing about a film, for example, and effective acting is one criterion, make sure you write down the names of principal actors, the characters they play, and details and bits of dialogue from scenes where their acting is particularly effective.

Use a three-column log to help you collect information on your topic. For a film review, two criteria might be as follows:

Subject: <u>Batman</u>

Criteria	Evidence	Judgment
Effective acting	The specific scenes of confrontation show the tension and drama, although Nicholson is too much a cartoon figure whose gags continue after his death.	Michael Keaton and Jack Nicholson are usually excellent as hero and villain.
Dramatic cinematography	The flights through the dark alleys of the city, the absence of sunshine and greenery, the dark costume and mask of Batman, and the final, eerie moonlight encounter reinforce the nighttime drama.	Director Tim Burton and cinematographer Roger Pratt dramatically re-create Gotham City at night.

Shaping Your Evaluating Essay

After you have collected some criteria and evidence, review the essays in this chapter. If you are evaluating a book, film, television show, commercial product, or an artistic performance, do the essays in this chapter suggest ways to organize your essay? Then test the following shaping strategies against your notes: Which of the following strategies will best organize and present your ideas for your audience?

Analysis by Criteria

Evaluations of consumer products are often organized by category or criteria. The writer states the criteria that are important for buyers of this particular item, gives a judgment in each area, and then supports each judgment with evidence.

Comparison/Contrast

Frequently, writers of evaluations compare two products, performances, or works of art. Comparisons (and contrasts) can add evidence and support to the writer's judgments, but they can also help shape or organize the whole essay.

Classification

Occasionally, a subject for evaluation contains several different types. An evaluation of the writing implements sold by most bookstores, for example, might classify (and then evaluate) each type: *mechanical pencils*, with their high-tech combination of metals and plastics and automatic lead-feed systems; *plastic ball-pen "pencils,"* with those rock-hard erasers that never erase anything; and the *multicolored ball pens*, with the outside plastic color matching the ink, in shades from yellow or aqua to lavender and burnt orange.

Chronological Order

Writers of reviews of books, films, and performances often follow the chronological order of the plot or main events, giving their judgments (and supporting evidence) as they describe the main events. However, be sure that your evaluation is *not* just a retelling of the film or book or performance. Any retelling of the plot should be brief and should show why the film or book is or is not good, effective, or memorable.

Drafting Your Evaluating Essay

You may simply start writing and see if a shape develops that will work for your particular subject and audience. Or you may prefer to outline your essay—using an appropriate shaping strategy—to see if all your evidence will fit before you start writing.

In either case, gather all your materials together. Reread your collecting and shaping notes. If you have an idea for a catchy title or lead-in, start there. Otherwise, start with the body of your paper and save your introduction for later. When you get stuck, reread what you have written so far or check your notes again, and keep writing.

Revising Your Evaluating Essay

Use the following guidelines as you give feedback to your peers and revise your own drafts. Revising is more than fixing spelling or changing the wording of a sentence or two. Revision often requires substantial changes in the overall claim, organization, amount of evidence, or appeal to the audience.

- **Review the title and lead-in.** Is the title just a label ("Netbooks") or does it describe the subject creatively ("All is Not Well in the Land of 'The Lion King'")? Which strategy would be best for the intended audience? Do the opening sentences or lead-in get the reader's attention?
- **Check the overall claim or thesis.** It should state an overall claim that *relates* to both the strengths and weaknesses discussed in the body of the essay.
- **Clarify the criteria for the audience.** Remember that criteria are standards of value or the ideal against which the writer measures the particular case. Categories (shopping shows, fishing shows, horror shows) are not necessarily criteria. Criteria should be ideal attributes: effective acting, exciting story line, or realistic settings.
- **Re-examine the appropriateness of the criteria for the audience.** Often evaluations do not use criteria appropriate for the subject and audience. Readers of *Time* magazine may check film reviews merely to see if a movie is entertaining and worth the price of admission; readers of *Film Quarterly* are much more interested in the craft and technical expertise of the director.
- **Check each criterion for judgment and supporting evidence.** For each major criterion, the writer should make a judgment (good or bad, effective or ineffective) and have specific details, description, testimony, test data, or other information to support the judgment.
- **Review data and direct quotations for accuracy.** Data, testimonies, or quotations from printed sources, interviews, or surveys must be *quoted accurately* and the sources must be referred to or cited in the essay.

- **Review transitions at the beginning of body paragraphs.** At the beginning of body paragraphs, use key words and transitional phrases to *signal* the major divisions in the evaluation.
- **Revise and edit sentences to improve clarity and avoid errors.** Use your peer readers' reactions and check your handbook to clarify sentences and correct errors in spelling, punctuation, or usage.

Postscript for Your Evaluating Essay

When you have finished your essay, answer the following questions. Be sure to hand in this response with your essay.

1. What *sources* of information provided most of your evidence: remembering experiences, observing the subject directly, or reading about the subject and interviewing other people?
2. What was your original opinion of your subject? How did that evaluation change as you wrote your essay? Cite one specific judgment that you *changed* or *discovered* as you wrote the essay.
3. Which of the *shaping strategies* described in this chapter were most helpful as you wrote this essay?
4. Where in the essay did you adapt your criteria, judgments, or evidence for your *audience*?
5. What do you like best about the essay? What problems did you have as you wrote? What would you revise if you had more time?

CONSUMER REPORTS

Laptops and Desktops

Prereading Journal Entry

Assume that you have decided to buy a new laptop computer. Which of the following criteria would be important in your choice: low price, light weight, long battery life, reliability, larger screen and keyboard, large memory, ability to run Windows 7, ability to play games? Explain which of these (or other) features you would want in a new laptop computer.

Consumer Reports *magazine reviews consumer products ranging from cameras, kitchen knives, and contact lenses to computers, washing machines, and automobiles. They maintain their integrity by accepting no advertising in their monthly issues. Since advertisements for products are rarely objective, consumers need information about the features, performance, price, and reliability of products that they might like to buy. In the following review of laptops and desktops,* Consumer Reports *evaluates the smaller netbooks alongside thirty-one conventional laptops and twenty-seven desktops. Although desktops and full-featured laptops have their place for some applications, netbooks fill a niche between the regular laptops and smaller devices like Apple's iPad.*

Laptops and Desktops: Netbooks Offer a Lighter, Cheaper Alternative to Traditional Laptops

1   It has long Been truism that a laptop can never be too thin or too light. And it has been just as true that such a slim-and-light model would set you back at least $1,500. But now, in the nick of time for cash-strapped consumers, net-books have come to the rescue.

2   You've probably started seeing net-books in airports, coffee shops, and just about anywhere people on the go congregate. Here's why: Although some net-books are thicker than many 13-inch slim-and-light laptops, the typical model weighs just 3 pounds, is about 10 inches wide, and costs $330 to $450—little more than a high-end iPhone.

3   These compact laptops are increasingly being positioned more as an additional mobile network-connected device than as a supplemental computer. AT&T, for example, recently began offering subsidized netbooks from Acer, Dell, and LG for $50 to $250 in a few markets. The catch: You have to sign up for a two-year wireless plan for the netbook. Verizon is planning a similar promotion.

4   The six netbooks we tested for this report all performed well enough for Web surfing and e-mail, but we found some major differences in battery life among them. One new netbook, the Dell Mini 10, arrived too late to test for this report. We'll test it in the near future.

5   In addition, we've rated 31 conventional laptops and 27 desktops, and we offer a First Look at two of the smallest and cheapest desktops on the market, built with the same technologies used in netbooks.

6   Unlike a smart phone, most netbooks have keyboards big enough for touch typing, and their displays are big enough to render a legible Windows desktop. (Some net-books run Linux, but those models aren't as popular.) True, typing on such a keyboard and sliding fingers across a small touch pad might strain your hands a bit, and focusing on the smaller display might take some getting used to. But for many people those compromises are worth the extraordinary price and portability.

7   Battery life is also surprisingly good, ranging from 3 to 9 hours, comparable with or better than a full-sized laptop. Most netbooks don't have built-in 3G communications. That's a costly extra. If you don't have it, you'll need a Wi-Fi connection to get online. The hard drive is usually 160 gigabytes, much smaller than most conventional laptops. The HP netbook in the Ratings came with a 16GB solid-state drive; it ran more slowly than the other netbooks we tested.

8   To use a netbook, you'll do without a built-in DVD or CD drive, live with just 1GB of memory (some models can be upgraded to more), and settle for less than blazing processing speed. But routine applications such as Web browsing, e-mail, and word processing should run fine. Forget about 3D gaming and video-editing, though. For those, you'll be much happier with a full-powered machine.

9   Netbooks first appeared under lesser-known brands, such as Asus. More recently, well-known brands such as Acer, Dell, HP, Lenovo, and Samsung have also gotten into the act.

10   The same inexpensive Intel processor, called the Atom, that made netbooks so compact and inexpensive is now finding its way into desktop computers, promising a new generation of cheaper home computers. (For a First Look at two of the first so-called net-tops—the $270 Compaq Presario CQ2009F and the $500 Averatec D1130—see "Nettops: Small, Affordable Desktops," on page 28.)

11   Because their designs differ so much from conventional laptops, we rated the netbooks separately. We considered portability to be very important because it's a key reason for choosing a netbook over a conventional laptop. We also did not hold ergonomics and performance to the same standard as we do for larger, heavier, and pricier laptops.

12   Thus, the netbook Ratings are intended to help you choose among netbooks, not to compare a netbook with a full-sized laptop. Keeping such limitations in mind, we found all of the netbooks quite usable for light work. Differences in areas such as battery life and features are noted in the Ratings.

Overview

Although all netbooks are suitable as secondary systems for performing routine tasks, you'll have to make compromises. The best offer better battery life.

☑ Recommended

These are models that stand out in our netbook tests for the reasons stated.

Best all-around netbooks:

1 **Samsung** $450
2 **Acer** $350
4 **Asus** $330

1 has very good portability and display, plus a 7-hour battery life. But it costs more than the others. **2** had a 9-hour battery life and very good portability. Its keyboard and trackpad were smaller, though. **4** performed well and was competitively priced, but it had the shortest battery life of the three.

1 Samsung   4 Asus

2 Acer

Ratings Netbooks

In performance order.

● Excellent
◑ Very good
○ Good
◒ Fair
● Poor

Recommendation	Rank	Brand & model	Price	Overall score	Portability	Ergonomics	Performance	Versatility	Display	Speakers	Battery life (hr.)	Weight (lb.)	Wi-Fi type (802.11)	Memory-card reader	Built-in webcam	VGA video out
				0 100 P | F | G | VG| E												
		10-INCH														
✓	1	**Samsung** NC10-14GB ①	$450 **53**		◑	○	○	○	◑	●	7	2.9	g	•	•	•
✓	2	**Acer** Aspire One A0D150-1165 ①	350 **52**		◑	◒	○	○	○	●	9	2.9	g	•	•	•
	3	**MSI** Wind U120-024US ①	350 **47**		○	◒	○	○	○	●	4½	2.8	g	•	•	•
✓	4	**Asus** Eee PC 1000H	330 **45**		○	○	○	○	○	●	3½	3.0	n	•	•	•
	5	**Averatec** Buddy N1030EA1E-1	480 **43**		○	○	○	○	◑	●	2¾	2.5	g	•	•	•
	6	**HP** Mini 1030NR ②	350 **40**		○	○	◒	○	○	◒	2¾	2.4	g	•	•	

① Tested with extended battery. ② 16GB solid-state drive.

QUESTIONS FOR DISCUSSION AND WRITING

1. *Consumer Reports* indicates test results from eight different criteria for evaluating netbooks. What are these criteria? Where does the article discuss or list these criteria?

2. The article discusses the advantages and disadvantages of netbooks. Cite two significant advantages that the netbooks have over conventional laptops or desktops. Then cite at least one disadvantage.

3. The article explains that in their evaluation, they did not hold netbooks to the same standard as they did for the larger or more expensive

laptops. Does this mean that the evaluation is not objective or biased? Explain.

4. Computers and smart phones evolve so quickly that information can quickly become out of date. Do an online search for other reviews of netbooks. Compare the information and evaluations you find online with this article from *Consumer Reports*. What new brands or styles of small netbooks are now available? Do these evaluations have tests to support their evaluations? Are these sites objective, or do they carry advertisements for computer products? Is the writer an expert or authority about computers?

5. Locate a copy of *Consumer Reports*. Scan through several articles. How is the writing different from another popular magazine you are familiar with—*Time* magazine, *Rolling Stone,* or *National Geographic?* Based on your comparison, describe characteristic features (target audience, subject matter, length, format, sentence style) of *Consumer Reports* articles.

DAVID SEDARIS

Today's Special

Prereading Journal Entry

If you have eaten out at a restaurant recently, write an entry describing your experience. Begin by describing the setting, layout, and décor of the restaurant. Was the restaurant quiet or noisy? Were the waiters helpful or rude? Then describe your meal. What did you have to eat and how was it prepared? If you had appetizers, an entrée, and dessert, describe how they were prepared. Overall, how would you judge your dining experience?

David Sedaris is a humorist and popular author of numerous essays and books, including Me Talk Pretty One Day *(2000),* Dress Your Family in Corduroy and Denim *(2004), and a recent* New York Times *bestseller,* When You are Engulfed in Flames *(2008). At age twenty, Sedaris began keeping a journal which became the source and inspiration for his later essays and National Public Radio spots. He is able to take ordinary, everyday topics—politics, restaurants, family members, sea turtles, foreign languages, smoking, gay relationships, travel—and turn them into entertaining commentaries on people, places, and events. With his sister, actress, comedienne,*

and author Amy Sedaris, he has authored several plays under the name,
"The Talent Family." He currently lives with his partner Hugh in Paris and
travels regularly to the United States. "Today's Special," taken from Me Talk
Pretty One Day, *uses humor as a way to evaluate an upscale New York*
restaurant while entertaining his readers.

1   It is his birthday, and Hugh and I are seated in a New York restaurant, awaiting the arrival of our fifteen-word entrees. He looks very
nice, dressed in the suit and sweater that have always belonged to him.
As for me, I own only my shoes, pants, shirt, and tie. My jacket belongs
to the restaurant and was offered as a loan by the maitre d', who apparently thought I would feel more comfortable dressed to lead a high
school marching band.

2   I'm worrying about the thick gold braids decorating my sleeves
when the waiter presents us with what he calls "a little something to
amuse the palette." Roughly the size and color of a Band-Aid, the
amusement floats on a shallow, muddy puddle of sauce and is topped
with a sprig of greenery.

3   "And this would be . . . what, exactly?" Hugh asks.

4   "This," the waiter announces, "is our raw Atlantic sword-fish served
in a dark chocolate gravy and garnished with fresh mint."

5   "Not again," I say. "Can't you guys come up with something a little
less conventional?"

6   "Love your jacket," the waiter whispers.

7   As a rule, I'm no great fan of eating out in New York restaurants. It's
hard to love a place that's outlawed smoking but finds it perfectly
acceptable to serve raw fish in a bath of chocolate. There are no normal restaurants left, at least in our neighborhood. The diners have all
been taken over by precious little bistros boasting a menu of indigenous American cuisine. They call these meals "traditional," yet they're
rarely the American dishes I remember. The patty melt has been
pushed aside in favor of the herb-encrusted medallions of baby arti-
choke hearts, which never leave me thinking, "Oh, right, those! I wonder if they're as good as the ones my mom used to make."

8   Part of the problem is that we live in the wrong part of town. SoHo
is not a macaroni salad kind of place. This is where the world's bright-
est young talents come to braise carmelized racks of corn-fed song-
birds or offer up their famous knuckle of flash-seared crappie served
with a collar of chided ginger and cornered by a tribe of kiln-roasted
Chilean toadstools, teased with a warm spray of clarified musk oil.

Even then they promise something simple, they've got to tart it up—the meatloaf has been poached in sea water, or there are figs in the tuna salad. If cooking is an art, I think we're in our Dada phase.

9   I've never thought of myself as a particularly finicky eater, but it's hard to be a good sport when each dish seems to include no fewer than a dozen ingredients, one of which I'm bound to dislike. I'd order the skirt steak with a medley of suffocated peaches, but I'm put off by the aspirin sauce. The sea scallops look good until I'm told they're served in a broth of malt liquor and mummified litchi nuts. What I really want is a cigarette, and I'm always searching the menu in the hope that some courageous young chef has finally recognized tobacco as a vegetable. Bake it, steam it, grill it, or stuff it into littleneck clams, I just need something familiar that I can hold on to.

10   When the waiter brings our entrees, I have no idea which plate might be mine. In yesterday's restaurants it was possible both to visualize and to recognize your meal. There were always subtle differences, but for the most part, a lamb chop tended to maintain its basic shape. That is to say that it looked chop-like. It had a handle made of bone and a teardrop of meat hugged by a thin rind of fat. Apparently, though, that was too predictable. Order the modern lamb chop, and it's likely to look no different than your companion's order of shackled pompano. The current food is always arranged into a senseless, vertical tower. No longer content to recline, it now reaches for the sky, much like the high-rise buildings lining our city streets. It's as if the plates were valuable parcels of land and the chef had purchased one small lot and unlimited air rights. Hugh's saffron linguini resembles a miniature turban, topped with architectural spires of shrimp. It stands there in the center while the rest of the vast, empty plate looks as though it's been leased out as a possible parking lot. I had ordered the steak, which, bowing to the same minimalist fashion, is served without the bone, the thin slices of beef stacked to resemble a funeral pyre. The potatoes I'd been expecting have apparently either been clarified to an essence or were used to stoke the grill.

11   "Maybe," Hugh says, "they're inside your tower of meat."

12   This is what we have been reduced to. Hugh blows the yucca pollen of his blackened shrimp while I push back the sleeves of my borrowed sport coat and search the meat tower for my promised potatoes.

13   "There they are, right there." Hugh uses his fork to point out what could easily be mistaken for five cavity-riddled molars. The dark spots must be my vegetable.

14   Because I am both a glutton and a masochist, my standard complaint, "That was so bad," is always followed by "And there was so little of it!"

15   Our plates are cleared, and we are presented with dessert menus. I learn that spiced ham is no longer considered just a luncheon meat and that even back issues of Smithsonian can be turned into sorbets.

16   "I just couldn't," I say to the waiter when he recommends the white chocolate and wild loganberry couscous.

17   "If we're counting calories, I could have the chef serve it without the crème fraîche."

18   "No," I say. "Really, I just couldn't."

19   We ask for the check, explaining that we have a movie to catch. It's only a ten-minute walk to the theater, but I'm antsy because I'd like to get something to eat before the show. They'll have loads of food at the concession stand, but I don't believe in mixing meat with my movies. Luckily there's a hot dog cart not too far out of our way.

20   Friends always say, "How can you eat those? I read in the paper that they're made from hog's lips."

21   "And . . . ?"

22   "And hearts and eyelids."

23   That, to my mind, is only three ingredients and constitutes a refreshing change of pace. I order mine with nothing but mustard, and am thrilled to watch the vendor present my hot dog in a horizontal position. So simple and timeless that I can recognize it, immediately, as food.

QUESTIONS FOR DISCUSSION AND WRITING

1. As a humorist, Sedaris looks for the amusing and absurd in people, places, and events. As a restaurant critic, however, Sedaris uses evaluation to make a serious point. He doesn't explicitly state his overall claim about this particular restaurant, but his opinion is evident throughout. What exactly does Sedaris like and dislike? Write your own three-column log for this essay. List the *criteria* (such as ambiance, food taste, service, presentation, etc.) that Sedaris uses in this review, the *evidence* he gives, and his *judgment* for each of the criteria. State in your own words Sedaris' overall judgment or claim.

2. In his essay, Sedaris claims to enjoy simple food like potatoes and hot dogs, yet he knows and uses the vocabulary of a sophisticated gourmand. List the words and phrases Sedaris uses to describe the cuisine of this particular restaurant. Does he use this vocabulary to praise the cuisine of this restaurant or to ridicule it? Explain, referring to specific sentences.

3. Review the techniques for observing and remembering in Chapters 3 and 4. Where in his essay does Sedaris give vivid and detailed descriptions or use images, similes, and metaphors? Where does Sedaris use narrative techniques such as scene setting, dialogue, and characterization? Support your response by citing specific sentences, phrases, or images.

4. Visit a local restaurant—preferably one you are already familiar with—for the purpose of writing a review. If you wish, bring some of your friends. Take notes during the meal so you won't miss any names of foods or service details. Then write two versions of your review. For the first one, write a straightforward, objective review of the restaurant, service, and meal. Organize your review by the criteria you choose. For your second version, write in a narrative fashion as Sedaris does, including scene description, key events, characters, and dialogue. When you finish, evaluate your reviews. Which do you like best? What newspaper, magazine, or Web site would be the best choice for each of your versions? Explain your choice(s).

RICHARD ALLEVA

Pocahokum

Prereading Journal Entry

If you have seen James Cameron's film, *Avatar*, write an entry describing your reaction to the film. What parts of the film did you like best and least? Think of several criteria you could use, such as story line, acting, cinematography, and themes, and explain why you liked (or didn't like) this film.

A film critic for Commonweal *magazine for over twenty years, Richard Alleva has a degree in drama from the University of Connecticut and an MFA in playwrighting from Catholic University. He has reviewed many contemporary films, including* Saving Private Ryan, The Lovely Bones, A Serious Man, Public Enemies, *and* The Hurt Locker. *In addition to reviewing films, Alleva has a significant career as an actor, touring the U.S. and Europe with the National Players, Catholic University's repertory company. In* Pocahokum, *Alleva argues that* Avatar, *while technically and visually a masterpiece, lacks sufficient characterization to carry the final hour of the film.*

Avatar

1   For more than a year TV and theater trailers have been promising that James Cameron's *Avatar* would change the way we look at movies, that its visuals would advance the art and the technology of film. No wonder the picture has broken all box-office records by earning more than a billion dollars within three weeks of its release. But has the promise been kept?

2   There is certainly a visual triumph to acknowledge here. Through my 3-D glasses (and by all means attend the 3-D version and not the conventional format also being shown), I found myself taking in imagery that literally deepened the innovations made by Orson Welles and his cameraman Greg Toland in 1941. The deep-focus cinematography of *Citizen Kane* gave its characters a richer, denser environment than any cast had previously enjoyed. When Welles, as Kane, stands in front of a huge fireplace in the background of one shot while his bored wife idles with a jigsaw puzzle in the foreground, husband and wife seem hundreds of feet removed from each other in their absurdly cavernous parlor, and this effect underlines her virtual imprisonment, his loneliness, and the comic monstrosity of Xanadu, the fortress-mansion. Unspoken emotions reach our minds by dazzling our eyes.

3   By contrast, the 3-D technology of the 1950s was gimcrack. It worked entirely by extrusion. Watch out! The witch doctor's spear is coming right at you! Yikes! Those scissors will put out your eyes! So adventitious were those tawdry thrills that when Hitchcock mounted a good, conventional suspense play, *Dial M for Murder*, in 3-D, he soon realized that his movie could be re-released in standard format without any loss in entertainment value.

4   But *Avatar*, along with the new *A Christmas Carol* and certain other recent 3-D productions, puts 3-D on track as a mainstream and potent innovation. It doesn't stick objects out of the screen but uses the process to make depth deeper. The world of *Avatar* doesn't leap out at us; we are lured into it.

5   That world is the planet Pandora, rainforest-like in landscape and inhabited by Na'vi, intelligent, blue-skinned, nine-foot-high beings. In the middle of the next century, human invaders, determined to claim Pandora's mineral resources, behave like the worst of European imperialists. If the native population can be moved away from the targeted areas, good. If not, they must be exterminated.

6   This invading army, though American, isn't our government's but a corporation's. Science may have advanced enough to fly humans to

other solar systems and equip soldiers with invincible tank-robots, but national economics back home are in a tailspin and the earth's resources have dried up. *Plus ça change. . .*

7   The invaders have been equipped with more than those tanks. It seems that a certain device can transport an individual's mind into a cloned body—an "avatar"—resembling the physique of a Na'vi. Jake Scully, a U.S. soldier who lost the use of his legs in combat and now serves with the mercenaries, is called upon to assume an avatar, mingle with the natives, and report their weaknesses to his brutal commander. If he succeeds, the corporation will pay for the high-tech operation that will end his paraplegia, something the impoverished U.S. Army can't afford. But Scully, adopted by a Na'vi tribe and in love with its leader's daughter, switches allegiance and leads the planet's population in a revolt against the invaders.

8   The first hour or so of this two-and-half-hour movie had me hoping that I was watching a genuine popular masterpiece, something of the caliber of *The Godfather* or *It's a Wonderful Life*. When Scully enters the Pandoran jungle, we are made to share his wonder at its strangeness. The 3-D process is crucial here, for though the planet's landscapes and animals have been designed by Rick Carter and Robert Stromberg with gusto and attention to detail, there is no startling originality in the results because the forests are simply earth's rainforests in floral overdrive, featuring flowers that close up at human touch and shrink back into the ground, vines that are a kudzu nightmare, and insects the size of small dogs. Similarly, the various beasts are just variations on dinosaurs and rhinos, and the flying reptiles that serve as steeds aren't much different from our medieval dragons. But all flora and fauna are given a new allure by the 3-D perspectives achieved by Joe Letteri. Everything seems more palpable and more dangerous than what we've seen in other movies that depend on special effects.

9   And the new sense of depth gives an extra charge to the action sequences. When characters walk on narrow cliff tops over deep canyons, the drop looks vertiginous in a way never seen before. When a jungle creature chases our hero, the distance between carnivore and prey seems *measurably* small.

10   However, when our hero makes contact with the tribe he will learn to love and respect, it is time for the movie to display not only visual flair but also some gift for characterization and what we might call mythic anthropology (think *The Lord of the Rings*, which had this in abundance). And it is precisely at this point that *Avatar* not only sags but positively

rots. The Na'vi aren't given any range of emotion, any humor, spontaneity, or flaws, but they perpetually exude an aura of noble-savage holiness. Worse, they are escapees from other movies: Disney's *Pocahontas* (for what is Scully's lady love but the famous savior of John Smith, and what is her father Eytukan but a blue-colored version of Chief Powhatan?), *Dances with Wolves, A Man Called Horse, The Last Samurai, The Emerald Forest, Broken Arrow*, and probably a score of others you've seen. They all share the same basic scenario: well-meaning but raw young white male meets fierce but ecologically wise tribe; recognizes the justice of their resistance to so-called civilization; wins their grudging respect and is adopted by them; falls in love with the tribe's princess, usually with a native rival for the maiden's hand glowering in the background; learns the wisdom, crafts, and fighting skills of his hosts; and leads the people in an uprising against the European or American land-grabbers.

11   Perhaps because they live and work within one of the epicenters of cutthroat (and wasteful) capitalism, Hollywood writers and directors love this story enough to tell it over and over again. It gives them everything they need to feel good about themselves: expiation (*The People are right, my civilization is poison*), self-righteousness (*I am wise enough to renounce my civilization and fight for The People*), and self-glorification (*Ah, but only I, and I alone, can lead The People to victory*). And there is always that great battle at the end to ensure attendance by testosterone-addled male adolescents.

12   But none of the movies I've listed above matches *Avatar* for thinness of characterization, predictability of plotting, and poverty of imagination. (Well, maybe *Pocahontas* made me groan more.) Embarrassment follows embarrassment (a nature-worshipping ceremony with the Pandorans linking arms and swaying from side to side looks like something the Esalen Institute would dream up), and cliché bumps up against cliché (there are networks of energy that glow through all living things).

13   So, does *Avatar* fulfill the promise that announced its coming? Yes. Thanks to James Cameron, this new, perfected version of 3-D is here to stay, and I expect more and more theaters will be equipped to handle the process, with TV, apparently, soon to follow. But isn't there an older, less splashy promise that every major film makes, whatever its technological capabilities? That the movie will reach our imaginations through the eyes, stir our emotions, and remain in our memories long enough to affect our lives? I believe there is such an implicit promise, and it is one that *Avatar* fails to keep. Because of its technical

innovation and financial success, even critics who resisted *Titanic* are now willing to proclaim Cameron a great director. For me, he remains strictly a great mechanic.

QUESTIONS FOR DISCUSSION AND WRITING

1. Film reviews usually have a double purpose: to give prospective viewers sufficient information about the film (without giving away the whole plot) and to evaluate the strengths and weaknesses of the film. What basic *who, what, when,* and *where* information does Alleva give?

2. Possible criteria for evaluating a film include good plot, effective acting, creative cinematography or special effects, vivid setting, memorable music, and meaningful themes. What criteria does Alleva use for his review of *Avatar*? Write out a three-column log, listing criteria, evidence, and judgments for each of Alleva's criteria.

3. Good film reviewers usually make comparisons to other films, to other performances by the actors or director, to other comparable films, or to contemporary cinematic trends. List the references and comparisons that Alleva makes. If you have seen the film, are there additional comparisons you might make? Explain.

4. In small groups in your class—groups that contain at least one person who has seen the film and one who has not—discuss whether Alleva's review is intended for readers who have seen the film or have not seen the film. Does Alleva's review help readers who have not seen the film decide whether to see the film? Does Alleva give away any crucial information that might spoil the film for those who have not yet seen it? For readers who have seen the film, does Alleva provide enough interesting new information or background material so that they learn something new about the film? Do they agree with Alleva's evaluation?

ABRAHAM LINCOLN

The Gettysburg Address

Prereading Journal Entry

The following selection begins with Abraham Lincoln's famous *Gettysburg Address*. Read this short 268 word speech that Lincoln delivered on the 4th of July, 1863, following the battle at Gettysburg. (Do not read the following article.) Read this speech at least twice, out loud if possible. Then write your comments, questions, and reactions.

1   Fourscore and seven years ago our fathers brought forth upon this continent a new nation, conceived in liberty, and dedicated to the proposition that all men are created equal.

2   Now we are engaged in a great civil war, testing whether that nation, or any nation so conceived and so dedicated, can long endure. We are met on a great battlefield of that war. We have come to dedicate a portion of that field as a final resting place for those who here gave their lives that that nation might live. It is altogether fitting and proper that we should do this.

3   But in a larger sense we cannot dedicate, we cannot consecrate, we cannot hallow this ground. The brave men, living and dead, who struggled here, have consecrated it far above our poor power to add or detract. The world will little note, nor long remember, what we say here, but it can never forget what they did here. It is for us the living, rather, to be dedicated here to the unfinished work which they who fought here have thus far so nobly advanced. It is rather for us to be here dedicated to the great task remaining before us, that from these honored dead we take increased devotion to that cause for which they gave the last full measure of devotion; that we here highly resolve that these dead shall not have died in vain; that this nation, under God, shall have a new birth of freedom; and that government of the people, by the people, and for the people, shall not perish from the earth.

GILBERT HIGHET

The Gettysburg Address

1   Fourscore and seven years ago. . . .

2   These five words stand at the entrance to the best-known monument of American prose, one of the finest utterances in the entire language, and surely one of the greatest speeches in all history. Greatness is like granite; it is molded in fire, and it lasts for many centuries. . . .

3   The dedication of the graveyard at Gettysburg was one of the supreme moments of American history. The battle itself had been a turning point of the war. On the 4th of July 1863, General Meade repelled Lee's invasion of Pennsylvania. Although he did not follow up his victory, he had broken one of the most formidable aggressive

enterprises of the Confederate armies. Losses were heavy on both sides. Thousands of dead were left on the field, and thousands of wounded died in the hot days following the battle. At first, their burial was more or less haphazard; but thoughtful men gradually came to feel that an adequate burying place and memorial were required. These were established by an interstate commission that autumn, and the finest speaker in the North was invited to dedicate them. This was the scholar and statesman Edward Everett of Harvard. He made a good speech—which is still extant: not at all academic, it is full of close strategic analysis and deep historical understanding.

4   Lincoln was not invited to speak, at first. Although people knew him as an effective debater, they were not sure whether he was capable of making a serious speech on such a solemn occasion. Buf one of the impressive things about Lincoln's career is that he constantly strove to *grow*. He was anxious to appear on that occasion and to say something worthy of it. (Also, it has been suggested, he was anxious to remove the impression that he did not know how to behave properly—an impression which had been strengthened by a shocking story about his clowning on the battlefield of Antietam the previous year.) Therefore when he was invited he took considerable care with his speech. He drafted rather more than half of it in the White House before leaving, finished it in the hotel at Gettysburg the night before the ceremony (not in the train, as sometimes reported), and wrote a fair copy next morning.

5   There are many accounts of the day itself, 19 November 1863. There are many descriptions of Lincoln, all showing the same curious blend of grandeur and awkwardness, or lack of dignity, or—it would be best to call it humility. In the procession he rode horseback: a tall lean man in a high plug hat, straddling a short horse, with his feet too near the ground. He arrived before the chief speaker, and had to wait patiently for half an hour or more. His own speech came right at the end of a long and exhausting ceremony, lasted less than three minutes, and made little impression on the audience. In part this was because they were tired, in part because (as eyewitnesses said) he ended almost before they knew he had begun, and in part because he did not speak the Address, but read it, very slowly, in a thin high voice, with a marked Kentucky accent, pronouncing "to" as "toe" and dropping his final R's.

6   Some people of course were alert enough to be impressed. Everett congratulated him at once. But most of the newspapers paid little attention to the speech, and some sneered at it. The *Patriot and Union* of Harrisburg wrote, "We pass over the silly remarks of the President; for the credit of the nation we are willing . . . that they shall no more be repeated or thought of"; and the London *Times* said, "The ceremony was rendered ludicrous by some of the sallies of that poor President Lincoln," calling his remarks "dull and commonplace." The first commendation of the Address came in a single sentence of the Chicago *Tribune*, and the first discriminating and detailed praise of it appeared in the Springfield *Republican*, the Providence *Journal*, and the Philadelphia *Bulletin*. However, three weeks after the ceremony and then again the following spring, the editor of *Harper's Weekly* published a sincere and thorough eulogy of the Address, and soon it was attaining recognition as a masterpiece.

7   At the time, Lincoln could not care much about the reception of his words. He was exhausted and ill. In the train back to Washington, he lay down with a wet towel on his head. He had caught smallpox. At that moment he was incubating it, and he was stricken down soon after he re-entered the White House. Fortunately it was a mild attack, and it evoked one of his best jokes: he told his visitors, "At last I have something I can give to everybody."

8   He had more than that to give to everybody. He was a unique person, far greater than most people realize until they read his life with care. The wisdom of his policy, the sources of his statesmanship—these were things too complex to be discussed in a brief essay. But we can say something about the Gettysburg Address as a work of art.

9   A work of art. Yes: for Lincoln was a literary artist, trained both by others and by himself. The textbooks he used as a boy were full of difficult exercises and skillful devices in formal rhetoric, stressing the qualities he practiced in his own speaking: antithesis, parallelism, and verbal harmony. Then he read and reread many admirable models of thought and expression: the King James Bible, the essays of Bacon, the best plays of Shakespeare. His favorites were *Hamlet, Lear, Macbeth, Richard III*, and *Henry VIII*, which he had read dozens of times. He loved reading aloud, too, and spent hours reading poetry to his friends. (He told his partner Herndon that he preferred getting the sense of any document by reading it aloud.) Therefore his serious speeches are important parts of the long and noble classical tradition of oratory

which begins in Greece, runs through Rome to the modern world, and is still capable (if we do not neglect it) of producing masterpieces.

10   The first proof of this is that the Gettysburg Address is full of quotations—or rather of adaptations—which give it strength. It is partly religious, partly (in the highest sense) political: therefore it is interwoven with memories of the Bible and memories of American history. The first and the last words are Biblical cadences. Normally Lincoln did not say "fourscore" when he meant eighty; but on this solemn occasion he recalled the important dates in the Bible—such as the age of Abraham when his first son was born to him, and he was "fourscore and six years old." Similarly he did not say there was a chance that democracy might die out: he recalled the somber phrasing in the Book of Job—where Bildad speaks of the destruction of one who shall vanish without a trace, and says that "his branch shall be cut off; his remembrance shall perish from the earth." Then again, the famous description of our State as "government of the people, by the people, for the people" was adumbrated by Daniel Webster in 1830 (he spoke of "the people's government, made for the people, made by the people, and answerable to the people") and then elaborated in 1854 by the abolitionist Theodore Parker (as "government of all the people, by all the people, for all the people").

11   Analyzing the Address further, we find that it is based on a highly imaginative theme, or group of themes. The subject is—how can we put it so as not to disfigure it?—the subject is the kinship of life and death, that mysterious linkage which we see sometimes as the physical succession of birth and death in our world, sometimes as the contrast, which is perhaps a unity, between death and immortality. The first sentence is concerned with birth:

Our *fathers brought forth* a new nation, *conceived* in liberty.

The final phrase but one expresses the hope that

this nation, under God, shall have a *new birth* of freedom.

And the last phrase of all speaks of continuing life as the triumph over death. Again and again throughout the speech, this mystical contrast and kinship reappear: "those who *gave their lives* that that nation might *live*," "the brave men *living* and *dead*," and so in the central assertion that the dead have already consecrated their own burial place, while "it is for us, the *living*, rather to be dedicated . . . to the great task remaining." The Gettysburg Address is a prose poem; it belongs to the same world as the great elegies, and the adagios of Beethoven.

12   Its structure, however, is that of a skillfully contrived speech. The oratorical pattern is perfectly clear. Lincoln describes the occasion, dedicates the ground, and then draws a larger conclusion by calling on his hearers to dedicate themselves to the preservation of the Union. But within that, we can trace his constant use of at least two important rhetorical devices.

13   The first of these is *antithesis*: opposition, contrast. The speech is full of it. Listen:

The world will little	*note*		
nor long	*remember*	what *we say*	here
but it can never	*forget*	what *they did*	here

And so in nearly every sentence: "brave men, *living* and *dead*"; "to *add* or *detract*." There is the antithesis of the Founding Fathers and men of Lincoln's own time:

```
Our fathers brought forth a new nation . . .

now we are testing whether that nation . . . can
long endure.
```

And there is the more terrible antithesis of those who have already died and those who still live to do their duty. Now, antithesis is the figure of contrast and conflict. Lincoln was speaking in the midst of a great civil war.

14   The other important pattern is different. It is technically called *tricolon*—the division of an idea into three harmonious parts, usually of increasing power. The most famous phrase of the Address is a tricolon:

government of the people
        by the people
        for the people

The most solemn sentence is a tricolon:

we cannot dedicate
we cannot consecrate
we cannot hallow this ground.

And above all, the last sentence (which has sometimes been criticized as too complex) is essentially two parallel phrases, with a tricolon growing out of the second and then producing another tricolon: a trunk, three branches, and a cluster of flowers. Lincoln says that it is for his hearers to be dedicated to the great task remaining before them. Then he goes on,

that from these honored dead

—apparently he means "in such a way that from these honored dead"—

we take increased devotion to that cause.

Next, he restates this more briefly:

that we here highly resolve. . . .

And now the actual resolution follows, in three parts of growing intensity:

that these dead shall not have died in vain
that this nation, under God, shall have a new birth of freedom

and that (one more tricolon)

government of the people
      by the people
      for the people
shall not perish from the earth.

Now, the tricolon is the figure which, through division, emphasizes basic harmony and unity. Lincoln used antithesis because he was speaking to a people at war. He used the tricolon because he was hoping, planning, praying for peace.

15   No one thinks that when he was drafting the Gettysburg Address, Lincoln deliberately looked up these quotations and consciously chose these particular patterns of thought. No, he chose the theme. From its development and from the emotional tone of the entire occasion, all the rest followed, or grew—by that marvelous process of choice and rejection which is essential to artistic creation. It does not spoil such a work of art to analyze it as closely as we have done; it is altogether fitting and proper that we do this: for it helps us to penetrate more deeply into the rich meaning of the Gettysburg Address, and it allows us the very rare privilege of watching the workings of a great man's mind.

QUESTIONS FOR DISCUSSION AND WRITING

1. Imagine that you are the mother of a soldier—actually just a fifteen-year-old boy—who died in battle at Gettysburg. You have been against the war from the start. You stand patiently throughout the long ceremony, but after listening to Lincoln's comments, you still believe your son died in vain. Write a short letter to Lincoln, responding to his address.

2. Read Lincoln's Gettysburg Address aloud. From your own point of view, do you agree with the original newspaper reports that found the speech "dull and commonplace," do you agree with Gilbert Highet's high praise, or are your judgments mixed? Brainstorm a list of *your* positive and negative reactions to this speech. Then write one sentence expressing your overall impression.

3. List the *criteria* Highet uses to evaluate Lincoln's Gettysburg Address. Then, following each criterion, jot down examples of the support or evidence he gives. Which criteria and supporting examples do you find *least* convincing? Which are *most* convincing? Explain.

4. Highet evaluates Lincoln's speech, but he also evaluates Lincoln himself. List the criteria he uses and cite the support he gives for his judgments.

5. Identify the following structural elements in Highet's essay. For each item, indicate the appropriate paragraph number or numbers:
   - Lead-in:
   - Thesis or overall claim:
   - Background description, information about Lincoln and Gettysburg:
   - Criterion #1: judgment and evidence:
   - Criterion #2: judgment and evidence:
   - Criterion #3: judgment and evidence:
   - Conclusion:

MARGARET LAZARUS

All's Not Well in Land of *The Lion King*

Prereading Journal Entry

It may have been awhile since you have seen Disney's *The Lion King*, but if you saw it and can remember, briefly describe the main characters and the plot. Who are the good and the evil characters, and how does the story end?

Margaret Lazarus is an Oscar-winning filmmaker with Cambridge Documentary Films in Massachusetts. One of her documentaries, Strong at the Broken Places: Turning Trauma into Recovery *(1998), deals with people's ability to overcome violence and trauma and use their experience to help society, but she is better known for her documentaries on the effect of advertising on women,* Killing Us Softly 3 *(1999) and its more recent version,* The Strength to Resist: Media's Impact on Women and Girls. *She is currently Senior Fellow at the Tisch School at Tufts University. In her review of* The Lion King, *Lazarus ignores typical film criteria —such as acting, directing, and cinematography—and focuses on the cultural stereotypes in the film that are communicated to the impressionable children in the audience.*

The "Disney magic," argues Lazarus, reinforces and reproduces bigoted and stereotyped views of minorities and women in our society.

1   It's official: Walt Disney's *The Lion King* is breaking box-office records. Unfortunately, it's not breaking any stereotypes.

2   My sons, along with millions of other kids around the world, joyously awaited *The Lion King*. I was intrigued because this time Disney appeared to be skipping the old folk-tales with their traditional and primal undercurrents.

3   I hoped Disney had grown weary of reinforcing women's subordinate status by screening fables about a beauty who tames an angry male beast or a mermaid who gives up her glorious voice and splits her body to be with a prince.

4   So off we went to the movies, figuring we would enjoy an original, well-animated story about animals on the African plain. Even before the title sequence, however, I started to shudder.

5   Picture this (and I apologize for spilling the plot): The golden-maned—that is, good—lion is presenting his first born male child to his subjects. All the animals in the kingdom, known as Pride Lands, are paying tribute to the infant son that will someday be their king. These royal subjects are basically lion food—zebras, monkeys, birds, etc.—and they all live together in supposed harmony in the "circle of life."

6   Outside the kingdom, in a dark, gloomy, and impoverished elephant graveyard, are the hyenas. They live dismally jammed together among bones and litter. The hyenas are dark—mostly black—and they are nasty, menacing the little lion prince when he wanders into their territory.

7   One of their voices is done by Whoopie Goldberg, in a clearly inner-city dialect. If this is not the ghetto, I don't know what is.

8   All is not perfect inside Pride Lands, however. The king's evil brother Scar has no lionesses or cubs. Scar has a black mane, and speaks in an effeminate, limp-pawed, British style done by Jeremy Irons—seemingly a gay caricature.

9   Scar conspires with the hyenas to kill the king and send the prince into exile. In exchange for their support, Scar allows the hyenas to live in Pride Lands. But property values soon crash: The hyenas overpopulate, kill all the game, and litter the once-green land with bones.

10 Already Disney has gays and blacks ruining the "natural order," and the stereotypes keep rolling. The lionesses never question whether they should be serving Scar and the hyenas—they just worry a lot. They are mistreated, but instead of fighting back these powerful hunters

passively await salvation. (Even my 7-year-old wondered why the young, strong lioness didn't get rid of Scar.)

11   The circle of life is broken; disaster awaits everyone. But then the first-born male returns to reclaim power. The royal heir kills the gay usurper, and sends the hyenas back to the dark, gloomy, bone-filled ghetto. Order is restored and the message is clear: Only those born to privilege can bring about change.

12   This is not a story about animals—we know animals don't behave like this. This is a metaphor for society that originated in the minds of Disney's creators. These bigoted images and attitudes will lodge deeply in children's consciousness.

13   I'm not sure I always understand the law of the Hollywood jungle, but my boys definitely don't. Scared and frightened by *The Lion King*, they were also riveted, and deeply affected. But entranced by the "Disney magic," they and millions of other children were given hidden messages that can only do them—and us—harm.

QUESTIONS FOR DISCUSSION AND WRITING

1. Lazarus says that *The Lion King* reinforces cultural, racial, and gender stereotypes. Specifically, what stereotypes does she discuss? What characters or scenes contain these stereotyped views?

2. What is the thesis or overall judgment in Lazarus's essay? What sentences most clearly express this thesis?

3. Write out a three-column log for this essay. What criteria does Lazarus use in her review? What is her most important criterion? What typical criteria for film reviews does she ignore?

4. The audience for Disney's *The Lion King* is primarily children. How does Lazarus account for that audience in her review? Is it fair that Lazarus, as an adult, assumes that "these bigoted images . . . will lodge deeply in children's consciousness" without actually reporting her children's impressions? Explain.

5. Lazarus uses informal, colloquial language to communicate with her readers. For example, she begins paragraph 4 with a breezy and conversational "So off we went to the movies. . . ." Find three other examples of her informal language. Is her tone effective in appealing to her readers? Explain.

6. Rent *The Lion King* from a video store and watch it one more time. Note where you find scenes or characters that illustrate (or refute) what Lazarus says about the film. Then write your own review of the film, taking Lazarus' opinion into account. What are your most important criteria? What evidence is relevant to each criterion? What is your overall judgment of the film?

The Two Best Letters on Television

Prereading Journal Entry

What is your favorite older or classic television series—think about *Seinfeld, Cheers, M*A*S*H, ER*, or other older TV series. First, write out your criteria for good television entertainment. Then give evidence from your favorite classic series, showing why it meets some of those criteria and does not meet other criteria.

Craig Cooley was born in Canyon, Texas, and majored in biology and premedical studies at Austin College. For one of his summer jobs, he was a Texas state-certified paramedic. When he decided to write this essay, he chose a subject—the classic television series ER *—that related to his own training and experience. As he explains, his purpose was "to show people what makes* ER *worth watching," and his audience is those people who have seen* ER *but don't watch it regularly. As you read his essay, see if Cooley convinces you that* ER *'s medical accuracy and dramatic action makes the program worthy of its reputation.*

Rough Draft

Is There an Actor in the House?

1 Several years ago, most TV analysts said that the one hour drama was on its way out. Since that time, however, the hour long drama has not only not faded, but is becoming more popular than many other television genres including news shows and, to some extent, comedy. In the fall of 1994, a new drama hit the airwaves. The title only consisted of two little letters, but it has become one of the most popular shows on television. Of course, I'm talking about *ER*. The creators of *ER* took a unique approach for a medical drama, they made it an action show. To make *ER* work, however, they had to walk a fine line and do more than give the viewer blood and guts every week. I feel that the creators have struck that balance beautifully. For the rest of this paper, I hope to illustrate the points of the show that not only make it popular, but also quality television.

2 The key to any action show is action. Although that seems like a stupid thing to say, too many dramas that are supposed to be action

based just aren't. Simply blowing things up or crashing cars does not make good action television. The viewer must feel like they are right alongside the heroes as they conquer evil. If a character is in some kind of danger or involved in a crisis, the people watching at home must feel truly concerned. They must have forgotten that it is only an actor and nothing bad will really happen. If these things can be accomplished, the show will be a successful action drama. ER does this excellently. Every time the paramedics roll in with an emergency patient and the doctors go to work you're right alongside pushing drugs and giving orders. The camera motions enhance this effect. The camera is never still, it always is moving and following the action. The realism comes from the almost jerky movements of the camera. It does not follow a scene as a camera filming a movie might. There are no grand majestic camera shots for ER. The camera for ER behaves like a person, it is the viewer sitting at home watching the show. Another thing that enhances the action of ER is the medical accuracy the actors are forced to use. Early interviews with Anthony Edwards (Dr. Mark Green) focused on all the medical jargon he had to learn for the part. Knowing lots of fancy words is not enough, however, they must be used correctly. The average viewer may not notice slip-ups, but health professionals will notice, including me. Being a paramedic, I know and perform many of the procedures in ER, and I can honestly say that the show is very medically accurate. It's not just accurate for my specialty, but it is also accurate according to many of the nurses and doctors I work with. Sure, it does have its inconsistencies. Personally, I've noticed that several of the procedures that would normally be done in the field by paramedics and EMTs conveniently are always performed by the doctors. I've heard similar complaints from some other health professionals. However, we all must realize that this is a medical drama, not a documentary. If you want complete accuracy, there is a PBS show on the weekends that shows actual surgeries, but trust me, it's boring.

3   Being medically accurate and full of action only goes so far. Seeing people having heart attacks and getting into car accidents would get old after awhile. Even a die-hard paramedic (which of course I am) does not want to see that all the time. The creators of ER also realize this. When the emergency is over, there is still lots of show left. Each of the doctors and nurses have lives, just like you and me. Much like soap operas, each episode jumps back and forth between the private lives of almost every character. Their lives are often as turbulent as the emergency room. Dr. Green and his wife have been having marriage troubles.

Dr. Benton's mother died last season. The medical student, Dr. Carter, gets into all sorts of personal problems. Unlike a soap opera, however, ER does not try to make every little side story pivotal to the main plot line. The show just follows the characters as if it were real life. I guess that is the key to the show's success, it's real life. OK, not exactly real life, but all the storylines are feasible. If doctors and nurses were surveyed around the country, someone would probably have a similar experience to each one of the episodes.

4   ER seems to have done what so many TV shows try to do, be a genuine hit. With a combination of action and realism, ER has gotten the chemistry just right. Thursday nights at nine should be filled with that strange theme song for many years to come.

Revision Plan:

1. Work on camera paragraph.
2. Fix last sentence: "The doctors of ER should be making house calls on Thursday nights at nine for many years to come."
3. Need examples of drama or cut from thesis.
4. Give more examples about realism.

Final Draft

The Two Best Letters on Television

1   Several years ago, most TV analysts said that the one-hour drama was on its way out. Since that time, however, the hour-long drama has not only not faded, but is becoming more popular than many other television genres including news shows and, to some extent, comedy. In the fall of 1994, a new drama hit the airwaves. The title consisted of only two little letters, but it has become one of the most popular shows on television. Its popularity parallels shows such as *Magnum P.I.*, *M*A*S*H*, and *Cheers*. Of course, I'm talking about *ER*. The creators of *ER* took a unique approach for a medical drama: they made it an action show. Unlike other medical dramas, such as *Diagnosis Murder* and *Marcus Welby M.D.* that use medicine as a backdrop, *ER* makes it one of the main characters. To make *ER* work, however, they had to walk a fine line between action and drama. There must be enough suspense to keep viewers on the edge of their seats, but the doctors of *ER* shouldn't feel like poor Ponch and John from *CHiPs*, who never made a traffic stop without a major pile-up on the California freeways. I feel that the creators struck that balance in the same way *M*A*S*H* combined comedy and the seriousness of war. For the rest of this paper, I hope to

illustrate how they've combined action and realism to make the show not only popular, but also a quality television program worthy of nine Emmy nominations.

2   The key to any action show is action. Too many dramas that claim to be action based just aren't. Simply blowing things up or crashing cars does not make good action television. The viewer must conquer evil right alongside the heroes. Furthermore, if a character faces some kind of danger or is involved in a crisis, the people watching at home must feel truly concerned. They should wonder if the bomb will be defused in time. The audience must forget that nothing bad will really happen to their hero. Once this is accomplished, the show has a chance to go down in TV history as great action television. *ER* has this chance.

3   Every time the paramedics roll in with an emergency patient and the doctors go to work, you're right there pushing drugs and giving orders. The camera moves with the doctors, looking over their shoulders for every procedure. The camera never sits still; it moves with the action wherever it goes. For instance, the cast shoots the scenes in Trauma 1 and 2 (the rooms with the nauseating yellow/green, tile walls) from start to finish without stopping the camera. Because of this, it must weave and dodge in between doctors, sometimes having to switch back and forth between the two rooms, and still get all the dialogue and important shots. The realism comes from these almost confused movements of the camera. In fact, the camera behaves like a person overwhelmed with the situation and unable to decide what to look at next. Viewers feel right there in the trauma room alongside the doctors.

4   Enhancing the action of *ER* is the accuracy in medical terminology and procedures. Early interviews with Anthony Edwards (Dr. Mark Greene) focused on all the medical jargon he and the other actors had to learn for their parts. The actors spent hours memorizing terms like Chem.-7, CBC, thorocotomy tray, cyanotic, and ventricular fibrillation—and these are the easy ones. The average viewer may not notice slip-ups, but health professionals, including myself, would notice in a heartbeat. Being a paramedic, I know how to perform many of the procedures used on *ER*, and I can honestly say that the show is very medically accurate. When the doctors work a cardiac arrest, they do everything correctly. They correctly charge the defibrillator to 200 Joules, and give epinephrine and atropine at the correct times, in the right doses—just like my Paramedic textbook said. Watching *ER* is

almost like having a refresher class every week. These little things make the difference for me. Nurses and doctors that I work with have also noticed this. Sure, it does have its inconsistencies. Dosages aren't always <u>perfect</u> and they sometimes perform procedures more for dramatic effect than medical need. Personally, I've noticed that several of the treatments that paramedics and EMTs normally do in the field, such as assisting a patient's breathing, conveniently get saved for the doctors. I have heard similar complaints from some other health professionals. However, we all must realize that this is a medical drama, not a documentary. If you want complete accuracy, PBS carries a show on the weekends that shows actual surgeries, but trust me, it has the suspense level of watching paint dry.

5   Being medically accurate and action-packed only goes so far. Seeing people having heart attacks and getting into car accidents would get old after a while. Even a die-hard paramedic who wishes he could work alongside Ponch and John all the time (which of course I do) does not want to see an hour of patients at death's door. The creators of *ER* also realize this. When the emergency is over, there is still lots of show left. Doctors and nurses have lives, just like you and me. The writers for *ER* give realistic lives to each of the characters. Each episode not only focuses on the emergency room, but spends considerable time showing the private lives of the characters. Their lives are often as turbulent as the *ER*. Dr. Greene and his wife have been having marriage troubles. Dr. Benton's mother died last season. The medical student, Carter, gets into all sorts of trouble. Finally, Nurse Hathaway has more problems with relationships than Liz Taylor. *ER* does not try to make every story line some grandiose affair with a cliffhanger ending each week. The show just follows the characters as if it were real life. For instance, you never know which patients will die or live on each episode, just like real life. Let's face it, real life is much stranger and more exciting than what a scriptwriter can usually dream up.

6   I guess that is the key to the show's success—it's real life. Okay, not exactly real life, but all the story lines are feasible. Doctors and nurses have been surveyed around the country and many have had similar experiences to each one of the episodes. *ER* seems to have done what so many TV shows try to do: be a genuine hit. With a combination of action and realism, *ER* has gotten the chemistry just right. The doctors of *ER* should be making house calls on Thursday nights at nine for many years to come.

QUESTIONS FOR DISCUSSION AND WRITING

1. What sentence(s) contain Cooley's overall claim? What are his main criteria?

2. Outline Cooley's essay. Does he begin with a lead-in to get the reader's interest? Where does he state his purpose and thesis? Where does he give the main criteria for his evaluation? Where does his conclusion begin? Does Cooley's organization work for his essay? Explain.

3. A writer's voice gives the reader the sense of listening to a real person telling a story or arguing a point. Where is Cooley's voice most apparent? Does his voice make the essay more interesting and convincing, or does it intrude too much? Explain your response.

4. Read Cooley's first draft and compare it to his final version. In his Postscript, Cooley says that he worked on avoiding passive voice, streamlining his writing, and adding more specific examples. (See also his revision plan at the end of his rough draft.) For each of these areas, find one place or sentence in the final version where Cooley's revisions improved his essay. (Did you find other changes that helped or hurt his final draft? Explain.)

5. Reread your Prereading Journal Entry. Do you have a favorite television series you would like to evaluate? First, compare your criteria to criteria your classmates used in their journal entries. Did they have some important criteria you didn't consider? Next, be sure that you have some negative comments as well as praise for your show. If you are not critical, your review will sound like the hype that the networks have written for their own shows. Finally, be sure to cite evidence from specific episodes as Cooley does.

CHAPTER 8

Problem Solving

Wᴇ ᴀʟʟ ᴄᴏᴍᴘʟᴀɪɴ ᴀʙᴏᴜᴛ ᴘʀᴏʙʟᴇᴍs ɪɴ ᴛʜᴇ ᴡᴏʀʟᴅ around us. As armchair critics, however, few of us think about solutions to problems. And even fewer propose practical, workable solutions. An old saying goes, "If you're so smart, why aren't you rich?" Indeed. If we all know how to make money, why aren't we as rich as Donald Trump? If we can all recognize the problems we face, why can't we put solutions into action? Why is that so tough?

Writing proposals to solve problems is difficult primarily because we are asking readers to change both their *beliefs* and their *behavior.* Proposals usually demand action: Writers persuade readers to **do** something—to clean up the environment, reform television programming, reduce handgun deaths, eliminate racist and sexist behavior, improve our schools, or conduct a war on drugs. In business, proposals might request owners or management to make the workplace more efficient or more attractive for customers. Many proposals request funding for a project, to study the effects of earthquakes on buildings and bridges, or to study how learning disabilities affect college students. Solving even those "minor" problems in our personal lives requires difficult changes. Persuading someone to stop smoking or fix up a personal relationship requires demonstrating that it *should* be done and then arguing that it *can* be done—that it is possible, practical, and feasible.

Problem solving requires several critical thinking and writing skills. Writers must accurately *observe* and describe the problem so that the reader agrees that the problem is serious—and that it should be solved.

Writers should *remember* and relate their own experiences to this problem. Writers must *evaluate* the problem or *explain how* it came about, or what its causes were. Writers then *investigate* possible solutions and *explain why* their proposal is better than other solutions. As support for their proposal, writers must show that the solution is feasible: It won't take too much time, use too many resources, or cost too much. The best proposals combine creativity with hard-headed, critical thinking.

Strategies for Reading and Writing Problem-Solving Essays

As you read the problem-solving essays in this chapter, watch for the following techniques or features. Note: Not *all* proposals have *all* of these features. Depending on the occasion or audience, they will place primary emphasis on the analysis of the problem, the proposed solution, or the analysis of alternative solutions.

- **Description of some event that calls attention to the problem.** Writers of proposals often begin with some incident or event that dramatizes the problem or shows why the problem is so acute right now. If the writer is proposing a solution to violence caused by automatic weapons, the proposal may open with a description of a recent news item: School children in California were killed by an attacker wielding an assault rifle.

- **Demonstration that the problem exists and is serious.** A proposal begins by describing exactly what the problem is. If the controversy is about gun control, perhaps the weapons are only part of the problem: Drugs, early release of convicts, or psychological instability may be part of the problem, too. (Often, describing the problem in a new way or with a different perspective becomes the basis for a creative solution.)

- **Proposal of solution(s) that will solve the problem.** A proposal clearly states the writer's solution(s). The solution states the combination of changes in belief and action that will remedy the situation. Usually, writers *limit* the problem and thus the solution: We cannot eliminate all gun-related violence, but we can reduce deaths of innocent bystanders by banning sales of certain high-powered weapons.

■ **Support for the proposal.** Writers use evidence and examples to show that their solution is more reasonable than alternative solutions and/or that it is practical and feasible. Since writers cannot support a possible future action with actual examples, they often draw comparisons (how reducing gun-related violence is like reducing dependency on drugs—it requires education as well as law enforcement), or they recall past events or precedents (how a solution did or did not work in a previous case or in another country).

Reading a Problem-Solving Essay

When you read the essays in this chapter, use the following strategies.

Prereading

Use the Prereading Journal Entry (or your own freewriting on the subject) to record what you already know about this problem and its possible solutions. Also think about the audience: Who is the author addressing? Who should the author address? What does the headnote about the author tell you about the occasion and the particular kind of proposal you are reading? Who is the writer? Is this a personal or business problem or a proposal advocating sweeping social reforms? Can you determine from the context whether this proposal is serious or humorous?

First Reading

As you read, assume the role of the intended audience. Read for information, analysis of the problem, and persuasiveness of the proposal. As you read, place a "?" next to a confusing or questionable passage, an "X" next to a passage you disagree with, and an "!" next to a surprising or striking passage. Highlight or place a wavy line under important passages. Underline any words or phrases you want to look up later. *When you finish, write in your own words the problem the writer describes and the proposed solution.*

Annotated Reading

As you read the essay a second time, write your own observations and reactions in the margin. "I think this is/is not a serious problem." "I believe/don't believe that this solution will work." "The writer seems to ignore the idea that . . . . " Also read from a writer's point of view. Note the key features of proposal writing. Place brackets [ ] around passages that illustrate the main features of proposals: introductory reference to current event; description of the problem; statement of the solution; and support for the proposal. Label each strategy in the margin near your brackets. If you see the writer using other strategies, label them. Note key features of style (is the language about right or too difficult for the audience to understand?) or format that are appropriate or inappropriate for the audience and situation.

Collaborative Reading

In the class or your small group, read each other's Prereading Journal Entries. What did other people in the class or your group think about this issue *before* reading the essay? (It's important to determine your various perspectives to decide whether the author successfully changed your beliefs or persuaded you to act.) Next, read each other's marginal annotations and compile a jointly annotated version of the essay. When you've finished an annotation that reflects a consensus (and also notes minority reactions to this essay), write one question or observation about this essay that you would like the class to discuss.

Writing a Problem-Solving Essay

Writing a problem-solving essay requires research, but if you think "I need to go to the library to write a research paper," you already have the wrong idea. Start your problem-solving essay by researching or "I-searching" your own *memory* and experiences. Write out specific experiences, set at a specific time and place, which demonstrated the problem for you. If these experiences made you aware of the problem, they will certainly make your readers see the problem.

You will, at some point, need to search for information online and find a few articles and books in the library for *background information* on your problem. After all, you shouldn't be reinventing the wheel. You should see if other people know about your problem. You should know who has already attempted to solve your problem and how successful their efforts have been. Finding sources is important, but don't allow these sources to control your essay.

Don't forget to *interview* classmates, friends, and family members about this problem: What memorable experiences have they had? Then research the problem with your own legs, ears, and eyes. Where can you go to *observe* the problem firsthand? Finally, ask yourself: "Who is my audience? Who needs this information?" Use your remembering, interviewing, and observing strategies to re-create the problem for your readers. They should be able to see it, touch it, and feel it.

When you start investigating your *solution,* use your observing, remembering, and interviewing strategies. Is there some place where you can observe these solutions in action? Write down your best solutions, but then test them against your memory. Would those solutions work in your experience? What do other people think about your solutions? Finding an expert or two (a friend, a teacher, a businessperson, a doctor, a parent, or someone who works daily with your problem) is essential. You may quote these experts in your paper, you may use their advice to help you find a good written source in the library or online, or you may revise your solution based on their advice and experience.

In summary, write out your own experiences. Observe the problem firsthand. Talk to people. Think about your audience. Go to the library. Research your topic online. But remember: Your purpose is not to summarize other people's solutions, but to synthesize all the information you gather into *your own proposal* to solve the problem.

Choosing a Subject for a Problem-Solving Essay

First brainstorm personal problems and then list public problems. Where your personal problems intersect with a larger social problem, you may have a workable topic.

Personal Topics

Brainstorm a "What's Bugging You" list: living space, mechanical objects, your environment, health, food, sleep, clothes, fitness, friends, music, sports, rules and regulations, courses, teachers, parents, social life, bosses, cars, parking, and jobs.

Public Topics

Brainstorm those aspects of the following large social problems that interest you: civil rights, the environment, climate change, health reform, treatment of minorities, education, automobiles, guns, government, computers, cell phone and distracted driving, alcohol, drugs, traffic laws, taxes, political campaigns, child care, sports, union labor, cities, military weapons, and sexist stereotypes.

Another strategy for public topics is the imaginative approach. If you were the president of the United States for a week, what one problem would you try to solve? If you were a millionaire, what local problem would you work on? If you had just $10,000 to improve one aspect of your campus, what would you do?

Collecting Ideas and Information

Focus

With a possible topic in mind, focus your subject by asking and answering the following "wh" questions:

Who, what, when, and where is the problem?
How or why does the problem exist?
Who, what, when, and where are the solutions?
What are the parts or steps in your solution?
Why will your solution work?
Who needs to know about this problem and its solution?
Who is the intended audience for the proposal?

Demonstrate That the Problem Exists

Use all of the following strategies to gather information:

Remember your own experiences with the problem.
Observe people, places, and events connected with the problem.
Interview people who know about the problem.
Read and copy a few articles or parts of books on the problem.

Examine Alternative Solutions

Use the following strategies to investigate possible solutions:

Remember your own experiences with possible solutions.
Observe people, places, and events that illustrate a possible solution.
Interview experts for their ideas about feasible solutions.
Read and photocopy articles or parts of books that describe solutions.

Investigate Drawbacks or Objections

Reread your notes and sources for possible drawbacks, feasibility problems, or contradictions. Be sure to ask experts *why, when,* or *where* their recommended solution(s) might *not* work.

Shaping Your Problem-Solving Essay

As you gather information and ideas for your essay, test your topic against each of the following shaping strategies. Which of the following ideas or patterns will help organize your presentation of the problem and solution for your particular audience?

Chronological Order

Sometimes writers discuss the *history* of their problem, showing how the problem developed over time. In "One Thing to Do About Food," Marion Nestle explains how the roots of childhood obesity can be traced to "farm subsidies, tariffs, and trade agreements" that now provide 3,900 calories per day, which is "700 calories a day higher than in 1980."

Causal Analysis

Problem solving requires writers to show how the changes they recommend would effect a solution. Eric Schlosser argues in his essay about fast food that simply creating "widespread public awareness" of how the system operates and how it mistreats animals would help stop abuses and help create "sustainable agriculture and real food."

Patterns for Problem Solving

The following patterns or brief outlines suggest four ways to organize your problem-solving essay. Perhaps one of these patterns will work for your topic and audience.

Problem-Solving Pattern

   I. Introduction
  II. The problem: identify and demonstrate
 III. The solution(s): evidence
  IV. Answering possible objections, costs, drawbacks
   V. Conclusion: implementation, call to action

Point-by-Point Pattern

   I. Introduction
  II. The overall problem: identify and demonstrate
 III. One part of the problem, its solution, evidence, feasibility
  IV. Second part of the problem, its solution, evidence, feasibility
   V. Third part of the problem, its solution, evidence, feasibility
  VI. Conclusion: implementation, call to action

Alternative Pattern

    I. Introduction
   II. The problem: identify and demonstrate
  III. Alternative solution one, why it's not satisfactory
  IV. Alternative solution two, why it's not satisfactory
   V. Alternative solution three, why it works best: evidence, feasibility
  VI. Conclusion: implementation, call to action

Step-by-Step Pattern

    I. Introduction
   II. The problem: identify and demonstrate
  III. Plan for implementing solution; how solution has worked in past
  IV. Step one: show why this step is necessary and feasible
   V. Step two: show why this step is necessary and feasible
  VI. Step three: show why this step is necessary and feasible
 VII. Conclusion

Drafting Your Problem-Solving Essay

Reread your collecting and shaping notes. Make sure your photocopies of articles are handy. If you prefer to write from a sketch outline, review your plan. Reconsider your audience—are you still comfortable writing to your selected audience? Once you begin drafting, write as much as you can. If you have to stop, write a few sections of the next paragraph so you know where to pick up again. Don't stop to check spelling or punctuation. If you are working on a computer, remember to save your file frequently and print out your draft when you finish.

Revising Your Problem-Solving Essay

Use the following strategies when revising your problem-solving essay:

- **Ask a reader to role-play your audience.** Ask your reader to read your solutions critically. What have you left out? Why, when, or where might the solution *not* work? What problems with feasibility have you left out?
- **Check your introductory paragraphs.** Do you have a *lead-in* that catches your reader's attention and dramatizes the problem? Do

you have a clear *thesis* statement about your problem and your recommended solution?

- **Review your proposal for key elements.** Have you stated the problem clearly, examined alternative solutions, proposed your solution, given evidence to show why it is feasible, answered objections to your proposal, and outlined steps for implementation? (Remember that not *all* proposals have all of these elements, but don't ignore one of these tactics if it is important for *your* proposal.)
- **Support your proposal with evidence.** Use specific examples from your experience and observations, information from your interviews, and ideas and statistics from written sources.
- **Check your facts and quotations from sources for accuracy.** Check your quotations for accuracy. Use accurate in-text citations and a "Works Cited" page.
- **Revise your essay for clarity.** Check your sentences for unnecessary words, imprecise phrasing, vague language, and unnecessary padding. Use transitions between paragraphs to clarify your organization for your reader.
- **Edit your essay.** Have a peer editor review your essay for problems in spelling, word choice, punctuation, usage, or mechanics.

Postscript for Your Problem-Solving Essay

Before you hand in your essay, answer the following questions. Hand in this postscript with your completed essay.

1. Which of the following strategies did you use in gathering information and ideas for this essay: *remembering* your own experiences, *observing* the problem (or solution) firsthand, *interviewing* friends and experts, *searching* for information online, and *reading* sources from the library? Which of these strategies was most useful?

2. What was the most difficult part of writing this essay: choosing a topic, collecting information and ideas, shaping and organizing, or revising and editing? How did you work through that difficult stage?

3. What are the best parts of your essay (the introduction, the demonstration of the problem, the proposal of your solution, the conclusion)? What parts still need more work?

4. If you had one more week to work on this paper, what would you do?

Solving for Pattern

Prereading Journal Entry

The Law of Unintended Consequences, attributed to sociologist Robert K. Merton, says that it is difficult to imagine all the possible consequences of an action that we take to solve a particular problem. The law not only applies in social and economic spheres, but also in our personal lives. Describe one event in your life when you tried to solve a problem, but the action you took led to consequences that you didn't anticipate or even imagined possible.

A native of Kentucky and Professor of English at the University of Kentucky, Wendell Berry is a prolific writer of poetry, fiction, and nonfiction. He is best known for his essays and books on agricultural and ecological topics, including The Unsettling of America: Culture and Agriculture *(1977),* The Gift of Good Land *(1981),* What are People For? *(1990),* The Way of Ignorance and Other Essays *(2005), and* Bringing It to the Table: On Farming and Food *(2009). In this selection from "Solving for Pattern," which appears in* The Gift of Good Land, *Berry discusses farming and agriculture, but he focuses on the nature of problem solving itself. Although many farm "solutions" (larger tractors, feed lots, overuse of fertilizers and pesticides) solve one problem, they create a host of destructive side effects. Good solutions, Berry argues, must not address problems in isolation. Good solutions must promote the harmony, health, and quality of the whole system.*

1   Our dilemma in agriculture now is that the industrial methods that have so spectacularly solved some of the problems of food production have been accompanied by "side effects" so damaging as to threaten the survival of farming. Perhaps the best clue to the nature and the gravity of this dilemma is that it is not limited to agriculture. My immediate concern here is with the irony of agricultural methods that destroy, first, the health of the soil and, finally, the health of human communities. But I could just as easily be talking about sanitation systems that pollute, school systems that graduate illiterate students, medical cures that cause disease, or nuclear armaments that explode in the midst of the people they are meant to protect. This is a kind of surprise that is characteristic of our time: The cure proves incurable; security

results in the evacuation of a neighborhood or a town. It is only when it is understood that our agricultural dilemma is characteristic not of our agriculture but of our time that we can begin to understand why these surprises happen, and to work out standards of judgment that may prevent them.

2   To the problems of farming, then, as to other problems of our time, there appear to be three kinds of solutions:

3   There is, first, the solution that causes a ramifying series of new problems, the only limiting criterion being, apparently, that the new problems should arise beyond the purview of the expertise that produced the solution—as, in agriculture, industrial solutions to the problem of production have invariably caused problems of maintenance, conservation, economics, community health, etc., etc.

4   If, for example, beef cattle are fed in large feed lots, within the boundaries of the feeding operation itself a certain factorylike order and efficiency can be achieved. But even within those boundaries that mechanical order immediately produces biological disorder, for we know that health problems and dependence on drugs will be greater among cattle so confined than among cattle on pasture.

5   And beyond those boundaries, the problems multiply. Pen feeding of cattle in large numbers involves, first, a manure-removal problem, which becomes at some point a health problem for the animals themselves, for the local watershed, and for the adjoining ecosystems and human communities. If the manure is disposed of without returning it to the soil that produced the feed, a serious problem of soil fertility is involved. But we know too that large concentrations of animals in feed lots in one place tend to be associated with, and to promote, large cash-grain monocultures in other places. These monocultures tend to be accompanied by a whole set of specifically agricultural problems: soil erosion, soil compaction, epidemic infestations of pests, weeds, and disease. But they are also accompanied by a set of agricultural–economic problems (dependence on purchased technology; dependence on purchased fuels, fertilizers, and poisons; dependence on credit)—and by a set of community problems, beginning with depopulation and the removal of sources, services, and markets to more and more distant towns. And these are, so to speak, only the first circle of the bad effects of a bad solution. With a little care, their branchings can be traced on into nature, into the life of the cities, and into the cultural and economic life of the nation.

6   The second kind of solution is that which immediately worsens the problem it is intended to solve, causing a hellish symbiosis in which problem and solution reciprocally enlarge one another in a sequence that, so far as its own logic is concerned, is limitless—as when the problem of soil compaction is "solved" by a bigger tractor, which further compacts the soil, which makes a need for a still bigger tractor, and so on and on. There is an identical symbiosis between coal-fired power plants and air conditioners. It is characteristic of such solutions that no one prospers by them but the suppliers of fuel and equipment.

7   These two kinds of solutions are obviously bad. They always serve one good at the expense of another or of several others, and I believe that if all their effects were ever to be accounted for they would be seen to involve, too frequently if not invariably, a net loss to nature, agriculture, and the human commonwealth.

8   Such solutions always involve a definition of the problem that is either false or so narrow as to be virtually false. To define an agricultural problem as if it were solely a problem of agriculture—or solely a problem of production or technology or economics—is simply to misunderstand the problem, either inadvertently or deliberately, either for profit or because of a prevalent fashion of thought. The whole problem must be solved, not just some handily identifiable and simplifiable aspect of it.

9   Both kinds of bad solutions leave their problems unsolved. Bigger tractors do not solve the problem of soil compaction any more than air conditioners solve the problem of air pollution. Nor does the large confinement-feeding operation solve the problem of food production; it is, rather, a way calculated to allow large-scale ambition and greed to profit from food production.

10   The real problem of food production occurs within a complex, mutually influential relationship of soil, plants, animals, and people. A real solution to that problem will therefore be ecologically, agriculturally, and culturally healthful.

11   Perhaps it is not until health is set down as the aim that we come in sight of the third kind of solution: that which causes a ramifying series of solutions—as when meat animals are fed on the farm where the feed is raised, and where the feed is raised to be fed to the animals that are on the farm. Even so rudimentary a description implies a concern for pattern, for quality, which necessarily complicates the concern for production. The farmer has put plants and animals into a relationship

of mutual dependence, and must perforce be concerned for balance or symmetry, a reciprocating connection in the pattern of the farm that is biological, not industrial, and that involves solutions to problems of fertility, soil husbandry, economics, sanitation—the whole complex of problems whose proper solutions add up to health: the health of the soil, of plants and animals, of farm and farmer, of farm family and farm community, all involved in the same interested, interlocking pattern— or pattern of patterns.

12   A bad solution is bad, then, because it acts destructively upon the larger patterns in which it is contained. It acts destructively upon those patterns, most likely, because it is formed in ignorance or disregard of them. A bad solution solves for a single purpose or goal, such as increased production. And it is typical of such solutions that they achieve stupendous increases in production at exorbitant biological and social costs.

13   A good solution is good because it is in harmony with those larger patterns—and this harmony will, I think, be found to have the nature of analogy. A bad solution acts within the larger pattern the way a disease or addiction acts within the body. A good solution acts within the larger pattern the way a healthy organ acts within the body. But it must at once be understood that a healthy organ does not—as the mechanistic or industrial mind would like to say—"give" health to the body, is not exploited for the body's health, but is a part of its health. The health of organ and organism is the same, just as the health of organism and ecosystem is the same. And these structures of organ, organism, and ecosystem belong to a series of analogical integrities that begins with the organelle and ends with the biosphere.

QUESTIONS FOR DISCUSSION AND READING

1. Berry's essay explains three kinds of solutions. What are these three types of solutions, and what, according to Berry, makes the third kind the best?

2. In paragraph 1, Berry says that he "could just as easily be talking about sanitation systems that pollute, school systems that graduate illiterate students, [or] medical cures that cause disease." Choose a common social problem facing your city or town and explain how Berry might analyze this problem.

3. Berry organizes his essay for his reader by analyzing solutions into three kinds, and then he signals his organization to the reader by making transitions at the beginning of key paragraphs to help guide the

reader. For example, he begins paragraph 6 by saying, "The second kind of solution is that which immediately worsens the problem . . . " Examine the beginnings of several other paragraphs in his essay. Where do you see him using key words and phrases that let the reader know a new or related topic is about to begin? Find at least four other examples. Then use your analysis to make an outline of Berry's essay.

4. An analogy is a comparison between two things or processes in which a simple or familiar thing helps to explain a complex or unfamiliar thing. For example, we can explain how the human heart works by drawing an analogy with a simple mechanical pump. In paragraph 13, Berry says that a "bad solution acts within the larger pattern the way a disease or addiction acts within the body." Explain Berry's analogy. Then apply this analogy to one specific problem that you discussed in Question 2, above, or that you discuss in class. Does Berry's organic analogy make sense in that particular case? Why or why not?

ERIC SCHLOSSER, MARION NESTLE, MICHAEL POLLAN, TROY DUSTER AND ELIZABETH RANSOM, PETER SINGER, AND JIM HIGHTOWER

One Thing to Do About Food

Prereading Journal Entry

The news has recently been full of stories about factory farming, childhood obesity, and the generally unhealthy diets of many Americans. Take an inventory of the food you, your family, or friends typically eat. Which of those foods would you label as healthy? Which would you call unhealthy? If you are currently on a diet, what foods are you eating and which are you avoiding?

It is well known that the United States faces an epidemic of problems related to food: childhood obesity, type II diabetes in adults, junk food advertising to children, unhealthy eating by adults, unhealthy living conditions for animals in factory farms, and overall ignorance on the part of the American public about how food is produced. In a forum edited by Alice Waters for The Nation magazine, the following seven authors were among a group of twelve writers contributing short responses about reforming food production, regulation, and consumption in the United States. Following each short response, Alice Waters provides a brief biographical sketch of each author. As you read each selection, consider how each author's proposal relates to his or her professional expertise and how all these potential solutions relate to each other and to an overall solution to the problem.

Eric Schlosser

Eric Schlosser is the author of Fast Food Nation: The Dark Side of the All-American Meal *and, with Charles Wilson,* Chew on This: Everything You Don't Want to Know About Fast Food *(both Houghton Mifflin).*

1   Every year the fast-food chains, soda companies and processed-food man ufacturers spend billions marketing their products. You see their ads all the time. They tend to feature a lot of attractive, happy, skinny people having fun. But you rarely see what's most important about the food: where it comes from, how it's made and what it contains, Tyson ads don't show chickens crammed together at the company's factory farms, and Oscar Mayer ads don't reveal what really goes into those wieners. There's a good reason for this. Once you learn how our modern industrial food system has transformed what most Americans eat, you become highly motivated to eat something else.

2   The National Uniformity for Food Act of 2005, passed by the House and now before the Senate, is a fine example of how food companies and their allies work hard to keep consumers in the dark. Backed by the American Beverage Association, the American Frozen Food Association, the Coca-Cola Company, ConAgra Foods, the National Restaurant Association, the International Food Additives Council, Kraft Foods, the National Cattlemen's Beef Association and the US Chamber of Commerce, among many others, the new law would prevent states from having food safety or labeling requirements stricter than those of the federal government. In the name of "uniformity," it would impose rules that are uniformly bad. State laws that keep lead out of children's candy and warn pregnant women about dangerous ingredients would be wiped off the books.

3   What single thing could change the US food system, practically overnight? Widespread public awareness—*of* how this system operates and whom it benefits, how it harms consumers, how it mistreats animals and pollutes the land, how it corrupts public officials and intimidates the press, and most of all, how its power ultimately depends on a series of cheerful and ingenious lies. The modern environmental movement began forty-four years ago when *Silent Spring* exposed the deceptions behind the idea of "better living through chemistry." A similar

movement is now gaining momentum on behalf of sustainable agriculture and real food. We must not allow the fast-food industry, agribusiness and Congress to deceive us. "We urgently need an end to these false assurances, to the sugar-coating of unpalatable facts," Rachel Carson famously argued. "In the words of Jean Rostand, 'The obligation to endure gives us the right to know.'"

Marion Nestle

Marion Nestle, Paulette Goddard Professor of Nutrition, Food Studies and Public Health at New York University, is the author of Food Politics *(California) and* What to Eat *(North Point).*

1   From a public health perspective, obesity is the most serious nutrition problem among children as well as adults in the United States. The roots of this problem can be traced to farm policies and Wall Street. Farm subsidies, tariffs and trade agreements support a food supply that provides 3,900 calories per day per capita, roughly twice the average need, and 700 calories a day higher than in 1980, at the dawn of the obesity epidemic. In this overabundant food economy, companies must compete fiercely for sales, not least because of Wall Street's expectations for quarterly growth. These pressures induce companies to make highly profitable "junk" foods, market them directly to children and advertise such foods as appropriate' for consumption at all times, in large amounts, by children of all ages. In this business environment, childhood obesity is just collateral damage.

2   Adults may be fair game for marketers, but children are not. Children cannot distinguish sales pitches from information unless taught to do so. Food companies spend at least $10 billion annually enticing children to desire food brands and to pester parents to buy them. The result: American children consume more than one-third of their daily calories from soft drinks, sweets, salty snacks and fast food. Worse, food marketing subverts parental authority by making children believe they are supposed to be eating such foods and they—not their parents—know what is best for them to eat.

3   Today s marketing methods extend beyond television to include Internet games, product placements, character licensing and word-of-mouth campaigns—stealth methods likely to be invisible to parents. When restrictions have been called for, the food industry has resisted, invoking parental responsibility and First Amendment rights, and proposing self-regulation instead. But because companies cannot be expected to act against corporate self-interest, government regulations

are essential. Industry pressures killed attempts to regulate television advertising to children in the late 1970s, but obesity is a more serious problem now.

4   It is time to try again, this time to stop all forms of marketing foods to kids—both visible and stealth. Countries in Europe and elsewhere are taking such actions, and we could too. Controls on marketing may not be sufficient to prevent childhood obesity, but they would make it easier for parents to help children to eat more healthfully.

Michael Pollan

Michael Pollan, Knight Professor of Journalism at the University of California, Berkeley, is the author of The Omnivore's Dilemma: A Natural History of Four Meals *(Penguin).*

1   Every five years or so the President of the United States signs an obscure piece of legislation that determines what happens on a couple of hundred million acres of private land in America, what sort of food Americans eat (and how much it costs) and, as a result, the health of our population. In a nation consecrated to the idea of private property and free enterprise, you would not think any piece of legislation could have such far-reaching effects, especially one about which so few of us—even the most politically aware—know anything. But in fact the American food system is a game played according to a precise set of rules that are written by the federal government with virtually no input from anyone beyond a handful of farm-state legislators. Nothing could do more to reform America's food system—and by doing so improve the condition of Americas environment and public health—than if the rest of us were suddenly to weigh in.

2   The farm bill determines what our kids eat for lunch in school every day. Right now, the school lunch program is designed not around the goal of children's health but to help dispose of surplus agricultural commodities, especially cheap feedlot beef and dairy products, both high in fat.

3   The farm bill writes the regulatory rules governing the production of meat in this country, determining whether the meat we eat comes from sprawling, brutal, polluting factory farms and the big four meat-packers (which control 80 percent of the market) *or* from local farms,

4   Most important, the farm bill determines what crops the government will support-—and in turn what kinds of foods will be plentiful and cheap, Today that means, by and large, corn and soybeans. These two crops are the building blocks of the fast-food nation: A McDonald's

meal (and most of the processed food in your supermarket) consists of clever arrangements of corn and soybeans—the corn providing the added sugars, the soy providing the added fat, and both providing the feed for the animals. These crop subsidies (which are designed to encourage overproduction rather than to help farmers by supporting prices) are the reason that the cheapest calories in an American super-market are precisely the unhealthiest. An American shopping for food on a budget soon discovers that a dollar buys hundreds more calories in the snack food or soda aisle than it does in the produce section. Why? Because the farm bill supports the growing of corn but not the growing of fresh carrots. In the midst of a national epidemic of dia-betes and obesity our government is, in effect, subsidizing the produc-tion of high-fructose corn syrup.

5   This absurdity would not persist if more voters realized that the farm bill is not a parochial piece of legislation concerning only the interests of farmers. Today, because so few of us realize we have a dog in this fight, our legislators feel free to leave deliberations over the farm bill to the farm states, very often trading away their votes on agricultural policy for votes on issues that matter more to their constituents. But what could matter more than the health of our children and the health of our land?

6   Perhaps the problem begins with the fact that this legislation is commonly called "the farm bill"—how many people these days even know a farmer or care about agriculture? Yet we all eat. So perhaps that's where we should start, now that the debate over the 2007 farm bill is about to be joined. This time around let's call it "the food bill" and put our legislators on notice that this is about us and we're paying attention.

Troy Duster and Elizabeth Ransom

Troy Duster, director of the Institute for the History of Production of Knowl-edge at New York University, holds an appointment as Chancellor's Professor at the University of California, Berkeley. Elizabeth Ransom is a sociologist at the University of Richmond whose work focuses on globalization, food and the changing structure of agriculture.

1   Strong preferences for the kinds of food we eat are deeply rooted in the unexamined practices of the families, communities and cultural groups in which we grow up. From more than a half-century of social science research, we know that changing people's habitual behavior—from smoking to alcohol consumption, from drugs to junk food—is a mighty task. Individuals rarely listen to health messages and then change their ways.

2   If we as a nation are to alter our eating habits so that we make a notable dent in the coming health crisis around the pandemic of childhood obesity and Type II diabetes, it will be the result of long-term
planning that will include going into the schools to change the way we
learn about food. With less than 2 percent of the US population engaged with agriculture, a whole generation of people has lost valuable
knowledge that comes from growing, preserving and preparing one's
own food. A recent initiative by the City of Berkeley, California, represents a promising national model to fill this void. The city's Uni-
fied School District has approved a school lunch program that is far
more than just a project to change what students eat at the noon
hour. It is a daring attempt to change the institutional environment
in which children learn about food at an early age, a comprehensive
approach that has them planting and growing the food in a garden,
learning biology through an engaged process, with some then cooking the food that they grow. If all goes well, they will learn about the
complex relationship between nutrition and physiology so that it is
an integrated experience—not a decontextualized, abstract, rote
process.

3   But this is a major undertaking, and it will need close monitoring
and fine-tuning. Rather than assuming that one size fits all in the
school, we will need to find out what menu resonates with schools that
are embedded within local cultures and climatic conditions—for example, teaching a health-mindful approach to Mexican, Chinese, Italian, Puerto Rican, Caribbean and Midwestern cuisine. Finally, we need
to regulate the kinds of food sold in and around the school site—much
as we now do with smoking, alcohol and drugs. The transition from
agrarian to modern society has created unforeseen health challenges.
Adopting an engaged learning approach through agricultural production and consumption will help future generations learn what it means
to eat healthy food and five healthy lives.

Peter Singer

*Peter Singer is a professor of bioethics at Princeton University. His most
recent book, co-written with Jim Mason, is* The Way We Eat: Why Our
Food Choices Matter *(Rodale).*

1   There is one very simple thing that everyone can do to fix the food
system. Don't buy factory-farm products.

2   Once, the animals we raised went out and gathered things we
could not or would not eat. Cows ate grass, chickens pecked at worms

or seeds. Now the animals are brought together and we grow food for them. We use synthetic fertilizers and oil-powered tractors to grow corn or soybeans. Then we truck it to the animals so they can eat it.

3   When we feed grains and soybeans to animals, we lose most of their nutritional value. The animals use it to keep their bodies warm and to develop bones and other body parts that we cannot eat. Pig farms use six pounds of grain for every pound of boneless meat we get from them. For cattle in feedlots, the ratio is 13:1, Even for chickens, the least inefficient factory-farmed meat, the ratio is 3:1.

4   Most Americans think the best thing they could do to cut their personal contributions to global warming is to swap their family car for a fuel-efficient hybrid like the Toyota Prius. Gidon Esliel and Pamela Martin of the University of Chicago have calculated that typical meat-eating Americans would reduce their emissions even more if they switched to a vegan diet. Factory farming is not sustainable. It is also the biggest system of cruelty to animals ever devised. In the United States alone, every year nearly 10 billion animals live out their entire lives confined indoors. Hens are jammed into wire cages, five or six of them in a space that would be too small for even one hen to be able to spread her wings. Twenty thousand chickens are raised in a single shed, completely covering its floor. Pregnant sows are kept in crates too narrow for them to turn around, and too small for them to walk a few steps. Veal calves are similarly confined, and deliberately kept anemic.

5   This is not an ethically defensible system of food production. But in the United States—unlike in Europe—the political process seems powerless to constrain it. The best way to fight back is to stop buying its products. Going vegetarian is a good option, and going vegan, better still. But if you continue to eat animal products, at least boycott factory farms.

Jim Hightower

Jim Hightower (www.jimhightower.com) is a syndicated newspaper columnist, a radio commentator and the author of six books including Thieves in High Places: They've Stolen Our Country–And It's Time to Take It Back *(Plume).*

1   In the very short span of about fifty years, we've allowed our politicians to do something remarkably stupid: turn America's food-policy decisions over to corporate lobbyists, lawyers and economists. These are people who could not run a watermelon stand if we gave them the melons and had the Highway Patrol flag down the customers for them—yet, they

have taken charge of the decisions that direct everything from how and where food is grown to what our children eat in school.

2   As a result, America's food system (and much of the world's) has been industrialized, conglomerated and globalized. This is food we're talking about, not widgets! Food, by its very nature, is meant to be agrarian, small-scale and local.

3   But the Powers That Be have turned the production of our edibles away from the high art of cooperating with nature into a high-cost system of always trying to overwhelm nature. They actually torture food—applying massive doses of pesticides, sex hormones, antibiotics, genetically manipulated organisms, artificial flavorings and color, chemical preservatives, ripening gas, irradiation . . . and so awfully much more. The attitude of agribusiness is that if brute force isn't working, you're probably just not using enough of it.

4   More fundamentally, these short-cut con artists have perverted the very concept of food. Rather than being both a process and product that nurtures us (in body and spirit) and nurtures our communities, food is approached by agribusiness as just another commodity that has no higher purpose than to fatten corporate profits.

5   There's our challenge. It's not a particular policy or agency that must be changed but the most basic attitude of policy-makers. And the only way we're going to get that done is for you and me to become the policy-makers, taking charge of every aspect of our food system—from farm to fork.

6   The good news is that this "good food" movement is already well under way and gaining strength every day. It receives little media coverage, but consumers in practically every city, town and neighborhood across America are reconnecting with local farmers and artisans to de-industrialize, de-conglomeratize, de-globalize—de-Wal-Martize—their food systems.

7   Of course, the Powers That Be sneer at these efforts, saying they can't succeed. But, as a friend of mine who is one of the successful pioneers in this burgeoning movement puts it: "Those who say it can't be done should not interrupt those who are doing it."

8   Look around wherever you are and you'll find local farmers, consumers, chefs, marketers, gardeners, environmentalists, workers, churches, co-ops, community organizers and just plain folks who are doing it. These are the Powers That Ought to Be—and I think they will be. Join them!

QUESTIONS FOR DISCUSSION AND READING

1. Choose one of the short essays and annotate it for the analysis of the problem and then for the author's proposed solution. For the author you choose, how much discussion is about the problem and how much about the solution? Which part—the discussion of the problem or the explanation of the solution—is more specific, detailed, and supported? What parts could be explained further to make the author's recommendations more persuasive? Be prepared to present your findings in class.

2. Find and underline each author's claim statement. What "one thing" does each author recommend should be done to address the problem? What reasons and evidence does each author offer in support of his or her claim? Explain.

3. Which of the short articles did you find most effective, most educational, or most persuasive? Which of the short articles did you find least effective? Defend your choice by analyzing the argument, reasons, and supporting evidence of the most effective essay and explain why its analysis of the problem or proposed solution is more effective than the article you thought least effective.

4. Assume that Alice Waters has asked you to contribute a short essay to this forum. Do some research on your library databases and on the Web on your chosen topic. Write a short essay that explains, for an audience similar to the readers of *The Nation*, what your position is about food production or eating habits and what solutions you would offer to the problems you describe.

MICHAEL BÉRUBÉ

How to End Grade Inflation: A Modest Proposal

Prereading Journal Entry

In your journal, reflect on the purpose of grades. Do grades help motivate students to study? Do grades really measure achievement? What is the difference, really, between "A," "B," and "C" grades? Should students receive a grade of "D" or "F" if they complete most of the assignments? Have grades become so inflated that a "C" grade is really a below average grade? Should something be done about inflated grading?

Michael Bérubé is the Paterno Family professor of literature at Pennsylvania State University and teaches American literature, cultural studies, and disability studies. He is the author of several books, including Life As We Know It: A Father, A Family, and an Exceptional Child *(1996),* Rhetorical Occasions: Essays on Humans and the Humanities *(2006), and* The Left at War *(2009). He also writes his own blog on a variety of subjects including politics, popular culture, current events, and hockey (he calls writing his hockey blogs "hogging"). He recently noted, with only minimal modesty, that his blog recently received its nine-millionth hit.* "How to End Grade Inflation: A Modest Proposal" *first appeared in the New York Times.*

1   Last month, Princeton University announced it would combat grade inflation by proposing that A-minuses, A's and A-pluses be awarded to no more than the top 35 percent of students in any course. For those of us in higher education, the news has come as a shock, almost as if Princeton had declared that spring in central New Jersey would begin promptly on March 21, with pleasant temperatures in the 60's and 70's through the end of the semester. For until now, grade inflation was like the weather: it got worse every year, or at least everyone said so, and yet hardly anybody did anything about it.

2   There is nothing inherently wrong with grade inflation. Imagine a system of scoring on a scale from 1 to 6 in which everyone gets a 5 and above, or a scale of 1 to 10 in which the lowest posted score is around 8.5. Such are the worlds of figure skating and gymnastics. If colleges employed similar scoring systems, the class valedictorian would come in with a 4.0, followed closely by hundreds of students above 3.95, trailed by the class clown at 3.4.

3   Critics would argue that we must be perilously close to such a system right now. Several years ago, Harvard awarded "honors" to 90 percent of its graduates. For its part, Princeton has disclosed that A's have been given 47 percent of the time in recent years, up from 31 percent in the mid-1970's. Perhaps grade inflation is most severe at the most elite colleges, where everyone is so far above average that the rules of the Caucus Race in "Alice in Wonderland" apply: everybody has won, and all must have prizes. At the school where I teach, Penn State, grade inflation over the same period has not been nearly so drastic. In the spring semester of 1975, the average G.P.A. was 2.86; in 2001 it had risen to only 3.02.

4   Still, we don't grade all that toughly. English departments have basically worked on the A/B binary system for some time: A's and A-minuses for the best students, B's for everyone else and C's, D's and F's for

students who miss half the classes or threaten their teachers with bodily harm. At Penn State, A's accounted for 47 percent of the grades in English in 2002. The numbers are similar for sociology, comparative literature and psychology—and indeed for the College of Liberal Arts as a whole. The sciences and engineering, notoriously, are stingier.

5   What to do? If we so desired, we could recalibrate grades at Penn State, at Princeton or at any college in the country. The principle is simple enough, and it's crucial to every diving competition: we would merely need to account for each course's degree of difficulty.

6   Every professor, and every department, produces an average grade—an average for the professor over her career and an average for the discipline over the decades. And if colleges really wanted to clamp down on grade inflation, they could whisk it away statistically, simply by factoring those averages into each student's G.P.A. Imagine that G.P.A.'s were calculated on a scale of 10 with the average grade, be it a B-minus or an A-minus, counted as a 5. The B-plus in chemical engineering, where the average grade is, say, C-plus, would be rewarded accordingly and assigned a value of 8; the B-plus in psychology, where the average grade might be just over B-plus, would be graded like an easy dive, adequately executed, and given a 4.7.

7   After all, colleges keep all the necessary statistics—by year, by course and by department. We know perfectly well which courses require a forward somersault with two and a half twists from the pike position for an A, and which courses will give B's for cannonballs. We could even encourage professors and entire departments to increase their prestige by lowering their average grade and thereby increasing their "degree of difficulty." Students who earn A's in difficult courses would benefit — as would students who earn B's.

8   Incorporating "degree of difficulty" into students' G.P.A.'s would turn campuses upside down; it would eliminate faculty capriciousness precisely by factoring it in; and it would involve nothing more than using the numbers we already have at our disposal. It would be confusing as hell. But it would yield a world in which the average grade was never anything more or less than the middle of the scale.

QUESTIONS FOR DISCUSSION AND WRITING

1. In paragraph two, Berube writes, "There is nothing inherently wrong with grade inflation." If that is the case, then why does he propose to end grade inflation? What problems, according to Berube, are associated with inflated grades?

2. Berube bases his argument on an analogy between giving grades and judging figure skating or diving. Examine this analogy. How is giving grades similar to determining scores for figure skating? In what ways are they different? Should Berube choose a different analogy in order to argue his point? Would his argument be more effective if he didn't use this analogy? Explain.

3. As part of his solution, Berube argues that we need to account for each course's "degree of difficulty." What problem associated with grade inflation would his system of "degree of difficulty" solve? Might this system have "unintended consequences" that might negatively effect students' educations?

4. Research different grading systems at different universities. Some use point systems, based on a 100 point scale. Some do not give grades at all, but just write performance evaluations. Write your own essay proposing grading reforms at your college or university, or just for your own major. What problems with current grading practices exist and how would you propose solving them? Assume that you are writing for your campus newspaper.

DEBORAH TANNEN

CrossTalk

Prereading Journal Entry

In a course you are currently taking where class discussions take place, take notes for a week on the following questions: How many people participate during the class? How many are men, how many women? Do you notice any differences between what males say in class and what females say? Specifically, do women ask more questions and preface their questions with disclaimers? Are men's comments longer and more assertive? Does the teacher or do the rest of the students respond differently to men versus women?

Deborah Tannen was born in Brooklyn, New York, and received her doctorate from the University of California at Berkeley. She is currently a professor of linguistics at Georgetown University and has written a variety of academic essays and popular books including You Just Don't Understand: Women and Men in Conversation *(1990),* Talking from 9 to 5 *(1994),* The Argument Culture: Moving from Debate to Dialogue *(1998),* You're Wearing

That?: Understanding Mothers and Daughters in Conversation *(2006)*, *and* You Were Always Mom's Favorite!: Sisters in Conversation Throughout Their Lives *(2009). In "CrossTalk," which appeared in* The Professional Communicator *and also in* Talking from 9 to 5, *Tannen focuses on how the conversational styles of women and men create communication breakdowns and how to solve those problems.*

1   A woman who owns a bookstore needed to have a talk with the store manager. She had told him to help the bookkeeper with billing, he had agreed, and now, days later, he still hadn't done it. Thinking how much she disliked this part of her work, she sat down with the manager to clear things up. They traced the problem to a breakdown in communication.

2   She had said, "Sarah needs help with the bills. What do you think about helping her out?" He had responded, "OK," by which he meant, "OK, I'll think about whether or not I want to help her." During the next day, he thought about it and concluded that he'd rather not.

3   This wasn't just an ordinary communication breakdown that could happen between any two people. It was a particular sort of breakdown that tends to occur between women and men.

4   Most women avoid giving orders. More comfortable with decision-making by consensus, they tend to phrase requests as questions, to give others the feeling they have some say in the matter and are not being bossed around. But this doesn't mean they aren't making their wishes clear. Most women would have understood the bookstore owner's question, "What do you think about helping her out?" as assigning a task in a considerate way.

5   The manager, however, took the owner's words literally. She had asked him what he thought; she hadn't told him to *do* anything. So he felt within his rights when he took her at her word, thought about it and decided not to help Sarah.

6   Women in positions of authority are likely to regard such responses as insubordination: "He knows I am in charge, and he knows what I want; if he doesn't do it, he is resisting my authority."

7   There may be a kernel of truth in this view—most men are inclined to resist authority if they can because being in a subordinate position makes them intensely uncomfortable. But indirect requests that are transparent to women may be genuinely opaque to men. They assume that people in authority will give orders if they really want something done.

8   These differences in management styles are one of many manifestations of gender differences in how we talk to one another. Women use language to create connection and rapport; men use it to negotiate their status in a hierarchical order. It isn't that women are unaware of status or that men don't build rapport, but that *the genders tend to focus on different goals.*

The Source of Gender Differences

9   These differences stem from the ways boys and girls learn to use language while growing up. Girls tend to play indoors, either in small groups or with one other girl. The center of a girl's social life is her best friend, with whom she spends a great deal of time sitting, talking and exchanging secrets. It is the telling of secrets that makes them best friends. Boys tend to play outdoors, in larger groups, usually in competitive games. It's doing things together that makes them friends.

10   Anthropologist Marjorie Harness Goodwin compared boys and girls at play in a black inner-city neighborhood in Philadelphia. Her findings, which have been supported by researchers in other settings, show that the boys' groups are hierarchical: high-status boys give orders, and low-status boys have to follow them, so they end up being told what to do. Girls' groups tend to be egalitarian: girls who appeared "better" than others or gave orders were not countenanced and in some cases, were ostracized.

11   So while boys are learning to fear being "put down" and pushed around, girls are learning to fear being "locked out." Whereas high-status boys establish and reinforce their authority by giving orders and resisting doing what others want, girls tend to make suggestions, which are likely to be taken up by the group.

Cross-Gender Communication in the Workplace

12   The implications of these different conversational habits and concerns in terms of office interactions are staggering. Men are inclined to continue to jockey for position, trying to resist following orders as much as possible within the constraints of their jobs.

13   Women, on the other hand, are inclined to do what they sense their bosses want, whether or not they are ordered to. By the same token, women in positions of authority are inclined to phrase their requests as suggestions and to assume they will be respected because of their authority. These assumptions are likely to hold up as long as both parties are women, but they may well break down in cross-gender communication.

14   When a woman is in the position of authority, such as the book-store owner, she may find her requests are systematically misunderstood by men. And when a woman is working for a male boss, she may find that her boss gives bold commands that seem unnecessarily imperious because most women would prefer to be asked rather than ordered. One woman who worked at an all-male radio station commented that the way the men she worked for told her what to do made her feel as if she should salute and say, "Yes, boss."

15   Many men complain that a woman who is indirect in making requests is manipulative: she's trying to get them to do what she wants without telling them to do it. Another common accusation is that she is insecure: she doesn't know what she wants. But if a woman gives direct orders, the same men might complain that she is aggressive, unfeminine or worse.

16   Women are in a double bind: *If we talk like women, we are not respected. If we talk like men, we are not liked.*

17   We have to walk a fine line, finding ways to be more direct without appearing bossy. The bookstore owner may never be comfortable by directly saying, "Help Sarah with the billing today," but she might find some compromise such as, "Sarah needs help with the billing. I'd appreciate it if you would make some time to help her out in the next day or two." This request is clear, while still reflecting women's preferences for giving reasons and options.

18   What if you're the subordinate and your boss is a man who's offending you daily by giving you orders? If you know him well enough, one potential solution is "metacommunication"—that is, talk about communication. Point out the differences between women and men, and discuss how you could accommodate to each other's styles. (You may want to give him a copy of this article or my book.)

19   But if you don't have the kind of relationship that makes metacommunication possible, you could casually, even jokingly, suggest he give orders another way. Or just try to remind yourself it's a cross-cultural difference and try not to take his curtness personally.

How to Handle a Meeting

20   There are other aspects of women's styles that can work against us in a work setting. Because women are most comfortable using language to create rapport with someone they feel close to, and men are used to talking in a group where they have to prove themselves and display what they know, a formal meeting can be a natural for men and

a hard nut to crack for women. Many women find it difficult to speak up at meetings; if they do, they may find their comments ignored, perhaps later to be resuscitated by a man who gets credit for the idea. Part of this is simply due to the expectation that men will have more important things to contribute.

21   But the way women and men tend to present themselves can aggravate this inequity. At meetings, men are more likely to speak often, at length and in a declamatory manner. They may state their opinions as fact and leave it to others to challenge them.

22   Women, on the other hand, are often worried about appearing to talk too much—a fear that is justified by research showing that when they talk equally, women are perceived as talking more than men. As a result, many women are hesitant to speak at a meeting and inclined to be succinct and tentative when they do.

Developing Options

23   Working on changing your presentational style is one option; another is to make your opinions known in private conversation with the key people before a meeting. And if you are the key person, it would be wise to talk personally to the women on your staff rather than assuming all participants have had a chance to express themselves at the meeting.

24   Many women's reticence about displaying their knowledge at a meeting is related to their reluctance to boast. They find it more humble to keep quiet about their accomplishments and wait for someone else to notice them. But most men learn early on to display their accomplishments and skills. And women often find that no one bothers to ferret out their achievements if they don't put them on display. Again, a woman risks criticism if she talks about her achievements, but this may be a risk she needs to take, to make sure she gets credit for her work.

25   I would never want to be heard as telling women to adopt men's styles across the board. For one thing, there are many situations in which women's styles are more successful. For example, the inclination to make decisions by consensus can be a boon to a woman in a managerial position. Many people, men as well as women, would rather feel they have influence in decision-making than be given orders.

26   Moreover, recommending that women adopt men's styles would be offensive, as well as impractical, because women are judged by the norms for women's behavior, and doing the same thing as men has a very different, often negative, effect.

A Starting Point

27   Simply knowing about gender differences in conversational style provides a starting point for improving relations with the women and men who are above and below you in a hierarchy.

28   The key is *flexibility*; a way of talking that works beautifully with one person may be a disaster with another. If one way of talking isn't working, try another, rather than trying harder by doing more of the same.

29   Once you know what the parameters are, you can become an observer of your own interactions, and a style-switcher when you choose.

QUESTIONS FOR DISCUSSION AND WRITING

1. According to Tannen, what different tendencies do men and women have in their conversational habits or styles? What is the source of these differences? What problems do these differences create? What does Tannen recommend to help avoid these problems in communication?

2. Tannen gives titles to each of the sections of her essay: "The Source of Gender Differences," "Cross-Gender Communication in the Workplace," and "How to Handle a Meeting." Is using these subheadings an effective organizational strategy, considering her purpose and audience? Explain. (Should you use subheadings in the essay you are currently writing? Why or why not?)

3. Tannen published this article in an academic journal called *The Professional Communicator*. Whom is she addressing in this essay: teachers and academics? Women working in the business or corporate world? Cite evidence from the article to support your explanation.

4. What exactly does the title of this essay—"CrossTalk"—mean or suggest? Is this an effective title for her essay? Explain.

5. Is Tannen using a feminine style in writing her article? Does she offer suggestions rather than make assertions? Does she encourage consensus building rather than telling her readers what to think and what to believe? Cite specific passages to support your answer.

6. At the beginning of her essay, Tannen refers to women in the third-person—"a woman who owns a bookstore," "most women," and "women in positions of authority." By the middle of the essay, however, Tannen refers to women in the first-person plural ("we" and "us") and in the second person ("you"). Find specific sentences where Tannen mixes third- and first-person, or uses first- and second-person address exclusively. What does your analysis tell you about her intended audience? Is she addressing only women? Do men have a role to play in helping to develop options to improve cross-gender communication?

7. Conduct your own observation of the conversational habits or styles of men and women. Do women you know ask indirect questions and work for consensus? Do the men you know make assertions and give orders in a hierarchical manner? Collect your own data from conversations and write a response to Tannen's essay.

A White Woman of Color

Prereading Journal Entry

Describe one time in your life when you tried to cross the boundaries between one culture and another or between one language and another. What were the conflicting cultures? Were you able to make the transition? What are your feelings as you look back on that event or period in your life?

Julia Alvarez was born in New York City, but was raised in the Dominican Republic. With the publication of novels such as How the García Girls Lost Their Accents *(1991),* In the Time of Butterflies *(1994),* Yo! *(1996), and* Return to Sender *(2009), she has become one of the best-known Latina writers. She has published fiction, essays, and poetry in dozens of journals and magazines, has an acclaimed volume of poetry,* Homecoming: New and Collected Poems *(1996), as well as several books for young readers including* How Tía Lola Learned to Teach *(2010). Alvarez writes that when she arrived in this country at the age of ten, she felt out of place, believing "that I would never belong in this world of Americans who were so different from me." Then, she says "magic happened" in her life when she discovered "an even better world: the one words can create in a story or poem." In this essay from* Half and Half: Writers on Growing Up Biracial and Bicultural *(1998), Alvarez recalls her early experiences with race and culture, beginning with her life in the Dominican Republic and continuing in the United States. As you read her essay, see how her experiences helped her realize a possible solution for racial and cultural differences in America.*

1   Growing up in the Dominican Republic, I experienced racism within my own family—though I didn't think of it as racism. But there was definitely a hierarchy of beauty, which was the main currency in our daughters-only family. It was not until years later, from the vantage

point of this country and this education, that I realized that this hierarchy of beauty was dictated by our coloring. We were a progression of whitening, as if my mother were slowly bleaching the color out of her children.

2   The oldest sister had the darkest coloring, with very curly hair and "coarse" features. She looked the most like Papi's side of the family and was considered the least pretty. I came next, with "good hair," and skin that back then was a deep olive, for I was a tomboy—another dark mark against me—who would not stay out of the sun. The sister right after me had my skin color, but she was a good girl who stayed indoors, so she was much paler, her hair a golden brown. But the pride and joy of the family was the baby. She was the one who made heads turn and strangers approach asking to feel her silken hair. She was white white, an adjective that was repeated in describing her color as if to deepen the shade of white. Her eyes were brown, but her hair was an unaccountable towheaded blond. Because of her coloring, my father was teased that there must have been a German milkman in our neighborhood. How could *she* be *his* daughter? It was clear that this youngest child resembled Mami's side of the family.

3   It was Mami's family who were *really* white. They were white in terms of race, and white also in terms of class. From them came the fine features, the pale skin, the lank hair. Her brothers and uncles went to schools abroad and had important businesses in the country. They also emulated the manners and habits of North Americans. Growing up, I remember arguments at the supper table on whether or not it was proper to tie one's napkin around one's neck, on how much of one's arm one could properly lay on the table, on whether spaghetti could be eaten with the help of a spoon. My mother, of course, insisted on all the protocol of knives and forks and on eating a little portion of everything served; my father, on the other hand, defended our eating whatever we wanted, with our hands if need be, so we could "have fun" with our food. My mother would snap back that we looked like *jibaritas* who should be living out in the country. Of course, that was precisely where my father's family came from.

4   Not that Papi's family weren't smart and enterprising, all twenty-five brothers and sisters. (The size of the family in and of itself was considered very country by some members of Mami's family.) Many of Papi's brothers had gone to the university and become professionals. But their education was totally island—no fancy degrees from Andover and Cornell and Yale, no summer camps or school songs in another

language. Papi's family still lived in the interior versus the capital, in old-fashioned houses without air conditioning, decorated in ways my mother's family would have considered, well, tasteless. I remember antimacassars on the backs of rocking chairs (which were the living-room set), garish paintings of flamboyant trees, ceramic planters with plastic flowers in bloom. They were *criollos*—creoles—rather than cosmopolitans, expansive, proud, colorful. (Some members had a sixth finger on their right—or was it their left hand?) Their features were less aquiline than Mother's family's, the skin darker, the hair coarse and curly. Their money still had the smell of the earth on it and was kept in a wad in their back pockets, whereas my mother's family had money in the Chase Manhattan Bank, most of it with George Washington's picture on it, not Juan Pablo Duarte's.

5 It was clear to us growing up then that lighter was better, but there was no question of discriminating against someone because he or she was dark-skinned. Everyone's family, even an elite one like Mami's, had darker-skinned members. All Dominicans, as the saying goes, have a little black behind the ears. So, to separate oneself from those who were darker would have been to divide *una familia*, a sacrosanct entity in our culture. Neither was white blood necessarily a sign of moral or intellectual or political superiority. All one has to do is page through a Dominican history book and look at the number of dark-skinned presidents, dictators, generals, and entrepreneurs to see that power has not resided exclusively or even primarily among the whites on the island. The leadership of our country has been historically "colored."

6 But being black was something else. A black Dominican was referred to as a "dark Indian" *(indio oscuro)*—unless you wanted to come to blows with him, that is. The real blacks were the Haitians who lived next door and who occupied the Dominican Republic for twenty years, from 1822 to 1844, a fact that can still so inflame the Dominican populace you'd think it had happened last year. The denial of the Afro-Dominican part of our culture reached its climax during the dictatorship of Trujillo, whose own maternal grandmother was Haitian. In 1937, to protect Dominican race purity, Trujillo ordered the overnight genocide of thousands (figures range from 4,000 to 20,000) of Haitians by his military, who committed this atrocity using only machetes and knives in order to make this planned extermination took like a "spontaneous" border skirmish. He also had the Dominican Republic declared a white nation despite the evidence of the mulatto senators who were forced to pass this ridiculous measure.

7   So, black was not so good, kinky hair was not so good, thick lips not so good. But even if you were *indio oscuro con pelo malo y una bemba de aquí a Baní,* you could still sit in the front of the bus and order at the lunch counter—or the equivalent thereof. There was no segregation of races in the halls of power. But in the aesthetic arena—the one to which we girls were relegated as females—lighter was better. Lank hair and pale skin and small, fine features were better. All I had to do was stay out of the sun and behave myself and I could pass as a pretty white girl.

8   Another aspect of my growing up also greatly influenced my thinking on race. Although I was raised in the heart of a large family, my day-to-day caretakers were the maids. Most of these women were dark-skinned, some of Haitian background. One of them, Misiá;, had been spared the machetes of the 1937 massacre when she was taken in and hidden from the prowling *guardias* by the family. We children spent most of the day with these women. They tended to us, nursed us when we were sick, cradled us when we fell down and scraped an elbow or knee (as a tomboy, there was a lot of this scraping for me), and most important, they told us stories of *los santos* and *el barón del cementerio,* of *el cuco and las ciguapas,* beautiful dark-skinned creatures who escaped capture because their feet were turned backwards so they left behind a false set of footprints. These women spread the wings of our imaginations and connected us deeply to the land we came from. They were the ones with the stories that had power over us.

9   We arrived in Nueva York in 1960, before the large waves of Caribbean immigrants created little Habanas, little Santo Domingos, and little San Juans in the boroughs of the city. Here we encountered a whole new kettle of wax—as my malapropping Mami might have said. People of color were treated as if they were inferior, prone to violence, uneducated, untrustworthy, lazy—all the "bad" adjectives we were learning in our new language. Our dark-skinned aunt, Tía Ana, who had lived in New York for several decades and so was the authority in these matters, recounted stories of discrimination on buses and subways. These Americans were so blind! One drop of black and you were black. Everyone back home would have known that Tía Ana was not black: she had "good hair" and her skin color was a light *indio.* All week, she worked in a *factoría* in the Bronx, and when she came to visit us on Saturdays to sew our school clothes, she had to take three trains to our nice neighborhood where the darkest face on the street was usually her own.

10   We were lucky we were white Dominicans or we would have had a much harder time of it in this country. We would have encountered a lot more prejudice than we already did, for white as we were, we found that our Latino-ness, our accents, our habits and smells, added "color" to our complexion. Had we been darker, we certainly could not have bought our mock Tudor house in Jamaica Estates. In fact, the African American family who moved in across the street several years later needed police protection because of threats. Even so, at the local school, we endured the bullying of classmates. "Go back to where you came from!" they yelled at my sisters and me in the playground. When some of them started throwing stones, my mother made up her mind that we were not safe and began applying to boarding schools where privilege transformed prejudice into patronage.

11   "So where are you from?" my classmates would ask.

12   "Jamaica Estates," I'd say, an edge of belligerence to my voice. It was obvious from my accent, if not my looks, that I was not *from* there in the way they meant being from somewhere.

13   "I mean *originally*."

14   And then it would come out, the color, the accent, the cousins with six fingers, the smell of garlic.

15   By the time I went off to college, a great explosion of American culture was taking place on campuses across the country. The civil rights movement, the Vietnam War and subsequent peace movement, the women's movement, were transforming traditional definitions of American identity. Ethnicity was in: my classmates wore long braids like Native Americans and peasant blouses from Mexico and long, diaphanous skirts and dangly earrings from India. Suddenly, my foreignness was being celebrated. This reversal felt affirming but also disturbing. As huipils, serapes, and embroidered dresses proliferated about me, I had the feeling that my ethnicity had become a commodity. I resented it.

16   When I began looking for a job after college, I discovered that being a white Latina made me a nonthreatening minority in the eyes of these employers. My color was a question *only* of culture, and if I kept my cultural color to myself, I was "no problem." Each time I was hired for one of my countless "visiting appointments"—they were never permanent "invitations," mind you—the inevitable questionnaire would accompany my contract in which I was to check off my RACE: CAUCASIAN, BLACK, NATIVE AMERICAN, ASIAN, HISPANIC, OTHER. How could a Dominican divide herself in this way? Or was I really a

Dominican anymore? And what was a Hispanic? A census creation—there is no such culture—how could it define who I was at all? Given this set of options, the truest answer might have been to check off OTHER.

17   For that was the way I had begun to think of myself. Adrift from any Latino community in this country, my culture had become an internal homeland, periodically replenished by trips "back home." But as a professional woman on my own, I felt less and less at home on the island. My values, the loss of my Catholic faith, my lifestyle, my wardrobe, my hippy ways, and my feminist ideas separated me from my native culture. I did not subscribe to many of the mores and constraints that seemed to be an intrinsic part of that culture. And since my culture had always been my "color," by rejecting these mores I had become not only Americanized but whiter.

18   If I could have been a part of a Latino community in the United States, the struggle might have been, if not easier, less private and therefore less isolating. These issues of acculturation and ethnicity would have been struggles to share with others like me. But all my North American life I had lived in shifting academic communities—going to boarding schools, then college, and later teaching wherever I could get those yearly appointments—and these communities reflected the dearth of Latinos in the profession. Except for friends in Spanish departments, who tended to have come from their countries of origin to teach rather than being raised in this country as I was, I had very little daily contact with Latinos.

19   Where I looked for company was where I had always looked for company since coming to this country: in books. At first the texts that I read and taught were the ones prescribed to me, the canonical works which formed the content of the bread-and-butter courses that as a "visiting instructor" I was hired to teach. These texts were mostly written by white male writers from Britain and the United States, with a few women thrown in and no Latinos. Thank goodness for the occasional creative writing workshop where I could bring in the multicultural authors I wanted. But since I had been formed in this very academy, I was clueless where to start. I began to educate myself by reading, and that is when I discovered that there were others out there like me, hybrids who came in a variety of colors and whose ethnicity and race were an evolving process, not a rigid paradigm or a list of boxes, one of which you checked off.

20   This discovery of my ethnicity on paper was like a rebirth. I had
been going through a pretty bad writer's block: the white page seemed
impossible to fill with whatever it was I had in me to say. But listening
to authors like Maxine Hong Kingston, Toni Morrison, Gwendolyn
Brooks, Langston Hughes, Maya Angelou, June Jordan, and to Lorna
Dee Cervantes, Piri Thomas, Rudolfo Anaya, Edward Rivera, Ernesto
Galarza (that first wave of Latino writers), I began to hear the language
"in color." I began to see that literature could reflect the otherness I was
feeling, that the choices in fiction and poetry did not have to be
bleached out of their color or simplified into either/or. A story could allow for the competing claims of different parts of ourselves and where
we came from.

21   Ironically, it was through my own stories and poems that I finally
made contact with Latino communities in this country. As I published
more, I was invited to read at community centers and bilingual programs. Latino students, who began attending colleges in larger numbers in the late seventies and eighties, sought me out as a writer and
teacher "of color." After the publication of *How the García Girls Lost
Their Accents,* I found that I had become a sort of spokesperson for Dominicans in this country, a role I had neither sought nor accepted. Of
course, some Dominicans refused to grant me any status as a "real"
Dominican because I was "white." With the color word there was also a
suggestion of class. My family had not been among the waves of economic immigrants that left the island in the seventies, a generally
darker-skinned, working-class group, who might have been the maids
and workers in my mother's family house. We had come in 1960, political refugees, with no money but with "prospects": Papi had a friend
who was the doctor at the Waldorf Astoria and who helped him get a
job; Mami's family had money in the Chase Manhattan Bank they
could lend us. We had changed class in America—from Mami's elite
family to middle-class spics—but our background and education and
most especially our pale skin had made mobility easier for us here. We
had not undergone the same kind of race struggles as other Dominicans; therefore, we could not be "real" Dominicans.

22   What I came to understand and accept and ultimately fight for
with my writing is the reality that ethnicity and race are not fixed con-
structs or measurable quantities. What constitutes our ethnicity and
our race—once there is literally no common ground beneath us to define it—evolves as we seek to define and redefine ourselves in new

contexts. My Latino-ness is not something someone can take away from me or leave me out of with a definition. It is in my blood: it comes from that mixture of biology, culture, native language, and experience that makes me a different American from one whose family comes from Ireland or Poland or Italy. My Latino-ness is also a political choice. I am choosing to hold on to my ethnicity and native language even if I can "pass." I am choosing to color my Americanness with my Dominicanness even if it came in a light shade of skin color.

23 I hope that as Latinos, coming from so many different countries and continents, we can achieve solidarity in this country as the mix that we are. I hope we won't shoot ourselves in the foot in order to maintain some sort of false "purity" as the glue that holds us together. Such an enterprise is bound to fail. We need each other. We can't afford to reject the darker or lighter varieties, and to do so is to have absorbed a definition of ourselves as exclusively one thing or the other. And haven't we learned to fear that word "exclusive"? This reductiveness is absurd when we are talking about a group whose very definition is that of a mestizo race, a mixture of European, indigenous, African, and much more. Within this vast circle, shades will lighten and darken into overlapping categories. If we cut them off, we diminish our richness and we plant a seed of ethnic cleansing that is the root of the bloodshed we have seen in Bosnia and the West Bank and Rwanda and even our own Los Angeles and Dominican Republic.

24 As we Latinos redefine ourselves in America, making ourselves up and making ourselves over, we have to be careful, in taking up the promises of America, not to adopt its limiting racial paradigms. Many of us have shed customs and prejudices that oppressed our gender, race, or class on our native islands and in our native countries. We should not replace these with modes of thinking that are divisive and oppressive of our rich diversity. Maybe as a group that embraces many races and differences, we Latinos can provide a positive multicultural, multiracial model to a divided America.

QUESTIONS FOR DISCUSSION AND WRITING

1. Alvarez is writing a narrative that is also a problem-solving essay. What is the problem she describes? Which sentence(s) most clearly state the problem? What is her solution? Which sentence(s) most clearly state her solution or recommendation?

2. In her final paragraph, Alvarez restates one of the main ideas for her essay. Work backwards, paragraph by paragraph, underlining

sentences which contain earlier versions of this theme or ideas related to this theme. Find—and write out—at least three earlier statements that relate to this theme. Explain how these sentences and ideas are similar to or different from her statement in the final paragraph.

3. At the beginning of her essay, Alvarez examines notions of race based on her childhood in the Dominican Republic. Beginning with paragraph 9, she then examines aspects of race in the United States. In light of her recommendations at the end of the essay, explain why it is effective for Alvarez to examine racism in her own country before she discusses race issues in the United States.

4. In the final paragraph of her essay, Alvarez refers twice to "we Latinos." Are Latinos the primary audience for the essay? What other groups are possible audiences for Alvarez's essay? Cite passages from the essay that might appeal to different groups.

5. Write an essay describing your own experiences in different or conflicting cultures. Have you made a difficult transition from one culture to another? Narrate one or two episodes from your life that illustrate the conflicts caused by the multiple cultures in your life. Do you have solutions that you can recommend?

JENNY SHARPE

The Problem of Dropouts Can Be Solved

Prereading Journal Entry

Explain what you know about friends of yours or students you know who dropped out of your high school. What seemed to be the causes? In your opinion, what might have kept them in school longer?

Jenny Sharpe grew up in Austin, Texas, and was a Spanish major at Austin College in Sherman, Texas. After completing her bachelor's degree, she planned to enroll in a teacher's program and receive her master's degree so she could return to Austin and teach. In her essay on the dropout problem, Sharpe's purpose was to encourage school reform by offering a three-step solution that would attack the problem from several angles. She hoped to address a general audience, including teachers, taxpayers, students, and parents.

Sketch Outline

  i. Introduction

  ii. Statement of the   violence (stats on prison population) teen
       problem: pregnancy vandalism during school hours

These problems stem from our school system and the dropout rate.

  iii. Step One: Target truancy
  iv. Step Two: Have alternative schools
  v. Step Three: Start early—Head start
  vi. Conclusion: These three combined will reach different kids
                        with different programs. Hopefully, all potential
                        dropouts will be affected by at least one of these
                        solutions.

Rough Draft

The Problem of Dropouts

Everyone will agree that the crime rate is out of hand, teen pregnancy is sky rocketing, gang violence is worsening, and welfare is being abused. Most of these problems stem from our lowered family values and our weakening school system. If we can lower the dropout rate, then we can curb many of these out of control figures. The only problem is that many Americans have given up on trying to solve our dropout problem. This is one reason it has gotten worse. People complain about the crime rate and the abuse of welfare, but rarely think about the causes. One statistic that shows the relationship between dropouts and the crime rate is that almost 40% of our state and federal prisoners do not have a high school diploma. With the combination of a strong truancy program, a wider selection of alternative schools, and a strengthened Head Start program, we can cut down on the problem of high school dropouts which eventually leads to problems such as high crime rates and teen pregnancies.

The first and most important step is to target the kids before they even start school. President Clinton wanted to start a program that began with prenatal care. This introduces parents to health care and gets them interested in helping their children. If parents invest a lot of time and energy in their kids, then they are more likely to continue pushing their kids to succeed. This parental involvement is essential in getting the students motivated. This prenatal program would carry into the

Head Start program for preschoolers. This prepares them for elementary school by teaching them the skills to be better listeners, more cooperative, and more able to learn at the same speed as other kids who receive more attention at home.

Head Start has the potential of reaching a lot of kids, even though it receives a lot of criticism. Those who fear investing too much money into a program that may still produce dropouts and criminals should look at some of the possible benefits. One of the first programs to target preschoolers was the Perry Preschool Program in the 1960s. 58 kids participated in this program for 1–2 years. The graduates were followed through the age of 27. "Researchers estimated the savings to society resulting from better social competence among Perry graduates, including reduced grade retention, welfare usage, and crime and increased school completion and employment rates" (128). They figured that "for every dollar spent on the preschool program, taxpayers saved $3 to $6 by age 19 and $7 by age 27" (128). This is the ideal system and it worked because it was so small and so well supported. Home visits made sure the parents were reinforcing what the kids learned in school. This type of close contact and communication between the parents and the school is imperative to a successful program. Head Start and other programs like it can only work if they have high standards. Head Start has met criticism because its standards have decreased. A poor program elicits poor results. Because of low funding, underpaid teachers, lack of coordinators, and little family support, the results of this system do not reflect its full potential.

Tightening the truancy policy should help also. We will definitely help the kids who go through early prevention programs if we stick with them through their school career, but what about those who don't enter the preschool system? Some of these kids who seem to be falling behind and don't have the benefit of a Head Start counselor to help them get back on track should be recognized by their teachers as "at risk." Pairing them with buddies or counselors or Big Brothers/Sisters might help, but so would a tough truancy program. Grayson County implemented a tough policy last January. After 10 absences, the school notifies Judge Gregory Middents. He sends the constable to the parents' place of employment to summon them to court. This is the first of a series of scare tactics. Once the family shows up to court, they are presented with three options: pay a $500 fine for each day missed (it can be lowered to $200), go to jail for $50 a day (the judge would decide the number of days), or attend a workshop one Saturday. Most families choose the workshop. The parents learn how to be better parents, how to take control of the family, and how to motivate their children. Students learn how to set goals for graduation and life in general, how to manage their time, and how to organize information. Approximately 80–90% of the students who go to court and attend the workshops go on to graduate without any problems. The other 10%, on the other hand, continue with the delinquent pattern and dropout.

There is another group of students who have not been addressed. Those who are failing, pregnant, troublesome, or disinterested. More alternative schools should be created to cater to the needs of these kids. Linda Woytasczyk, a counselor at the Fred Douglass School (an alternative learning center here in Sherman), insists that some students can't work in such a structured environment as our present schools. The Fred Douglass School has a self-paced curriculum which allows the students to get caught up or graduate early. Many of the students at this school support themselves and their own children so the school has two sessions to accommodate such varied schedules. There are 40 students in the morning session and 40 in the afternoon. This small size allows the students to get to know their teachers and form real relationships with them. They know that the teachers care. The flexible system gives the students more freedom. They pick their schedule, work at their own pace, and don't go by bells. It is this freedom and attention that encourage the students to work hard and reach their goal to graduate. Although this type of program might not be for everyone, neither is the traditional school system. The addition of new alternative or technical schools would reach more students, especially the ones who would probably end up dropping out of the traditional school system. We need more options for our students because not all of them are college bound and ready for careers.

No matter how well all of these programs work, they will never be able to "overpower the effects of poor living conditions, inadequate nutritional and health care, negative role models, and substandard schools," but good programs can enhance the student's likeliness of succeeding in school. Already, the Head Start programs have proven to be successful. Strengthening them can only improve the results. The alternative learning centers are also quite capable of stunting the dropout rate. Although the truancy policy is still new, it too seems to be working. The combination of these three ideas can only improve our dropout dilemma. The need is there, but the support is lacking.

Implementing these programs involves a risk that few people are willing to take. We have put this off long enough, though. It is time to take this risk and invest our tax dollars into our children's future.

Final Draft

The Problem of Dropouts

1   Quick glances at today's paper or this week's issue of any news magazine will bombard us with headlines that read: *Violence in Our Cities, Babies Having Babies, Another Gang Bang Haunts Our Streets.* These issues and ones like them are a part of our everyday lives. We see pictures of devastated parents and shocked teachers. We hear statistic after statistic about our rising crime rate and our delinquent youth. We spend hours debating the causes of these problems, but rarely come up with solutions. How will we know if there is an answer if we don't test a few of the options? One solution to lowering these disturbing statistics is to lower the dropout rate. One statistic that shows the relationship between dropouts and the crime rate is that almost 40% of our state and federal prisoners do not have a high school diploma (U.S. Department of Justice, Bureau of Justice Statistics, 1994). So many children turn to crime because they don't have anything else going for them. There are few consequences that can dissuade children from committing crimes when they don't have a future to look forward to; but if we can help them in school, they might have a better chance at succeeding in life. With the combination of a strengthened Head Start program, a strong truancy program, and a wider selection of alternative schools, we can reduce the problem of high school dropouts, which might eventually lead to problems such as high crime rates and teen pregnancies.

2   The first and most important step to lowering the dropout rate is to target the kids before they even start school. President Clinton wanted to start a program that began with prenatal care. This introduces parents to health care and gets them interested in helping their children. The more time and energy parents put forth in the early stages of childhood, the more likely they will be to continue to push their kids to succeed through high school. Parental involvement is essential in getting the students motivated. The prenatal program would carry into the Head Start program which prepares preschoolers for elementary school by teaching them the skills to be better listeners, to be more cooperative, and to be more able to learn at the same speed as other kids who receive more attention at home.

3   The main problem with implementing a prenatal care program is its cost. Many critics of the Head Start program would oppose this earlier start because they haven't seen any of the rewards from Head Start. We must realize though, that Head Start and other programs like it can only work if they have high standards. Head Start has met criticism because its standards have decreased. A poor program elicits poor results. Because of low funding, underpaid teachers, lack of coordinators, and little family support, the results of this system do not reflect its full potential. We do not even know its full potential because we have not invested enough money into it to test it. Those who fear investing too much money into a program that may still produce dropouts should look at some of the possible benefits.

4   The best system to look at when considering possible benefits is the Perry Preschool Program which was one of the first programs to target preschoolers. During the 1960s, 58 kids participated in this program for 1–2 years. The graduates were followed through the age of 27. This program underwent many tests, one of which "estimated the savings to society resulting from better social competence among Perry graduates, including reduced grade retention, welfare usage, and crime and increased school completion and employment rates" (Zigler 128). The researchers figured that "for every dollar spent on the preschool program, taxpayers saved $3 to $6 by age 19 and $7 by age 27" (Zigler 128). This is the ideal system and it worked because it was so small and so well supported. Home visits made sure the parents were reinforcing what the kids learned in school. The type of close contact and communication between the parents and the school is imperative to a successful program.

5   Head Start can work, with enough reform, to raise its standards and draw better teachers. The program could also be strengthened by following its graduates through elementary school and high school. This continued connection with the students might keep them on the right track because often they start with strong skills but get shuffled around and lost in the crowd. Kids, especially those at risk, need lots of attention and support. They need a role model and someone they can trust. Maybe, if we are willing to invest the time and money, the Head Start program can incorporate counselors to keep up with the graduates and plan weekend retreats and workshops. We need to keep these kids involved and let them know that we still care about them. As the program exists now, the kids move on to elementary school and are quickly swallowed by the big classes. They lose the individual encouragement

that drives them to succeed. Counselors could offer this encouragement and help ease the transition and continue to reinforce parental involvement and student participation.

6   We will definitely help the kids who go through early prevention programs if we stick with them through their school career, but what about those who don't enter the preschool system? Some of these kids, who seem to be falling behind and don't have the benefit of a Head Start counselor to help them get back on track, should be recognized by their teachers as "at risk." One solution might be to pair them with buddies, counselors, or Big Brothers/Sisters. Another, more accessible, solution could be the installation of a tough truancy program. I spoke to the Justice of the Peace, Gregory Middents, to learn more about the tough policy that Grayson County implemented last January. After 10 absences, the school notifies Judge Middents. He sends the constable to the parents' place of employment to summon them to court. Once the family shows up to court, they are presented with three options: pay a $500 fine for each day missed (it can be lowered to $200), go to jail for $50 a day (the judge would decide the number of days), or attend a workshop one Saturday (Middents). Judge Middents informed me that most families choose the workshop. One of his flyers for the workshops explained that the parents learn how to be better parents, how to take control of the family, and how to motivate their children. Students learn how to set goals for graduation and life in general, how to manage their time, and how to organize information. One of the many tests Judge Middents has run showed that approximately 80–90% of the students who go to court and attend the workshops go on to graduate without any problems. The other 10%, on the other hand, continue with the delinquent pattern and dropout (Middents).

7   There is another group of students who have not been addressed, those who are failing, pregnant, troublesome, or disinterested. More alternative schools should be created to cater to the needs of these kids. One example of a very successful alternative program is the Fred Douglass School (an alternative learning center here in Sherman). Linda Woytasczk, one of the counselors at the school, insists that some students can't work in such a structured environment as our present schools. She explained that the Fred Douglass School's self-paced curriculum allows the students to get caught up or graduate early. She said that many of the students at her school support themselves and their own children so the school has two sessions to accommodate such varied schedules. There are 40 students in the morning session and 40 in

the afternoon. This small size allows the students to get to know their teachers and form real relationships with them. According to Linda, the students know and appreciate the fact that the teachers care about them. The flexible system gives the students more freedom. For example, they pick their schedule, work at their own pace, and are not regulated by bells. It is this freedom and attention that encourage the students to work hard and reach their goal to graduate. That is the goal of alternative schools, to encourage the students to take an interest in school and to graduate. Although this type of program might not be for everyone, neither is the traditional school system. The addition of new alternative or technical schools would reach more students, especially the ones who would probably end up dropping out of the traditional school system. We need more options for our students because not all of them are college bound and ready for careers.

8   Implementing any one of these programs, much less all three, will be costly. However, we must look at it as an investment, not a loss. Any investment involves risk, but avoiding the risk means avoiding a possible solution too. Unfortunately, no matter how well all of these programs work, they will never be able to "overpower the effects of poor living conditions, inadequate nutritional and health care, negative role models, and substandard schools," but good programs can enhance the student's likelihood of succeeding in school (Zigler 129). Already, the Head Start programs have proven to be successful. Strengthening them can only improve the results. The alternative learning centers are also quite capable of stunting the dropout rate. Although the truancy policy is still new, it too seems to be working. The combination of these three ideas can only improve our dropout dilemma. The need is there, but the support is lacking. Implementing these programs involves a risk that few people are willing to take. We have put this off long enough, though. It is time to take this risk and invest our tax dollars into our children's future.

WORKS CITED

Middents, Gregory. Personal interview. 11 Oct. 1995.

Woytasczyk, Linda. Personal interview. 13 Oct. 1995.

Zigler, Edward Frank. "Head Start: Criticisms in a Constructive Context." *American Psychologist.* Feb. 1994: 127–32.

QUESTIONS FOR WRITING AND DISCUSSION

1. What exactly is the problem that Sharpe addresses? What are Sharpe's three steps to reducing the dropout rate? What drawbacks or feasibility difficulties does Sharpe anticipate in solving the dropout problem?

2. In what order does Sharpe discuss her three steps to reducing the dropout rate? Is there a reason or logic for her order? Should she revise this order? Explain.

3. Following a traditional strategy for problem-solving essays, Sharpe concludes with a "call to action." Is this concluding strategy effective? Explain why or why not.

4. Sharpe suggests that her audience might include students, parents, teachers, or taxpayers. What specific sentences in her essay are directed toward members of each of these groups?

5. List any possible solutions that Sharpe does not consider. Why doesn't she mention them? Should she add them to her revision? Why or why not?

Arguing

W E HAVE ALL HAD ARGUMENTS WITH FRIENDS, CASUAL acquaintances, or even strangers about politics, sports, diets, classes, or music. We usually enjoy hearing their viewpoints and expressing our own beliefs. At the end of some discussions, however, we feel frustrated at our inability to convince others. Sometimes we wish we had been quick enough to think of a better response. And sometimes we realize that we simply don't know enough to argue the issue intelligently. Written argument, however, gives us a second chance to learn about the issue, to list the pro and con arguments, to think of good examples for our arguments, and to arrange our argument effectively for our audience.

Written argument is a formalized, written debate in which we play both sides, imagining the opposing arguments and then countering them with our best ideas and evidence. Role-playing is therefore essential for effective argumentative writing. We cannot merely assert our belief in the "truth" and expect to change our readers' minds. The art of persuasion requires imagining how the opposition will react to our position and tailoring our arguments and evidence specifically for our readers.

Like a formal debate, written argument has specific rules and regulations. Participants in this game play to win—to persuade their readers—but their argument must follow certain rules of "fair play." Writers must use appeals to logic to persuade their readers. Writers also use appeals to their own good character to bolster the argument. And finally, writers may use emotional appeals, but only if those appeals do not unfairly distort the issue.

Although written argument has clear rules, writers do not always know if they are "winning." Referees do not blow a whistle and shout: "Unsportsmanlike conduct! You have unfairly characterized the opposing argument," or "Illegal procedure! You have no evidence to support your claim." In actual practice, every reader is a silent referee who, instead of blowing a whistle, simply remains unconvinced by a poor argument. When writers do represent the opposing positions and argue fairly, however, they can increase the chances of persuading their audience.

It is no secret that argument is the most important kind of writing practiced in colleges and universities. As the most public of all forms of writing, argument is a cornerstone of democracy. Our political, social, and individual freedoms depend on our ability to articulate multiple points of view, on our skill at arguing fairly for a position, and on our willingness to reach a consensus or compromise position. As you read the essays in this chapter, notice how the authors not only argue their positions but also invite you to participate in the ongoing public debate.

Strategies for Reading and Writing Arguing Essays

As you read the argumentative essays in this chapter, look for the following arguing strategies.

- **Introduction that sets the context for the argument.** Argumentative essays often begin with a description or an example that shows *who* is for this issue, *how* or *when* the argument developed, and *why* the whole controversy is important. An argumentative essay about unnecessary violence or injury in sports, for example, might begin with a single, memorable incident.
- **Statement of a debatable thesis or claim.** Early in the essay, the writer states a *claim* usually involving a cause and effect, a statement of value, or a proposal to solve a problem. The claim must be debatable: Both sides of the argument must have some merit. If the writer argues that professional hockey is too violent, there must be a reasonable argument that says that some controlled violence is a legitimate part of the game.
- **Representation of the opposing arguments.** Writers of argument describe the important opposing arguments fairly. Usually writers

will represent and then attempt to refute the opposing arguments as they develop their own arguments.

- **Use of evidence to refute the opposition and support the claim.** Mere assertions of belief or disagreement will not persuade readers. Effective arguments refute the opposing arguments and support the writer's claim with evidence: specific examples, detailed description, quotations from authorities, facts, or statistics.
- **Writing in a reasonable tone.** Writers of argument treat their opponents—and their readers—with respect. They argue reasonably and avoid illogical statements or inflammatory language.

Reading an Arguing Essay

Prereading

Before you read each essay, write out your position on that issue in the Prereading Journal Entry. Then read the headnote to determine the background and context for the controversy. Does the writer have some relevant experience with this issue? Does any of the biographical information—or the title of the essay—lead you to expect the writer to be either pro or con on this topic?

First Reading

First, analyze yourself as the audience for this topic. Are you sympathetic to the writer's stance? Are you indifferent or just uninformed? Do you disagree with the writer's claim? As you read, decide whether the writer is intending the essay for someone who agrees, is undecided, or disagrees. In the margin, place an "X" next to a statement you disagree with; place a "?" next to a passage that has questionable logic or support. Use an "!" for a striking passage or passage you agree with. Highlight or place a wavy line under key sentences. Underline any words you want to look up later. When you finish, write in your own words the writer's claim.

Annotated Reading

As you read the essay a second time, write your own reactions in the margin. What is the writer's best argument? The best piece of evidence? Where is the writer's argument weakest? What opposing argument is omitted? Reread the "Strategies for Reading and Writing

Arguing Essays." Place brackets [ ] around passages that illustrate the main features of argumentative essays. In the margin, label at least one passage illustrating each feature, and outline the essay by noting the thesis and the major arguments against and for the writer's claim. Finally, note features of style: sentences or vocabulary that are effective, too simple, or too difficult. Where was the writing clear, and where was it difficult to track? Where was the language appropriate or inappropriate for the writer's intended audience?

Collaborative Reading

In class or in a small group, share your journal entries and annotations. What did your group or the class think about this essay before you read it? How many agreed, disagreed, or were uninformed or undecided? Did the article change any readers' minds? Share and then compile a jointly annotated version of the essay. At the end of the essay, write out the writer's claim or thesis. Finally, write one question about this essay for the class to discuss in more detail.

Writing an Arguing Essay

Depending on your assignment, your purpose, and your intended audience, you may write one of several kinds of arguing essays. The most common kind of arguing essay uses **traditional argument,** which assumes that there are "pro" and "con" positions. In traditional argument, you argue for your side and against the other side. In this kind of argument, you take an adversarial stance: You marshal all the evidence for your side and you expose the weaknesses in the other side. Traditional argument works best when you are in a debate environment, when you want your readers to vote one way or another, or when you want to persuade your readers that only one point of view is right.

A second kind of argument, which we might call **constructive argument,** tries to avoid the "pro" versus "con" tactics altogether. It is most useful for complex topics that require examining the multiple positions that people or stakeholders take on difficult issues. A writer using constructive argument assumes that we need to know more about many different points of view in order to think intelligently about a complex issue. Like Rogerian argument (which follows), it avoids adversarial confrontation but its goal is to gain the widest possible perspective on a topic before recommending one possible stance or solution.

Finally, in a third kind of argument, so-called **Rogerian argument,** the goal is to avoid confrontation and threat, and thereby reduce conflict by opening the lines of communication between both sides. Rogerian argument—named after psychologist Carl Rogers—is a non-adversarial or negotiated argument where mutual understanding and compromise are the ultimate goals.

Traditional Argument

Traditional arguments assume that there are really only two sides to an issue. Your goal as a writer is to persuade your readers that your position is right and the opposite position is wrong. Writing traditional argument first requires that you have a claim that is debatable. **Your claim or thesis must have reasonable arguments on both sides:** "Although smoking cigarettes is still legal, our public health demands that we ban smoking in all public and commercial places." Second, in traditional argument you choose to argue a claim of fact, of cause and effect, of value, or of policy—or some combination. A **claim of fact** distinguishes between myths or false perceptions and the reality: "Although abusive men often think their actions are justified and abused women sometimes think they deserve punishment, both need counseling in order to restore a healthy relationship." A **claim of cause and effect** says that something has caused or will cause a particular effect: "If American schools are to improve, we need a workable system to guarantee choice to parents and children." A **claim of value** leads to an evaluating essay that examines both sides of the argument: "*Out of Africa* is a great film, not just because of its beautiful cinematography, but because it portrays the spirit of a courageous woman." A **claim of policy** leads to a problem-solving essay that examines both sides of the argument: "Although some Americans claim that laws against cell phone use in cars infringe on their right of free speech, the safety of the public demands tough, nation-wide legislation." For each of these claims, you must present both sides of the issue.

Third, as you collect evidence to support your claim, pay attention to how this evidence will appeal to your reader. Writers of all kinds of argument use **appeals to reason, to character, and to emotion.** Frequently, your evidence will support an **appeal to reason.** By giving facts, statistics, citations from authorities, quotations, examples, and personal experience, you demonstrate that A logically causes B, that movie A is great because it meets clearly defined criteria, or that tougher seat belt legislation is the best policy. You may also **appeal to your good character** by using reliable evidence, by using a reasonable and rational tone, by fairly and accurately describing opposing arguments, and by citing relevant personal experience. If your readers see that you have some experience with the issue and have treated opposing positions fairly, your good character will help convince them. Although an **appeal to emotion** can backfire, if you avoid inflammatory rhetoric and do not use emotional appeals that distort or manipulate the truth, your emotional appeals may also persuade your readers.

Constructive Argument

Constructive argument, unlike traditional argument, is not adversarial or polarized. In "The Argument Culture," which appears later in this chapter, Deborah Tannen argues that we need to find "constructive ways of settling differences." One way to do this is to become aware that almost every topic people argue about has more than just a "pro" and a "con" side. Constructive argument looks at all sides of an argument. Instead of trying to "debate" the issue, constructive argument's goal is to open the conversation among all points of view.

Most traditional arguments can be reframed by looking for multiple positions rather than just the "pro" or "con" sides. In the abortion debate, for example, instead of being for or against abortion, find out about other possible positions, about gray areas, or about specific cases or circumstances. Perhaps the dialogue should be about deciding how much counseling and education should be available to everyone involved—the potential mother, the father, the family members, the doctors, the pastors, or priests. Perhaps the conversation should center on how much sex education should take place in the public schools before students reach high school age. By refusing to see any argument in terms of just two sides, by talking to a variety of people instead of just the two polarized political groups, and by actively looking for alternative solutions, writers can take the first steps toward writing a constructive argument.

Constructive argument, like traditional argument, makes a claim and uses appeals, but it considers several alternative arguments. It educates readers by explaining the many possible perspectives and then convinces them that genuine communication rather than adversarial debate is the blueprint for a workable solution. In order to avoid traditional adversarial tactics and promote a constructive resolution, use the following strategies:

- **Avoid polarizing arguments into just two opposing positions.** Find three or four different positions or points of view. Accurately describe all of these positions early in your argument.
- **Analyze the context of each of these positions.** Who advocates each position? When, where, or why does this position have merits? When, where, or why does each position have problems?
- **Find the common ground that exists among these positions.** What underlying values, principles, or beliefs do these positions share (or not share)?
- **Work toward destabilizing the traditional pro–con debate.** Focus on building wider perspectives that value cooperation rather than confrontation.
- **Recommend a position or solution that encourages further education, discussion, and dialogue.**

Constructive argument, then, requires withholding your own convictions about a topic until you have more fully educated yourself about the complexities and multiple positions involved. It requires that you understand the context of each different position and have analyzed its merits and problems. Finally, it requires a genuine openness about the topic—a willingness to listen to several points of view, a readiness to educate yourself about the topic, and a desire to promote further dialogue and conversation.

Rogerian Argument

Traditional argument is confrontational and adversarial. Writers engage in a verbal "war" whose goal is to "defeat" the arguments of the opposition. In contrast, Rogerian argument is nonadversarial. Following the recommendations of psychologist Carl Rogers, Rogerian argument is nonthreatening and nonconfrontative. Its goal is not to "win" an argument, but to open the lines of communication and to establish common ground in order to reach a compromise. To do that, writers must be sympathetic to different points of view and—this is crucial—willing to modify their own position. Once the reader sees that the writer is open to change, the reader may become more flexible and more willing to accept compromise, too.

Once both sides are more flexible, a compromise position or solution becomes a possibility. As Rogers says, "This procedure gradually achieves a mutual communication . . . pointed toward solving a problem rather than toward attacking a person or group." Rogerian argument, then, is not a courtroom debate typical of traditional argument, but is more of a negotiating session whose goal is compromise. Whereas constructive argument examines multiple points of view in order to defuse the "pro" versus "con" mentality, Rogerian argument deals directly with two opposing points of view by reducing threat and seeking compromise. And unlike traditional argument, which intends to change the actions or beliefs of the opposition, Rogerian argument works toward changes in *both sides* as a means of establishing common ground and reaching a solution.

Rogerian argument, like traditional argument, makes a claim and considers opposing arguments, but its strategies are entirely different. In order to avoid adversarial tactics and promote open communication, use the following strategies:

- **Avoid a confrontational stance.** Confrontation threatens your audience and increases their defensiveness.
- **Present your character as someone who understands the opposition.** Show that you are fully informed by restating the opposing position fairly and sympathetically.
- **Establish common ground with the opposition.** Indicate the underlying beliefs and values that you share.
- **Be willing to change your views.** Show where your own position may not be reasonable and then modify your original position.
- **Direct your argument toward a compromise or workable solution.** Show how this solution meets the goals of both sides.

Note, however, that an argument does not have to be either entirely adversarial or entirely Rogerian. For example, you may want to use Rogerian strategies for the most sensitive points in a traditional argument. Similarly, you may want to use some of the strategies of constructive argument for parts of a traditional argument. Let your purpose and your intended audience be your guide.

Choosing a Subject for Your Arguing Essay

The ideal topic is one that has generated public debate and controversy, but one that connects to your own experience. Try listing controversial topics in one column, and your authority list or experiences in the other. Where they match, you may have a workable topic.

Controversial Topics	Authority List/Personal Experience
High college tuition	
Alcohol consumption at sporting events	
Outlawing texting in cars	
Health-care legislation	
Profiling at security checkpoints	
Climate change legislation	
High stakes testing in high schools	
DWI laws	
Responding to terrorism	
Concealed weapons on campus	
Immigration reform	
Prejudice in the workplace	

Brainstorm additional topics for the left-hand column. Then list your own interests, hobbies, or important experiences in the right-hand column. Where both topics match or intersect, you may have a workable topic.

Collecting Arguments and Examples

For this essay, you will need information from books and articles in your library, but don't forget your field research. Whom can you interview on your topic? Would an informal survey of reactions of your friends, family, or classmates give you ideas or information? Be sure to make photocopies of the important sources you uncover in the library. If you interview an authority, take along a tape recorder.

As you gather information, keep thinking about the big picture. What exactly is your purpose? Are you going to use traditional argument and write a pro–con essay? Are you going to do a constructive argument, where you examine multiple positions on a controversial topic and recommend a solution? Might Rogerian argument be appropriate? **Which of these strategies would work best considering your topic, your audience, and your purpose?** Keep coming back to the big picture as you gather information and do your research. Remember to check out the research appendix if you are doing library or Internet research.

Shaping Your Arguing Essay

One of the oldest outlines for argumentative essays comes from classical rhetoric. Use the following outline as a **guide** rather than a rigid plan for your own topic.

I. **Introduction:** Announces the subject; gets your audience's interest and attention; creates positive appeal to your good character
II. **Narration:** Gives background, context, statement of problem, or definition of key terms
III. **Partition:** States your claim or thesis; outlines or maps out your arguments
IV. **Argument:** Presents the arguments and evidence for your claim
V. **Refutation:** Counters the arguments of your opposition
VI. **Conclusion:** Summarizes arguments, suggests your solution (if appropriate), or ties back into the introduction

Most argumentative essays have these six parts or features, but they do not necessarily occur in this order. Some writers refute the opposing arguments *before* giving their own reasons and evidence. Since most short argumentative essays combine the introduction, narration, and partition in a few short introductory paragraphs, use the following abbreviated outlines as possible patterns for your own topic.

Outline 1	Intro (attention getter, background, claim, and map)
	Your arguments
	Refute opposing arguments
	Conclusion
Outline 2	Intro
	Refute opposing arguments
	Your arguments
	Conclusion
Outline 3	Intro
	Refute first opposing argument, which leads to your first argument
	Refute second opposing argument, which leads to your second argument
	Refute third opposing argument, which leads to your third argument, etc.
	Your additional arguments
	Conclusion

Test each of these patterns against your topic. Which will work best for your claim, your evidence, and your audience?

Drafting Your Arguing Essay

Especially if you are doing extended research for this essay, start writing your ideas as soon as possible in your journal. Don't think you need to do all of your research and then start writing. Whenever you get an idea, start writing, and leave a blank space or draw a line in your draft where you need more evidence. Your goal is not to patch together seventeen quotations from articles in books, magazines, or newspapers. Your goal is to use your research to learn what has already been said about your topic and then decide what you think. Write your own ideas and arguments as soon as you decide what you believe.

When you have gathered sufficient evidence, collect all your photocopies of sources, your notes from interviews, and your prewriting. If you've tested one of the argumentative outlines, use that to sketch out a plan. If you prefer to start writing first and organize later, then get started. If you have a good example, description, set of facts, or statistics for your lead-in, start there. If not, start with your claim and worry about your lead-in later. If you have to quit drafting temporarily, stop in the middle of a paragraph where you know what is coming next. Then write a note to yourself about what you will say next.

Revising Your Arguing Essay

Use the following guidelines as you revise and edit your essay.

- **Reconsider your audience.** Ask a friend or classmate to role-play your audience. What additional arguments can he or she imagine? Where is your argument or evidence the weakest? Do you address your arguments to your intended audience?
- **Review your introduction.** Do you catch your reader's attention with a startling example or statistic, a vivid description, a quotation, or a specific example from your own experience? Do you state your claim clearly by the end of your opening paragraphs?
- **Establish the background for your claim.** Have you defined key terms? Have you explained the problem? Have you described the subject you are evaluating?

- **Respond to opposing arguments.** If you have only given your side, you haven't really written an argumentative essay. Make sure that you represent and then respond to key opposing arguments.
- **Give supporting evidence for each reason.** Make sure that every assertion you make is supported by facts, statistics, observations, quotations from authorities, examples, and/or your own personal experience.
- **Make clear transitions between paragraphs.** Signal the major arguments or counterarguments in your essay. Your reader should be able to follow your argument just by reading the first sentence or two in each paragraph.
- **Check in-text citations for accuracy.** Quote directly when the writer's original words are more exact or more persuasive than your paraphrase might be. Use ellipsis points (. . .) to omit unimportant words from a long direct quotation. When you use a writer's exact words, when you paraphrase, or when you use facts or statistics, cite the source in your text at the end of the sentence (see sample student essays for MLA format). Failure to cite your sources properly constitutes plagiarism.
- **Revise and edit your essay.** Revise sentences to improve conciseness and clarity and reduce wordiness and clutter. Review for problems in grammar, usage, spelling, and mechanics.

Postscript for Your Arguing Essay

When you have finished your essay, answer the following questions. Hand in this postscript with your essay.

1. What did you *learn* about your subject as you researched it? On what points did you change your mind? What was the most surprising bit of evidence you found?

2. Which of the opposing arguments is the strongest? Which of your arguments is the strongest? Where is your evidence strongest and where weakest?

3. Describe how you think a reader who totally *disagrees* with your position will react to your essay.

4. If you had two more days to gather evidence, which of the following would you do: Find more articles or books in the library? Interview another authority? Observe a place, action, or person? Use more of your own experience? Explain.

DEBORAH TANNEN

The Argument Culture

Prereading Journal Entry

The introduction to this chapter says that written argument is like a debate, with pro and con sides. Think of an issue or argument which has more than two different points of view or sides. Write out an issue or question and then explain how there could be three or four different "sides" or positions you could take on this issue.

A professor of linguistics at Georgetown University, Deborah Tannen is also a best-selling author of many books on discourse and gender, including You Just Don't Understand: Women and Men in Conversation *(1990),* Talking from 9 to 5 *(1994),* The Argument Culture: Moving from Debate to Dialogue *(1998),* You're Wearing That?: Understanding Mothers and Daughters in Conversation *(2006), and* You Were Always Mom's Favorite!: Sisters in Conversation Throughout their Lives *(2009). Throughout her career, Tannen has focused on how men and women have different conversational habits and assumptions, whether they talk on the job or at home. In the following essay, taken from* The Argument Culture, *Tannen tries to convince her readers that adversarial debates with only two sides represented may not be a constructive way of resolving differences of opinion. As a culture, we would be much more successful, Tannen believes, if we didn't always think of argument as a war or a fight but as a dialogue among a variety of different positions.*

1   Balance. Debate. Listening to both sides. Who could question these noble American traditions? Yet today, these principles have been distorted. Without thinking, we have plunged headfirst into what I call the "argument culture."

2   The argument culture urges us to approach the world, and the people in it, in an adversarial frame of mind. It rests on the assumption that opposition is the best way to get anything done: The best way to discuss an idea is to set up a debate; the best way to cover news is to find spokespeople who express the most extreme, polarized views and present them as "both sides"; the best way to settle disputes is litigation that pits one party against the other; the best way to begin an essay is to attack someone; and the best way to show you're really thinking is to criticize.

3   More and more, our public interactions have become like arguing with a spouse. Conflict can't be avoided in our public lives any more than we can avoid conflict with people we love. One of the great strengths of our society is that we can express these conflicts openly. But just as spouses have to learn ways of settling their differences without inflicting real damage, so we, as a society, have to find constructive ways of resolving disputes and differences.

4   The war on drugs, the war on cancer, the battle of the sexes, politicians' turf battles—in the argument culture, war metaphors pervade our talk and shape our thinking. The cover headlines of both *Time* and *Newsweek* one recent week are a case in point: "The Secret Sex Wars," proclaims *Newsweek*. "Starr at War," declares *Time*. Nearly everything is framed as a battle or game in which winning or losing is the main concern.

5   The argument culture pervades every aspect of our lives today. Issues from global warming to abortion are depicted as two-sided arguments, when in fact most Americans' views lie somewhere in the middle. Partisanship makes gridlock in Washington the norm. Even in our personal relationships, a "let it all hang out" philosophy emphasizes people expressing their anger without giving them constructive ways of settling differences.

Sometimes You Have to Fight

6   There are times when it is necessary and right to fight—to defend your country or yourself, to argue for your rights or against offensive or dangerous ideas or actions. What's wrong with the argument culture is the ubiquity, the knee-jerk nature, of approaching any issue, problem or public person in an adversarial way.

7   Our determination to pursue truth by setting up a fight between two sides leads us to assume that every issue has two sides—no more, no less. But if you always assume there must be an "other side," you may end up scouring the margins of science or the fringes of lunacy to find it.

8   This accounts, in part, for the bizarre phenomenon of Holocaust denial. Deniers, as Emory University professor Deborah Lipstadt shows, have been successful in gaining TV air time and campus newspaper coverage by masquerading as "the other side" in a "debate." Continual reference to "the other side" results in a conviction that everything has another side—and people begin to doubt the existence of any facts at all.

9   The power of words to shape perception has been proved by researchers in controlled experiments. Psychologists Elizabeth Loftus and John Palmer, for example, found that the terms in which people are asked to recall something affect what they recall. The researchers showed subjects a film of two cars colliding, then asked how fast the cars were going; one week later they asked whether there had been any broken glass. Some subjects were asked, "How fast were the cars going when they bumped into each other?" Others were asked, "How fast were the cars going when they smashed into each other?"

10   Those who read the question with "smashed" tended to "remember" that the cars were going faster. They were also more likely to "remember" having seen broken glass. (There wasn't any.) This is how language works. It invisibly molds our way of thinking about people, actions and the world around us.

11   In the argument culture, "critical" thinking is synonymous with criticizing. In many classrooms, students are encouraged to read someone's life work, then rip it to shreds.

12   When debates and fighting predominate, those who enjoy verbal sparring are likely to take part—by calling in to talk shows or writing letters to the editor. Those who aren't comfortable with oppositional discourse are likely to opt out.

How High-Tech Communication Pulls Us Apart

13   One of the most effective ways to defuse antagonism between two groups is to provide a forum for individuals from those groups to get to know each other personally. What is happening in our lives, however, is just the opposite. More and more of our communication is not face to face, and not with people we know. The proliferation and increasing portability of technology isolates people in a bubble.

14   Along with the voices of family members and friends, phone lines bring into our homes the annoying voices of solicitors who want to sell something—generally at dinnertime. (My father-in-law startles phone solicitors by saying, "We're eating dinner, but I'll call you back. What's your home phone number?" To the nonplused caller, he explains, "Well, you're calling me at home; I thought I'd call you at home, too.")

15   It is common for families to have more than one TV, so the adults can watch what they like in one room and the kids can watch their choice in another—or maybe each child has a private TV.

16   E-mail, and now the Internet, are creating networks of human connection unthinkable even a few years ago. Though e-mail has enhanced communication with family and friends, it also ratchets up the anonymity of both sender and receiver, resulting in stranger-to-stranger "flaming."

17   "Road rage" shows how dangerous the argument culture—and especially today's technologically enhanced aggression—can be. Two men who engage in a shouting match may not come to blows, but if they express their anger while driving down a public highway, the risk to themselves and others soars.

The Argument Culture Shapes Who We Are

18   The argument culture has a defining impact on our lives and on our culture.

- **It makes us distort facts,** as in the Nancy Kerrigan-Tonya Harding story. After the original attack on Kerrigan's knee, news stories focused on the rivalry between the two skaters instead of portraying Kerrigan as the victim of an attack. Just last month, Time magazine called the event a "contretemps" between Kerrigan and Harding. And a recent joint TV interview of the two skaters reinforced that skewed image by putting the two on equal footing, rather than as victim and accused.

- **It makes us waste valuable time,** as in the case of scientist Robert Gallo, who co-discovered the AIDS virus. Gallo was the object of a groundless four-year investigation into allegations he had stolen the virus from another scientist. He was ultimately exonerated, but the toll was enormous. Never mind that, in his words, "These were the most painful and horrible years of my life." Gallo spent four years fighting accusations instead of fighting AIDS.

- **It limits our thinking.** Headlines are intentionally devised to attract attention, but the language of extremes actually shapes, and misshapes, the way we think about things. Military metaphors train us to think about, and see, everything in terms of fighting, conflict and war. Adversarial rhetoric is a kind of verbal inflation—a rhetorical boy-who-cried-wolf.

- **It encourages us to lie.** If you fight to win, the temptation is great to deny facts that support your opponent's views and say only what supports your side. It encourages people to misrepresent and, in the extreme, to lie.

End the Argument Culture by Looking at All Sides

19   How can we overcome our classically American habit of seeing issues in absolutes? We must expand our notion of "debate" to include more dialogue. To do this, we can make special efforts not to think in twos. Mary Catherine Bateson, an anthropologist at Virginia's George Mason University, makes a point of having her class compare three cultures, not two. Then, students are more likely to think about each on its own terms, rather than as opposites.

20   In the public arena, television and radio producers can try to avoid, whenever possible, structuring public discussions as debates. This means avoiding the format of having two guests discuss an issue. Invite three guests—or one. Perhaps it is time to re-examine the assumption that audiences always prefer a fight.

21   Instead of asking, "What's the other side?" we might ask, "What are the other sides?" Instead of insisting on hearing "both sides," let's insist on hearing "all sides."

22   We need to find metaphors other than sports and war. Smashing heads does not open minds. We need to use our imaginations and ingenuity to find different ways to seek truth and gain knowledge through intellectual interchange, and add them to our arsenal—or, should I say, to the ingredients for our stew. It will take creativity for each of us to find ways to change the argument culture to a dialogue culture. It's an effort we have to make, because our public and private lives are at stake.

QUESTIONS FOR DISCUSSION AND WRITING

1. What is "the argument culture," as Tannen defines it? What examples does she give to illustrate how our culture is adversarial?

2. In her essay, Tannen uses claims of value, cause/effect, and policy. Find examples from her essay illustrating each of these claims. State the claim in your own words and list the examples or evidence Tannen uses to support each claim. Which of these claims best represents her overall thesis?

3. Read Tannen's advice in the final four paragraphs of her essay. Does she follow her own advice in writing this essay? Which pieces of advice does she follow and which does she ignore? Cite examples from the essay to support your analysis. Would her essay be more effective if she did follow her own advice? Explain.

4. As a professor of linguistics, Tannen can write in an academic style, but she can also write in an informal style for general audiences. In this essay, is Tannen writing for academics or for anyone interested in culture and communication? Find examples of Tannen's "academic" style as well as her informal style. Does she successfully integrate the two or is she too informal or too academic? Explain.

5. Choose one of the other essays in the Arguing or Problem Solving chapters and analyze the strategies for argument used by the author of the essay. Does that author follow the recommendations Tannen gives in the last four paragraphs of her essay? Cite specific examples from the essay to support your analysis.

DAVID KAROLY

Climate Change Science Misinformation

Prereading Journal Entry

Before you read this article (or the following one) on climate change, write a journal entry explaining what you know or have read about climate change. In your opinion, has global warming increased due to natural variations or due to increased carbon emissions by human beings?

An internationally-recognized and award-winning expert on climate change, David Karoly helped to prepare the Fourth Assessment Report of the Intergovernmental Panel on Climate Change (IPCC) and is the author of several technical and popular articles about climate change. He is a Federation Fellow in the School of Earth Sciences at the University of Melbourne, a member of the Wentworth Group of Concerned Scientists, and Chair of Victoria's Climate Change Reference Group. The following article, "Climate Change Science Misinformation," appeared over a year before "Climategate" hit the news in late 2009; but because Professor Karoly was heavily involved in the latest IPCC report, he is often referred to in articles that charge climate scientists with manipulation of climate data based on information obtained from an alleged hacking of over 1,000 email exchanges of the Climatic Research Unit at the University of East Anglia.

1   Science is about developing an understanding of natural and physical systems and testing that understanding using observations and modelling. Questioning and scepticism are fundamental aspects of science. Scientific theories are accepted understandings that have stood the test of time after extensive critical analysis.

2   The arena for proposing new scientific ideas and their subsequent testing is through peer-reviewed scientific journals. New science is not based on a single scientific publication, but on the accumulation of evidence from many published studies.

3   Over the last two decades, there have been thousands of peer-reviewed scientific studies of climate variability and change, leading to understanding of the causes of recent global warming. This understanding is reported in the assessments of the Intergovernmental Panel on Climate Change (IPCC), as well as by other scientific bodies including the US National Academy of Sciences, the British Royal Society, the US Climate Change Science Program, and the Australian Academy of Science.

4   Over the last decade, they have all reached the same conclusion - the observed increase in global-average surface temperature since the mid-20th century is mainly due to the increase in greenhouse gases in the atmosphere caused by human activity.

5   Recently, there has been an increase in opinion pieces in the media questioning the scientific understanding of global warming. This is not reflected in a surge of scientific publications suggesting that increasing greenhouse gases are not the cause of recent global warming. Instead, the vast majority of scientific studies support and strengthen this conclusion.

6   I do not know the reason for this increase in media coverage of so-called "global warming sceptics", where a common trend is to select a small amount of information to give credit to a misleading conclusion. Whatever the agenda, they have a number of common statements.

7   *The IPCC is a political body and does not provide balanced assessments.* This is untrue. While the members of the IPCC are government representatives, its assessment reports are written by hundreds of scientific experts from many fields. These reports are required to be policy-neutral and contain no recommendations. Each report takes more than three years to prepare and goes through multiple stages of independent expert and government review. This is the most thorough review process undertaken for any scientific assessment.

8   *Carbon dioxide is such a minor atmospheric constituent that it can't affect global climate.* This is untrue. While carbon dioxide makes up only 0.038% of the atmosphere, it is vital in the energy balance of the Earth's surface and atmosphere. If the atmosphere contained no greenhouse gases, the surface temperature would be about 30°C colder.

9   The most important greenhouse gas is water vapour, but its concentration is determined by the temperature of the atmosphere and not emissions from human activity. Carbon dioxide concentrations in the atmosphere vary due to natural and human sources.

10   *Temperature increases from ice ages to interglacial periods occur before increases in carbon dioxide, so carbon dioxide increases don't cause warming.* This is another false conclusion. Temperature increases from ice ages to interglacial warm periods over the last half million years are initiated by variations in the Earth's orbit around the Sun, leading to changes in the amount of sunlight in summer at high latitudes.

11   These temperature increases are followed by increases in atmospheric concentrations of carbon dioxide, as the warmer ocean waters lose some dissolved carbon dioxide. However, the warmth of interglacial periods is only possible with the warming influence of the carbon dioxide increases, which amplifies the initial warming.

12   *Increases in carbon dioxide over the last hundred years are due to natural sources.* This is another untruth. The observed increase in carbon dioxide in the atmosphere is due to burning fossil fuels, industrial activity and land clearing.

13   Observed changes in the relative abundance of different isotopes of carbon in carbon dioxide and small reductions in the amount of oxygen in the atmosphere are not consistent with natural sources, such as volcanoes or losses from the ocean. Observed carbon dioxide concentrations are now 30% higher than any time over the last half million years.

14   *Global average temperatures have dropped from 2002 to 2008, while carbon dioxide has increased, so carbon dioxide can't cause long-term warming.* This is another false conclusion. There are large natural year-to-year variations in climate. The warming influence due to increasing greenhouse gases is at global scales and cumulative over many years.

15   At short time scales, natural variability can offset that warming influence and cause short-term cooling. Global average temperatures have fallen over the last six years, due to natural variations, with the warmth in 2002 and in 1998 due to El Niño events and the recent La Niña causing colder temperatures in 2007 and 2008. The long-term warming trend is unequivocal.

16   *Climate models are untested and unreliable.* This is untrue. Global climate models are important physically-based tools for studying climate variability and change, with more than twenty different models developed independently around the world. They simulate well the magnitude of observed global-scale temperature variations. The long-term warming trend over the 20th century simulated by climate models agrees with that observed only when increasing greenhouse gases are included in the models.

17   *The observed spatial pattern of warming does not show the fingerprint of increasing greenhouse gases.* This is not true. The spatial fingerprint of the response to increasing greenhouse gases includes warming at the surface and in the lower atmosphere and cooling in the upper atmosphere, with larger warming at the surface in high latitudes and in the tropics at heights around 10 km.

18   This spatial fingerprint agrees well with the observed pattern of surface temperature changes over the last hundred years and with temperature changes up to heights of 30 km over the last four decades, when observational data are available. Any differences between the observed pattern and the greenhouse fingerprint are consistent with natural climate variability.

19   *The best explanation for recent global warming is variations of the sun or cosmic rays.* This is untrue. The spatial pattern of responses to increasing solar intensity is warming at the surface and warming in the upper atmosphere, which is not consistent with the observed cooling in the upper atmosphere.

20   Increasing solar intensity is also not consistent with the observed greater warming in winter and at night, when sunlight is less important. There are no observed increases in solar intensity or in cosmic rays over the last three decades, a period of pronounced global warming. The largest variations of solar intensity and in cosmic rays are associated with the eleven-year solar sunspot cycle. However, global-average temperature shows a long-term trend and no pronounced eleven–year cycle linked to the sunspot cycle.

21   In summary, let me emphasise that the pattern and magnitude of observed global-scale temperature changes since the mid-20th century cannot be explained by natural climate variability, are consistent with the response to increasing greenhouse gases, and are not consistent with the responses to other factors. Hence, it is very likely that increasing greenhouse gases are the main cause of the recent observed global-scale warming.

QUESTIONS FOR DISCUSSION AND WRITING

1. Karoly begins his essay with a definition of science. How does he define science? Why might Karoly emphasize that "questioning and skepticism" are key parts of the scientific method in this article for general readers?

2. Arguing essays should represent alternate or opposing views and then respond to them with reasons and supporting evidence. List the eight opposing views that Karoly responds to. What evidence does he provide to support his responses?

3. Karoly's essay, which appeared on an ABC news site, is written for the general public, not primarily for climate scientists. Find examples in Karoly's vocabulary, sentence structure, and organization of his essay that indicate he is writing for a general audience. How effectively does he appeal to and attempt to persuade his audience?

4. Reread your Prereading Journal Entry. If you had questions or doubts about climate change, did Karoly's essay address any of your concerns? Explain why you were or were not persuaded by Karoly's arguments.

5. On the Internet or in your library databases, find information about "climategate" and other current questions about climate change research. Is the "debate" about climate change science helping the general public understand climate change science? Is science immune from cultural or political forces? Is the IPCC responding to charges of possible manipulation of data? Write your own essay on the current state of climate change that provides evidence for the most reasonable response to climate change controversies.

GREGG EASTERBROOK

Some Convenient Truths

Prereading Journal Entry

News agencies like to run stories about emergencies, crises, and bad news, so often any good news about a current topic receives less attention than the bad news. Search online and in your library databases for recent positive news about the development of alternative energies or the reduction of greenhouse gasses. What information can you find that suggests that America and other parts of the world are making progress on developing new energy sources and reducing carbon emissions? For a start, visit the Climate Progress Web site at http://climateprogress.org.

Educated at Colorado College and Northwestern University, Gregg Easterbrook writes on a variety of topics including sports, the environment, progress, and globalization. He has written for The New Republic, The Atlantic Monthly, *and* The Washington Monthly. *Among his half-dozen published books are* A Moment on the Earth *(1995),* The Here and Now *(2002),* The Progress Paradox *(2003), and* Sonic Boom: Globalization at Mach Speed *(2009). Although Easterbrook was skeptical about the initial global warming fears, he is now a convert, agreeing that "the science has changed from ambiguous to near-unanimous," proving that man is contributing significantly to climate change. "Some Convenient Truths" appeared in* The Atlantic Monthly.

1   Runaway global warming looks all but unstoppable. Maybe that's because we haven't really tried to stop it.

2   If there is now a scientific consensus that global warming must be taken seriously, there is also a related political consensus: that the issue is Gloom City. In *An Inconvenient Truth*, Al Gore warns of sea levels rising to engulf New York and San Francisco and implies that only wrenching lifestyle sacrifice can save us. The opposing view is just as glum. Even mild restrictions on greenhouse gases could "cripple our economy," Republican Senator Kit Bond of Missouri said in 2003. Other conservatives suggest that greenhouse-gas rules for Americans would be pointless anyway, owing to increased fossil-fuel use in China and India. When commentators hash this issue out it's often a contest to see which side can sound more pessimistic.

3   Here's a different way of thinking about the greenhouse effect: that action to prevent runaway global warming may prove cheap, practical, effective, and totally consistent with economic growth. Which makes a body wonder: Why is such environmental optimism absent from American political debate?

4   Greenhouse gases are an air pollution problem—and all previous air pollution problems have been reduced faster and more cheaply than predicted, without economic harm. Some of these problems once seemed scary and intractable, just as greenhouse gases seem today. About forty years ago urban smog was increasing so fast that President Lyndon Johnson warned, "Either we stop poisoning our air or we become a nation [in] gas masks groping our way through dying cities." During Ronald Reagan's presidency, emissions of

chlorofluorocarbons, or CFCs, threatened to deplete the stratospheric ozone layer. As recently as George H. W. Bush's administration, acid rain was said to threaten a "new silent spring" of dead Appalachian forests,

5   But in each case, strong regulations were enacted, and what happened? Since 1970, smog-forming air pollution has declined by a third to a half. Emissions of CFCs have been nearly eliminated, and studies suggest that ozone-layer replenishment is beginning. Acid rain, meanwhile, has declined by a third since 1990, while Appalachian forest health has improved sharply.

6   Most progress against air pollution has been cheaper than expected. Smog controls on automobiles, for example, were predicted to cost thousands of dollars for each vehicle. Today's new cars emit less than 2 percent as much smog-forming pollution as the cars of 1970, and the cars are still as affordable today as they were then. Acid-rain control has cost about 10 percent of what was predicted in 1990, when Congress enacted new rules. At that time, opponents said the regulations would cause a "clean-air recession"; instead, the economy boomed.

7   Greenhouse gases, being global, are the biggest air-pollution problem ever faced. And because widespread fossil-fuel use is inevitable for some time to come, the best-case scenario for the next few decades may be a slowing of the rate of greenhouse-gas buildup, to prevent runaway climate change. Still, the basic pattern observed in all other forms of air-pollution control—rapid progress at low cost—should repeat for greenhouse-gas controls.

8   Yet a paralyzing negativism dominates global-warming politics. Environmentalists depict climate change as nearly unstoppable; skeptics speak of the problem as either imaginary (the "greatest hoax ever perpetrated," in the words of Senator James Inhofe, chairman of the Senate's environment committee) or ruinously expensive to address.

9   Even conscientious politicians may struggle for views that aren't dismal. Mandy Grunwald, a Democratic political consultant, says, "When political candidates talk about new energy sources, they use a positive, can-do vocabulary. Voters have personal experience with energy use, so they can relate to discussion of solutions. If you say a car can use a new kind of fuel, this makes intuitive sense to people. But global warming is of such scale and magnitude, people don't have any commonsense way to grasp what the solutions would be. So political candidates tend to talk about the greenhouse effect in a depressing way."

10   One reason the global-warming problem seems so daunting is that the success of previous antipollution efforts remains something of a secret. Polls show that Americans think the air is getting dirtier, not cleaner, perhaps because media coverage of the environment rarely if ever mentions improvements. For instance, did you know that smog and acid rain have continued to diminish throughout George W. Bush's presidency?

11   One might expect Democrats to trumpet the decline of air pollution, which stands as one of government's leading postwar achievements. But just as Republicans have found they can hash Democrats by falsely accusing them of being soft on defense, Democrats have found they can bash Republicans by falsely accusing them of destroying the environment. If that's your argument, you might skip over the evidence that many environmental trends are positive. One might also expect Republicans to trumpet the reduction of air pollution, since it signifies responsible behavior by industry. But to acknowledge that air pollution has declined would require Republicans to say the words, "The regulations worked."

12   Does it matter that so many in politics seem so pessimistic about the prospect of addressing global warming? Absolutely. Making the problem appear unsolvable encourages a sort of listless fatalism, blunting the drive to take first steps toward a solution. Historically, first steps against air pollution have often led to pleasant surprises. When Congress, in 1970, mandated major reductions in smog caused by automobiles, even many supporters of the rule feared it would be hugely expensive. But the catalytic converter was not practical then; soon it was perfected, and suddenly, major reductions in smog became affordable. Even a small step by the United States against greenhouse gases could lead to a similar breakthrough.

13   And to those who worry that any greenhouse-gas reductions in the United States will be swamped by new emissions from China and India, here's a final reason to be optimistic: technology can move across borders with considerable speed. Today it's not clear that American inventors or entrepreneurs can make money by reducing greenhouse gases, so relatively few are trying. But suppose the United States regulated greenhouse gases, using its own domestic program, not the cumbersome Kyoto Protocol; then America's formidable entrepreneurial and engineering communities would fully engage the problem. Innovations pioneered here could spread throughout the world, and suddenly rapid global warming would not seem inevitable.

14   The two big technical advances against smog—the catalytic converter and the chemical engineering that removes pollutants from gasoline at the refinery stage—were invented in the United States. The big economic advance against acid rain—a credit-trading system that gives power-plant managers a profit incentive to reduce pollution—was pioneered here as well. These advances are now spreading globally. Smog and acid rain are still increasing in some parts of the world, but the trend lines suggest that both will decline fairly soon, even in developing nations. For instance, two decades ago urban smog was rising at a dangerous rate in Mexico; today it is diminishing there, though the country's population continues to grow. A short time ago declining smog and acid rain in developing nations seemed an impossibility; today declining greenhouse gases seem an impossibility. The history of air pollution control says otherwise.

15   Americans love challenges, and preventing artificial climate change is just the sort of technological and economic challenge at which this nation excels. It only remains for the right politician to recast the challenge in practical, optimistic tones. Gore seldom has, and Bush seems to have no interest in trying. But cheap and fast improvement is not a pipe dream; it is the pattern of previous efforts against air pollution. The only reason runaway global warming seems unstoppable is that we have not yet tried to stop it.

QUESTIONS FOR DISCUSSION AND WRITING

1. Like most writers of effective arguments, Easterbrook begins his essay by reviewing the controversy about global warming and climate change. Then he states his main claim, followed by supporting evidence. What is his claim and what events does he cite for his evidence?

2. Easterbrook bases his argument on a comparison between solving air pollution in the 1980s and solving greenhouse gas emissions in the twenty-first century. Are these, however, really comparable situations or similar problems? Explain how these two situations are similar but also how they are different. Do the differences mean that Easterbrook's argument is not valid or effective? Explain.

3. Writing for a non-scientific magazine, The Atlantic Monthly, Easterbrook presents his argument using comfortable, informal language designed to appeal to American citizens rather than atmospheric scientists. Reread the first three paragraphs of his essay. Underline sentences, words, and phrases that show Easterbrook using an informal, colloquial language that appeals to his audience. Does this language help him convince his readers of his thesis? Explain.

4. Assume that you are writing a response to Easterbrook's article to appear in *The Atlantic Monthly.* Reread your journal entry and do some more online and library research on the current state of climate change. Focus your essay on the optimism versus pessimism debate. Is there still a reason to be optimistic or is it too early to know how significant our progress has been?

NEIL L. WATERS

Why You Can't Cite Wikipedia in My Class

Prereading Journal Entry

On your computer, open up the document containing the last paper you wrote which required online or library research. Did you use Wikipedia as one of your sources? Did you use it for background research, or did you quote and cite what you found on the page? Briefly explain how you used the information that you found in the final version of your paper.

Neil L.Waters is Kawashima Professor of Japanese Studies and Professor of History at Middlebury College. He graduated from Middlebury College, served in the Peace Corps in South Korea, and received his doctorate in Japanese History from the University of Hawaii. His publications include articles in the Journal of Japanese Studies and the Journal of Asian Studies, as well as two books, Japan's Local Pragmatists (1983) and Beyond the Area Studies Wars (2000). "Why You Can't Cite Wikipedia in My Class" appeared in Communications of the ACM after the history department at Middlebury adopted a policy stating that students could not cite Wikipedia in their papers for their departmental courses. As Waters explains in his essay, the story was picked up by the local, national, and international media at a time when Wikipedia citations began appearing in students' essays. For teachers and students in many disciplines, Waters' essay opened the dialogue on the proper uses of open-source materials in the research process.

1   The case for an online open-source encyclopedia is enormously appealing. What's not to like? It gives the originators of entries a means to publish, albeit anonymously, in fields they care deeply about and provides editors the opportunity to improve, add to, and polish them, a

capacity not afforded to in-print articles. Above all, open sourcing marshals legions of unpaid, eager, frequently knowledgeable volunteers, whose enormous aggregate labor and energy makes possible the creation of an entity—Wikipedia, which today boasts more than 1.6 million entries in its English edition alone—that would otherwise be far too costly and labor-intensive to see the light of day. In a sense it would have been technologically impossible just a few years ago; open sourcing is democracy in action, and Wikipedia is its most ubiquitous and accessible creation.

2 Yet I am a historian, schooled in the concept that scholarship requires accountability and trained in a discipline in which collaborative research is rare. The idea that the vector-sum products of tens or hundreds of anonymous collaborators could have much value is, to say the least, counterintuitive for most of us in my profession. We don't allow our students to cite printed general encyclopedias, much less open-source ones. Further, while Wikipedia compares favorably with other tertiary sources for articles in the sciences, approximately half of all entries are in some sense historical. Here the qualitative record is much spottier, with reliability decreasing in approximate proportion to distance from "hot topics" in American history [1]. For a Japan historian like me to perceive the positive side of Wikipedia requires an effort of will.

3 I made that effort after an innocuous series of events briefly and improbably propelled me and the history department at Middlebury College into the national, even international, spotlight. While grading a set of final examinations from my "History of Early Japan" class, I noticed that a half-dozen students had provided incorrect information about two topics—the Shimabara Rebellion of 1637–1638 and the Confucian thinker Ogyu Sorai—on which they were to write brief essays. Moreover, they used virtually identical language in doing so. A quick check on Google propelled me via popularity-driven algorithms to the Wikipedia entries on them, and there, quite plainly, was the erroneous information. To head off similar events in the future, I proposed a policy to the history department it promptly adopted: "(1) Students are responsible for the accuracy of information they provide, and they cannot point to Wikipedia or any similar source that may appear in the future to escape the consequences of errors. (2) Wikipedia is not an acceptable citation, even though it may lead one to a citable source."

4 The rest, as they say, is history. The Middlebury student newspaper ran a story on the new policy. That story was picked up online by *The Burlington Free Press*, a Vermont newspaper, which ran its own story. I was

interviewed, first by Vermont radio and TV stations and newspapers, then by the *New York Times,* the *Asahi Shimbun* in Tokyo, and by radio and TV stations in Australia and throughout the U.S., culminating in a story on NBC Nightly News. Hundreds of other newspapers ran stories without interviews, based primarily on the *Times* article. I received dozens of phone calls, ranging from laudatory to actionably defamatory. A representative of the Wikimedia Foundation (www.wikipedia.org), the board that controls Wikipedia, stated that he agreed with the position taken by the Middlebury history department, noting that Wikipedia states in its guidelines that its contents are not suitable for academic citation, because Wikipedia is, like a print encyclopedia, a tertiary source. I repeated this information in all my subsequent interviews, but clearly the publication of the department's policy had hit a nerve, and many news outlets implied, erroneously, that the department was at war with Wikipedia itself, rather than with the uses to which students were putting it.

5   In the wake of my allotted 15 minutes of Andy Warhol-promised fame I have tried to figure out what all the fuss was about. There is a great deal of uneasiness about Wikipedia in the U.S., as well as in the rest of the computerized world, and a great deal of passion and energy has been spent in its defense. It is clear to me that the good stuff is related to the bad stuff. Wikipedia owes its incredible growth to open-source editing, which is also the root of its greatest weakness. Dedicated and knowledgeable editors can and do effectively reverse the process of entropy by making entries better over time. Other editors, through ignorance, sloppy research, or, on occasion, malice or zeal, can and do introduce or perpetuate errors in fact or interpretation. The reader never knows whether the last editor was one of this latter group; most editors leave no trace save a whimsical cyber-handle.

6   Popular entries are less subject to enduring errors, innocent or otherwise, than the seldom-visited ones, because, as I understand it, the frequency of visits by a Wikipedia "policeman" is largely determined, once again, by algorithms that trace the number of hits and move the most popular sites to a higher priority. The same principle, I have come to realize, props up the whole of the Wiki-world. Once a critical mass of hits is reached, Google begins to guide those who consulted it to Wikipedia before all else. A new button on my version of Firefox goes directly to Wikipedia. Preferential access leads to yet more hits, generating a still higher priority in an endless loop of mutual reinforcement.

7   It seems to me that there is a major downside to the self-reinforcing cycle of popularity. Popularity begets ease of use, and ease of use begets

the "democratization" of access to information. But all too often, democratization of access to information is equated with the democratization of the information itself, in the sense that it is subject to a vote. That last mental conflation may have origins that predate Wikipedia and indeed the whole of the Internet.

8   The quiz show "Family Feud" has been a fixture of daytime television for decades and is worth a quick look. Contestants are not rewarded for guessing the correct answer but rather for guessing the answer that the largest number of people have chosen as the correct answer. The show must tap into some sort of popular desire to democratize information. Validation is not conformity to verifiable facts or weighing of interpretations and evidence but conformity to popular opinion. Expertise plays practically no role at all.

9   Here is where all but the most hopelessly postmodernist scholars bridle. "Family Feud" is harmless enough, but most of us believe in a real, external world in which facts exist independently of popular opinion, and some interpretations of events, thoroughly grounded in disciplinary rigor and the weight of evidence, are at least more likely to be right than others that are not. I tell my students that Wikipedia is a fine place to search for a paper topic or begin the research process, but it absolutely cannot serve subsequent stages of research. Wikipedia is not the direct heir to "Family Feud," but both seem to share an element of faith—that if enough people agree on something, it is most likely so.

10   What can be done? The answer depends on the goal. If it is to make Wikipedia a truly authoritative source, suitable for citation, it cannot be done for any general tertiary source, including the *Encyclopaedia Britannica*. For an anonymous open-source encyclopedia, that goal is theoretically, as well as practically, impossible. If the goal is more modest— to make Wikipedia more reliable than it is—then it seems to me that any changes must come at the expense of its open-source nature. Some sort of accountability for editors, as well as for the originators of entries, would be a first step, and that, I think, means that editors must leave a record of their real names. A more rigorous fact-checking system might help, but are there enough volunteers to cover 1.6 million entries, or would checking be in effect reserved for popular entries?

11   Can one move beyond the world of cut-and-dried facts to check for logical consistency and reasonableness of interpretations in light of what is known about a particular society in a particular historical period? Can it be done without experts? If you rely on experts, do you pay them or depend on their voluntarism?

I suppose I should now go fix the Wikipedia entry for Ogyu Sorai (en.wikipedia.org/wiki/Ogyu_ Sorai). I have been waiting since January to see how long it might take for the system to correct it, which has indeed been altered slightly and is rather good overall. But the statement that Ogyu opposed the Tokugawa order is still there and still highly misleading [2]. Somehow the statement that equates the samurai with the lower class in Tokugawa Japan has escaped the editors' attention, though anyone with the slightest contact with Japanese history knows it is wrong. One down, 1.6 million to go.

REFERENCES

1. Rosenzweig, R. Can history be open source? *Journal of American History 93*, 1 (June 2006), 117–146.
2. Tucker, J. (editor and translator). *Ogyu Sorai's Philosophical Masterworks.* Association for Asian Studies and University of Hawaii Press, Honolulu, 2006, 12–13, 48–51; while Ogyu sought to redefine the sources of Tokugawa legitimacy, his purpose was clearly to strengthen the authority of the Tokugawa shogunate.

QUESTIONS FOR DISCUSSION AND WRITING

1. Although Waters' position is clear in the title of his essay, the first few paragraphs of his essay are devoted not to arguing his claim, but to providing context and background for his argument about the proper use of Wikipedia in research. What is this context for his argument? What led up to his decision? How does his even-handed review of this context help establish him as a reasonable person, interested in informing and educating his readers as much as persuading them?

2. Waters grounds much of his argument on his distinction between the "democratization of access to information" versus the "democratization of the information itself." Explain what he means by this difference. Why is this distinction crucial to his argument that Wikipedia should not be used as an authoritative source in the research process? Explain.

3. In paragraph 8, Waters introduces his example about the quiz show, "Family Feud." How is this example relevant to his argument? Are Wikipedia and "Family Feud" similar, or are there key differences?

4. Near the end of his argument, Waters proposes that Wikipedia could become a truly authoritative source if it made a few key changes. What are those changes and how might that help the reliability and authoritativeness of Wikipedia?

Professors Should Embrace Wikipedia

Prereading Journal Entry

On your computer, open up the document containing the last paper you wrote which required online or library research. Did you use Wikipedia as one of your sources? Did you use it for background research, or did you quote and cite what you found on the page? Now, look at some of the other online sources you may have cited. How reliable is the information in those sources? What person or entity is responsible for this page? Are the authors of the page an authority on this particular topic? Do they have a particular bias? Is this site as reliable as Wikipedia? Is it as reliable as an academic journal article on the same topic?

Mark A. Wilson is the Lewis and Marian Nixon Professor of Natural Sciences in the Department of Geology at the College of Wooster. He received his PhD in paleontology from the University of California, Berkeley, and is the author of numerous articles about evolutionary paleontology and geology. His article, "Professors Should Embrace Wikipedia" appeared in Inside Higer Ed, *an online journal dedicated to providing the "best news and information possible" about the world of higher education. As Wilson explains, Wikipedia quickly became an online site for his students to investigate, learn, and communicate about the field of geology. The question remains, however, whether any wiki site, which can be changed by anyone regardless of agenda or (lack of) professional background, can serve to promote the goals of academic knowledge. As you read Wilson's essay consider the feasibility of his recommendations.*

1   When the online, anyone-can-edit Wikipedia appeared in 2001, teachers, especially college professors, were appalled. The Internet was already an apparently limitless source of nonsense for their students to eagerly consume—now there was a Web site with the appearance of legitimacy and a dead-easy interface that would complete the seduction until all sense of fact, fiction, myth and propaganda blended into a popular culture of pseudo intelligence masking the basest ignorance. An *Inside Higher Ed* article just last year on Wikipedia use in the academy drew a huge and passionate response, much of it negative.

2   Now the English version of Wikipedia has over 2 million articles, and it has been translated into over 250 languages. It has become so massive that you can type virtually any noun into a search engine and the first link will be to a Wikipedia page. After seven years and this exponential growth, Wikipedia can still be edited by anyone at any time. A generation of students was warned away from this information siren, but we know as professors that it is the first place they go to start a research project, look up an unfamiliar term from lecture, or find something disturbing to ask about during the next lecture. In fact, we learned too that Wikipedia is indeed the most convenient repository of information ever invented, and we go there often—if a bit covertly—to get a few questions answered. Its accuracy, at least for science articles, is actually as high as the revered *Encyclopedia Britannica,* as shown by a test published in the journal *Nature.*

3   It is time for the academic world to recognize Wikipedia for what it has become: a global library open to anyone with an Internet connection and a pressing curiosity. The vision of its founders, Jimmy Wales and Larry Sanger, has become reality, and the librarians were right: the world has not been the same since. If the Web is the greatest information delivery device ever, and Wikipedia is the largest coherent store of information and ideas, then we as teachers and scholars should have been on this train years ago for the benefit of our students, our professions, and that mystical pool of human knowledge.

4   What Wikipedia too often lacks is academic authority, or at least the perception of it. Most of its thousands of editors are anonymous, sometimes known only by an IP address or a cryptic username. Every article has a "talk" page for discussions of content, bias, and organization. "Revert" wars can rage out of control as one faction battles another over a few words in an article. Sometimes administrators have to step in and lock a page down until tempers cool and the main protagonists lose interest. The very anonymity of the editors is often the source of the problem: how do we know who has an authoritative grasp of the topic?

5   That is what academics do best. We can quickly sort out scholarly authority into complex hierarchies with a quick glance at a vita and a sniff at a publication list. We make many mistakes doing this, of course, but at least our debates are supported with citations and a modicum of civility because we are identifiable and we have our reputations to maintain and friends to keep. Maybe this academic culture can be added to the Wild West of Wikipedia to make it more useful for everyone?

6   I propose that all academics with research specialties, no matter how arcane (and nothing is too obscure for Wikipedia), enroll as

identifiable editors of Wikipedia. We then watch over a few wikipages of our choosing, adding to them when appropriate, stepping in to resolve disputes when we know something useful. We can add new articles on topics which should be covered, and argue that others should be removed or combined. This is not to displace anonymous editors, many of whom possess vast amounts of valuable information and innovative ideas, but to add our authority and hard-won knowledge to this growing universal library.

7   The advantages should be obvious. First, it is another outlet for our scholarship, one that may be more likely to be read than many of our journals. Second, we are directly serving our students by improving the source they go to first for information. Third, by identifying ourselves, we can connect with other scholars and interested parties who stumble across our edits and new articles. Everyone wins.

8   I have been an open Wikipedia editor now for several months. I have enjoyed it immensely. In my teaching I use a "living syllabus" for each course, which is a kind of academic blog. (For example, see my History of Life course online syllabus.) I connect students through links to outside sources of information. Quite often I refer students to Wikipedia articles that are well-sourced and well written. Wikipages that are not so good are easily fixed with a judicious edit or two, and many pages become more useful with the addition of an image from my collection (all donated to the public domain). Since I am open in my editorial identity, I often get questions from around the world about the topics I find most fascinating. I've even made important new connections through my edits to new collaborators and reporters who want more background for a story.

9   For example, this year I met online a biology professor from Centre College who is interested in the ecology of fish on Great Inagua Island in the Bahamas. He saw my additions and images on that Wikipedia page and had several questions about the island. He invited me to speak at Centre next year about evolution-creation controversies, which is unrelated to the original contact but flowed from our academic conversations. I in turn have been learning much about the island's living ecology I did not know. I've also learned much about the kind of prose that is most effective for a general audience, and I've in turn taught some people how to properly reference ideas and information. In short, I've expanded my teaching.

10   Wikipedia as we know it will undoubtedly change in the coming years as all technologies do. By involving ourselves directly and in large numbers now, we can help direct that change into ever more

useful ways for our students and the public. This is, after all, our sacred charge as teacher-scholars: to educate when and where we can to the greatest effect.

QUESTIONS FOR DISCUSSION AND WRITING

1. Wilson's essay argues for a proposal to change how teachers and scholars use Wikipedia. What does Wilson recommend and where does Wilson state this claim most clearly?

2. In support of his recommendation, Wilson cites several advantages for students, scholars, and researchers. What are the advantages that Wilson cites?

3. Typically, arguing essays respond to alternate or opposing ideas. What are possible disadvantages to Wilson's proposal? Search online or in your library's databases for responses to Wilson's ideas. How might Wilson respond to these objections?

4. As a student, have you participated in a wiki site? What in your experience were the advantages and disadvantages of communicating in a wiki format? Are there some situations where a wiki format is helpful but others where it is not so productive? Explain.

5. Write your own essay on Wikipedia. How, in fact, are Wikipedia sites organized? What rules do you have to follow to add or revise information on the site? What controls exist to monitor Wikipedia sites? Are there some topics or sites that are "locked down," as Wilson suggests? Has the information on Wikipedia sites become more reliable and authoritative? Using the information you gather, write your own essay recommending a policy that teachers and students should follow when using or citing Wikipedia.

MIKE ROYKO

Endorsements Just a Shell Game

Prereading Journal Entry

If someone offered you a substantial amount of money to endorse a product that you personally disliked or objected to, would you agree to do the endorsement? Would it depend on the exact product? Would it depend on how much money the advertiser offered you? Choose a particular product that you do not like and explain why you would or would not do the endorsement.

Mike Royko was born in Chicago, grew up on the northwest side, and attended Wright Junior College, the University of Illinois, and Northwestern University. After a stint in the Air Force, Royko began his long and distinguished career as a columnist. Writing primarily for the Chicago Daily News *and the* Tribune, *Royko soon became Chicago's best-known and best-loved columnist. He received numerous awards including the Ernie Pyle Memorial Award, the H. L. Mencken Award, and the Heywood Broun Award—in addition to winning a Pulitzer Prize in 1972. He published several books, including* Boss: Richard J. Daley of Chicago *and* Sez Who? Sez Me. *In* "Endorsements Just a Shell Game," *Royko relies on one of his favorite side-kicks, Slats Grobnik, to create an entertaining dialogue about the ethics of advertising. As you read this essay, consider whether Royko has written an effective argumentative essay or just created an entertaining ethical dialogue about advertising.*

1   The man from an advertising agency had an unusual proposition.

2   His agency does the TV commercials for a well-known chain of Mexican restaurants in Chicago.

3   "You may have seen our commercials," he said. "They include a cameo appearance by Lee Smith and Leon Durham of the Cubs. It shows them crunching into a tortilla."

4   No, I somehow missed seeing that.

5   "Well, anyway, we'd like to have you in a commercial."

6   Doing what?

7   "Crunching into a tortilla."

8   I thought tortillas were soft. I may be wrong, but I don't think you can crunch into a tortilla. Maybe you mean a taco.

9   "Well, you'd be biting into some kind of Mexican food."

10   What else would I have to do?

11   "That's it. It would be a cameo appearance. You'd be seen for about four seconds. You wouldn't have to say anything."

12   I'd just bite into a piece of Mexican food?

13   "Right. For a fee, of course."

14   How big a fee?

15   He named a figure. It was not a king's ransom, but it was more than walking-around money.

16   "It would take about 45 minutes to film," he said.

17   Amazing. In my first newspaper job almost 30 years ago, I had to work 12 weeks to earn the figure he had mentioned.

18   It was a small, twice-a-week paper, and I was the only police reporter, the only sports reporter, the only investigative reporter, the assistant political writer, and on Saturday I would edit the stories going into the entertainment page. The publisher believed in a day's work for an hour's pay.

19   Now I could make the same amount just for spending 45 minutes biting into a taco in front of a TV camera.

20   "Well, what do you think?" he asked.

21   I told him that I would think about it and get back to him.

22   So I asked Slats Grobnik, who has sound judgment, what he thought of the deal.

23   "That's a lot of money just to bite a taco on TV. For that kind of scratch, I'd bite a dog. Grab the deal."

24   But there is a question of ethics.

25   "Ethics? What's the ethics in biting a taco? Millions of people bite tacos every day. Mexicans have been biting them for hundreds of years. Are you saying that Mexicans are unethical? Careful, some of my best friends are Mexicans."

26   No, I'm not saying that at all. I like Mexicans, too, although I'm opposed to bullfighting.

27   "Then what's unethical?"

28   The truth is, I can't stand tacos.

29   "What has that got to do with it? I can't stand work, but I do it for the money."

30   It has everything to do with it. If I go on TV and bite into a taco, won't I be endorsing that taco?

31   "So what? You've endorsed politicians and I've never met a politician that I liked better than a taco."

32   But endorsing a taco I didn't like would be dishonest.

33   "Hey, that's the American way. Turn on your TV and look at all the people who endorse junk. Do you think they really believe what they're saying?"

34   Then it's wrong. Nobody should endorse a taco if they don't like a taco.

35   "Then tell them you'll bite something else. A tortilla or an enchilada."

36   But I don't like them, either. The truth is, I can't stand most Mexican food. The only thing I really like is the salt on the edge of a margarita glass.

37   "Can't you just bite the taco and spit it out when the camera is turned off?"

38   That would be a sham. Besides, even if I liked tacos or tortillas, what does it matter? Why should somebody eat in a restaurant because they see me biting into that restaurant's taco? Am I a taco expert? What are my credentials to tell millions of people what taco they should eat? I'm not even a Mexican.

39   "You're as Mexican as Jane Byrne, and she's doing it."

40   To get the Hispanic vote, she would go on TV and eat a cactus.

41   "Well, you're a sucker to turn it down. Why, it's almost un-American. Do you think that in Russia any newsman would ever have an opportunity to make that much money by biting into a pirogi."

42   That may be so.

43   But maybe someday a food product will come along that I can lend my name to, something I can truly believe in.

44   "I doubt it. Not unless they start letting taverns advertise shots and beers on TV."

QUESTIONS FOR DISCUSSION AND WRITING

1. What is Royko's purpose in writing this essay? To entertain the reader? To write about an interesting event in his life? To explain why he dislikes Mexican food? To argue that ethics should be important in business? Defend your choice(s) with reference to the essay.

2. Argumentative essays present both (or several) sides to an issue. What arguments does Royko give for not accepting the offer? What arguments does Slats give for accepting the advertising deal?

3. Royko wrote this column for the Chicago *Tribune*. What kind of *Tribune* reader might find this essay most interesting? Would you read this essay if you saw it in the newspaper? Why or why not?

4. Analyze Royko's reasons for hesitating to do the taco commercial. Is it because he doesn't like tacos? Is it because he feels guilty for earning so much money so easily? Is it because he's not Mexican? Which of these—or other—reasons is foremost in Royko's mind?

5. Write out your definition of an effective written argument. List the major criteria for an argumentative essay. Does Royko's essay meet that definition and satisfy those criteria? Support your answer with specific references to Royko's essay.

6. Recall a situation where you were asked to do something you felt was ethically wrong or irresponsible. Describe the situation. What were the pro and con arguments at the time? What decision did you make? In retrospect, do you believe you made the right decision? Explain.

Letter from Birmingham Jail

Prereading Journal Entry

Without reading the following headnote, write in your journal what you know about Martin Luther King. What do you know about his life or death? What did he mean by "civil disobedience" or nonviolent protest? How is Martin Luther King Day celebrated in your town or city? What current public figure is most active in nonviolent protest for civil rights of minorities?

In 1955, an unknown Baptist minister named Martin Luther King organized a Negro boycott of the segregated bus system in Montgomery, Alabama. To the dismay of the white citizens, the boycott lasted 381 days. From 1955 until his assassination in 1968, King was the acknowledged leader of the American Civil Rights Movement. Born the son of a Baptist minister, King earned degrees from Morehouse College, Crozer Theological Seminary, Boston University, and Chicago Theological Seminary. King's writings include Why We Can't Wait *(1964) and* Where Do We Go from Here: Chaos or Community? *(1967). Although King's most dramatic moment was the delivery of his "I Have a Dream" speech to 200,000 civil rights protesters at the Lincoln Memorial, his legacy to America is the defense of civil disobedience in "Letter from Birmingham Jail," a document that echoes Plato's* Apology, *Henry David Thoreau's "Civil Disobedience," and Mahatma Gandhi's* Nonviolent Resistance.

"Letter from Birmingham Jail" was written in April 1963, while King was in jail in Birmingham, Alabama, for acts of civil disobedience. King is responding to a letter signed by eight Jewish, Catholic, and Protestant clergymen appealing for "Law and Order and Common Sense." In their statement, the clergymen express concern about "unwise and untimely" demonstrations "led in part by outsiders." They call for "honest and open negotiation of racial issues" and deplore the "extreme measures" that, though technically peaceful, might incite "hatred and violence." They then praise law enforcement officials for their "calm manner" and request that "our own Negro community" withdraw from the demonstrations. "When rights are consistently denied," the clergymen conclude, "a cause should be pressed in the courts and in negotiations among local leaders, and not in the streets." In his letter, King replies to each of these statements.

My Dear Fellow Clergymen:

1   While confined here in the Birmingham city jail, I came across your recent statement calling my present activities "unwise and untimely." Seldom do I pause to answer criticism of my work and ideas. If I sought to answer all the criticisms that cross my desk, my secretaries would have little time for anything other than such correspondence in the course of the day, and I would have no time for constructive work. But since I feel that you are men of genuine good will and that your criticisms are sincerely set forth, I want to try to answer your statement in what I hope will be patient and reasonable terms.

2   I think I should indicate why I am here in Birmingham, since you have been influenced by the view which argues against "outsiders coming in." I have the honor of serving as president of the Southern Christian Leadership Conference, an organization operating in every southern state, with headquarters in Atlanta, Georgia. We have some eighty-five affiliated organizations across the South, and one of them is the Alabama Christian Movement for Human Rights. Frequently we share staff, educational, and financial resources with our affiliates. Several months ago the affiliate here in Birmingham asked us to be on call to engage in a nonviolent direct-action program if such were deemed necessary. We readily consented, and when the hour came we lived up to our promise. So I, along with several members of my staff, am here because I was invited here. I am here because I have organizational ties here.

3   But more basically, I am in Birmingham because injustice is here. Just as the prophets of the eighth century B.C. left their villages and carried their "thus saith the Lord" far beyond the boundaries of their home towns, and just as the Apostle Paul left his village of Tarsus and carried the gospel of Jesus Christ to the far corners of the Greco-Roman world, so am I compelled to carry the gospel of freedom beyond my own home town. Like Paul, I must constantly respond to the Macedonian call for aid.

4   Moreover, I am cognizant of the interrelatedness of all communities and states. I cannot sit idly by in Atlanta and not be concerned about what happens in Birmingham. Injustice anywhere is a threat to justice everywhere. We are caught in an inescapable network of mutuality, tied in a single garment of destiny. Whatever affects one directly, affects all indirectly. Never again can we afford to live with the narrow, provincial

"outside agitator" idea. Anyone who lives inside the United States can never be considered an outsider anywhere within its bounds.

5   You deplore the demonstrations taking place in Birmingham. But your statement, I am sorry to say, fails to express a similar concern for the conditions that brought about the demonstrations. I am sure that none of you would want to rest content with the superficial kind of social analysis that deals merely with effects and does not grapple with underlying causes. It is unfortunate that demonstrations are taking place in Birmingham, but it is even more unfortunate that the city's white power structure left the Negro community with no alternative.

6   In any nonviolent campaign there are four basic steps: collection of the facts to determine whether injustices exist; negotiation; self-purification; and direct action. We have gone through all these steps in Birmingham. There can be no gainsaying the fact that racial injustice engulfs this community. Birmingham is probably the most thoroughly segregated city in the United States. Its ugly record of brutality is widely known. Negroes have experienced grossly unjust treatment in the courts. There have been more unsolved bombings of Negro homes and churches in Birmingham than in any other city in the nation. These are the hard, brutal facts of the case. On the basis of these conditions, Negro leaders sought to negotiate with the city fathers. But the latter consistently refused to engage in good-faith negotiation.

7   Then, last September, came the opportunity to talk with leaders of Birmingham's economic community. In the course of the negotiations, certain promises were made by the merchants—for example, to remove the stores' humiliating racial signs. On the basis of these promises, the Reverend Fred Shuttlesworth and the leaders of the Alabama Christian Movement for Human Rights agreed to a moratorium on all demonstrations. As the weeks and months went by, we realized that we were the victims of a broken promise. A few signs, briefly removed, returned; the others remained.

8   As in so many past experiences, our hopes had been blasted, and the shadow of deep disappointment settled upon us. We had no alternative except to prepare for direct action, whereby we would present our very bodies as a means of laying our case before the conscience of the local and the national community. Mindful of the difficulties involved, we decided to undertake a process of self-purification. We began a series of workshops on nonviolence, and we repeatedly asked ourselves: "Are you able to accept blows without retaliating?" "Are you able to endure the ordeal of jail?" We decided to schedule our

direct-action program for the Easter season, realizing that except for Christmas, this is the main shopping period of the year. Knowing that a strong economic-withdrawal program would be the by-product of direct action, we felt that this would be the best time to bring pressure to bear on the merchants for the needed change.

9   Then it occurred to us that Birmingham's mayoral election was coming up in March, and we speedily decided to postpone action until after election day. When we discovered that the Commissioner of Public Safety, Eugene "Bull" Connor, had piled up enough votes to be in the run-off, we decided again to postpone action until the day after the run-off so that the demonstrations could not be used to cloud the issues. Like many others, we wanted to see Mr. Connor defeated, and to this end we endured postponement after postponement. Having aided in this community need, we felt that our direct-action program could be delayed no longer.

10   You may well ask, "Why direct action? Why sit-ins, marches, and so forth? Isn't negotiation a better path?" You are quite right in calling for negotiation. Indeed, this is the very purpose of direct action. Nonviolent direct action seeks to create such a crisis and foster such a tension that a community which has constantly refused to negotiate is forced to confront the issue. It seeks so to dramatize the issue that it can no longer be ignored. My citing the creation of tension as part of the work of the nonviolent resister may sound rather shocking. But I must confess that I am not afraid of the word "tension." I have earnestly opposed violent tension, but there is a type of constructive, nonviolent tension which is necessary for growth. Just as Socrates felt that it was necessary to create a tension in the mind so that individuals could rise from the bondage of myths and half-truths to the unfettered realm of creative analysis and objective appraisal, so must we see the need for nonviolent gadflies to create the kind of tension in society that will help men rise from the dark depths of prejudice and racism to the majestic heights of understanding and brotherhood.

11   The purpose of our direct-action program is to create a situation so crisis-packed that it will inevitably open the door to negotiation. I therefore concur with you in your call for negotiation. Too long has our beloved Southland been bogged down in a tragic effort to live in monologue rather than dialogue.

12   One of the basic points in your statement is that the action that I and my associates have taken in Birmingham is untimely. Some have asked: "Why didn't you give the new city administration time to act?"

The only answer that I can give to this query is that the new Birmingham administration must be prodded about as much as the outgoing one, before it will act. We are sadly mistaken if we feel that the election of Albert Boutwell as mayor will bring the millennium to Birmingham. While Mr. Boutwell is a much more gentle person than Mr. Connor, they are both segregationists, dedicated to maintenance of the status quo. I have hoped that Mr. Boutwell will be reasonable enough to see the futility of massive resistance to desegregation. But he will not see this without pressure from devotees of civil rights. My friends, I must say to you that we have not made a single gain in civil rights without determined legal and nonviolent pressure. Lamentably, it is an historical fact that privileged groups seldom give up their privileges voluntarily. Individuals may see the moral light and voluntarily give up their unjust posture; but, as Reinhold Niebuhr has reminded us, groups tend to be more immoral than individuals.

13   We know through painful experience that freedom is never voluntarily given by the oppressor; it must be demanded by the oppressed. Frankly, I have yet to engage in a direct-action campaign that was "well timed" in the view of those who have not suffered unduly from the disease of segregation. For years now I have heard the word "Wait!" It rings in the ear of every Negro with piercing familiarity. This "Wait" has almost always meant "Never." We must come to see, with one of our distinguished jurists, that "justice too long delayed is justice denied."

14   We have waited for more than 340 years for our constitutional and God-given rights. The nations of Asia and Africa are moving with jet-like speed toward gaining political independence, but we still creep at horse-and-buggy pace toward gaining a cup of coffee at a lunch counter. Perhaps it is easy for those who have never felt the stinging darts of segregation to say, "Wait." But when you have seen vicious mobs lynch your mothers and fathers at will and drown your sisters and brothers at whim; when you have seen hate-filled policemen curse, kick, and even kill your black brothers and sisters; when you see the vast majority of your twenty million Negro brothers smothering in an airtight cage of poverty in the midst of an affluent society; when you suddenly find your tongue twisted and your speech stammering as you seek to explain to your six-year-old daughter why she can't go to the public amusement park that has just been advertised on television, and see tears welling up in her eyes when she is told that Funtown is closed to colored children, and see ominous clouds of inferiority beginning to form in her little mental sky, and see her beginning to

distort her personality by developing an unconscious bitterness toward white people; when you have to concoct an answer for a five-year-old son who is asking, "Daddy, why do white people treat colored people so mean?"; when you take a cross-country drive and find it necessary to sleep night after night in the uncomfortable corners of your automobile because no motel will accept you; when you are humiliated day in and day out by nagging signs reading "white" and "colored"; when your first name becomes "nigger," your middle name becomes "boy" (however old you are) and your last name becomes "John," and your wife and mother are never given the respected title "Mrs."; when you are harried by day and haunted by night by the fact that you are a Negro, living constantly at tiptoe stance, never quite knowing what to expect next, and are plagued with inner fears and outer resentments; when you are forever fighting a degenerating sense of "nobodiness" — then you will understand why we find it difficult to wait. There comes a time when the cup of endurance runs over, and men are no longer willing to be plunged into the abyss of despair. I hope, sirs, you can understand our legitimate and unavoidable impatience.

15   You express a great deal of anxiety over our willingness to break laws. This is certainly a legitimate concern. Since we so diligently urge people to obey the Supreme Court's decision of 1954 outlawing segregation in the public schools, at first glance it may seem rather paradoxical for us consciously to break laws. One may well ask: "How can you advocate breaking some laws and obeying others?" The answer lies in the fact that there are two types of laws: just and unjust. I would be the first to advocate obeying just laws. One has not only a legal but a moral responsibility to obey just laws. Conversely, one has a moral responsibility to disobey unjust laws. I would agree with St. Augustine that "an unjust law is no law at all."

16   Now, what is the difference between the two? How does one determine whether a law is just or unjust? A just law is a man-made code that squares with the moral law or the law of God. An unjust law is a code that is out of harmony with the moral law. To put it in the terms of St. Thomas Aquinas: An unjust law is a human law that is not rooted in eternal law and natural law. Any law that uplifts human personality is just. Any law that degrades human personality is unjust. All segregation statutes are unjust because segregation distorts the soul and damages the personality. It gives the segregator a false sense of superiority and the segregated a false sense of inferiority. Segregation, to use the terminology of the Jewish philosopher Martin Buber, substitutes an

"I-it" relationship for an "I-thou" relationship and ends up relegating persons to the status of things. Hence segregation is not only politically, economically, and sociologically unsound, it is morally wrong and sinful. Paul Tillich has said that sin is separation. Is not segregation an existential expression of man's tragic separation, his awful estrangement, his terrible sinfulness? Thus it is that I can urge men to obey the 1954 decision of the Supreme Court, for it is morally right; and I can urge them to disobey segregation ordinances, for they are morally wrong.

17   Let us consider a more concrete example of just and unjust laws. An unjust law is a code that a numerical or power majority group compels a minority group to obey but does not make binding on itself. This is *difference* made legal. By the same token, a just law is a code that a majority compels a minority to follow and that it is willing to follow itself. This is *sameness* made legal.

18   Let me give another explanation. A law is unjust if it is inflicted on a minority that, as a result of being denied the right to vote, had no part in enacting or devising the law. Who can say that the legislature of Alabama which set up that state's segregation laws was democratically elected? Throughout Alabama all sorts of devious methods are used to prevent Negroes from becoming registered voters, and there are some counties in which, even though Negroes constitute a majority of the population, not a single Negro is registered. Can any law enacted under such circumstances be considered democratically structured?

19   Sometimes a law is just on its face and unjust in its application. For instance, I have been arrested on a charge of parading without a permit. Now, there is nothing wrong in having an ordinance which requires a permit for a parade. But such an ordinance becomes unjust when it is used to maintain segregation and to deny citizens the First Amendment privilege of peaceful assembly and protest.

20   I hope you are able to see the distinction I am trying to point out. In no sense do I advocate evading or defying the law, as would the rabid segregationist. That would lead to anarchy. One who breaks an unjust law must do so openly, lovingly, and with a willingness to accept the penalty. I submit that an individual who breaks a law that conscience tells him is unjust, and who willingly accepts the penalty of imprisonment in order to arouse the conscience of the community over its injustice, is in reality expressing the highest respect for law.

21   Of course, there is nothing new about this kind of civil disobedience. It was evidenced sublimely in the refusal of Shadrach, Meshach,

and Abednego to obey the laws of Nebuchadnezzar, on the ground that a higher moral law was at stake. It was practiced superbly by the early Christians, who were willing to face hungry lions and the excruciating pain of chopping blocks rather than submit to certain unjust laws of the Roman Empire. To a degree, academic freedom is a reality today because Socrates practiced civil disobedience. In our own nation, the Boston Tea Party represented a massive act of civil disobedience.

22 We should never forget that everything Adolf Hitler did in Germany was "legal" and everything the Hungarian freedom fighters did in Hungary was "illegal." It was "illegal" to aid and comfort a Jew in Hitler's Germany. Even so, I am sure that, had I lived in Germany at the time, I would have aided and comforted my Jewish brothers. If today I lived in a Communist country where certain principles dear to the Christian faith are suppressed, I would openly advocate disobeying that country's antireligious laws.

23 I must make two honest confessions to you, my Christian and Jewish brothers. First, I must confess that over the past few years I have been gravely disappointed with the white moderate. I have almost reached the regrettable conclusion that the Negro's great stumbling block in his stride toward freedom is not the White Citizen's Counciler or the Ku Klux Klanner, but the white moderate, who is more devoted to "order" than to justice; who prefers a negative peace which is the absence of tension to a positive peace which is the presence of justice; who constantly says, "I agree with you in the goal you seek, but I cannot agree with your methods of direct action"; who paternalistically believes he can set the timetable for another man's freedom; who lives by a mythical concept of time and who constantly advises the Negro to wait for a "more convenient season." Shallow understanding from people of good will is more frustrating than absolute misunderstanding from people of ill will. Lukewarm acceptance is much more bewildering than outright rejection.

24 I had hoped that the white moderate would understand that law and order exist for the purpose of establishing justice and that when they fail in this purpose they become the dangerously structured dams that block the flow of social progress. I had hoped that the white moderate would understand that the present tension in the South is a necessary phase of the transition from an obnoxious negative peace, in which the Negro passively accepted his unjust plight, to a substantive and positive peace, in which all men will respect the dignity and worth of human personality. Actually, we who engage in nonviolent direct

action are not the creators of tension. We merely bring to the surface the hidden tension that is already alive. We bring it out in the open, where it can be seen and dealt with. Like a boil that can never be cured so long as it is covered up but must be opened with all its ugliness to the natural medicines of air and light, injustice must be exposed, with all the tension its exposure creates, to the light of human conscience and the air of national opinion, before it can be cured.

25   In your statement you assert that our actions, even though peaceful, must be condemned because they precipitate violence. But is this a logical assertion? Isn't this like condemning a robbed man because his possession of money precipitated the evil act of robbery? Isn't this like condemning Socrates because his unswerving commitment to truth and his philosophical inquiries precipitated the act by the misguided populace in which they made him drink hemlock? Isn't this like condemning Jesus because his unique God-consciousness and never-ceasing devotion to God's will precipitated the evil act of crucifixion? We must come to see that, as the federal courts have consistently affirmed, it is wrong to urge an individual to cease his efforts to gain his basic constitutional rights because the quest may precipitate violence. Society must protect the robbed and punish the robber.

26   I had also hoped that the white moderate would reject the myth concerning time in relation to the struggle for freedom. I have just received a letter from a white brother in Texas. He writes: "All Christians know that the colored people will receive equal rights eventually, but it is possible that you are in too great a religious hurry. It has taken Christianity almost two thousand years to accomplish what it has. The teachings of Christ take time to come to earth." Such an attitude stems from a tragic misconception of time, from the strangely irrational notion that there is something in the very flow of time that will inevitably cure all ills. Actually, time itself is neutral; it can be used either destructively or constructively. More and more I feel that the people of ill will have used time much more effectively than have the people of good will. We will have to repent in this generation not merely for the hateful words and actions of the bad people, but for the appalling silence of the good people. Human progress never rolls in on wheels of inevitability; it comes through the tireless efforts of men willing to be co-workers with God, and without this hard work, time itself becomes an ally of the forces of social stagnation. We must use time creatively, in the knowledge that the time is always ripe to do right. Now is the time to make real the promise of democracy and

transform our pending national elegy into a creative psalm of brotherhood. Now is the time to lift our national policy from the quicksand of racial injustice to the solid rock of human dignity.

27   You speak of our activity in Birmingham as extreme. At first I was rather disappointed that fellow clergymen would see my nonviolent efforts as those of an extremist. I began thinking about the fact that I stand in the middle of two opposing forces in the Negro community. One is a force of complacency, made up in part of Negroes who, as a result of long years of oppression, are so drained of self-respect and a sense of "somebodiness" that they have adjusted to segregation; and in part of a few middle-class Negroes who, because of a degree of academic and economic security and because in some ways they profit by segregation, have become insensitive to the problems of the masses. The other force is one of bitterness and hatred, and it comes perilously close to advocating violence. It is expressed in the various black nationalist groups that are springing up across the nation, the largest and best-known being Elijah Muhammad's Muslim movement. Nourished by the Negro's frustration over the continued existence of racial discrimination, this movement is made up of people who have lost faith in America, who have absolutely repudiated Christianity, and who have concluded that the white man is an incorrigible "devil."

28   I have tried to stand between these two forces, saying that we need emulate neither the "do-nothingism" of the complacent nor the hatred and despair of the black nationalist. For there is the more excellent way of love and nonviolent protest. I am grateful to God that, through the influence of the Negro church, the way of nonviolence became an integral part of our struggle.

29   If this philosophy had not emerged, by now many streets of the South would, I am convinced, be flowing with blood. And I am further convinced that if our white brothers dismiss as "rabble-rousers" and "outside agitators" those of us who employ nonviolent direct action, and if they refuse to support our nonviolent efforts, millions of Negroes will, out of frustration and despair, seek solace and security in black-nationalist ideologies—a development that would inevitably lead to a frightening racial nightmare.

30   Oppressed people cannot remain oppressed forever. The yearning for freedom eventually manifests itself, and that is what has happened to the American Negro. Something within has reminded him of his birthright of freedom, and something without has reminded him that it can be gained. Consciously or unconsciously, he has been caught up

by the *Zeitgeist*, and with his black brothers of Africa and his brown and yellow brothers of Asia, South America, and the Caribbean, the United States Negro is moving with a sense of great urgency toward the promised land of racial justice. If one recognizes this vital urge that has engulfed the Negro community, one should readily understand why public demonstrations are taking place. The Negro has many pent-up resentments and latent frustrations, and he must release them. So let him march; let him make prayer pilgrimages to the city hall; let him go on freedom rides—and try to understand why he must do so. If his repressed emotions are not released in nonviolent ways, they will seek expression through violence; this is not a threat but a fact of history. So I have not said to my people, "Get rid of your discontent." Rather, I have tried to say that this normal and healthy discontent can be channeled into the creative outlet of nonviolent direct action. And now this approach is being termed extremist.

31   But though I was initially disappointed at being categorized as an extremist, as I continued to think about the matter I gradually gained a measure of satisfaction from the label. Was not Jesus an extremist for love: "Love your enemies, bless them that curse you, do good to them that hate you, and pray for them which despitefully use you, and perse-cute you." Was not Amos an extremist for justice: "Let justice roll down like waters and righteousness like an ever-flowing stream." Was not Paul an extremist for the Christian gospel: "I bear in my body the marks of the Lord Jesus." Was not Martin Luther an extremist: "Here I stand; I cannot do otherwise, so help me God." And John Bunyan: "I will stay in jail to the end of my days before I make a butchery of my conscience." And Abra-ham Lincoln: "This nation cannot survive half slave and half free." And Thomas Jefferson: "We hold these truths to be self-evident, that all men are created equal. . . ." So the question is not whether we will be extrem-ists, but what kind of extremists we will be. Will we be extremists for hate or for love? Will we be extremists for the preservation of injustice or for the extension of justice? In that dramatic scene on Calvary's hill three men were crucified. We must never forget that all three were crucified for the same crime—the crime of extremism. Two were extremists for immorality, and thus fell below their environment. The other, Jesus Christ, was an extremist for love, truth, and goodness, and thereby rose above his environment. Perhaps the South, the nation, and the world are in dire need of creative extremists.

32   I had hoped that the white moderate would see this need. Perhaps I was too optimistic; perhaps I expected too much. I suppose I should

have realized that few members of the oppressor race can understand the deep groans and passionate yearnings of the oppressed race, and still fewer have the vision to see that injustice must be rooted out by strong, persistent, and determined action. I am thankful, however, that some of our white brothers in the South have grasped the meaning of this social revolution and committed themselves to it. They are still all too few in quantity, but they are big in quality. Some—such as Ralph McGill, Lillian Smith, Harry Golden, James McBride Dabbs, Ann Braden, and Sarah Patton Boyle—have written about our struggle in eloquent and prophetic terms. Others have marched with us down nameless streets of the South. They have languished in filthy, roach-infested jails, suffering the abuse and brutality of policemen who view them as "dirty nigger-lovers." Unlike so many of their moderate brothers and sisters, they have recognized the urgency of the moment and sensed the need for powerful "action" antidotes to combat the disease of segregation.

33   Let me take note of my other major disappointment. I have been so greatly disappointed with the white church and its leadership. Of course, there are some notable exceptions. I am not unmindful of the fact that each of you has taken some significant stands on this issue. I commend you, Reverend Stallings, for your Christian stand on this past Sunday, in welcoming Negroes to your worship service on a non-segregated basis. I commend the Catholic leaders of this state for integrating Spring Hill College several years ago.

34   But despite these notable exceptions, I must honestly reiterate that I have been disappointed with the church. I do not say this as one of those negative critics who can always find something wrong with the church. I say this as a minister of the gospel, who loves the church; who was nurtured in its bosom; who has been sustained by its spiritual blessings and who will remain true to it as long as the cord of life shall lengthen.

35   When I was suddenly catapulted into the leadership of the bus protest in Montgomery, Alabama, a few years ago, I felt we would be supported by the white church. I felt that the white ministers, priests, and rabbis of the South would be among our strongest allies. Instead, some have been outright opponents, refusing to understand the freedom movement and misrepresenting its leaders; all too many others have been more cautious than courageous and have remained silent behind the anesthetizing security of stained glass windows.

36   In spite of my shattered dreams, I came to Birmingham with the hope that the white religious leadership of this community would see

the justice of our cause and, with deep moral concern, would serve as the channel through which our just grievances could reach the power structure. I had hoped that each of you would understand. But again I have been disappointed.

37   I have heard numerous southern religious leaders admonish their worshipers to comply with a desegregation decision because it is the law, but I have longed to hear white ministers declare: "Follow this decree because integration is morally right and because the Negro is your brother." In the midst of blatant injustices inflicted upon the Negro, I have watched white churchmen stand on the sideline and mouth pious irrelevancies and sanctimonious trivialities. In the midst of a mighty struggle to rid our nation of racial and economic injustice, I have heard many ministers say: "Those are social issues, with which the gospel has no real concern." And I have watched many churches commit themselves to a completely otherworldly religion which makes a strange, un-Biblical distinction between body and soul, between the sacred and the secular.

38   I have traveled the length and breadth of Alabama, Mississippi, and all the other southern states. On sweltering summer days and crisp autumn mornings I have looked at the South's beautiful churches with their lofty spires pointing heavenward. I have beheld the impressive outlines of her massive religious-education buildings. Over and over I have found myself asking: "What kind of people worship here? Who is their God? Where were their voices when the lips of Governor Barnett dripped with words of interposition and nullification? Where were they when Governor Wallace gave a clarion call for defiance and hatred? Where were their voices of support when bruised and weary Negro men and women decided to rise from the dark dungeons of complacency to the bright hills of creative protest?"

39   Yes, these questions are still in my mind. In deep disappointment I have wept over the laxity of the church. But be assured that my tears have been tears of love. There can be no deep disappointment where there is not deep love. Yes, I love the church. How could I do otherwise? I am in the rather unique position of being the son, the grandson, and the great-grandson of preachers. Yes, I see the church as the body of Christ. But, oh! How we have blemished and scarred that body through social neglect and through fear of being noncon-formists.

40   There was a time when the church was very powerful—in the time when the early Christians rejoiced at being deemed worthy to suffer

for what they believed. In those days the church was not merely a thermometer that recorded the ideas and principles of popular opinion; it was a thermostat that transformed the mores of society. Whenever the early Christians entered a town, the people in power became disturbed and immediately sought to convict the Christians for being "disturbers of the peace" and "outside agitators." But the Christians pressed on, in the conviction that they were "a colony of heaven," called to obey God rather than man. Small in number, they were big in commitment. They were too God-intoxicated to be "astronomically intimidated." By their effort and example they brought an end to such ancient evils as infanticide and gladiatorial contests.

41   Things are different now. So often the contemporary church is a weak, ineffectual voice with an uncertain sound. So often it is an arch defender of the status quo. Far from being disturbed by the presence of the church, the power structure of the average community is consoled by the church's silent—and often even vocal—sanction of things as they are.

42   But the judgment of God is upon the church as never before. If today's church does not recapture the sacrificial spirit of the early church, it will lose its authenticity, forfeit the loyalty of millions, and be dismissed as an irrelevant social club with no meaning for the twentieth century. Every day I meet young people whose disappointment with the church has turned into outright disgust.

43   Perhaps I have once again been too optimistic. Is organized religion too inextricably bound to the status quo to save our nation and the world? Perhaps I must turn my faith to the inner spiritual church, the church within the church, as the true *ekklesia* and the hope of the world. But again I am thankful to God that some noble souls from the ranks of organized religion have broken loose from the paralyzing chains of conformity and joined us as active partners in the struggle for freedom. They have left their secure congregations and walked the streets of Albany, Georgia, with us. They have gone down the highways of the South on tortuous rides for freedom. Yes, they have gone to jail with us. Some have been dismissed from their churches, have lost the support of their bishops and fellow ministers. But they have acted in the faith that right defeated is stronger than evil triumphant. Their witness has been the spiritual salt that has preserved the true meaning of the gospel in these troubled times. They have carved a tunnel of hope through the dark mountain of disappointment.

44   I hope the church as a whole will meet the challenge of this deci-
sive hour. But even if the church does not come to the aid of justice,
I have no despair about the future. I have no fear about the outcome of
our struggle in Birmingham, even if our motives are at present misunderstood. We will reach the goal of freedom in Birmingham and all
over the nation, because the goal of America is freedom. Abused and
scorned though we may be, our destiny is tied up with America's
destiny. Before the pilgrims landed at Plymouth, we were here. Before
the pen of Jefferson etched the majestic words of the Declaration of
Independence across the pages of history, we were here. For more
than two centuries our forebears labored in this country without
wages; they made cotton king; they built the homes of their mas-
ters while suffering gross injustice and shameful humiliation—and
yet out of a bottomless vitality they continued to thrive and develop. If
the inexpressible cruelties of slavery could not stop us, the opposition
we now face will surely fail. We will win our freedom because the
sacred heritage of our nation and the eternal will of God are embodied
in our echoing demands.

45   Before closing I feel impelled to mention one other point in your
statement that has troubled me profoundly. You warmly commended
the Birmingham police force for keeping "order" and "preventing violence." I doubt that you would have so warmly commended the police
force if you had seen its dogs sinking their teeth into unarmed, nonviolent Negroes. I doubt that you would so quickly commend the policemen if you were to observe their ugly and inhumane treatment of
Negroes here in the city jail; if you were to watch them push and curse
old Negro women and young Negro girls; if you were to see them slap
and kick old Negro men and young boys; if you were to observe them,
as they did on two occasions, refuse to give us food because we wanted
to sing our grace together. I cannot join you in your praise of the
Birmingham police department.

46   It is true that the police have exercised a degree of discipline in
handling the demonstrators. In this sense they have conducted themselves rather "nonviolently" in public. But for what purpose? to preserve the evil system of segregation. Over the past few years I have
consistently preached that nonviolence demands that the means we
use must be as pure as the ends we seek. I have tried to make clear that
it is wrong to use immoral means to attain moral ends. But now I must
affirm that it is just as wrong, or perhaps even more so, to use moral

means to preserve immoral ends. Perhaps Mr. Connor and his policemen have been rather nonviolent in public, as was Chief Pritchett in Albany, Georgia, but they have used the moral means of nonviolence to maintain the immoral end of racial injustice. As T. S. Eliot has said, "The last temptation is the greatest treason: To do the right deed for the wrong reason."

47   I wish you had commended the Negro sit-inners and demonstrators of Birmingham for their sublime courage, their willingness to suffer, and their amazing discipline in the midst of great provocation. One day the South will recognize its real heroes. They will be the James Merediths, with the noble sense of purpose that enables them to face jeering and hostile mobs, and with the agonizing loneliness that characterizes the life of the pioneer. They will be old, oppressed, battered Negro women, symbolized in a seventy-two-year-old woman in Montgomery, Alabama, who rose up with a sense of dignity and with her people decided not to ride segregated buses, and who responded with ungrammatical profundity to one who inquired about her weariness: "My feets is tired, but my soul is at rest." They will be the young high school and college students, the young ministers of the gospel and a host of their elders, courageously and nonviolently sitting in at lunch counters and willingly going to jail for conscience' sake. One day the South will know that when these disinherited children of God sat down at lunch counters, they were in reality standing up for what is best in the American dream and for the most sacred values in our Judaeo-Christian heritage, thereby bringing our nation back to those great wells of democracy which were dug deep by the founding fathers in their formulation of the Constitution and the Declaration of Independence.

48   Never before have I written so long a letter. I'm afraid it is much too long to take your precious time. I can assure you that it would have been much shorter if I had been writing from a comfortable desk, but what else can one do when he is alone in a narrow jail cell, other than write long letters, think long thoughts, and pray long prayers?

49   If I have said anything in this letter that overstates the truth and indicates an unreasonable impatience, I beg you to forgive me. If I have said anything that understates the truth and indicates my having a patience that allows me to settle for anything less than brotherhood, I beg God to forgive me.

50   I hope this letter finds you strong in the faith. I also hope that circumstances will soon make it possible for me to meet each of you, not as an integrationist or a civil-rights leader but as a fellow clergyman and a Christian brother. Let us all hope that the dark clouds of racial prejudice will soon pass away and the deep fog of misunderstanding will be lifted from our fear-drenched communities, and in some not too distant tomorrow the radiant stars of love and brotherhood will shine over our great nation with all their scintillating beauty.

Yours for the cause of Peace and Brotherhood,

MARTIN LUTHER KING, JR.

QUESTIONS FOR DISCUSSION AND WRITING

1. King's letter replies to the charges made by eight clergymen. How many of their points does he respond to? Identify the paragraphs containing his response to each charge.

2. Two of King's most important arguments answer the charge that his actions are "untimely" and "unlawful." What arguments and evidence does he use to answer these two charges?

3. In which paragraphs does King use appeals to reason, to character, and to emotion? Which of these appeals did you find most effective? Explain.

4. In his essay, King supports his argument with facts, personal experience, quotations by authorities, and biblical references. Which of these kinds of evidence does he use most frequently? Which is most effective?

5. King is firm in his position, but his tone is often courteous and accommodating in his replies to the clergy. Find three examples where his tone is courteous or respectful. Does this moderate, reasonable tone make his argument more effective? Explain.

6. King's immediate audience is the eight clergymen, but his larger audience includes members of the Southern Christian Leadership Conference, the people who participated in the demonstrations, the white moderate, other members of "the church," and the public at large. Where does King refer to or appeal to each of these groups?

7. In the library or online, find out about recent actions of political or environmental protest groups. Focus on one group that has made recent headlines. Compare their tactics to the "four basic steps" for nonviolent civil disobedience King outlines in paragraphs 6 through 9. Has this group followed King's procedure? In your opinion, are their methods timely, just, and nonviolent? Are their methods effective?

Immigration

Prereading Journal Entry

Do you have someone in your family or circle of friends who immigrated to the United States? When did they come? What country did they come from? What is the story of their life in America?

After reading an essay entitled "Can We Still Afford to Be a Nation of Immigrants?" by David Kennedy, a professor of American History at Stanford University, Emily Sintek decided to write her arguing essay on the debate surrounding the immigration issue in the United States. Instead of arguing for one side or the other, however, she decided to examine the arguments on both sides and then find some common ground that the two sides might agree on. Since virtually all Americans were immigrants at one time or another, she reasons, perhaps we can use our common heritage as immigrants to work out a policy that would help both the "natives and [the] newcomers" achieve the American Dream.

1   He works in a corporate office in Houston, Texas, as a prominent investment banker. His wife is blonde, blue-eyed, educated, the wife of a millionaire. This man, drawing up images of the American dream, was once a small child growing up in Pakistan, surrounded by war, poverty, and political turmoil. He is my uncle; he is an immigrant; he is an American. Although few on either side of the immigration debate would deny his contribution to our country, some might dismiss his case as rare, unrepresentative of the current stream of immigrants entering America, while others might claim it is our moral duty to take in as many as we can, regardless of character, in order to provide a refuge in the midst of chaos. It is true that many who come do not have the outcome my uncle did, but the question remains: Whose side should one take in the immigration debate? There is a middle ground.

2   Guttentag and Parent, authors of *Immigrant Rights Demand Attention* from the *Forum for Applied Research and Public Policy*, emphasize our "history of giving political refuge to the persecuted, economic opportunity to the impoverished, and personal liberty to the oppressed," as strong supporters of increased immigration. Indeed, we are a "nation of immigrants." Such supporters identify a trend

towards blaming our social and economic ills on immigration during times of economic difficulty and social uncertainty. They claim immigrants provide moral, social, and economic benefits, that the number of people entering the country should be increased, in cases of oppression particularly, and that many of the contentions of the other side are merely misconceptions. According to their calculations, the number of illegal immigrants entering the country each year is smaller than most think, the fear that immigrants are taking U.S. jobs is unfounded, and the idea that many immigrants are dependent on social programs has been refuted. The focus of much of this side of the argument centers on immigrant rights, contending "as a nation we must adopt policies that reflect our values, protect individual rights, address the needs of our citizens, acknowledge the contribution of immigrants to our economy and culture, and reject the biases and stereotypes that frequently infect our immigration policies" (Guttentag and Parrent).

3   On the other hand, according to the article *News that Misfits* from the *National Review*, there is an urgent need for immigration reform, specifically immigration reduction, with "profound problems resulting from the post-1965 influx" of newcomers into America. They believe the current immigration has produced little or no net economic gain for the country, that instead it is "inflicting significant fiscal costs on native-born Americans" (*National Review*). Many on this side believe "current immigrants show deteriorating skill levels, on average, relative to natives" and that "current immigration is responsible for an overall wage loss of perhaps 1.2 percent" (*National Review*). They fear natives are experiencing difficulties as immigrants soak up the resources available in the United States, benefits that would otherwise go to those already living in America who need it. Such facts are readily available, and now, widely known, they claim, so that "they (immigration enthusiasts) can run but they can't hide" anymore (*National Review*).

4   Although the two sides appear incredibly opposed, there is much common ground between them. No matter which side one is on, most likely those involved in the debate are either immigrants themselves or descendants of immigrants. It is our heritage. Human life is also valued on both sides. Those who want increased immigration value lives that could be much improved by their arrival into our country, given opportunity and refuge from often oppressive governments elsewhere; but also being natives themselves, they value America's

stability and the lives of those already living in the country, counting their family, friends, and selves among those. Those who want decreased immigration value the lives of those already in America in hopes that they might make a life for themselves; but they also must value the lives of newcomers because they, too, are descended from immigrants, valuing the contributions they have made and continue to make to our country. Both sides want to improve the lives of natives and newcomers and both want to improve America itself—politically, economically, and culturally—continuing the tradition of opportunity, stability, and freedom.

5   The solution, then, is finding a balance. A middle ground of optimum benefits must be found. Too much immigration results in chaos. If the United States doesn't have enough resources to accommodate these newcomers, to give them a stable foundation at which to start, these people would be no better off than if they had stayed in their home country. Natives would grow resentful of newcomers who take jobs and resources they desperately need. Too little immigration results in lost opportunities. They are those we could have helped to escape oppression, those who have skills and hard work to offer, those who might help to create a more culturally diversified country, a more intriguing place to live.

6   Stricter policies for illegal immigrants must be enforced in order to ensure those who arrive legally can get all the benefits they need for a good start in America as well as to make it easier to make a more accurate estimate of how many immigrants our country can hold per year, so that, perhaps, as illegal immigration decreases, legal immigration may increase. The government needs to determine what resources, programs, and assistance are available for these groups in order to determine how many immigrants our nation can take in, take care of, and help be successful within our society. Hard facts must be established as to the impact immigration has on the country, both positive and negative, so that the incoming number may be manipulated to create maximum benefits for the country.

7   Immigrants can be a positive addition to our country or a failed investment, much depends on the number allowed in. Currently, the illegal immigration policies are not working and, it seems, the negative impacts of immigration are too high. Both of these factors signal the need for reform. Stricter policies and fewer immigrants might create the balance necessary to create an equilibrium so that those who are here, both natives and newcomers, are in reach of the American Dream.

WORKS CITED

Guttentag, Lucas, and Ann Parrent. "Immigrant Rights Demand Protection." *Forum for Applied Research and Public Policy.* Volume 10 (Fall 1995). 17 April 2002, <http://newfirstsearch.oclc.org>.

"News that Misfits." *National Review.* Volume 49 (June 1997). 17 April 2002, <http://newfirstsearch.oclc.org>.

QUESTIONS FOR DISCUSSION AND WRITING

1. According to Sintek, why might some people want to limit or halt immigration in the United States? What problems do they think immigrants cause?

2. For those who think immigration benefits both individuals and the country, what reasons or evidence do they give based on Sintek's evidence?

3. What exactly is the basis for the "middle ground" that might, according to Sintek, bring the two sides together?

4. Where in Sintek's essay do you see her state her purpose most clearly? Where do you see her, for example, explaining how our shared experiences as immigrants might help us find a solution that benefits everyone?

5. In order to work toward a middle ground in a contested debate, negotiators need to treat each side with respect and eliminate any inflated rhetoric or accusations. Where do you see Sintek being neutral and even-handed as she represents both sides of this argument?

6. Although Sintek begins with a personal example about her uncle, she discusses the two sides in this debate and suggests a solution without further reference to herself or her family. Assume that you are a member of the intended audience for this essay. Would you have preferred to see other references to Sintek's family or her uncle? Or do you think that keeping her approach more objective at the end is the best way to reach a workable solution? Explain.

7. On the Internet or in your library's databases, collect additional articles about the current debate about immigration. What are current trends in handling immigration? Is it becoming easier or more difficult to immigrate? Write an essay that balances the sources you find and suggests a workable solution for the next decade.

credits

PHOTOS

index of authors and titles

A

Adler, Mortimer , How to Mark a Book, 20

Alexie, Sherman, The Joy of Reading and Writing, 25

Alleva, Richard, Pocahokum, 251

All's Not Well in Land of The Lion King (Lazarus) , 262

Altschuler, Glenn C., The E-Learning Curve, 180

Alvarez, Julia , A White Woman of Color, 301

Argument Culture, The (Tannen), 330

B

Barthes, Roland , Toys, 102

Beauty Behind Beauty Pageants, The (White), 185

Berry, Wendell, Solving for Pattern, 280

Bérubé, Michael, How to End Grade Inflation: A Modest Proposal , 292

C

Campbell, SueEllen, Layers of Place, 106

Cat Bathing as a Martial Art (Herron), 224

Climate Change Science Misinformation (Karoly), 335

Consumer Reports, Laptops and Desktops, 243

Cooley, Craig, The Two Best Letters on Television, 265

Corbett. Sarah, Rick Steves's Not-So-Lonely Planet, 174

Day Language Came into My Life, The (Keller), 134

CrossTalk (Tannen), 295

D

Day Language Came into My Life, The (Keller), 134

Dillard, Annie, Lenses, 92

Does Obesity Rehab Work? (Suddath/Reedley), 169

Drivers on Cell Phones Are as Bad as Drunks (University of Utah New Center), 165

Duster, Troy et al., One Thing to Do About Food, 284, 288

E

Easterbrook, Gregg, Some Convenient Truths, 340

Elbow , Peter, Freewriting, 56

E-Learning Curve, The (Altschuler), 180

Endorsements Just a Shell Game (Royko), 353

F

Fetal Pig (Weston), 113

Freewriting (Elbow), 56

G

Gettysburg Address, The (Lincoln), 255

Gettysburg Address, The (Highet), 256

Goedeker, Walter, The Wake-Up Call, 150

Goodman, Ellen, Honor Society Hypocrisy, 15

Gregory, Dick, Shame, 125

H

Haiti: A Survivor's Story (Wagner), 129

Heat-Moon, William Least, West Texas, 88

Herron, Bud, Cat Bathing as a Martial Art, 224

Highet, Gilbert, The Gettysburg Address, 256

Hightower, Jim et al., One Thing to Do About Food, 284, 290

Honor Society Hypocrisy (Goodman), 15

Houston, Jeanne Wakasuki, Living in Two Cultures, 144

How to End Grade Inflation: A Modest Proposal (Bérubé), 292

How to Mark a Book (Adler), 20

How to Take Control of Your Credit Cards (Orman), 201

I

Immigration (Sintek), 373

J

Jesus Is a Brand of Jeans (Kilbourne), 214

Jones, Michael J., Wine Tasting: How to Fool Some of the People All of the Time, 228

Joy of Reading and Writing, The (Alexie), 25

K

Karoly, David, Climate Change Science Misinformation, 335

Keller , Helen, The Day Language Came into My Life, 134

Kilbourne, Jean, Jesus Is a Brand of Jeans, 214

King, Jr. , Martin Luther, Letter from Birmingham Jail, 356

King, Stephen, Why We Crave Horror Movies, 221

381

L

Lamott, Anne, *Shitty First Drafts*, 60
Laptops and Desktops (Consumer Reports), 243
Layers of Place (Campbell), 106
Lazarus, Margaret, *All's Not Well in Land of* The Lion King, 262
Learning to Read (Malcolm X), 29
Lenses (Dillard), 92
Letter from Birmingham Jail (King, Jr.), 356
Lincoln, Abraham, *The Gettysburg Address*, 255
Living in Two Cultures (Houston,) 144
Los Pobres (Rodriguez), 137

M

Maker's Eye: Revising Your Own Manuscripts, The (Murray), 65
Malcolm X, *Learning to Read*, 29
Mircos. Nicolle, *My Sister, Kari*, 50
Mother Tongue (Tan), 71
Murray, Donald M., *The Maker's Eye: Revising Your Own Manuscripts*, 65
My Sister, Kari (Mircos), 50

N

Nestle, Marion et al., *One Thing to Do About Food*, 284, 286

O

One Thing to Do About Food (Duster and Ransom, et al.), 284, 288
One Thing to Do About Food (Hightower et al.), 284, 290
One Thing to Do About Food (Nestle et al.), 284, 286
One Thing to Do About Food (Pollan et al.), 284, 287
One Thing to Do About Food (Schlosser et al.), 284, 285
One Thing to Do About Food (Singer et al.), 284, 289

Orman. Suze, *How to Take Control of Your Credit Cards*, 201
Our Barbies, Ourselves (Prager), 104
Pocahokum (Alleva), 251

P

Pollan, Michael et al., *One Thing to Do About Food*, 284, 287
Prager, Emily, *Our Barbies, Ourselves*, 104
Problem of Dropouts Can Be Solved, The (Sharpe), 309
Professors Should Embrace Wikipedia (Wilson), 349

R

Ralli, Tania, *Who's a Looter?*, 37
Ransom, Elizabeth et al., *One Thing to Do About Food*, 284
Rick Steves's Not-So-Lonely Planet (Corbett), 174
Rodriguez, Richard, *Los Pobres*, 137
Royko, Mike, *Endorsements Just a Shell Game*, 352

S

Schlosser, Eric et al., *One Thing to Do About Food*, 284, 285
Scudder, Samuel H., *Take This Fish and Look at It*, 96
Sedaris, David, *Today's Special*, 247
Shame (Gregory), 125
Sharpe, Jenny, *The Problem of Dropouts Can Be Solved*, 309
Shitty First Drafts (Lamott), 60
Singer, Peter et al., *One Thing to Do About Food*, 284, 289
Sintek, Emily, *Immigration*, 373
Solving for Pattern (Berry), 280
Some Convenient Truths (Easterbrook), 340
Suddath/Reedley, Claire, *Does Obesity Rehab Work?*, 169

T

Take This Fish and Look at It (Scudder), 96
Tan, Amy, *Mother Tongue*, 71
Tannen, Deborah, *The Argument Culture*, 330
Tannen, Deborah, *CrossTalk*, 295
Today's Special (Sedaris), 247
Toys (Barthes), 102
Two Best Letters on Television, The (Cooley), 265

U

University of Utah News Center, *Drivers on Cell Phones Are as Bad as Drunks*, 165

V

Von Drehle, David, *Why Crime Went Away*, 207

W

Wagner, Laura, *Haiti: A Survivor's Story*, 129
Wake-Up Call, The (Goedeker), 150
Waters , Neil L., *Why You Can't Cite Wikipedia in My Class*, 344
Weston, Elizabeth, *Fetal Pig*, 113
West Texas (Heat-Moon), 88
White, Mary, *The Beauty Behind Beauty Pageants*, 185
White Woman of Color, A (Alvarez), 301
Who's a Looter? (Ralli), 37
Why Crime Went Away (Von Drehle), 207
Why We Crave Horror Movies (King), 221
Why You Can't Cite Wikipedia in My Class (Waters), 344
Wilson, Mark, *Professors Should Embrace Wikipedia*, 349
Wine Tasting: How to Fool Some of the People All of the Time (Jones), 228

NOTES

NOTES

NOTES

NOTES